STATE OF THE CONTINENT

State of the Continent

A Mid-Century Assessment of Political Performance in Africa

John M. Fobanjong

SPEARS
MEDIA PRESS

DENVER

Spears Media Press LLC
DENVER
7830 W. Alameda Ave, Suite 103-247 Denver, CO 80226
United States of America

First Published in 2018 by Spears Media Press
www.spearsmedia.com
info@spearsmedia.com
Information on this title: www.spearsmedia.com/shop/state-of-the-continent

Library of Congress Control Number: 2018964401

ISBN: 978-1-942876-34-2 (Paperback)
ISBN: 978-1-942876-36-6 (eBook)

Typeset by Spears Media Press in 10/13pt Georgia

Dedicated to

Philip Fobanjong & Hans Spoerri

Contents

Acknowledgement   ix

Preface   xi

Chapter 1   1
Historical Backdrop

Chapter 2   11
Understanding Africa from a Comparative Perspective

Chapter 3   27
Global Challenges the West has Won with the Help of Africa

Chapter 4   51
Pondering Africa's Failures

Chapter 5   79
Could Africa be Saying No to Modernity?

Chapter 6   91
Assessing the Performance of Internal Influences

Chapter 7   131
Assessing the Performance of External Influences

Chapter 8   171
Reordering the African Public Sector

Chapter 9   199
Reordering the African Private Sector

Appendix 1. U.S. President Barack Obama's
First Official Address to Africa   247

Appendix 2. U.S. President Barack Obama's
Second Official Address to Africa   255

Appendix 3. Ghanaian President, Nana Akufo–Addo's
Address to the West   267

Index   273

Illustrations

FIGURES

Figure 1. The Continent that Fell Asleep xv
Figure 2.1. Retracing the European Voyages that Led to the
European Discovery of Africa and the Americas 12

TABLES

Table 6.1. Status of Democracy in Africa at the Half Century Mark 112

BOX

Box 8.1: African Corruption in Comparative Perspective – An Anecdote 193

Acknowledgement

The inspiration for this book came from my family, my friends and my professional colleagues. The two people that very early on placed me on the track to writing a book on Africa are my two older brothers, Philip Nji Fobanjong and Hansheirri Spoerri. Their love and passion for Africa is unparalleled. These two men are principally responsible for every mountain I have climbed and every feat I have surmounted. Their trust and brotherly love made it possible for me to survive the rigors of higher education. If anyone ever taught me that the definition of brotherliness goes beyond blood to include endearing and enduring love, it was my Swiss brother Hans Spoerri. I have never had any two more affectionate cheer-leaders.

Above all else is the love and support I receive every day from my darling wife, Antoinette, who is the center of my existence and the wind beneath my wings. If angels do come to the world in human form, Antoinette is a true angel. I could never have imagined life without her.

Among my most cherished blessings are my children, Collins & Abigail Fobanjong, Costa & Emmanuel Fombe, Siri Fobanjong, Tizi Fobanjong; and my grandchildren Amalie Fobanjong, Sims-G Fobanjong, Martin Fomum and Goddy Fombe. Some of them may be still too young to read this book, but it is my fervent wish that when they all read it when they come of age it will inspire them to develop the same love and passion for writing and for higher education as their grandfather had.

Throughout my career in higher education, many of the colleagues that I have worked with have left a lasting mark in my heart. Among them are John Carroll, Richard Lobban, Carolyn Lobban and Jean Doyle. Not only were Professors Carroll and Doyle my twin mentors, they were also, in their time, twin visionaries at the University of Massachusetts Dartmouth. They were as concerned with the education of the next generation of students as they were with building the careers of the next generation of faculty. John and Jean succeeded in shepherding a department that was rocked by tremendous interpersonal challenges into one of the most stable and most highly respected departments at the University of Massachusetts Dartmouth.

If it is true that one is never too old to learn, it should also be true that one is never too old to have a mentor. As by manifest design, just as Professors Carroll and Doyle were moving on to enjoy their well-deserved retirement,

Professors Richard Lobban and Carolyn Lobban, of the United States Naval War College were stepping in to continue as both as my mentors and my very close friends. Passionate Africanists and indefatigable global crusaders for justice, Richard and Carolyn have for more than a half century put their hearts, their lives and their professional expertise to the service of Africa. Until we began working together, almost all of my previous publications were on Civil Rights and American public policy. With Richard, my publications began to gradually focus on Africa. This book is a reflection of the influence Richard and Carolyn have had on me.

My professional career was naturally preceded by my student career. On my American journey as a student, I was showered with kindness and generosity by some very special persons. It is impossible to remember all of them. I am however able to remember those whose acts have and will remain indelible in my memory. The Dobys (Troy, Jane, Toby and Bob) were my first American family. They were the loveliest and most loving family of any family in America. The only suiting word I can find to describe Mrs. Jane Doby is that she was an angel. Besides the care and genuine love they gave me, they also provided me with a home away from home. Thank you Troy (Dad), Jane (Mom), brothers Toby and Bob.

On campus, at Berea College, Kentucky, an incredibly loving young couple, Larry and Jean Baker, staff employees for the College, picked me out among some 1,500 students as their international student favorite. They took me into their warm and loving home every weekend, to help me avoid the monotony of eating cafeteria food every day. Thank you, Larry, Jean and Heather.

To "he" that much is given, much is expected. Among the students that I have mentored and worked with over the years, Dominique Nkengfack distinguishes himself as the most trusted and the most disciplined. An avid reader and student of international relations, he calls me every Sunday, and has been doing so since 1983 to discuss international affairs.

Preface

One of the expressions of accountability in democratic societies is in annual "state-of-the-state" addresses. In a democratic nation such as the United States, this accountability is constitutionally mandated and given every January in what is referred to as the "State of the Union" address. Because most countries in Africa are not democratic, annual state-of-the-state addresses are generally not constitutionally mandated. To find out how a given African country has performed in a given year, a reader is forced to turn to reports by the World Bank, the IMF and other outside sources. Here, the reader is limited to reading reports that only give account of annual performance. As a continent, a majority of the countries in Africa have had more than fifty years of independence and self-rule. Crossing the half-century mark is a milestone that deserves scholarly attention. While it may be true that the World Bank and IMF regularly produce annual reports on economic performance in Africa, there is no indication that they have conducted or are interested in conducting a half-century study of the continent's performance. This book therefore may be the very first major work to conduct an assessment of Africa's political performance since the countries in Africa achieve independence a half-century ago. By virtue of being the first publication that studies, the political performance of a continent in a half century, there is no doubt that the book is going to inspire follow-up publications – if not on Africa, on other regions in the international system. In some cases, it may actually inspire some publishing houses to organize the publication of a book series on "century" or "half-century" political performance in other regions of the world.

Unlike for the democratic state where accountability or political assessment is an annual rite, for a continent, and for the African continent in particular, we see a half-century as a more meaningful cutoff mark. Hence the book's title, *State of the Continent: A Mid-Century Assessment of Political Performance in Africa*. It is but appropriate that at the end of Africa's first half century, we take time out to examine the "state-of-the-continent." Ordinarily, when asked how far Africa has come in the past half century, some people may say "Africa has come a long way." Others might say "Africa has not come far enough." Depending on one's perspective, both responses could be correct. To fully understand how far Africa has come in its first half century of independence, however, the reader needs a response that goes beyond a simple one-liner. The purpose of this book is to go beyond such bland one-line responses to more closely examine how Africa has performed politically since gaining independence. For individuals as well as for nation states, an understanding of present conditions requires an in-depth knowledge of past conditions.

While the title and focus of the book is primarily on the post-colonial period when Africans recaptured their lost liberties and became architects of their political destiny, to fully understand today's Africa, we need to take a brief look at the continent's colonial and pre-colonial past. This should give us the background that will help develop new hypotheses in this study. In other words, to fully understand the forces that have influenced Africa's performance in the last half century, we would need first to understand the forces that were at play in Africa's colonial and pre-colonial past.

While colonial rule in Africa may have lasted for a mere three-quarter of a century (1884-1960s), it made a mark that will endure into the distant future. In its first half century of independence and self-rule, post-colonial African rule has equally made a mark that deserves scholarly scrutiny. In this book, our assessment is going to be primarily qualitative. Many of the programs and organizations that collect and disseminate quantitative data on Africa today – from *Afrobarometer* to *Freedom House, Transparency International,* and *World Development Index* – did not exist when the independence process in Africa began half a century ago. Even for programs that existed, the data they collected did not measure the same issues that are measured by data that is collected today. Corruption, AIDS, failed states, foreign aid and the debt crisis that stand in the way of development in Africa today were not indexed. Any attempt to longitudinally assess how AIDS, debt and corruption have impacted Africa since the late 1950s would therefore be conceptually flawed. AIDS, debt and corruption did not become an epidemic in Africa until the 1980s.

Assessing Africa's performance in the past half century of independence should produce lessons that would allow us to better predict the continent's performance in the next half century. In essence, this is what this book is about. It provides two lenses – a lens to the past and a lens to the future. It develops critical and sometimes provocative thoughts that are of interest not only to students of Africa, but to anyone who is interested in the study of the growth and transformation of nation-states – African as well non-African. The student who is interested in the knowledge of how the United States evolved from an agrarian colonial territory to a global, knowledge-based super-state will find the analysis in this book intellectually penetrating. And the student who is interested in understanding how political systems fail or succeed will equally find the explanatory theories here useful. But most importantly, policy-makers with interest in Africa – from foreign policy-makers, to diplomats, foreign investors, military planners, international financial institutions to the curious intellectual – are going to find the lessons in this book insightful. Indispensable to sound policy-making is a good understanding of history. What has happened in the past, how and why it happened, and how what happened in the past impacts what is happening today, are all thoughts that must be pondered. Not only am I hoping that the reader will find answers to some of these questions, I am hoping that the book will prod the reader to critically pose more questions beyond the questions that are posed in this book.

Much of the material in the book is presented from a comparative perspective. It is only by measuring the leap that one has taken in relation to the leap that others have taken that one can determine if one has taken a great leap. Studying Africa in isolation to developments in other parts of the world cannot fully produce critically important lessons. It is only by studying Africa in relation to developments in other regions of the world that one would understand if the continent is leaping forward, leaping backward or remaining stagnant.

In October 2016, Nigeria celebrated the 56th anniversary of its independence. In the same month, Lesotho also celebrated the 50th anniversary of its independence. Nigeria is the largest country in Africa, and Lesotho is one of the smallest countries in Africa. Despite their dissimilarity, what both countries have in common is that they have both had more than a half-century of independence and self-rule. But what is worth noting for both countries is that the celebration of their independence was heralded with pessimism. Media headlines in Nigeria read that "Nigerians feel pride and despair on 56th Independence;" and reminisced that "There was a time we actually had a nation that was near greatness. What we have now is nothing compared to that. Are we going forward or are we moving backward?"[1] On Lesotho, the media headline was a question, and the question was, "But is the country really free?"[2] These are two countries on the same continent. Will a look at two countries on other continents or regions of the world produce a similar sense of exasperation? Cross-continentally, will a comparative study of Africa and America – two continents that interfaced with Europe within the same decade – produce similar findings?

[1]   Chika Oduah, *Nigerians feel pride and despair on 56th Independence*, http://www.aljazeera.com/indepth/features/2016/10/nigerians-feel-pride-despair-56th-independence-161001082955779.html, (accessed October 12, 2016).

[2]   Deutsche Welle, Lesotho: real freedom after 50 years of independence? http://www.dw.com/en/lesotho-real-freedom-after-50-years-of-independence/a- 35949091?utm_source=Media+Review+for+October+4%2C+2016&utm_campaign=DMR-+EN+-+10%2F04%2F2016&utm_medium=email. (Accessed 10/25/2016).

Beyond the scholarly world and its hypothetical abstractions, political performance in Africa in the past half century has also pricked the attention of the outside world. One of the continent's important external stakeholder – the United States – has openly expressed concern over the continent's political performance (see appendixes 1-2). Going beyond verbal expressions of concern, the United States initiating policies that it hopes will address the challenges of governance and economic development on the continent. In August 2014, it hosted a summit of African and American leaders. The theme of the summit was *Investing in the Next Generation*. It was the first such summit in the history of the two regions, and its theme reflected the vast opportunities that Africa presents to the United States and to the rest of the outside world. The continent's middle class is projected to grow past one billion within the next 50 years.[3] For democracy and for economic growth, this is good news. The middle class is the engine of economic development. To transform this coming demographic boom into an engine of growth and development, Africa needs to begin making the necessary investments today. To make sure the investments are wise, Africa would need to begin first by assessing the continent's political performance in the past fifty years to avoid past missteps as the continent embarks on the second half of its first century of independence. For humans, half a century is a long time. For some, it could actually be a lifetime. For a continent however, a half century is a very short time. As short as it may be, it is an interval that gives us an opportunity to pause and take a look at our accomplishments and our missteps; what was achieved and what is yet to be achieved.

The famous American poet, Langston Hughes once referred to Africa as a "sleeping giant." The image in the picture below vividly captures that poetic prognosis. The image depicts a delegation of African conference participants noticeably dosing off. It is a continent that has enigmatically remained asleep since coming into contact with the outside world. Poetry is an art. Very often, it is art that sees a reality that lay persons do not see. For obvious reasons, even the West which was optimistic on Africa's development prospects in the early years of independence had by the early 2000 grown disillusioned by the continent's post-colonial economic and political performance. But for the continent's resources, the growing Chinese presence, and the global war against terrorism, the West would have long given up on Africa. For a continent whose share of world trade at the turn of the 21st century remained at under 2%, and whose share of global scientific output is below 0.03%, why should anyone care?

---

3   http://blogs.worldbank.org/futuredevelopment/making-middle-class-africa, (Accessed November, 6, 2016).

Figure 1. The Continent that Fell Asleep

Source: Author

Since gaining independence as many as two-fifths of the countries in Africa have at one time or another been embroiled in conflict. Life expectancy has been declining, as the continent celebrated the first half century of independence, the lifespan of the average African was down to below fifty years. On the economy, hundreds of billions of dollars in aid transferred to Africa have produced no perceptible impact in the quality of life of the average African. Citizens of the Democratic Republic of Congo, Sudan, Somalia and the Central African Republic, since achieving independence, never enjoyed a single decade of peace and stability. Today, the finger of blame that was directed at the West by the now anachronistic dependency school of thought in the first three decades of independence, would by Africa's first half-century of independence be pointedly redirected at Africa's rulers. Africa's youths today have actually gone beyond disillusionment to actually holding their leaders responsible for the underdevelopment of the continent.

Afrocentric scholars generally write and talk wistfully about the continent's past greatness – the era when Africa had great emperors and great kings such as King Mansa Musa of Mali, Queen Nzinga of the Bakongo, and Queen Zaria of Nigeria. Until now, there has been no explanation on how and why these past accomplishments fell apart. Contemporary African behavior, as depicted in the above photo does appear to provide a clue: the continent fell into a comatose slumber.

Our attempt to assess Africa's political performance in this book is supplemented by the assessment of eminent observers – President Barack Obama of the United States and President Nana Akufo-Addo. In two separate keynote addresses delivered on the African continent and directed at the continent's political leadership, President Obama makes an open assessment of the political performance of African leaders, and goes on to recommend better approaches to good governance. The text of the two speeches are included in the appendix. In return, an African voice – that of President Akufo-Addo – would call the West to reexamine its foreign aid policies to Africa, and look into reforming it and/or possibly weaning Africa off it completely. The full text of his address is equally included in the appendix. Africa needs a roadmap as it begins the second half of its first century of independence. Classroom discussions and writing assignments that will result from the study of this book and the attached appendixes should help develop the critical thinking that will sketch out this roadmap.

Chapter 1

Historical Backdrop

"Africa doesn't need strong men; it needs strong institutions"
(Barack Obama)

The transition from the Cold War to what was ephemerally described as the New World Order relieved Africa of the proxy wars that made the continent a battlefield for the superpowers. While the tension that characterized superpower rivalry remained peaceful and "cold" between the superpowers, it went devastatingly "hot" in Africa. The use of Africa as a battlefield for venting superpower tensions denied Africa the opportunity to enjoy the honeymoon that should have come with its independence. Decrying Africa's helplessness in the face of these proxy wars, the eminent statesman and Tanzania's founding president, Julius Nyerere, noted that "when elephants fight, it is the grass that suffers."[1] In serving as an outlet for the relief of superpower tension, Africa kept the superpowers from directly engaging in a "hot" war, and thus may have helped prevent the outbreak of World War III. As the international system celebrated the sudden shift of superpower relations from conflict to cooperation in the early 1990s, the euphoria that heralded the end of the Cold War quickly flickered into oblivion. By the end of the nineties decade and the start of the first decade of the 21st century, events surrounding the 9/11 Attack had brought levels of tension in the international community back to what they were at the height of the Cold War. Instead of "the new world order", the state of the international system was now being referred to as "the new world disorder."[2]

While the euphoria over the proclamation of the new world order may have been short-lived, and despite the global security challenges that lay ahead, globalization and the growing integration of the global economy remained forward-looking. It was this new integration and its growing

---

1   Walters, Eric & Arian Bradbury, *When Elephants Fights*, Custer, WA: Orca Book Publishers; Reprint edition (February 1, 2012)
2   Tzvetan Todorov, *The New World Disorder: Reflections of a European*, New York: Polity; 1st Edition (January 14, 2005)

sustainability that would become the engine for the new global economy. Previous world orders, from mercantilism to capitalism brought nothing but predation on Africa. Will globalization be any different from previous world orders? This is a question that critiques suspicious that globalization is going to be a lineal replay of the past. Are there steps Africa can take that will prevent globalization from rehashing the predatory trends of the past? In examining Africa's political performance in the first half-century, these are some of the questions that must be raised. Can Africa take advantage of the growing globalization of the international economy and restructure itself in ways that would allow her to now receive benefits that were denied her in previous global economic systems?

In other parts of the world, including North America, decolonization was liberating and empowering. In Africa, decolonization was neither liberating nor empowering. If it were at all empowering, it was empowering only to the new African rulers to whom the reins of power were handed. On acquiring power, these rulers moved to transform themselves into Leviathans – Leviathans that were more predatory than the imperial forces they replaced. Thus, as predatory as colonial rule was, post-colonial rule turned out to be more predatory. The breed of African leaders that inherited power from imperial rulers went on to rule Africa as if they themselves were non-Africans. Indeed, independence in Africa can in many ways be aptly seen as the wholesale transfer of authority from one predatory system to another. To make up for the lack of legitimacy in post-independent Africa, excessive powers were given to security forces. These forces resorted to the use of the same oppressive strategies that were used in colonial times. Mobutu's treatment of Lumumba was not much different from the treatment King Leopold gave to the indigenous people of Congo in the 19th century. The same could be said of Uganda's Idi Amin, Burkina Faso's Blaise Compaore, Central Africa Republic's Jean-Bédel Bokassa, Cameroon's Paul Biya and Sudan's Al Bashir. What these rulers did to their citizens is comparable and, in some cases worse than what European colonial rulers did to Africans. Had Nelson Mandela been the citizen of an African country other than South Africa, he would never have lived to see prison walls, much less become president of his country. He most likely would have been summarily executed the way Congo's first head of state, Lumumba and Nigeria's first democratically elected president, Abiola were executed.

On the whole, while decolonization may have rid Africa of foreign rule, it was soon replaced by a new form of exploitation, now internal, that operated through an entangled web of political and bureaucratic scheming. Today, much of Africa remains internally colonized. As the end of the Cold War and the growing globalization of the international system heralded a newfound sense of optimism across much of the world, in Africa it brought an exasperating sense of pessimism. And as the outside world was euphoric over the new economic opportunities that globalization was going to bring to Africa, critiques of globalization saw it as nothing but a replay of the previous expressions of optimism when Africa was being forcibly integrated into similar past global economic models. As an economic model, colonialism was justified as a *civilizing mission*. In place of civilization, it brought untold repression. In the end, the euphoria and promise of hope that heralded colonial rule turned into untold misery.

At the end of colonial rule in the 1960s, the transfer of governing power to African rulers produced yet another sense of euphoria. The outgoing colonialists and the newly liberated masses of the continent were both hopeful and optimistic about Africa's ability to achieve development. But instead of achieving development, the continent embarked on a destructive course that would be marked by corruption and domestic instability. Here again, optimism flickered into pessimism.

In post-colonial African history, nothing brought greater hope and a greater feeling of euphoria than Nelson Mandela's release from prison in 1990. This momentous political event was celebrated by Africans and friends of Africa as the new dawn of an "African renaissance." The Renaissance in Europe was that era when Europe pulled itself out of the dark ages and embarked on a path to modernity. For those who hoped that the "African renaissance" was going to bring the same transformation to the continent, they were disappointed. In less than four years, the Rwanda Genocide - the worst humanitarian crisis of post-independent Africa – produced a throwback that went beyond pessimism to despondency. The genocide produced a domino effect in the region, with the breakout of civil conflict across the continent – from diamond-funded civil wars in West Africa, to genocidal persecutions in Darfur, secessionist wars in Eritrea and South Sudan, and *warlordism* in Somalia and in the Democratic Republic of Congo.

The third manifestation of euphoria in Africa began in the late 2000s when it was revealed that the continent's vast oil reserves presented an alternative to Middle Eastern oil. International investors immediately became bullish on Africa. During the global financial crisis of 2008-2010, as the economies of Western nations were in the negative, African economies were actually growing at the impressive rate of 5 to 6%. For reasons that are well known to the international community (corruption, debt, resource-based extractive economies, the colonial legacy), the growth did nothing to improve living conditions for Africa's masses. As Africa celebrated its first half century of independence, more than 50% of the continent's population continued to live on less than $1 a day. For the continent's youth, hope could only be found by leaving the continent. In October 2013, on their way in search of hope outside the continent, 360 African youths drowned off the coast of the Italian Island of Lampedusa. Ever since then, Africans struggling to run away from the continent's man-made hardship would continue to die in their hundreds. These realities stood in stark contrast to the much talked about economic growth that globalization was purportedly going to bring.

Assessing the Colonial Relationship Between Africa and Europe

In more than half a millennium, Africa has been a vital asset for the West. Africa's importance for the West became even more obvious in the middle of the 20th century, when the world was polarized into two fiercely competing ideological poles. Among Africa's contributions during this period was the supply of rare strategic minerals to the West. The minerals contributed to helping the West win the Cold War. It was a period during which the West saw Africa as a zone of strategic importance and was prepared to go to war to keep her Soviet rival from extending its influence to the region. Africa became a testing ground for battles that the superpowers would have otherwise directed at each other. Hundreds of thousands of African lives were lost. The 1960's, the decade when much of Africa became independent, was the height of the Cold War. Leaders of resource rich African countries who refused to take sides, and/or who were suspected of pursuing an independent nationalist agenda were either ostracized or summarily eliminated. As French President, Charles de Gaulle moved to ostracized Guinea's Sekou Touré for refusing to sign a neocolonial pact with France, the United States connived to eliminate Patrice Lumumba for obstinately opting to pursue a nationalist path. Not only did superpower-sponsored proxy wars render the independence of several African countries stillbirth, the wars contributed to their collapse into failed states. The collapse was most acute in the Democratic Republic of Congo, where more than six million people were killed and tens of thousands of women raped between the 1990s and 2010. Described as the world's bloodiest war since World War II, the Congolese conflict morphed into a foreign backed civil war for control of the country's $24 trillion mineral reserves.[3]

Despite the role that the proxy wars in Africa played in deflecting direct confrontation away from the two superpowers, barely ten years after the Cold War was over, Western leaders soon dismissed Africa as a region that had no strategic importance for the West. At a 2000 televised debate, U.S. Presidential candidate, George W. Bush, stated that Africa had no strategic importance to the United States.[4] This was pre-September 2011 era. Many

3   http://www.globalpost.com/dispatch/news/regions/africa/110527/congo-sex%20slaves-girl-soldiers-helped-resume-normal-lives, accessed, May 12, 2016.

4   Donald Rothchild & Edmond J. Keller, *Africa-US Relations: Strategic Encounters*, Lynne Reiner Publishers, New York, 2006, p. 49.

in the United States probably shared his view. He won the elections. But looking back at the billions of dollars that were spent during the Cold War to deny Soviet expansion in Africa and looking at the billions the US was to spend in the post-9/11 era to combat terrorism on the African continent, one cannot help but see how myopic such thinking was.

Before the modern era, Africa and its coastlines provided an alternate sea route for Western merchants to the spice islands of Asia. As early as in the 17th century, Africa began providing the West with the human resources that enabled Europe to not only catch up, but to overtake China's technological lead. Without the contributions that free labor from Africa made to the development of the New World, capitalism would never have taken off in the United States. Prior to this partnering between Africa's labor and Europe's entrepreneurship, China and the Ottoman empires were technologically and militarily ahead of the West. The partnership enabled the West to overtake these two powerful empires.

The end of the Cold War witnessed the wholesale disengagement of the superpowers from Africa. The disengagement provided a unique opportunity for Africans. During the Cold War, a period when the territorial scramble for Africa by Western powers was replaced by an ideological scramble by the superpowers, Africans were not free to independently determine their political destiny. With the two superpowers now disengaged and no longer resolved to using Africa as a battlefield for their proxy wars, this presented a unique opportunity for Africa to permanently place Africa's interests ahead of outside interests. Sadly, Africans failed to make good use of this opportunity.

Politically, economically and geographically, Africa needed reconfiguring at independence. Just as America was reconfigured at independence, first as a confederation of 13 states, and later as a union of states, Africa needed a similar reconfiguration. Unfortunately, the leadership that should have negotiated the reconfiguration of Africa into a politically strong and united continent was more concerned in jealously protecting their newly acquired sovereignties. Any attempt to change or reconfigure Africa was perceived as attempts at negotiating their power away. The only three African leaders who saw the need for a reconfigured Africa were Ghana's Kwame Nkrumah, Congo's Patrice Lumumba and Guinea-Bissau's Amilcar Cabral. Unfortunately, all three would be eliminated. Their lives were cut short by deadly conspiracies that were masterminded by Africa's external stakeholders. In the main, what betrayed Africa were its selfish and visionless leaders, and a Europe that quickly found a neocolonial backdoor to maintaining its influence on the continent. Today, unless Africa's colonially distorted structures are dismantled and/or reconfigured, the quest for stability and economic development will continue to remain elusive.

Assessing the Claim that Africa Cannot Govern Itself

There is a commonly held view that Africans cannot efficiently govern themselves. While this may be true in the context of the modern nation-state system, it must not be forgotten that prior to coming into contact with the West, Africa was self-governing. All throughout the continent, there were stable and efficient systems of government that dated back thousands of years. In his book, *Which Way Africa?*, the British historian Basil Davidson describes an African state along the Zambezi River which was effectively and efficiently governed by a king. The authority of the king was guided by democratic principles. He was accountable to his electorate and ran the risk of getting deposed if he abused that authority.[5] According to Davidson, Africa's past is both long and interesting. It contains a record of continuous and successful development over several thousand years – development that gives no grounds for any assumption of natural inferiority or failure in achievement.[6] Across parts of the continent, traditional forms of African democracy seemed to predate and even cast convincing doubt on the relevance of Western parliamentary models. Unlike in Western legislative processes where decision making is by majority vote, decision making in early Africa was often by consensus. Members of the community would assemble in the courtyard of an elderly clansman and deliberate until they all came into agreement. The British writer and statesman, Lord William Malcolm Hailey reveals that prior to the coming of European rule, it was rare to find any form of authoritarian rule in Africa.[7] As illustrated in the writings of a Portuguese writer in 1837, "The government of Bailundu (a clan in today's Angola) is democratic. These heathen mix with the infamous humility of the Orientals and the unbridled coarseness of the English people at election time in England. The kings defer to and flatter their counselors: these are they who elevate a king to the throne and also cast him down."[8]

The British anthropologist, Margaret Fields, pointedly observed that, "the notion that Britain brought democracy to West Africa is quite erroneous. On the contrary, Britain did much to destroy indigenous democracy. Neither is the idea of an opposition a new one. Alongside every chief (in Ashanti) was a *Mankrado* or *Krontinhene* of whom it was said, 'every *Mankrado* is opposed to the chief.'"[9]

---

5 Basil Davidson, *Which Way Africa? The Search for a New Society*. 3rd Edition, Baltimore, Maryland, Penguin Books, 1971, pp. 23-24

6 Davidson, p, 42

7 Lord Hailey, *Native Administration in the British African Territories*, London, H.M. S. O., 1951, part 4, p. 2

8 G.M. Childs, *Umbundu Kinship and Character*, London, 1949, p. 23.

9 Margaret J. Field, *Search for Security: An Ethno-Psychiatric Study of Rural Ghana*, London, W.W. Norton & Company, 1960 p. 26.

Similar standards of democratic accountability were detected among several Ashanti rulers of West Africa. They had rules that checked the powers of the monarch. Recorded in the laws and constitution of the Ashanti State, the rules were not too different from the restrictions that are inscribed in the American Bill of Rights. They read:

Tell him that
We do not wish for greediness
We do not wish that he should curse us
We do not wish that his ears should be hard of hearing
We do not wish that he should call people fools
We do not wish that he should act on his own initiative
We do not wish things done as in Kumasi
We do not wish that it should ever be said
'I have no time. I have no time'
We do not wish personal abuse
We do not wish personal violence.[10]

In Western Africa, democratic governance reached political sophistication as early as in the year 1062, when Ghana under Emperor Tunka Manin adopted economic policies that raised adequate revenues to respond to the expansive needs of the empire, while at the same time keeping inflation under control.[11] Africa's perceived inability to govern itself today may have more to do with the fact that not only are the modern structures and institutions of government in place still relatively new, these institutions were developed externally and superimposed from the top-down. The forced imposition of a system that both fragments and merges heterogeneous ethnicities under one centralized rule was bound to produce social and political instability. Attempts to correct for this instability have included proposals for federal arrangements that recognize and value ethnic diversity within the territorial boundaries of the nation-state as formalized by the contemporary independence era.[12] Decentralization rather than centralization of political power is practically more effective in overcoming ethnic conflict and ensuring the success of participatory democracy.[13] Under decentralized political systems, local needs become the basis of government policies and programs of development.[14]

---

10 Ibid.
11 Davidson, pp. 24-25
12 Peter Schraeder, *African Politics and Society: A Mosaic of Transformation*, New York: Bedford/St. Martin Press, 2000, p. 37.
13 Ibid. P. 38.
14 Ibid.

The Paradox of Poverty in Wealth

On the basis of natural resource, Africa is undeniably the wealthiest continent. It has as much as 40% of the world's natural resources. For observers of Africa, reconciling this contradiction between the vast abundance of natural resources and the growing prevalence of poverty in Africa is perplexing. It is not uncommon to hear avid Africanists assert that London, Paris and New York were built with wealth that was acquired from the exploitation and sale of Africa's natural and human resources. The question they fail to address however is that if Africa were able to generate resources that contributed to the development of these great metropolitan capitals, why has Africa not been able to direct some of these resources to the development of Africa? This is a question that is easier asked than answered. Hopefully, on the completion of this book, the reader will be in a better position to answer the question.

Sharing the Blame

To say that Africa has failed to live up to expectation is an understatement. But who is to blame for this failure? Liebenow argues that the European powers that governed Africa for more than three quarter of a century refuse to accept blame for Africa's failure, preferring instead to "lament the destruction or erosion of the alleged legacy of democracy and development they claim to have left behind." Meanwhile, on their part, African leaders refuse to accept blame for their failed policies, preferring instead to "lay all of their problems at the door steps of the former colonialists."[15] He defends the view that there are enough blames to go around, and holds both Africa and the West to blame for Africa's failure.

The wholesale castigation of the West for the underdevelopment of Africa is not only a distortion, it is an abnegation of the responsibilities of African leaders. A systematic assessment of the performance of African governments in the post-independent era would reveal that many of Africa's problems are man-made. That African leaders must be held responsible for Africa's failure does not however vindicate the West of the historic role it played in contributing to that failure.

At independence, Africa had much of what it needed to provide for a smooth and steady economic development. Prior to independence, Africa's resources – both natural and human – contributed and continue to contribute to the development of Europe and the Americas. For a complex range of inexplicable reasons, these resources have failed to produce similar results in Africa. Corruption, mismanagement, ethnic cleavages and lingering colonial

---

15   J. Gus Liebenow, *African Politics: Crises and Challenges*, Indiana University Press, 1986, p. 3.

interests are among the excuses often given for Africa's failure. These vices are present in other regions of the world. Yet, countries in these regions have successfully achieved development. Here, apologists for the continent would argue that the difference between Africa and the other regions of the world is that the fragmentation and exploitation that began in the fifteenth century in the form of slavery continued through to the twentieth and twenty-first centuries under various nomenclatures - colonialism, neocolonialism, globalization and debt bondage.

While most of Africa's current problems are arguably self-inflicted, it would be appropriate to say that Africa's debt crisis is inflicted by international financial institutions which, like the Merchant of Venice, are bent on extolling interest payments from the poorest of the world's poor by any means necessary. There is no other valid explanation for why anyone would want to continue to loan money to countries that are ostensibly insolvent? Curiously, these are loans that are made by institutions that employ some of the best minds in economics and whose decisions are based on the careful study of the credit worthiness of the recipient countries. Credit worthiness implies the ability to repay. That most African countries end up not being able to repay these loans, there is no arguing who is to blame here.

Despite the known hardship that loan payments cause on the masses in Africa, when asked to cancel them, international financial institutions were initially reluctant to do so. Up until the mid-2000s, the standard policy was to reschedule loan payments by granting additional loans, so the indebted countries could keep making interest payments on the principal owed. Resources that should have been directed to developing schools, hospitals, and highways were directed at making interest payments to the World Bank, to the IMF and to various other foreign creditors. When a country is advised to give greater priority to interest repayment to foreign creditors than to investments in education, child nutrition and healthcare, the consequences would naturally be stagnation, underdevelopment and a reduced lifespan. No doubt therefore that Africans have the lowest lifespan.

In the late 1990s to the mid-2000s, it took repeated public demonstrations by civil society organizations in the West for international financial institutions to develop a conscience that allowed them to finally agree to a policy of loan forgiveness. Respite from the cancelled debt was however short-lived. By the late 2000, as a result of the subprime loan crisis, Africa's debt burden was back up to 24.5% in 2009 from 22.4% the year before. The debt-service to export ratio also increased to 16.2% from 15.9% in 2008, raising fears of slipping back to the unsustainable high debt levels the continent experienced before debt forgiveness.[16]

---

16   United Nations Economic Commission for Africa; www.uneca.org/dpmd/publications/
      mrde2009/docs/15_External_Debt.pdf, (accessed June 5, 2016).

Chapter 2

Understanding Africa from a Comparative Perspective

> The state of Africa is a scar on the conscience of the world.
> (British Prime Minister, Tony Blair in 2001)

This chapter provides a historical overview of Africa and North America – two regions whose destinies were tied together at founding, but which have evolved along two very different trajectories. One is democratic, stable and prosperous, while the other is poor, unstable and underdeveloped. While the political and economic institutions of North America have become a model for the world, Africa's political and economic institutions remain an embarrassment. Looking at the two regions individually, it is hard to believe that they both were brought into the European orbit in the same decade.

The Serendipitous Discovery of Africa and the Americas

The fifteenth century was a fateful period in the history of the world. It was the century when Europe unexpectedly came into contact with two previously unknown worlds – Africa and the Americas. The biggest military threat to Europe at the time was the Ottoman Empire. It was the age of mercantilism, and the Ottoman Empire's threatening presence at the crossroads of East-West trade routes forced Europeans to look for alternate routes to the spice islands of Asia. In 1488, the Portuguese explorer, Bartholomew Dias was appointed by King John of Portugal to head an expedition that would sail southeasterly, in search of such an alternate. He would become the first European to make land contact with Africans, when he circumnavigated as far south as the Cape of Good Hope.

Four years later, in 1492, a Spanish explorer by name Christopher Columbus was granted a charter by the King of Spain to sail out Westerly in search of an alternate route to Asia. The skills that were most sought after at the time were cartography and navigation. Cartographic and maritime navigational skills were for the 1490s what computer programming and space exploration skills were for the late twentieth to early twenty-first century. Christopher Columbus was in many ways the Neil Armstrong of his day. With the charter from the king of Spain, he set out sailing west. On

October 12, 1492, he arrived Central America. To mark the discovery of this previously unknown landmass, he planted the Spanish flag.

Four years later, in 1497, another skilled Portuguese navigator, Vasco da Gama, was granted a charter by the King of Portugal to find an alternate route to India by sailing southerly along the African coastline. He set out and discovered a route to India that was shorter and a lot more accurate.

Figure 2.1. Retracing the European Voyages that Led to the European Discovery of Africa and the Americas

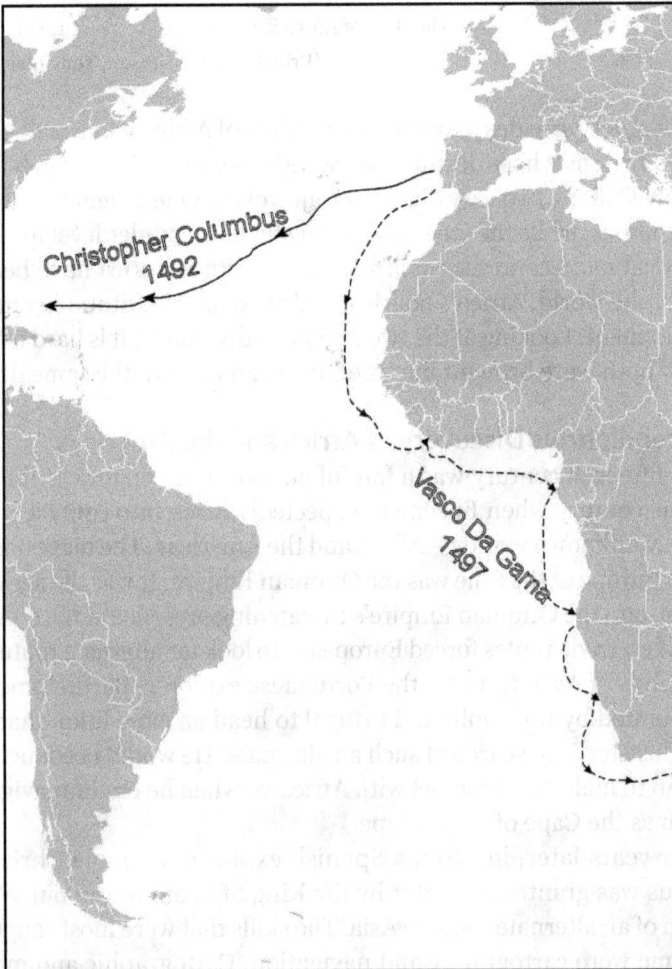

Source: Author

Along the way, Vasco da Gama and his crew frequently stopped on the coastal shores of Africa to replenish their ships with fresh supplies of food and water. The explorers were welcomed with warmth and extraordinary hospitality. Africans have always lived by the biblical teaching in Hebrews 13:2 that says, "do not forget to entertain strangers, for by so doing some people have entertained angels without knowing it." Not only did the hospitality of Africans facilitate the journey, it gave the navigators hope to continue on to Asia. The naming of a port city in South Africa "the Cape of Good Hope" was in expression of that hope. The hospitality of Africans gave European explorers the hope that they needed to carry out with their mission. That city is today called Cape Town.

While the new trade route to India was used to trade spices and other commodities, the trade route to the Americas would be used to enslave and trade the very people whose hospitality helped the European explorers complete their mission. There was indeed an alternative to the slave trade. In lieu of enslavement, Europeans could have hired Africans' migrant labor. Had Africans been hired and brought to the New World as paid migrant workers, just as Chinese workers were brought to on the trans-America railroad, not only would it have been ethically more humane, it would have been a win-win for all. With this option, African migrant laborers would have, at the end of their contract in the Americas, had the option and opportunity to return home to Africa, bringing back with them the new knowledge and skills learned during their sojourn in the Americas. To a large extent, this would have contributed to bringing parallel development to Africa.

Shared Colonial Experiences – Africa and the United States

While the colonization of the United States began in the sixteenth century, colonial rule in Africa did not begin until the nineteenth century. Unlike Africa which was colonized by as many as eight competing European powers (Belgium, Britain, France, Germany, Italy, the Netherlands, Portugal, and Spain), the United States was colonized by one European power. Under British rule, the American colonies were given significant autonomy in self-government, religious worship, and economic organization. For more than 140 years, the system worked relatively well.[1] In Africa, European rule was harsh, repressive, and autocratic. There was no tolerance for individual or group rights. Political freedom and the right to self-determination were simply unthinkable. Instead, there was a systemic and concerted effort to eradicate and supplant everything African with everything European.

While the United States was a settler colony with a common linguistic, cultural and religious identity, Africa's colonial subjects were largely indigenous. The group of eight competing European nations, all with different

---

1   D.W. Meining, *The Shaping of America, Vol. 1: Atlantic America, 1492-1900*, New Haven, CT, Yale University Press, 1986.

languages and cultures, systematically worked to impose their cultural and religious beliefs on Africans. That Africa remains geographically balkanized and culturally heterogeneous today, is attributable to the wide variety of imperial powers that colonized the continent. North America would be unstable today if it too had been colonized and arbitrarily balkanized into unsustainable micro-states by eight fiercely competing European countries.

In the United States, the colonial experience was lived for several hundred years. In Africa, it lasted for a mere seventy-five years. European colonial rule in Africa was long enough to disrupt the old order, but not long enough to establish and embed a new order. Had Africa been colonized by one, rather than by eight competing European powers, or had colonial rule lasted for as long it lasted in the Americas, it possibly would have instilled values that would have led to the establishment of a political system as stable and as enduring as America's.

Ultimately, independence for both Africa and Britain's North American colonies came about as a result of the bankruptcy of the former colonial powers. In North America, Britain was bankrupted by the French and Indian wars. In Africa Europe was bankrupted by World War II. Cash strapped, the bankrupted colonizer of North America sought to raise money by imposing taxes on tea, sugar, stamps and other common American staples. The colonists mobilized to challenge the new taxes. Britain declared war. The colonists fought back, and the fighting led to victory and independence for the American colonists.

Fast forward to the 20th century, independence for a good number of African countries was gained under somewhat similar circumstances. Equally bankrupted by war - World War II, imperial Europe no longer had the financial or administrative resources to continue the administration of its African colonies. African nationalists seized the opportunity and began a campaign for independence. Noticing that China and the Soviet Union had newly emerged as ideological challengers to the West, African nationalists turned to them for military support. The support led to victory and independence for several African countries – from Algeria to Angola to Mozambique.

Though independence for Africa and the United States came almost three centuries apart, they each coincided with rather two unusual historical phenomena. America's independence in 1776 coincided with the publication of Adam Smith's landmark book, *The Wealth of Nations*, which laid out the theoretical underpinnings of capitalism, while Africa's independence in the post-World War II era coincided with the push to propagate and internationalize communism. Karl Marx published his book, the *Communist Manifesto* (1883), exactly one hundred and seven years after the publication of Adam Smith's *The Wealth of Nations*. Communism had for goal the dismantling of capitalism through a revolutionary uprising by the proletariat. Inspired by Marx's ideas, Russian peasants mobilized in 1917, very much like the American colonists did at the Boston Tea Party in 1776 and overthrew their ruler. The Soviet push to internationalize communism at the end of World War II set international communism on a collision course with international capitalism. Rivalry between the two ideologies led to a cold war between the two superpowers. Here is a question that is worth pondering: What if the ideas of Karl Marx had come before Adam Smith's? Had the *Communist Manifesto* been published before 1776 when America was still being exploited by the British Crown, would it have turned the Boston Tea Party communist uprising? We are aware that, right after winning its independence, America adopted a governing ideology that was radically different from monarchic rule and from anything the British and the rest of the world had ever known. In 1776, republicanism and constitutional democracy were so radically abstract and different, it was universally disdained by European monarchies. Indeed, republicanism was as distant from monarchic rule as communism was from capitalism when it was adopted by Russia in 1917. So, had Karl Marx come before Adam Smith and had America adopted communism, what would the world be like today? This is a question that is difficult to answer, but a question that is worth asking.

In the meantime, the political reality is that independence in many African countries came through negotiated settlements. In almost every case, independence that is achieved by negotiated settlement always inevitably morphs into neocolonialism – a new and more resilient form of colonial exploitation. It is a system that is particularly present in French-speaking African countries. Agreements and treaties that were signed at independence gave the French oversight, and sometimes veto powers over the internal and external policies of its "former" African colonies. The colonies were obligated to sign over ownership of the resources in the subsoil to France, hold 40% of their foreign reserves with the French Central Bank in Paris, and have their national currencies printed by France and pegged to the French national currency, the French franc. Had the United States achieved independence through a peacefully negotiated agreement, it similarly would have remained subjected to various forms of British neocolonial exploitation.

While positivists may be opposed to violence and revolutions as a political tool, violence is in reality a dialectic for democratic development. Historically, self-determination and democracy have most often evolved from revolutionary action. This is as true for America as it is for Africa. Most African countries whose independence was achieved by revolution have on the whole fared better than countries whose independence was negotiated and peaceably granted.

The Task of Nation Building

The campaign for independence is an affirmative demand for self-rule. After independence comes the more daunting task of nation-building. It is a task in which America has made astounding strides, but a task in which Africa has woefully failed. While the United States rose from the ashes of colonial subjugation to overtake its former colonizer, Africa emerged from the devastation of colonial rule and became hobbled by stagnation and underdevelopment. Euphemistically described as developing countries, African countries are in reality countries that are underdeveloped and under-developing steadily. Developing countries are countries where one sees everyday change on all fronts – economic, scientific, and technological. If Africa were developing, the quality of life would be much better today than it was at independence. Every current statistic on the continent shows that economically and politically, the quality of life in Africa was much better in the first decade of independence than today.

In both Africa and North America, the task of nation-building started out as an exercise at trial and error. America took a path that was radically different from that of the mother country. Besides adopting republicanism over monarchic rule, the newly independent nation started out by boycotting trade with its former colonial ruler. It then turned inwards and proceeded to developing the political and technological foundations on which it was going to base its development. Unlike in Africa, the nation-builders of the new American State were of European descent. They were inspired by the "radical" philosophies of the likes of John Locke, Thomas Hobbes, Montesquieu and Jean-Jacques Rousseau. After a failed experiment with the Articles of Confederation, the 13-member states called a Constitutional Convention to reassess and redefine the future of the young nation. The Convention successfully put together a new social contract that over time enabled America to weather the Civil War, survive the Great Depression, accommodate the Civil Rights Movement and win the Cold War. Had America at independence adopted a system of government that was similar to what was in Britain, it may never have been able to stand on its own, just as French-speaking Africa has been unable to stand on its own.

For African countries, however, after achieving independence, they all continued to maintain close economic and political ties with the very powers they liberated themselves from and adopt the very governing structures that were used to colonize and exploit them. In his book, *The Black Man's Burden*, Basil Davidson decries the plight of the African freedom fighters who, schooled mostly in Western ways, could only imagine an African future inspired by the very West whose shackles they fought so hard to break, turning their backs on experiences that might have been useful for governing in their pre-colonial African past.[2]

The suffix "mental" in "developmental" implies that development is a mental process rather than an external or physical process. Sustainable development cannot be externally driven. It must come from the mind. As long as the ideas, thoughts and the vision for political and economic development are not internally driven, the push to develop and modernize Africa will continue to be an exercise in futility.

Among the forces that continue to impede development in Africa are Africa's continuous hold to the old order – i.e., traditional values. At America's independence, there was no old order or competing traditional values on the continent. This made the establishment of a republic less conflicting. In post-colonial Africa, the process of nation-building was carried out by Africans who were caught up between the conflicting values of tradition and modernity. In their struggle to build a new order, the old order was still actively in place, competing and sometimes obstructing the establishment of the new order. If forced to choose between the unwritten tradition of his society and the modern republican constitution that he took an oath to respect, the typical African ruler will without doubt choose the former. No such dilemma was present in the U.S. at its founding.

At independence, as soon as the thirteen new American states realized that holding on separately to their newly acquired sovereignties was going to make them potentially vulnerable to future external and internal threats, they decided to come together and form a union. With vision and a determined quest for national grandeur, the thirteen newbies would grow into fifty states. While one of the factors that continues to inhibit development in Africa is Africa's balkanization into unsustainable micro-states, African leaders know that they can overcome this by restructuring and reorganizing themselves into a strong and dynamic union.

The accelerated growth of the United States from thirteen to fifty states was the deliberate result of visionary leadership. From the westward expansion to the Louisiana purchase, to the purchase of Alaska, the leaders of the United States were genuinely interested and committed to founding a greater America that extended from the Atlantic to the Pacific. If a similar vision were present in Africa, it equally could have led to the development of a continental federation.

What may have impaired the development of a similar vision in Africa would be the fact that while the United States is governed by institutions, Africa is governed by a personality cult. In Africa, presidential power is irrevocably placed in the person and in the bureaucracy that serves that person.

---

2   Basil Davidson, *The Black Man's Burden: Africa and the Curse of the Nation-State*, Three Rivers Press, New York, 1993

This concentration of power is often responsible for the social and political instability that defines today's Africa. Meanwhile, it is clearly known that the legitimacy of individual leaders can be more readily challenged than the legitimacy of institutions. It is easier to overthrow an individual from power than to overthrow an institution of government such parliament or a democratically elected president. When so much power is concentrated in one individual, it makes that individual a vulnerable target of military coup or assassination.

Finally, as a nation of immigrants, the nation-building effort in the United States was pivoted by an Anglo-Saxon core. All other immigrant groups had to assimilate culturally and linguistically into this core population. English cultural values became the values of all later immigrants. In African countries, however, there is rarely an influential or pioneering core ethnic group whose legitimacy is commonly accepted, and into which all other ethnic groups willingly assimilate. Unfortunately, in African countries, there are many competing core groups, and with the prevalence of many competing cores, political order is characterized more by centrifugal than by centripetal forces.

Legitimacy and the Task of Nation Building in Africa

The primary obstacle to nation-building in Africa is the challenge of legitimacy. At independence, the United States knew how important this challenge was going to be and immediately went to work to address it. It produced a "social contract" that not only guaranteed freedom and equality, but that also foreshadowed any pretensions of tyranny by either the majority or the minority. Today, many see the American constitution as a symbol of America's political stability and its source of authority. In the U.S. Constitution, the structure of government is clearly defined, functions and powers horizontally separated among the various federal branches of government, and vertically distributed among the various state and local levels of government. The powers defined in the constitution are assigned not to the occupant of the office, but to the office.

In much of Africa, up until the 1990s, the constitution was frequently regarded not so much as a social contract, but as the will of the head of state. Written by him and rubber-stamped by his handpicked parliament, it requires no input from, or ratification by, the electorate. It is amended at the president's will and can be violated when it interferes with his self-interest. While power is in theory clearly defined and assigned to three branches of government, in practice, all three branches of government are controlled by the president. With supreme and unquestionable authority over the constitution and over the three branches of government, this gives African rulers absolute powers. In the 1970s and 1980s, the people of Zaire actually went beyond the belief that their president had absolute power, to actually promoting the myth that his rule was pre-ordained and therefore divine. The president himself, Mobutu Sese Seko, actively promoted the myth that he was the reincarnation of Jesus Christ.[3] The same was true with the President of Equatorial Guinea, Obiang Ngeuma. In a nationwide broadcast, the government radio station announced that President Obiang Ngeuma was in "permanent contact with the almighty" and could therefore "kill anyone without being called to account."[4]

While constitutional interpretation is the prerogative of supreme courts in Western societies, in Africa the Supreme Court must defer to the will of the president. Ultimately, the constitution of the typical African country is what the president says it is. Any supreme court judge whose interpretation of the constitution goes at odds with the president's runs the risk of dismissal and/or prosecution. In 2001, Zimbabwe's President Robert Mugabe did just that. He dismissed supreme court judges whose interpretation of the constitution were at odds with his land reform policies.

Elsewhere in Africa, Cameroon's President Ahmadou Ahidjo, on the eve of his retirement in 1982 secretly amended the constitution to hand power over to his handpicked successor. On coming to power, the new president, Paul Biya, also amended the national constitution, single-handedly trans-forming Cameroon from a union of two states – "the United Republic of Cameroon" to a single centralized state – "the Republic of Cameroon." In 1996, he again amended the constitution extending the presidential term of office from five to seven years. Bent on staying in power for life, Biya yet again amended the constitution in 2008, abolishing term limits. As added guarantee, the amended constitution included a provision that granted him immunity from prosecution for crimes committed while he was in office. Using the constitution to protect oneself against prosecution even before one is accused and/or indicted is no doubt an *a priori* admission of guilt.

Several African states at independence embraced multiparty democracies for a brief moment. Before long, they all adopted one-party systems on the pretext that one-party systems were necessary in keeping their diverse ethnic and religious populations united. Behind the façade of welding together diverse ethnic populations, was a design to consolidate the president's powers and avoid political competition. Despite America's distinctive ethnic diversity, legitimacy was achieved not by instituting one-party rule but by promoting pluralism. The rigidity that was inherent in the one-party political systems in Africa soon became a fragmenting rather than a unifying force. In the early 1990s, when "the winds of democracy" inexplicably blew into Africa

---

3   Video, *Mobutu Sese Seko, Roi du Congo*, Directed by Thierry Michel, 1999.
4   www.guardian.co.uk/world/.../equatorialguinea.danglaister (accessed 02/02/2010)

from the East, they opened up a Pandora Box of irredentism and competing claims to territorial and ethnic autonomy. The question that remains unanswered to this day is that, why did a continent that was colonized by Western democracies that practice multiparty politics at home emerged at independence to adopt single party authoritarian political systems that were reminiscent of the centralized single party systems of the Communist East? In a related question, why did the 1990s winds of democracy blow into Africa from the East rather than from the West? While the colonial powers may have practiced democracy at home, in Europe, what it left behind in Africa was a legacy of autocratic rule. "Indigenous sociopolitical arrangements in most other targeted societies were replaced not by participatory, quasi self-government, but by military rule, the purpose of which was to institutionalize mercantilism and extract raw materials."[5] Noticing how effective autocratic rule was, the communist East rushed to adopt it in the first half of the 20th century. As critical as Western democracies may have been of these centralized, single-party autocratic systems of the East, the West actually saw them as an effective governance model and allowed their handpicked African rulers to adopt them. In almost every case where Europe has had to exercise governing power anywhere outside of the West over non-westerners, that exercise has always been autocratic.

This paradox is vividly captured by Caroline Elkins, in her reaction to the December 2007 bloody fallout in the disputed Kenyan elections:

> If you're looking for the origins of Kenya's ethnic tensions, look to its colonial past... It's no wonder that newly independent countries such as Kenya maintained and even deepened the old imperial heritage of authoritarianism and ethnic division. The British had spent decades trying to keep the Luo and Kikuyu divided, quite rightly fearing that if the two groups ever united, their combined power could bring down the colonial order. Indeed, a short-lived Luo-Kikuyu alliance in the late 1950s hastened Britain's retreat from Kenya and forced the release of Jomo Kenyatta, the nation's first president, from a colonial detention camp. But before their departure, the British schooled the future Kenyans on the lessons of a very British model of democratic elections. Britain was determined to protect its economic and geopolitical interests during the decolonization process, and it did most everything short of stuffing ballot boxes to do so. That set dangerous precedents.

---

5   Edward J. Dodson, Third World Problems: A Post-Colonial Legacy? www.coperativeindividualism.org/dodson_third_world_problems.html (accessed 11/01/2011)

Among other maneuvers, the British drew electoral boundaries to cut the representation of groups they thought might
cause trouble and empowered the provincial administration
to manipulate supposedly democratic outcomes.

... Fears of ethnic ascendancies, power-hungry political elites,
undemocratic processes and institutions - all are hallmarks of
today's Kenya, just as they were during British colonial rule.
... the democratic historical trajectory that Kenya has been
moving along was launched at the inception of British colonial
rule more than a century ago. It's not hard to discern similar
patterns - deliberately stoked ethnic tensions, power-hungry
elites, feeble democratic traditions and institutions - in other
former British colonies such as Pakistan, Zimbabwe and Iraq
that share similar imperial pasts. In retrospect, the wonder is
not that Kenya is descending into ethnic violence. The wonder
is that it didn't happen sooner.[6]

The answer to our second question on why the winds of democracy came
in from the East and not from the West would be because at the collapse of
the Soviet Empire, East bloc states were quick to realize that while centralized single-party rule had been working to benefit the centralized Soviet
hegemony, it was doing little to advance the welfare of the satellite states.
They therefore had to do away with it. It was a realization that African states
could not on their own come to. Looking at the practice of democracy on
the continent today, one is still able to tell that the imprints are from the
East. These imprints are seen in the persistence of vote rigging, political
intolerance, and the manipulation of the public will through the abolition
of term limits and the institution life/dynastic presidencies.

Challenging the forced legitimacy and years of deprivation that were
imposed on them by one-party rule, most ethnic populations took advantage
of the democratic winds that blew into Africa in the 1990s to begin reassert-
ing their autonomy and ethnic identities. The challenge of the old order and
the search for legitimacy would plunge Africa into a multiplicity of inter-
ethnic wars. In parts of Africa where indignation for the injustices of the old
order were most deeply felt, some of the inter-ethnic conflicts turned into
genocidal wars. A series of African countries, including Somalia, Liberia,
Sierra Leone, the Cote d'Ivoire, the Democratic Republic of Congo, Rwanda
and Uganda disintegrated along ethno-regional conclaves and, under the
command of competing warlords, they fought for control of national power.

6   Caroline Elkins, *The Washington Post*, Sunday, January 6, 2008; B03

A similar phenomenon was witnessed in other parts of the world that were previously kept under leash by authoritarian one-party rule. Challenges to the legitimacy of the Yugoslavian central government and the reassertion of ethnic self-rule added the phrase "ethnic cleansing" to the vocabulary of international politics in the 1990s.

In every regard, ethnicity and ethnic affinity in Africa is a lot stronger than national identity. Because it is a combination of one's heritage and one identity, it remains so defining that any disregard for it can only but trigger an aggressive pushback. Still influenced by traditional forms of government that go back thousands of years, most Africans remain uncompromising and intolerant of the authority and rule of leaders that are not from their ethnic background. The idea of choosing a leader by a ballot remains abstract for most traditionalists. For traditional Africans, the modern electoral process is seen as a gamble. For them leadership is of such divine importance, it cannot be decided by casting pieces of papers in ballot boxes. No doubt therefore that modern democratic rule has been slow to take hold in Africa. In much of traditional Africa, when you are a ruler, your rule is for life. Not only is the idea of an elected ruler absurd, the idea that a ruler should step down after serving in office is for them outrightly ridiculous. They see it as tantamount to getting the British monarch to agree to a new political arrangement where he/she is elected to serve for one or two terms and then forced to step down. Basically, what is at play here are the forces of tradition competing against the forces of modernity. Democracy and electoral systems are modern. Chieftaincy and inherited monarchic rule are traditional. Pit them against each other and it will result in the chronic instability that we find in Africa today.

For most traditional Africans, there has to be a certain mystic about a ruler. It is this mystic that makes his rule divine. It is a tradition that has been around since the beginning of organized society. The mystic does not apply to leaders who are elected, and particularly to leaders who are from a different ethnic group. Absent such mystic, the legitimacy of elected African rulers is frequently questioned and challenged. These challenges are often expressed through military coups, warlordism and factional warfare.

In Africa, as elsewhere in the world, legitimacy is a precondition for stability, and stability is in turn a precondition for development. But in societies where there is greater respect for tradition than for the written constitution, how do we establish legitimacy? The problem was solved in Britain by integrating the new institutions of democracy with the traditional institutions of the monarchy to come up with what is referred to today as Britain's "unwritten Constitution." In Africa, instead of following the same model that had so well succeeded in merging the new order with the old order in Britain, Europeans sought first to eradicate and replace the traditional governance institutions they met in Africa with colonial autocracies. As soon as this was done, things fell apart and ever since then, Africa has not been able to find focus.

Ultimately, it does appear that to establish legitimacy in Africa, we may need to begin by reestablishing the old order that colonial rule worked so hard to erase. Once that is established and granted respect similar to the respect the British enjoy under dual monarchic/democratic rule, it is then that it would be appropriate to integrate and/or superimpose a new order in the form of constitutional democracy. In other words, legitimacy and nation-building in Africa does need to follow a path similar to the path that it followed in Britain. For Africans as for Britons, there has to be a certain mystic about a ruler. The same is true for the peoples of Japan, Thailand and other democracies where elected heads of states work alongside ceremonial heads of states. The successful wedding of the old and the new in such traditional societies has produced some of the most enduring guarantees of political and economic stability.

No matter how well educated or westernized an African is, there is always the tendency to show respect to "the elder" or traditional ruler. If given the choice between respect for traditional rules and respect for constitutional rule, most modern African rulers will show greater respect to traditional rules. This explains why African leaders who so very readily amend their national constitutions to advance their personal agenda would, when given the opportunity, be afraid to tamper with the rules in their tradition. Indeed, the very governmental leaders who majestically stand up high at the national scene are likely to bow low before their traditional village rulers when they visit their villages. And in most cases, the edicts of a traditional ruler – though unwritten – are sometimes more revered than the mandates of the written constitution. To establish a modern constitutional democracy in Africa therefore, it may actually be necessary to begin first by consolidating and codifying the highly revered traditional norms that governed Africa for thousands of years prior to the institution of modern constitutional rule.

Africa's Long Walk with Globalization

Globalization emerged as the reigning political and economic paradigm of the early 21st century. Many see it as a new paradigm. In reality, it is a paradigm that is as old as the inception of the modern global system. Since the 15th century, Africa has been an integral part of the global system. Forcibly brought into the system by slavery, it evolved into colonialism, neocolonialism and now, globalization. As a new global paradigm, globalization starts out where imperialism left off. With the evolutionary transformation of the international economy from trade to industry to technology and information technology, Africa appears poised once again to be relegated to the fringes of the global economy. This is evidenced in Africa's negligible contribution to the emerging global economy. Prior to independence, Africa's contribution to the global economy was actually more significant than it is today. At independence, the continent failed to industrialize and diversify its export economy. As a result, its share of contribution to the globalizing international economic system fell from 5% in the pre-independence period to 2% today.[7]

Despite optimistic claims that "Africa seems increasingly to be the final frontier for economic globalization",[8] it does appear that Africa is thus far not well poised to derive much benefits from the current globalizing world economy. To take advantage of the opportunities that globalization has to offer, Africa is missing one very important advantage – the ability to derive economies of scale. This is an advantage that accrues largely to Western multinationals and regionally integrated economies such as NAFTA and the EU. From the onset, it was evident that the drivers of globalization were big corporations and regional trading blocs. So far, there are no known multi-national corporations in Africa (no African versions of Shell, Exxon/Mobile, CitiGroup and Chevron/Texaco) and no viable regional trading blocs. It is very likely therefore that Africa's role in the globalizing international system is going to remain that of a passive observer rather than that of an active participant.

Economies of scale are derived primarily from size. A majority of the states in Africa are micro-states, and therefore lacking the advantage of size. Despite sustained efforts to establish regional economic blocs, the national boundaries that were established during colonial rule continue to be defining and restrictive. Western Europe on the other hand realized very early on in the late 1940s that to overcome the multiplicity of development challenges that lay ahead, it needed to continentally pull the economies of its member states together. When it did so, it was able to take advantage of the economies of scale that are enjoyed by bigger states. Had the EU not integrated its economies, there definitely would be no Air-Bus plane manufacturing in Europe today. The United States realized the importance of an integrated economy much earlier, in 1787, and developed a political system that brought together under one national government, the thirteen economies that have grown into fifty prosperous states today. By the time globalization emerged in the 21st century, these two regions - the United States and the European Union - were well poised to taking advantage of it.

Economies that have not had the opportunity to perform regionally in

---

7   Nicolas Van de Walle, "Africa and the World Economy: Continued Marginalization or Re-engagement?" in John W. Harbeson and Donald Rothchild, Eds. *Africa in World Politics*, Colorado: Westview Press, 2000 p. 265.

8   2010 Report on Africa, Tom Cargill, *Our Common Interests: Africa's Role in the Post-G8 World*, Royal Institute of International Affairs, Chatham House, London.

the minor leagues of economic competition will not be able to perform in the major leagues of global economic competition. Economic performance in the major leagues is driven primarily by big multinational corporations. Knowing that globalization is an economic system that comes with a decreasing role for sovereign states and an increasing role for multinationals, micro-states such as Sao Tome, Equatorial Guinea, Cape Verde are simply never going to be able to effectively regulate the economic activities of major multinational companies which are doing business in their territories. Now as in the past, it is obvious that the playing field is not level. If with all its resources and regulatory powers the United States government was unable to regulate the fraudulent business practices of Enron and MCI-Worldcom, it is doubtful that such micro-states as Cape Verde and Sao Tome are going to be able to exercise any regulatory oversight over the activities of multinational corporations that do business on their countries. Fragmented and balkanized into unsustainable microstates, not only does Africa lack the regulatory capacity, it lacks the financial, technical and technocratic wherewithal to monitor the activities of multinationals and possibly go after corporations that violate contractual and/or environmental policies.

On top of the powers of multinational corporations, are the powers of Western governments. While talking about the virtues of free trade and free competition, and preaching to Africans about the virtues of economic liberalism, the US and the EU continue to promote domestic policies that pay subsidies to their farmers. Not only do such policies give Western producers an undue advantage, they make it impossible for the African farmer to compete in the global marketplace.

While the U.S. has over hundreds of years honed and perfected its regulatory powers, most African states are still too small and too weak to develop the legal and technical abilities that would enable them to effectively monitor and regulate corporate malfeasance. This is particularly true if we see globalization as the unleashing of Western corporate power to compete in a world whose economies are weak, under-capitalized, and underdeveloped. Allegorically, globalization could in some ways be seen as the "waltmartization" of the international economy. If the current globalizing trend continues, fledgling Third World businesses are going to regrettably go the way the "mom & pop" stores in the United States went when a Walmart store opened in their local communities.

With the growing marginalization of Africa, we cannot help but ponder: Could globalization be the continuation of colonial domination by another name and in another form? Is today's playing field level? If it is not, what can be done to make it level, so Africa can effectively compete? How truly global would the global economy be if it globalizes without Africa? In other words, what would the globalization of the international economy look like

25

without the full participation of one-seventh of its population that lives on the African continent? There are obviously no easy answers to these questions. But a cursory look at the evolution of the global system should give us some insights to the role Africa has played in past economic systems.

Chapter 3

Global Challenges the West has Won with the Help of Africa

Interest does not tie nations together; it sometimes separates them. But sympathy and understanding does unite them.

Woodrow Wilson[1]

The history of Africa's interaction with the West is long, detailed and acrimonious. Despite this acrimony, historical evidence shows that the two regions have over the centuries partnered to produce some of the evolutionary forces that have powered the international economy. In his study of *Capitalism and Slavery*, Eric Williams discovered that from the vast fortunes that plantation owners, shipbuilders and transporters accumulated in the slave trade, they were able to fund the establishment of the banks and heavy industries that led to the success of the Industrial Revolution in Europe.[2] In a follow up book on the causes of the British Industrial Revolution, Joseph E. Inikori reveals too that both as consumers and as producers, Africans on both sides of the Atlantic were instrumental to the success of the Industrial Revolution. Where previously English merchants sold continental and Asian-made goods, they were now selling British manufactured goods in Africa and in the Americas. This structural shift and the resultant industrial revolution were fueled by the flow of raw materials from Africa, and the processing of finished and semi-finished goods by Africans in the New World.[3] He provides archival evidence that shows that "export production in French America (today's Haiti) ... was 100% produced by Africans.[4]

Outside of the economic sphere, Africa has helped the West win many global historical challenges. We will here attempt to identify some of these

1   Woodrow Wilson, http://strangewondrous.net/browse/subject/i/international+relatio ns?start=10, Accessed 2/22/2016.
2   Erick Williams, *Capitalism and Slavery*, University of North Carolina, 1994.
3   Joseph E. Inikori, *Africans and the Industrial Revolution in England: A Study in International Trade and Economic Development*. Cambridge: Cambridge University Press, 2002, p. 478.
4   ibid, p. 191.

challenges.

Helping the West Tame the American Wilderness

To properly understand why Europeans went through the costly burden of taking people from as far-away as Africa and bringing them to the America's, we would have to start by taking a look at Darwin's classic thesis on the survival of the fittest. Here, we see that they made this costly investment because they saw Africans as fit and as capable of helping transform the forests and the swamps of the American wilderness into a developed and livable state. Here was a Europe that had unexpectedly stumbled on a vast, wild and resource-rich wilderness in an age when there were no earth-moving or tree-felling caterpillars or tractors. Attempts to employ Native Americans and European indentured servants proved futile. Mortality rates among non-African racial groups were high, so on the advice of Pope Nicolas V, Africans were shipped in as early as in the 15th century.[5] They provided more than just physical labor. They became the tractors that did the digging, the ploughing and the clearing that helped in the conquering and taming of the American wilderness. Prior to the development of tractors and bulldozers therefore, Africans were the tractors and bulldozers of the New World. The survival rate of African labor was better. On the basis of Darwin's *survival of the fittest* thesis therefore, of all population groups whose labor was put to test in the taming of the American wilderness, Africans were "the fittest" and the most helpful.

Helping the West Overtake China

There is agreement among historians that prior to the European discovery of Africa, China was technologically more advanced than the West. Through slavery and colonial exploitation, the West was able to combine Africa's human and material resources with her entrepreneurship to not only catch up, but to effectively overtake China. As early as in the 15th century, decades before Europe discovered Africa, there were active friendly ties between Africa and China. In expression of that friendship, gifts were exchanged. Among them were giraffes, zebras, rhinos, leopards, and ostriches sent to the Chinese Ming Emperor Yongle between 1405 and 1433.[6] As an imperial power at the time, China had the ability to colonize and exploit Africa; and had it done so, the proceeds of that exploitation would have

---

5   Davenport, Frances Gardiner. Ed. *European Treaties bearing on the History of the United States and its Dependencies to 1648.* Carnegie Institution of Washington, Washington, D.C.: 1917, p. 23.

6   Sally Church, The Giraffe of Bengal; A Medieval Encounter in Ming China, The Medieval *History Journal* April 2004 vol. 7 no. 1 1-37; Dale Peterson, *Giraffe Reflections*, University of California Press (September 9, 2013)

gone to strengthen and maintain China's economic and technological lead. Internally and regionally, China was resource-rich, and the need to colonize or exploit a continent that was far away from its shores did not occur to her at the time.

Thus, while China's interest in Africa is viewed as a recent development, it actually predates the European conquest of Africa. Over time, as European colonial and imperial power increased and China's diminished, the Chinese largely disappeared from the continent until their return in the second half of the 20th century. Today, the discovery of "pillar graves" in southern Africa, along with Chinese porcelain embedded in stone graves is indication that trade existed between Africa and China[7] well before the arrival of Europeans.

From the active economic ties China began developing with Africa in the early 21st Century, it would appear that China may have come to the realization too that to catch up with the West, it too has to partner with Africa. What in 1884 was described as the European scramble for Africa had by the early 21st century become the Chinese scramble for Africa. Chinese presence would be felt in almost every sector of the African economy – minerals, energy, mining, manufacturing, finance, trade, telecommunications, agriculture and fisheries. Behind closed doors, Western policy-makers became jittery about the growing Chinese presence in Africa. In some circles, the American/Chinese rivalry in Africa was referred to as the new cold war. In this new contention the U.S. chose to counter the growing Chinese economic presence in Africa with a military presence. Using the global war against terrorism as subterfuge, the United States government in February 2007 authorized the establishment of a U.S. Combatant Command for Africa. From the U.S. perspective, the expectation was that if the West is ever going to win the global war against terrorism, and/or the new "cold war" against China, it was going to have to re-partner with Africa. This was exactly what it did. Yet, while China is unconditionally investing in Africa, the United States is conditioning its assistance on "countries whose governments are judged as heading in a positive direction in terms of institutional and economic development and U.S. security interests."[8]

Helping the West Neutralize and Disintegrate the Ottoman Empire

Before the emergence of communism and fascism, the biggest political and military threat to the West was the Ottoman Empire. Pope Urban II's

---

7   UNESCO, http://www.worldheritagesite.org/tags/tag623.html (accessed 01/19/2010)
8   http://www.foreignpolicy.com/story/cms.php?story_id=3098&print=1(accessed 12/08/2011).

authorization of an all-out Western crusade against the spread of Islam in 1095 led to a fierce war between Christians and Muslims. By 1453, Muslims had taken over and occupied Constantinople. Positioned on the southeastern frank of Western Europe, it controlled strategic trade routes between East and West. The vital economic resources of the day included spices. Conducting trade in these resources was rendered difficult by the hostile presence of the Ottoman Empire on the land and sea trade routes that went from Europe across the Middle East to Asia. The West was forced to come up with an alternative route that would avoid passing through the Middle East. In the process of finding that route, Africa was discovered. Not only did Africa provide a friendlier bypass route to Asia, it later provided slave labor, minerals and raw materials that enabled the West to defeat and neutralize the Ottoman threat. By the end of World War I – a war in which Africans and Black Americans fought on the side of the West – the Ottoman Empire was completely neutralized, with many of its former provinces, including all of North Africa, forcibly brought under the colonial tutelage of the West.

Helping Europeans Expel Muslims from East Africa

Before the European slave trade, Arabs enjoyed virtual monopoly over the trade in African slaves. The monopoly was facilitated by two factors. First, Africa south of the Sahara was largely unknown to Europeans. Secondly, sub-Sahara Africa was geographically closer to the Arab world. These two advantages were taken away when the Portuguese defeated and expulsed their Arab colonizers. Inspired by their victory over the Arabs, the West declared a global war against Islam, taking the conflict beyond the outer peripheries of Europe and North Africa. In the process, Portuguese explorers discovered and made friends with African rulers in central and western Africa, establishing diplomatic ties with some. Both on land and by sea, Africans gave safe passage to the Portuguese, enabling them to circumnavigate southeasterly to the continent's eastern coastline, where they militarily uprooted remnants of Muslim influence. Without this expedition, much of what is today's Swahili Africa – the region from Kenya south to Mozambique – would continue to remain an Arab/Muslim enclave. A Muslim presence along the East African coast would have, with time, eventually extended to southern Africa. Portugal's global war against Islam paved the way for David Livingstone and other Christian missionaries to freely travel to the region promote Western influence and the Christian religion. Cecil Rhodes and other European capitalists who later forcibly settled the region would never have been able to do so, had Africans not given the Portuguese safe passage to expel Arabs from Eastern Africa.

Helping America win the Revolutionary War Against Great Britain

Both sides in the American Revolutionary War needed Blacks to win the war. Both Britain and America actively recruited Blacks into their armies; but it was the side that recruited the larger number of Blacks that won the war. That side was America. Long before the war started, the author of the Declaration of Independence, Thomas Jefferson knew that Blacks were going to be instrumental in winning the war. In the preamble to the Declaration of Independence, he writes that "All Men are Created Equal." This was a call directed not just at rallying the white masses, but at mobilizing the slave population as well. The original text of the Declaration of Independence was even more pointed. While the final text was an indictment on inequality, the original text was a more pointed indictment on slavery. It read:

> He has waged cruel war against human nature itself, violating its most sacred rights of life & liberty in the persons of a distant people who never offended him, captivating & carrying them into slavery in another hemisphere, or to incur miserable death in their transportation thither. This piratical warfare, the opprobrium of *infidel* powers, is the warfare of the CHRISTIAN king of Great Britain. Determined to keep open a market where MEN should be bought & sold, he has prostituted his negative for suppressing every legislative attempt to prohibit or to restrain this execrable commerce: and that this assemblage of horrors might want no fact of distinguished die, he is now exciting those very people to rise in arms among us, and to purchase that liberty of which he has deprived them, & murdering the people upon whom he also obtruded them; thus paying off former crimes committed against the *liberties* of one people, with crimes which he urges them to commit against the *lives* of another. In every stage of these oppressions we have petitioned for redress in the most humble terms; our repeated petitions have been answered by repeated injury. a prince whose character is thus marked by every act which may define a tyrant, is unfit to be the ruler of a people who mean to be free. Future ages will scarce believe that the hardiness of one man, adventured within the short compass of 12 years only, on so many acts of tyranny without a mask, over a people fostered & fixed in principles of liberty.[9]

---

9   Thomas Jefferson, The Declaration of Independence, http://www.wsu.edu/~dee/AMERICA/DECLAR.HTM

This is an intensely vitriolic indictment of the British. Slaves saw it as a genuine call for freedom and equality. They took up arms and valiantly fought alongside their white counterparts. They helped win the victory that won independence for America. The outcome may have been different had they refused to fight or had they allied and fought but for Britain. Indeed, Britain had made a similar appeal to the enslaved Blacks, promising to grant freedom to slaves who joined the British military. A special regiment known as the Lord Dunmore's Ethiopian Regiment,[10] was established for slaves who answered the call. Unfortunately for the British but fortunately for the colonists, less than 1000 slaves answered the call. Victory would be won by the side which enlisted more Black troops – the American colonies. Thanks to the contributions of the peoples of African descent, that victory was won and celebrated by America's founding fathers and documented in hundreds of publications, including a publication entitled "An Historical Research: Opinions of the Founders of the Republic on Negroes as Slaves, as Citizens and as Soldiers."[11]

Helping the North Win the American Civil War

In the second major war that was fought to prevent the collapse and disintegration of the United States, Blacks again played a decisive role. Despite persisting skepticisms, including skepticisms by Abraham Lincoln on the ability of blacks to serve as soldiers,[12] Union Generals actively recruited both freed and enslaved Blacks to fight for the Union Army. General James H. Lane who organized, trained and put into action two regiments of Black soldiers,[13] and in a letter to Secretary of War Stanton, General Benjamin Butler declared that "I shall call on Africa to intervene, and I do not think I shall call in vain."[14]

Within two years into the war, as many as fifty thousand black soldiers were fighting for the Union army. Written accounts published at the end of the civil war included such comments as: "You have no idea how my prejudices with regard to the Negro troops have been dispelled ... The brigade of Negroes behave magnificently and fought splendidly; could not have done better. They are far superior in discipline to the White troops and just as

10 Benjamin Quarles, *The Negro in the American Revolution*, Chapel Hill: University of North Carolina Press, p. 19; see also Gordon S. Woods, *The Radicalism of the American Revolution*, New York: Knopf, 1992, pp. 176-8.

11 George Livermore, *An Historical Research: Opinions of the Founders of the Republic on Negroes as Slaves, as Citizens and as Soldiers*, Charleston, SC: Nabu Press, 2010

12 Leon F. Litwack, *Been in the Storm So Long: The Aftermath of Slavery* (New York: Vintage Books, 1979, p. 66

13 Benjamin Quarles, *The Negro in the Civil War*, New York: Da Capo Press, 1953, 1989 p. 114.

14 Ibid, p. 116-117.

brave."[15] Even Judge Joseph Hold and former Secretary of War would point out that "In view of the loyalty of the race and of the obstinate courage which they have shown themselves to possess, they certainly constitute a most powerful and reliable arm of the public defense."[16] Views such as "I never believed in niggers before, but by Jasus, they are a hell for fighting," were commonly expressed by white troops.[17] Even the abolitionist writer, Frederick Douglas wrote that let the black man get "bullets in his pocket, and there is no power on earth which can deny that he has earned the right to citizenship in the United States.[18]

Helping with America's Westward Expansion of the United States

As America modernized and began to expand westward, it was confronted with yet another challenge. It was faced with the challenge of overcoming resistance from American Indians. In the conflict, America's secret weapon was a contingent of Black soldiers of the 9th and 10th Calvary Regiments. They were deployed in an area that extended from Texas to Montana and through the Southwest. They fought more than 177 combats. Awed by their bravery and agility in the battlefield, American Indians referred to them as "Buffalo Soldiers" – a term of endearment and reverence in American Indian culture. Contingents of African Americans were also assigned the task of escorting the settlers and providing security to railroad workers.

Besides serving as the vanguard in the United States westward expansion, African Americans were again recruited to fight in the Spanish-American War, the Philippine Insurrection, the Mexican Expedition and the Korean Police Action.[19]

Helping America Win Worlds War I & II

Historians rightly refer to the two major European wars of the 20th century as world wars. But for the Japanese and American involvement, they would have remained intra-European wars. And it would have been nothing new, as the history of Europe had up until the 20th century, been largely a history of wars. This was why, up to the 20th century, leaders of the young American nation adopted an avowedly isolationist foreign policy. Longer and more severe wars were fought in Europe prior to the 20th century. They included the 30-Year War; the 100-Year War; and the

---

15   Dudley Taylor Cornish, *The Sable Arm: Negro Troops in the Union Army*, 1861-1865, New York: W. W. Norton, 1966, p. 142-143.
16   Ibid, p. 156.
17   Joseph T. Glatthaar, "Black Glory: The African-American Role in Union Victory," in Gavor S. Boritt, ed. *Why the Confederacy Lost*, New York: Oxford University Press, 1992, p. 156.
18   Quarles, p. 184
19   Buffalo Soldiers, http://www.buffalosoldiers.com/

Napoleonic Wars. None of them were referred to as world wars. By the 20th century, however, Africa had come under the orbit of Europe. As Europe went to war, so too did Africa. In the first half of the 20th century, when the United States was finally forced to abandon its isolationist policy and join in the two world wars, it too took its own Africans (who had now become African-Americans) along.

When the United States was invited to take part in World War I, among the resources mobilized to answer the call to combat was its African American population. African American contributions to the war included troops and money. Some 400,000 African American troops were deployed, and as much as $250 million was privately raised within the African American community for the war effort.[20] This was at a time when most African Americans worked mainly in low wage menial jobs or as exploited sharecroppers. In today's dollars, the value of what African Americans contributed to the First World War would be in the billions of dollars. Prior to America's participation in the War, continental Africans were already fighting alongside British, French, German troops. As with the enslaved Africans who fought in America's westward expansion, Africans were in the vanguard. They dug the trenches, performed the physically tasking assignments and were frequently sent ahead to scout out for the enemy. In the process, they took heavy casualties. It was a war in which Africans were killing Africans, as the Africans who were fighting in the German army were shooting at Africans who were fighting in the British army. Eventually, with the help of Africans, the Allied Forces won. In the treaty that ended the War, all of Germany's African colonies were seized and divided up among the victorious European powers. Africans who fought for the winning side did not have the opportunity to savor victory. As with slaves in the United States who fought in the American Revolution but later denied freedom when America gained independence, Africans who helped to liberate France from Germany's defeat and occupation were denied freedom.

In many ways, the scramble for Africa was an extension of the perennial rivalry that characterized intra-European relations over the centuries. The 1884 Berlin Conference was organized to establish the rules that will bring discipline and orderliness in the competing territorial claims that various European powers were making in Africa. Without the Berlin Conference, the intra-European rivalry that was now extended to Africa in the form of the scramble for territorial acquisition would have caused World War I to break out much sooner - most probably in 1884 rather than in 1917. An earlier outbreak of conflict was similarly averted in 1494 when Pope Alexander VI

---

20 E. David Cronon, *Black Moses: The Story of Marcus Garvey and the Universal Negro Improvement Association*, Madison: University of Wisconsin Press, 1955, 1969, pp. 27-28.

brought two competing imperial European states, Portugal and Spain, to sign a treaty – the Treaty of Tordesillas – establishing a demarcation line as the two competed for territorial acquisition in Africa and in the Americas.

In his recent book on *African Development*, former World Bank staff and Vice President for the Center for Global Development, Todd J. Moss, points to 1898, as the year when Britain and France crossed paths in Africa, and came very close to going to war:

> Britain pushed into Africa from two points, Cape Colony on the far south and Egypt in the north. Cecil Rhode's dream was to link British colonies right across the continent "from the Cape to Cairo." At the same time, France was seeking to build an east-west empire to connect its holdings in Senegal across the Sahara to the Niger River and on to the Nile and as far as on the Red Sea. Indeed, these two imperial axes crossed at Fashoda in southern Sudan, where the French and British came to the verge of war in 1898. But, as at Berlin, in the end they backed down and agreed to separate spheres of influence.[21]

As with the First World War, Africans on the continent and Africans in the Americas fought with the West in 1945 to prevent the rise of fascism in Europe and Japanese imperialism in Asia. Indeed, on the Pacific front, one of the first heroes of the War was Doris Miller, a Black mess-man and son of a Texas Sharecropper. A crewman on the battleship West Virginia the day Japanese warplanes attacked Pearl Harbor, he first helped carry his mortally wounded captain from the ship's burning bridge, and then returned to shut down invading Japanese airplanes, using an anti-aircraft machine gun for which he had no prior training. Thanks to his efforts, the lives of hundreds of American troops were saved.[22] In recognition of this, U.S. President Ronald Reagan would decades later recount the story of "a Negro Sailor whose total duties involved kitchen type duties ... He cradled a machine gun in his arms ... and stood on the end of a pier blazing away at Japanese airplanes that were coming down and strafing him and that

21   Todd J. Moss, *African Development*, New York: Lynne Rienner Publishers, 2011, p. 25
22   Gordon W. Prange, December 7, 1941: The Day the Japanese Attacked Pearl Harbor, New York: McGraw-Hill, 1988, pp. 149, 153; Gordon W. Prange, At Dawn We Slept: The Untold Story of Pearl Harbor, New York: McGraw-Hill, pp. 514-5; Bernard C. Nalty, Strength for the Fight: *A History of Black Americans in the Military*, New York: Free Press, 1986, p. 186. Dennis D. Nelson, The Integration of the Negro into the U.S. Navy, New York: Octagon Books, 1982, p. 25.

(segregation) was all changed."[23]

On the Atlantic front, the all black 99th Pursuit Squadron, famously known as the "Tuskegee Airmen," performed so well against the German Air Force that the U.S. Air Force rushed to add three more squadrons. Designated the 332nd Fighter Group, the four squadrons became the Air Force of choice for ground troops who wanted air cover as they advanced into enemy positions. The Group shut down 111 enemy planes and never lost a single bomber under its escort to enemy air attack. They were among the most decorated pilots in the war, earning 865 Legion of Merit, 95 Distinguished Flying Crosses, 1 Silver Star, 14 Bronze Stars, 744 Air Medals, 8 Purple Hearts, and a Presidential Citation.[24]

In Europe, continental African troops fought alongside British and French forces against German forces. One of the most celebrated Africans who contributed to America's victory in World War II was a woman from Congo named Augusta Chiwy. Discovered by historian Martin King, she was nicknamed "the black nurse from the Congo" in the HBO mini-series, "Band of Brothers." Born in the Belgian Congo in 1921, Augusta volunteered to work with US Army medic Dr. John Prior, in December 1944, at the Battle of the Bulge, the largest and bloodiest battle of World War II, in the town of Bastogne. Eyewitness accounts say that Chiwy risked her life, running out into the battlefield to retrieve and nurse wounded U.S. troops, even as the ground around her was being raked up by intense German mortars and heavy machine gun shelling. Blown through the wall by one of the explosions, she survived, got up, and went right back to work tending wounded American soldiers. In early 2011, Augusta Chiwy was knighted "Lady Chiwy" by King Albert II of Belgium. Later that year, in November 2011, she was given the US Army's Civilian Award for Humanitarian Service. Colonel JP McGee, the U.S. Commander of the 101st Airborne Division, who gave the award had nothing but the highest praises for Lady Chiwy: "M'aam, you embody what is best and most kind in all of us. It is an honor to share the stage with you and to be able to say on behalf of US veterans everywhere — thank you. The number of lives that you touched is incalculable. There are men and women in America who would never have a father or grandfather if you hadn't been there to provide them basic medical care."[25]

On the Asian front, the performance of African troops in Britain's Fourteenth Army Battalion in "the Burma Campaign," led to decisive victory against Japan. The British press at the time refused to write about the

23 Lou Cannon, Reagan, New York: G. P. Putnam's Sons, 1982, p. 20.
24 Bernard C. Nalty, Strength for the Fight: A History of Black Americans in the Military, New York: Free Press, 1986, p.153.
25 PRI, Nurse Honored for Bravery, http://www.theworld.org/2011/12/nurse-honored-augusta-chiwy/ By Clark Boyd December 16, 2011.

extraordinary performance of the African troops. It was not until research-ers later dug up the facts that British historians referred to these African fighters as "the Forgotten Army."[26]

While European colonialism was denying freedom and independence to Africans at home, the very Africans were being recruited to help liberate Europe from two "isms" – Nazism and Fascism. A third "ism" – the "ism of colonialism - continued to harangue Africa, forcing a Ghanaian newspaper, the Gold Coast Independent, speak out in defense of the more than 3000 Ghanaians who fought in World War I to "if they were good enough to fight and die in the Empire's cause, they were good enough ... to have a share in the government of their countries."[27]

A dialog between an African nationalist and a British colonial admin-istrator in the aftermath of World War II provides a sarcastic but revealing parody that surrounded the denial of freedom to the Africans who sacrificed their lives to win freedom for Europe:

> "Away with Hitler! Down with him!" said the British officer (appealing for Africans to fight against Hitler).
>
> "What's wrong with Hitler?" asked the African.
>
> "He wants to rule the whole world," said the British officer.
>
> "What's wrong with that?"
>
> "He is German, you see," said the British officer, trying to appeal subtly to the African's tribal consciousness.
>
> "What's wrong with his being German?"
>
> "You see," said the British officer, trying to explain in terms that would be conceivable to the African mind, "it is not good for one tribe to rule another. Each tribe must rule itself. That's only fair. A German must rule Germans, an Italian, Italians, and a Frenchman, French people."[28]

26 *The Guardian*, https://www.theguardian.com/world/video/2015/aug/10/forgotten-army-world-war-two-west-african-soldiers-burma-video
27 David Kimble, *Political History of Ghana*, Oxford: Oxford University Press, 1963, p. 545.
28 Ndabaningi Sithole, *African Nationalism*, Oxford, Oxford University Press 1959, p. 20.

Africans who fought for the French were referred to as the *Tirailleurs*.[29] Placed in the vanguard and generally assigned the more dangerous missions, they fought with distinction. Despite their bravery and the sacrifices they made to liberate France from German occupation, the pensions they received were far less than what was paid to their French counterparts. Senegalese veterans who dared mutiny in expression of this unfair treatment were summarily massacred by French troops in 1945 at Camp Thiaroye in Dakar. Between 1956 and 1962, the independence of former French colonies in Africa further led to the freezing of military pensions for all former African soldiers who fought for France. Pensions paid to their French counterparts continued to grow at the rate of inflation. After watching a 2006 movie, *Indigenes*, that depicted the plight of the African soldiers, French President Jacques Chirac signed an order in September 2006 authorizing past-due pension payments to the Tirailleurs.[30] The redress came sixty years too late. A majority of the Africans who fought for France in World War II were already dead.

While Africa rushed to help Europe in the First and Second World Wars, when Africa was faced with a similar challenge, Europe was reluctant to step up with the same courage that Africans fought with in Worlds War I and II. In *Stealth Conflicts: Africa's World War in the DRC and International Consciousness*, Virgil Hawkins, decries Europe's failure to come to Africa's help in the 1998 civil war in the Democratic Republic of Congo. Described as Africa's First World War, it was a conflict that involved eight foreign countries – all of them African – costing about as many lives as were lost in World War II.

The President of the International Relief Committee, George Rupp, lamented that the death toll in the Congo Civil War had, by 2010, risen to six million people, surpassing any other conflict since World War II, to become the world's deadliest documented conflict.[31] Despite this enormity, Europe did not act with the same sense of urgency with which Africa acted to help save Europe from its own 1945 world war.

Helping America Win the Cold War

The ideological rivalry that characterized the Cold War was in essence a campaign to win over much of the world. One of the major regions of the

29   Blackpast, http://www.blackpast.org/?q=gah/tirailleurs-senegalais, (accessed June 12, 2018)

30   Mathew Saltmarsh, *New York Times*, 08/18/2008, Colonial Soldiers Want More from France http://www.nytimes.com/2009/08/13/world/europe/13iht-vets.html?_r=0

31   Haider Rizvi, DRC: In Congo, staggering death toll and a move toward peace, http://www.reliefweb.int/rw/rwb.nsf/db900sid/KKAA-7BA5H2?OpenDocument, (accessed 05/05/2018)

world that was coveted and heavily contested was Africa. Both superpowers invested tremendous material, diplomatic and political resources to keep each other from gaining control of Africa. Africans who sought to remain ideologically independent or nonaligned were either assassinated or forced into exile. Famous among them was the first Prime Minister of Congo, Patrice Lumumba, who was assassinated for speaking out against foreign influence in Africa; and Ghana's Kwame Nkrumah, who was forced into exile for aggressively pursuing a pan-Africanist agenda. Throughout the Cold War, Lumumba's handpicked replacement, Mobutu Sese Seko, faithfully allied with the West, giving it access to the country's rare strategic minerals – minerals that helped the West gain edge over the East in strategic weapons systems. Thanks to Africa's alliance with the West, the West won the Cold War. The outcome of the War would have been different had Africa allied with the Soviet Union. In the post-Cold War era, even as the West mobilized to fight yet another war – this time a war against global terrorism – it once again saw Africa as an indispensable ally. This was seen in the 2007 establishment of Africom.

Helping America in the Global War Against Terrorism

Despite Africa's documented support for the West, in response to a question in the 2000 U.S. Presidential debate, then candidate George Bush stated that Africa was not a foreign policy priority for the United States.[32] By 2007 however, he would sign a presidential order establishing a U.S. Military Command for Africa. In announcing the establishment of the Command, President Bush stressed the strategic importance of Africa to U.S. national security. And at the October 1, 2008 inauguration ceremony for the Command, Defense Secretary Robert Gates stipulated that the Command was going to focus on the three D's: defense, diplomacy and development. The announcement produced strong opposition across Africa, and intense polarization among African intellectuals. Proponents of the policy argued that the new command reflected Africa's growing strategic importance. Critics saw the Command as a self-serving move by the United States to secure combat terrorism, contain China and secure Africa's oil and minerals.

Terrorism is the second global threat that has given great powers the excuse to extend their influence to Africa. The first threat was communism. When the Soviet Union emerged after World War II and declared its intention to expand communism beyond its national borders, the United States spent hundreds of billions of dollars to contain its expansion. Among the assets developed to contain Soviet expansion were United States Combatant

---

32 Commission on Presidential Debates, http://www.debates.org/index. php?page=october-11-2000-debate-transcript

Commands. Every major geographic region in the world was assigned a combatant command. None was established for Africa. Yet, this was one of the regions of the world where the Cold War rivalry between the superpowers actually went hot. Had a U.S. Combatant Command been established for Africa during the Cold War, the U.S. would have been in a better position to contain Soviet expansionism, and it wouldn't have raised as much opposition in Africa as it did when it was established in 2007.

More importantly, had Africom been created before the 1990s, the twin attacks that destroyed two American embassies in East Africa in 1998 would never have happened; 9-11 would never have happened; the Afghanistan and the Iraqi wars would never have been fought; and ISIS, Al Qaeda and their affiliates would probably never have been established. How? Why? When Osama was driven from Saudi Arabia, he moved to Africa where he sought refuge in Sudan. While there, he organized, plotted and carried out synchronized attacks against the two US embassies in East Africa. Looking back, it was all but evident that the attacks were a rehearsal for the World Trade Center that was to come three years later, on September 11, 2001. So, what happened after the East Africa attacks? The U.S. government pressured the Sudanese government to disassociate itself with Osama. When Osama was forced to leave Sudan, he was welcomed to Afghanistan and given a safe haven. From here, he plotted and launched the September 2001 attack.

But what if Africom had existed prior to all of these attacks? First, Osama would not have sought refuge in Africa when he was exiled from Saudi Arabia. Secondly, Africom's intelligence services would have picked up early warning signals of the pending plot against the two U.S. embassies in East Africa and would have moved to thwart them. Thirdly, instead of the diplomatic pressure on the government of Sudan to disassociate itself with Osama, Africom would have militarily neutralized Osama.

Back in the first decade of the 20th century, US President Woodrow Wilson was a strong advocate for the "colonized peoples of the world." Had the US moved to establish an African military command to enforce Wilson's anti-colonialism doctrine, just as Britain deployed its Navy in the 19th century to enforce the ban on the trans-Atlantic slave trade, it certainly would not have raised the opposition it did when the Command was established in 2007.

Coming at a time when Africa had suffered through the experiences of colonial and neocolonial exploitation, African policy-makers quickly saw Africom as a neocolonial subterfuge to secure oil interests and counterbalance China's growing influence on the continent. Just as no Africans were represented at the 1884-1885 Berlin Conference, no Africans were represented or consulted in the 2007 decision-making that announced the establishment of Africom. Most Africans were of the impression therefore that America was out to militarize the continent. Many saw it as a new colonial force that was coming in the guise of goodwill. Out of concern that they would be branded spies by their host countries, international nongovernmental organizations, including U.S. nongovernmental organizations were increasingly reluctant to develop working ties with Africom. Even America's premier international aid agency, USAID, saw Africom as a potential spoiler of the trust and goodwill that it had worked over the years to build with African countries. Given their past experiences with slavery, colonialism and neocolonial, Africans appear to have become quick at recognizing when they were being manipulated. Convincing them to believe in America's version of the truth was a tough call. After being told that colonialism was a "civilizing mission," and slavery a "journey to the holy land," getting Africans to believe that Africom was going to be a "goodwill" purveyor of defense, diplomacy and development (Defense Secretary Gates' three Ds) was a difficult sell. For obvious reasons, Africans on the whole have a very negative view of their militaries. They see them as human rights abusers. So for America to launch a military institution and present it as the foremost institution that was to collaborate with African governments on defense, diplomacy and development matters could only be seen with suspicion in Africa.

On the basis of nomenclature, had the U.S. Central Command bore the name "Middle East Command," and had the U.S. Pacific and the U.S. Southern Commands been named US-Asia Command and US-Latin America Command, they equally would have evoked similar fears and similar resistance. This is to say that had Africom gone by any other name than "Africa Command," it probably wouldn't have raised much resistance. Substitute the word "command" for any other word – cooperation, partnership, goodwill, friendship, etc. – and African states would have rushed to actively welcome Africom. For example, right after the launching of Africom, another U.S. military program called the Africa Partnership Station (APS) was launched. Run by the U.S. Navy, the program patrols the coastal waters of the West Coast of Africa and Gulf of Guinea, in collaboration with African states. If there is one reason why the Africa Partnership Station was welcomed, and the African Command was not, it all had to do with the name. One was seen as a "partnership"; the other was seen as "command." What do combatant commands do? They fight wars. No doubt Africans were so vehemently opposed to the establishment of Africom. Given their past experience with slavery and colonialism, the word "command" in the name was literarily seen by Africans as renewed effort to reestablish imperialism on the continent. For them, a military command established by a former imperial power on their continent would have no other objective but to "command" Africa. This was the immediate conclusion a majority of Africans made.

The launching of Africom was all the more controversial because it was done unilaterally. As was the case with the 1884 Berlin Conference

that divided up Africa among competing European states, African governments were not consulted. For a continent that was yet to recover from the
destabilizing effects of European colonization and the destructive impact
of superpower rivalry during the Cold War, such a unilateral decision was
both naïve and insensitive. It was not until after an intense international
opposition that U.S. policy-makers backtracked and began to redefine Africom as a command whose mission was going to revolve around four core
tenets – security, development, diplomacy and prosperity.[33] Privately, however, the United States Naval Center for Contemporary Conflict continued
to see international terrorism, the increasing importance of African oil to
American energy needs, and growth in the Chinese presence in Africa as
reasons for concern.[34] With the lessons learned from the friendship that
developed between Afghanistan and Al Qaeda after Afghanistan became a
failed state, the U.S. was quick to come to the realization that failed states
were potential threats to US national security interests. With the increased
ability of transnational syndicates to organize through "virtual" mediums
such as the internet, cell phones or text messaging, the lesson was all too
ominous. For a continent characterized by widespread corruption and porous
national borders, there was the looming potential that it could serve as a
safe haven or launching ground for terrorists and as a possible incubator
for anti-Americanism.

David Ignatius of the *Washington Post* thinks that "the real puzzle with
Africom is understanding its purpose. Some advocates propose pragmatic
strategic goals, from containing China's influence in Africa to countering
terrorism to protecting African oil supplies."[35] Some Africans worry that
these pretenses mask a hidden agenda of establishing what could amount
to American neocolonialism... Its nation-building goal sounds noble, but
so did European imperialism in 1884.[36]

That Africans were initially opposed to Africom actually had something
to do with the lack of convincing results in America's declaration that Africa's
security was the rationale for the establishment of Africom. Despite the
presence of a US Military base in Djibouti, and despite the deployment of
US Special Forces in Uganda in 2011, piracy activities were still going on in
Somalia, and the Lord's Resistance Army was still at large. In February 2012,
Somali President Sheikh Sharif Ahmed openly criticized foreign navies for
failing to stop piracy in the waters off Somalia and the Horn of Africa. "As
you know, there are many foreign navies around us but these have failed to

33 United States European Command, http://www.eucom.mil/africom/, (accessed 1/8/2018)
34 Strategic Insights, January 2007.
35 http://www.realclearpolitics.com/articles/2008/01/
more_us_involvement_needed_in.html
36 ibid

eliminate piracy along our waters."[37] While some pirates were arrested by the international navy, the business continued to thrive.

The litmus test for Africom was its ability to combat the growing piracy threat in the Horn of Africa and beyond. Up until 2012, Africom had not succeeded in taming the threat. If anything, piracy and terrorist activities went on the rise rather than on the decline. In 2012, the Gulf of Guinea actually overtook Somalia to become the world's piracy hot-spot with 966 sailors attacked compared to Somalia's 851, with the International Maritime Bureau placing the cost of goods stolen at between $33 million to $100 million.[38] Africans monitoring the continuous threat of piracy on the coast of Somalia silently ponder how America was going to be able to succeed in eliminating the threat of piracy in the Gulf of Guinea, when it had so far not succeeded in stemming the threat in the Horn of Africa. In addition, terrorist cells were multiplying on the continent. There was Al Qaeda in the Maghreb (AQIM), Al Shabab in the Horn of Africa and Boko Haram in northern Nigeria. Gen. Carter F. Ham, head of the United States Africa Command, saw the growing activism as an attempt by Boko Haram, AQIM and Al Shabab to establish a loose partnership across Africa.[39]

Three years after the establishment of Africom, the International Maritime Bureau (IMB) reported in the first quarter of 2011 that worldwide pirate attacks were the highest ever recorded. Of the 142 attacks reported, 97 of them were carried out off the coast of Somalia - a 127% increase from the previous year. This is despite a multilateral effort by NATO, Russia, China, India and Iran to curb the problem.[40] For the year 2010, the International Maritime Organization reported 45 piracy attacks in the Gulf of Guinea; and 64 attacks in 2011.

Just as the threat of global terrorism was the primary driving force for U.S. foreign policy in Africa, so too was U.S. interest in African oil. In 2000, sub-Sahara Africa produced more than 4 million barrels of oil a day. This was more oil than the total volume of oil that is produced by Iran, Venezuela or Mexico. Nigeria alone was among the top five suppliers of oil to the United

---

37 Abdulkadir Khalif, Africa Review (Kenya), Somalia President Calls for Tougher Anti-Piracy Action,http://www.africareview.com/News/Somalia+President+asks+foreign+navies+to+step+up+war+on+piracy/-/979180/1324558/-/g76hqmz/-/ (Accessed February 11, 2012)

38 Adeniyi Adeijimi Osinowo, "Combating Piracy in the Gulf of Guinea," African Center for Strategic Studies, http://news.yahoo.com/african-leaders-unite-combat-gulf-guinea-piracy-192335204.html, Accessed October 30, 2013.

39 Adam Nossiter, New York Times, "Islamist Group With Possible Qaeda Links Upends Nigeria," http://www.nytimes.com/2011/08/18/world/africa/18nigeria.html?pagewanted=2&_r=2&nl=todaysheadlines&emc=tha2 (accessed August 20, 2011).

40 Aljazeera, Dubai hosts anti-piracy conference, http://english.aljazeera.net/news/middleeast/2011/04/20114186721819166.html (accessed 04/04/2011)

States. Algeria, Angola, and Gabon were among the top fifteen.[41] Overall, the United States imported more oil from Africa than from the Middle East in the post 9/11 era. "However, while all countries need and buy oil today, only a few send their troops to control the sources."[42]

Damage Control on a Fumbled Foreign Policy

To deflect strong African opposition to Africom, the U.S. moved to locate the headquarters in Stuttgart, Germany. With a staff of 2000 administrative personnel in Stuttgart, with some 5,000 Special Operations troops that provide training and logistics across the 54-nation continent, and cooperative security locations at several "Forward Operating Sites" known as "lily pads" across the continent, Africom is the newest, but also the smallest of the Pentagon's six regionally focused commands. By comparison, U.S. Central Command has a base force of some 150,000 troops and oversees security planning for 20 countries - less than half the number of countries on the continent of Africa.[43] Besides, it is obvious that something is lost in not locating Africom in the environment it was set up to manage. An American living in Germany has a standard of living well above that of the average African. They enjoy good roads, well-stocked supermarkets, clean running water and a stable political environment. Naturally, they will lack empathy for the African experience. General Accounting Office report GAO-10-794 dated July 2010 found that one of the reasons the command had difficulty implementing activities was because its personnel have limited knowledge about cultural issues in Africa. An American in Germany is only guessing at what might be best for Africa. Only once Africom is on the continent and its personnel assimilated can the Command get on with the business of making the best decisions for its partnership with Africa.

After spending hundreds of billions of dollars to defeat the Soviets in Africa, the United States turned its back on the continent as soon as the Soviets were booted out. The same was true with Afghanistan, where the U.S. spent hundreds of billions of dollars to deny the expansion of Soviet influence to Western Asia. As soon as the Soviets were forced out of Afghanistan, the United States too turned its back on the country. Almost immediately, Afghanistan became a safe haven for Muslim fundamentalism and anti-American sentiment. Instead of packing to leave after its successful defeat of the Soviets, had the U.S. stayed and invested economically and socially in Africa and Afghanistan, it would have made it difficult for the two regions

---

41   Christian Science Monitor, May 23, 2002.

42   Phebe Eckfeldt, *Workers World*, July 27, 2007

43   Kristina Wong, *The Washington Times*, US's Africom trains host nation's forces to battle terrorism, http://www.washingtontimes.com/news/2012/feb/8/as-demand-for-special-operation-forces-rises-will-/ (Accessed February 8, 2012)

to become vulnerable to anti-American propaganda and demagoguery. In turning its back on Africa, and in failing to embrace Africa as an economic partner, the U.S. made Africa attractive to a renewed anti-Americanism that culminated in the 1989 synchronized attacks on U.S. Embassies in East Africa.[44]

Even when U.S. retaliation forced Osama Bin Laden to leave Africa and seek sanctuary in Afghanistan, U.S. policy-makers were still not quick enough to come up with a plan that would win the hearts and minds of Africans and promote lasting pro-American sentiments in the continent. It took almost ten years for the U.S. to finally figure out that a combatant command is what was needed to enhance American security interests in the region.

The presidential order that authorized the establishment of Africom was careful to reassure Africa that this was not going to be another bid for the re-imposition of Western imperialism. This time around, he was diplomatic in his choice of language – repeatedly referring to Africa as "our partners," highlighting the need to "promote *our common goals* of development, health, education, democracy and economic growth ..." and the need to *consult* "with African leaders to seek their thoughts on how Africa Command can respond to security challenges and opportunities in Africa" (emphasis added). Even though the language of the text was very carefully chosen, African states on the whole were still reluctant to embrace the idea of a Western military command on the continent. Multiple reassurances that Africom was going to have a humanitarian focus, while serving as a security shield, with Africa as America's "co-partner" failed to allay suspicions among Africans that the U.S. had neocolonial ambitions. Combatant Commands (or Cocoms), as the name indicates, are established to control military operations. The inherent contradiction in the description of Africom as a security shield, while stating at the same time that it was not going to be involved in combat only raised renewed skepticism. The skepticism contributed to a concerted opposition among major nation-state players on the continent. Nigeria, South Africa and the Muslim states of North Africa were among the lead detractors. Nigeria and South Africa, the two most influential countries in sub-Sahara Africa came out immediately to say "No." Establishing an American military command on the continent would be tantamount to meddling in their zone of influence.

In a move to allay their concerns, Africom's first commanding General, "Kip" Ward, averred that he did not "envision kinetic operations for United

---

44   David Ignatius, "Into Africa Without a Map," Washington Post, Sunday, January 6, 2008; B07, http://www.washingtonpost.com/ac2/related/topic/China

States forces"[45] This only triggered skepticism. The skeptics were proven right when, four years later Africom was given the mission to command an air campaign against the military defenses of Gaddafi's Libya. Contrary to the General's remarks, Africom went kinetic here. Overthrowing Gaddafi was Africom's most visible achievement so far. This did not sit well with Africans. Detractors of US foreign policy in Africa, including what I would call "Africom-skeptics", felt vindicated. As a sitting head of state, Gaddafi was a member of the fraternity of African heads of states. His overthrow was an ominous reminder to others that they too could be overthrown should any of them fall out of favor with the West

The Muslim states of North Africa were primarily concerned that a U.S. Military Command on their territory would do to their regimes what the U.S. base in Saudi Arabia did to the Saudis – produced new Muslim radicals in the likes of Osama Bin Laden, who was bent on destabilizing Saudi Arabia and bringing down the Saudi Royalty.

China vs. the US in Africa – Who Has it Right?

As anti-Americanism made the extraction and shipment of oil from the Middle East both risky and costly, Africa suddenly became a more appealing alternative. With respect to China, while the U.S. does not see its growing presence in Africa as an immediate military threat, it is reminded by history that rapidly rising nations have the potential to readily transform acquired economic capabilities into military capabilities. Sitting quietly as China acquires increased economic capabilities in Africa would be leading China in that direction. The response? An ostentatious strategic military alliance with Africa in the form of a United States-Africa Command. While its stated purpose is to fend off potential terrorist threats and provide security for Africa's energy resources, its unstated purpose is the stealth monitoring of the growing influence of China on the continent of Africa.

Prior to the establishment of Africom, the U.S. government's strategic take on Africa had long been that, "we have no compelling interests in Africa, and we sure as hell do not want anybody else to have any either." American policy-makers came to the realization, rather belatedly, that the presence of China in Africa was only exceeded by the absence of America. In early 2007, after Ethiopia received a $500 million concessional loan from China, followed by a $1.5 billion investment in telecommunications infrastructure and another $1.5 billion in short term trade credits, Western nations complained that Chinese loans to Africa (granted mostly without conditions)

---

45 Danielle Skinner, U.S. Africa Command public affairs office, House Armed Services Committee Discusses U.S. Africa Command in Annual Fiscal Report, (accessed 2/18/20120 http://www.realclearpolitics.com/articles/2008/01/more_us_involvement_needed_in.html

were undermining Western aid conditionality.[46]

Curiously, as China interfaced with Africa economically, the U.S. chose to interface with Africa militarily. Whose paradigm will be right in the long run, it will be up to historians to decide. What appears paradoxical however is that a nation which was founded on the ideals of private enterprise, opted to use a public sector/military led initiative as its foreign policy instrument of choice on a continent where the military is regarded with distrust and profound suspicion. One would have expected such a public sector driven instrument of foreign policy would come from China – a nation whose founding ideals were based centralized public sector planning. Here was the United States which fought a 50-year Cold War to prevent the introduction of Soviet and Chinese inspired central planning and military driven solutions to development in Africa. In an unexpected reversal of roles, while the U.S. is embracing Africom as a development facilitator in Africa, China embraced capitalism and capitalist investments as its foreign policy instrument of choice in Africa. China's oil purchases generally come with a commitment to finance major infrastructural development such as highways, railroads, parliament buildings. Pondering why a nation that was founded on free enterprise and private sector solutions to societal problems would now resort a military/public sector driven solution for Africa, critiques of U.S. foreign policy in Africa rushed to invoke Abraham Maslow's thought that "if the only thing one has left in hand is a hammer, everything one sees would look like a nail." Proponents of Africom argue however that given the pressing need to partner with Africa and the strategic importance of such partnership, it was but appropriate for the mission to be assigned to the most efficient and most well-funded of America's institutions – the military.

Opponents of the military driven policy argue on the other hand that Africom is a mission whose goals and objectives were not clearly defined. In his campaign for the presidency, the very president who would sign the order to establish Africom was strongly opposed to the use of the American military in nation-building. That the same President would later commit U.S. troops to a nation-building assignment in Africa leaves one to believe that U.S. foreign policy for Africa is driven by reactionary rather than by visionary considerations. American policy makers have historically shown no strategic interest in Africa until another foreign power or competing ideology shows interest in the region. Hence our argument above that the Chinese presence in Africa is only exceeded by the absence of the United States. Actually, among those who denounced the new Africom as a blatant

---

46   The Financial Times, September 23, 2007, www.ft.com/com/s/cb811a48-b586-11db-a5a5-0000779e2340._i_rssPage=fc3334c0-217a-11da-8b51-00000e2511c8.html (accessed 01/12/2011)

move to "step up military infiltration in Africa," was a scholar at the People's Liberation Army (PLA) Academy of Military Sciences, Lin Zhiyuan. He, like all Chinese policy-makers see the growing US military presence around the world, including in China's own backyard, as both unwarranted and misguided.[47]

We started this section with China. We argued that Europe's strategic alliance with Africa made it possible for the West not only to catch up, but to technologically overtake China. In working silently to grow its presence in Africa, it does appear that China has come to the same realization. Since the late 1970s, China been systematically making investments in all sectors of the African economy that are expressly long term. In failing to aggressively invest in Africa right after its Cold War defeat of the Soviet Union, the West left a void. China stepped in to fill the void and is now fully capitalizing on it.

China sees Africa not just as a market for raw materials, but as market for consumer goods as well. Lured by the rush to loot the continent, European colonizers saw Africa in colonial times mainly as a market for raw materials. Given the intra-European rivalry that was going on at the time, European powers were driven more by the rush to increase their national capabilities with Africa's raw materials than by the need to develop consumer markets in Africa. "I better get all the resources I can get before my fellow European rival gets them." Developing a market for consumer goods would have meant making the social investments that would have enabled the development of an African middle class. But concerned that such investments would enlighten and raise awareness that could lead to demands for democracy and political self-determination, the colonial powers chose not to take the risk. Had Europe invested in the development of a middle class in Africa, it would today have a consumer market of one billion-plus consumers. This would have translated to one of the largest consumer markets for Western products in the world. Such a market would provide full employment for American and European factories. Today, there would be no place in Africa for China. Looking back, it is obvious that in failing to develop a middle class and a consumer market in Africa, the West short-changed itself.

When China saw the void in Africa, it decided to fill it on two fronts. It developed a mutually beneficial balance between a raw material market and a consumer market - exporting consumer goods and infrastructural development to Africa and importing minerals and natural resources from the continent. This enabled China to overtake the West as Africa's largest trading partner. If the 21st century is going to be China's century, we can affirmatively say that this was precipitated by Western myopia.

---

47   Asia Times, Sreeram Chaulia, "Dragon tries to slay US military," http://www.atimes. com/atimes/China/MH16Ad02.html (accessed 08/20/2011)

Unlike in the past therefore, the West today has an economic competitor in Africa. The 21st century will belong to whoever manages this competition successfully. In a manner reminiscent of a long-term investor, China's investment strategy in Africa focuses on addressing Africa's infrastructural needs, as it extracts Africa's natural resources.

In the final analysis, if the United States government in general and Africom in particular are going to succeed in their mission in Africa, several basic things must change. There must be a greater hard power/soft power balance in U.S. foreign policy and there must be demonstrable willingness to collaborate internationally as well as at the interagency level in producing win-win outcomes in America's relations with Africa.

Chapter 4

Pondering Africa's Failures

> In Africa, promise and opportunity sit side by side with disease, war, and desperate poverty. This threatens both a core value of the United States - preserving human dignity and our strategic priority - combating global terror.
>
> US National Security Strategy 2002

On most every measurable development index, not only does Africa fall short, it falls behind the rest of the World. For a continent whose past is described by historians as the cradle of civilization, and whose present is described by economists as replete with a vast array of natural resources, this gives reason to ponder. While the continent is replete with natural resources, it is paradoxically also devoid of management and organizational know-how. It is not uncommon to hear exasperated young Africans pontificate wistfully that if only the continent were somehow magically handed over to a Western country such as the United States, Africa would in a very short time be transformed from desolation into an oasis of prosperity. But why have Africans not been able to work to transform the continent themselves? Much of Africa's governing elite either schooled in the West or have spent time there. Some may have actually been schoolmates with some of the elite that now govern Western countries. One would expect them to apply in Africa the lessons and experiences they gained living in the West. But they have not done so. In this chapter, we are going to examine some of the reasons that account for Africa's failure.

The literature on failed states is extensive. While failed states are found in almost every region of the world, a disproportionately high number of them are found in Africa. Of the 26 countries listed on the World Bank's list of failed and failing states in 2006, 14 of them were in Africa.[1] Because a majority of the world's failed states are in Africa, it would not be out of place to refer to Africa as a failed continent.

---

1   Karen DeYoung, Washington Post, Sept 15, 2006, World Bank Lists Failing Nations That Can Breed Global Terrorist (accessed 3/18/2008) Washingtonpost.com/wp-dyn/content/article/.../14/AR2006091401859.html

Ordinarily, a failed African continent would not have meant much to the West. But these are no ordinary times. Africa's failure did not just happen overnight. For decades, the continent was a sinking ship. In 1994, months of trauma and bloodletting in the failing state of Rwanda did not raise an eyebrow in the capital of any Western nation. It took years of international outcry for the West to finally intervene to end a nearly 20-year bloodletting that typified the failure of the Liberian state. It was not until the West realized that a failed Africa had the potential to become an incubator for global terrorism that it finally decided to invest militarily and economically in capacity-building on the continent. The investments were made in response to a 2002 National Security Strategy study that revealed that the U.S. was threatened more by failed and failing states than by conquering states. The study's findings were echoed by the UN Secretary General's warning that "ignoring failed states creates problems that sometimes come back to bite us;" and by French President Jacques Chirac, who cautioned about "the threat that failed states carry for the world's equilibrium." Somehow, "failed states have made a remarkable odyssey from the periphery to the very center of global politics."[2]

By 2007, the international community had gone from talking about failed states in Africa to talking about phantom states. In an article entitled *Central African Republic: Anatomy of a Phantom State*, Africa Report No. 136 of December 13 2007 stated that "The Central African Republic (CAR) is if anything worse than a failed state: it has become virtually a phantom state, lacking any meaningful institutional capacity at least since the fall of Emperor Bokassa in 1979." Independent for more than a half century, it was not until 1993 that the country had its first democratic elections. As in much of Africa, balloting was along tribal lines, leading to a series of uprisings and rebellions that quickly plunged the country into a state of permanent rebellion with disastrous humanitarian consequences.[3]

As we ponder Africa's failures, we are primarily going to look at two spheres – the political and economic spheres. Politics and economics are the twin propellers of stability and prosperity. In his campaign for the independence and unity of Africa, Ghana's first President, Kwame Nkrumah once cautioned that, "*seek ye first the political kingdom,*" and the rest will follow.[4] For over half a century, Africans have had control of the political kingdom. "The rest" has however failed to follow. Could Nkrumah have been

2   The National Security Strategy, September 2002, (accessed 3/09/2011) http://www.foreignpolicy.com/story/cms.php?story_id=3098&print=1

3   The Crisis Group, Central African Republic: Anatomy of a Phantom State, Report No 136, (assessed, 05/12/2012), http://www.crisisgroup.org/home/index.cfm?id=5220&l=1

4   Public Broadcasting Service, Commanding Heights, (accessed 02/14/2018), http://www.pbs.org/wgbh/commandingheights/shared/minitextlo/prof_kwamenkrumah.html

mistaken here? Prior to Nkrumah, Karl Marx cautioned that between the infrastructure and the superstructure, we must seek to gain control of the infrastructure first. The infrastructure here, for Marx, is the economy. Should Africa have sought first the economic kingdom before seeking the political kingdom? Under the political conditions of the day, this was not possible. In colonial times, Africans were economically marginalized. They therefore did not have the means to gain economic control at independence. Working first to take control of the political kingdom as Nkrumah had hinted, was the only realistic option at the time. It is the political kingdom, that is, the superstructure that sets the rules within which the infrastructure operates. If properly conceived, these rules should shape and provide the path that would eventually lead to the realization of the infrastructure.

It is important not to discount the importance of ideas in shaping history. Social scientists love to search for structures that determine history, but sometimes agency (human action) plays a determining role. What failed Africa may have been its failure to define and articulate an ideological or philosophical roadmap for Nkrumah's vision. When America's founding fathers declared free enterprise as the vision for their newly independent state, and when China's modern founders, Mao Tse Tung and Deng Xiaoping educed peasant and later pragmatic socialism as the vision for the new China, a succession of American and Chinese leaders respectively interpreted and produced the philosophical roadmaps that have led to the material realization of these visions. Proclaiming a grand vision is the duty of a statesman. Defining and articulating that vision becomes the responsibility of intellectuals and policymakers. Very few debates have been conducted in African intellectual circles to define and articulate Nkrumah's "*seek ye first the political kingdom*" vision. In failing to redefine and re-articulate Nkrumah's vision, African leaders failed Nkrumah. This has led to disastrous consequences for the political and economic emancipation of the continent, producing what Larry Diamond refers to as the "swollen" state phenomenon.[5] In the absence of political visionaries, political opportunists have emerged to give Nkrumah's vision a bad name. Disillusioned by the performance of corrupt rulers in Africa, the African masses are now left with the impression that the push for political independence or the acquisition of the political kingdom was misguided.

But could the derailment of Nkrumah's vision by kleptocratic rulers equally be to blame? Can we genuinely say that the political kingdom that is under the rule of corrupt African rulers today is the political kingdom that Nkrumah envisioned? This is a question that cannot be answered in

---

5   Larry Diamond (1987). Class Formation in the Swollen African State. *The Journal of Modern African Studies*, 25, pp 567-596.

the affirmative. The corrupt regimes that have ruled Africa since independence are not in any way a reflection of what Nkrumah had in mind when he proclaimed the primacy of the political kingdom. Africa was and still remains caught in an inextricable quagmire; and until it goes back to clearly articulating and fully understanding from a strict constructionist perspective what Nkrumah meant by "the political kingdom," it may never get out of this quagmire.

Back to our unanswered question: Why has the acquisition of political independence not brought stability and prosperity to Africa? In other words, why has the democratic experiment failed in Africa? This is where we are going to turn our attention to next.

A Short-lived Colonial Experience

Unlike in the Americas and in India where colonial rule lasted for several hundred years, the colonial experiment in Africa was just long enough to destabilize and disorientate. Colonial rule in Africa was just long enough to cut Africa off from its past, extinguishing thousands of years of experience in political organization, but not long enough to replace the extinguished past with an enlightened path to the future. Sub-Sahara Africa was colonized in 1884. Ghana inaugurated the independence process in 1957, but the wholesale acquisition of independence did not come until the 1960s. When added up, it comes out to a mere 76 years of European colonial occupation. If we decide to factor in a series of intervening global shocks that redirected attention and resources away from the colonial enterprise, the duration of the colonial experience in Africa was even shorter than the 76 years. For example, World War I which lasted from 1914 to 1919 briefly took away five years of attention from the colonial enterprise. The Great Depression, which lasted from 1929 to 1933 redirected four years of attention and resources away from development efforts in Africa to economic recovery efforts in Europe. Finally, the outbreak of World War II which lasted six years, once again caused Europe to redirect attention and resources away from its empire building enterprise in Africa to fighting for its survival at home. When this is all added up, it takes away a total of 15 years from the 76 years of European imperial efforts in Africa. This brings the net duration of colonial rule in Africa to a mere 61 years.

Sixty-one years is a very short time for any people to abandon their traditional culture and acquire a new culture. Even if Europe were sincere about its "civilizing mission," its 61-year presence in Africa was simply not enough to carry it out. To describe Africa as a half-baked cake therefore will not be out of place. Somehow, just when the cake-maker mixes and places the cake in the oven, he is forcibly removed from the kitchen by circumstance beyond his control. A cake that is abandoned would either rot or go sour.

This seems to be what has happened to Africa. The two events that forcibly removed Europe out of the kitchen – World War II and the decolonization campaigns – unexpectedly came too soon. As a result, colonial rule was just long enough to stir up the continent and allow it to go sour.

A quick look at regions of Africa where the colonial experience lasted for extended periods of time, such as in Cape Verde and South Africa, would show a stable political culture. Colonial rule in Cape Verde lasted from 1462 to 1975 (513 years). In South Africa, it went from 1652 to 1994. Both colonies had settler European populations. And to use our cake-making metaphor, here the baker was not abruptly disrupted or forcibly removed from the kitchen. Because the colonial enterprise lasted for several hundred years, the colonizers had time to fully replace the indigenous culture with a new European culture. Today, Africans from mainland Africa travel to Cape Verde and to South Africa to look for economic opportunities.

The case of Cape Verde is especially noteworthy. With a population of a mere 500,000 in 2010, and a topography marked by volcanic rocks and sand dunes, the country can barely produce enough food to feed itself. Much of mainland Africa in the meantime is fertile and endowed with abundant natural resources. The mainland should be providing employment and other economic opportunities to Cape Verdeans; not the other way round. Of course, had colonial rule in the mainland lasted as for long as it did in Cape Verde, there is no doubt that it would have instilled the values that would have led to full acculturation and the full replacement of African traditional values with the modern values of democratic governance and efficient economic management.

Blind Respect for Colonially Imposed Boundaries

At independence, under the auspices of the Organization of African Unity (OAU), African rulers agreed to politically embed and make permanent the arbitrary boundaries that were forcibly imposed on them by European colonial powers. These are boundaries that were drawn not to advance the interest of Africans, but to advance the competing interests of European powers. Had the United States similarly decided to honor and make permanent the colonial boundaries of the thirteen colonies that were inherited from Britain, the United States would never have evolved to become that global power that it is today. Such landlocked states as Illinois, Ohio, Michigan, Wisconsin, Colorado, Montana, and the Dakotas, though not part of the initial 13 States, would today be as poor and as unstable as the landlocked states of Chad, Niger, Burundi, Mali and South Sudan. Once America realized at independence that the territorial boundaries that divided the newly independent thirteen states were an obstacle to national security, trade, economic growth and political development, it quickly voted to replace them with a federal system that provided for a seamless geographic and political union. This instantaneously made the sum of its parts stronger than its constitutive parts. The reverse is true for Africa today – where the sum of the whole is weaker than its constitutive parts. Despite tepid efforts by the African Union and the Organization of African Union before it, at continental policy-making, colonially imposed boundaries continue to impede trade, travel, and political unity.

Intra-African boundaries translate into barriers to intra-African trade, and the lack of trade translates into the lack of employment. The single most important "push" force that is causing the emigration of Africa's youth from the continent is unemployment. Unemployment in Africa is so alarmingly high, it has been referred to as a political and social "time-bomb." According to the International Labor Organization, in the first decade of the 21st century, nearly two-thirds of the population under 25 is unemployed. Even for those who are employed, a 2006 United Nations Economic Commission for Africa reported that Sub-Saharan Africa was "the only region where the total number of young workers living on less than a dollar a day had constantly increased from 36 million in 1995 to 45 million in 2005."[6] The implication here is that finding work was not even a guarantee for life without poverty.

Failed Democratic Experiments

In the previous chapter we saw that the failure to build the new order of modern democratic rule over the old order of traditional rule was largely responsible for the failure of democracy in Africa. Unlike in Britain where the old order was retained and used as a foundation on which the new order was built, in Africa there was a systemic but inconclusive effort to obliterate the old order. For the European colonizer, everything that had to do with traditional African institutions, (i.e., the old order) was deemed primitive and thus wrong; and had to be replaced. Nowhere was this more glaring than in French colonial rule in Africa. Following the revolution that resulted in the assassination of the French King and the dismantling of monarchic rule in France, the French came to Africa with a mindset that was anti-monarchic, and thus worked to systematically get rid of any form of governance that had to do with traditional or monarchic rule.

In the place of traditional/monarchic rule, the French established autocratic bureaucracies that subjugated and exploited colonial subjects. At independence, these institutions were inherited by African rulers, and cloaked in one-party political systems characterized by corruption, kleptocracy and bureaucratic inefficiency.

6   Unemployment a Time Bomb in Africa, http://www.unmultimedia.org/radio/english/detail/102006.html.

Had France and other colonial powers simply taken time to examine how pre-colonial Africa was governed, they would have discovered that not only did Africans have sophisticated institutions of governance, they had a workable system for ensuring individual and collective security. Among the Nuer, a confederation of ethnic people that extends from Southern Sudan to Western Sudan, no one individual had the legal authority to declare war or call for a cease-fire.[7] It was not until several thousand years later that a similar law was passed in the United States, the 1973 War Powers Act, to prohibit a single individual - the President - from declaring war. According to Basil Davidson, the major states of Africa and Europe were divided by no cultural gap of any great significance. "Law and order in the Western Sudan were probably superior under the emperor of Mali than in contemporary France and England, while the scholarship of Timbuktu and Djenne could possibly have given points to that of Oxford or Paris."[8] As with the rest of the world, Africans had established structures of government that served them well. As European powers sought to impose their version of government on Africa, they consciously chose to ignore existing African traditions. The result is what we have today – economic and political decay.

Peter Schraeder has documented a rich mosaic of political institutions – an embodiment of political and economic sophistication - that existed in Africa prior to the imposition of European rule.[9] Among them is a diversity of "segmented political systems" with no recognized central political authority. The governance structure was highly decentralized, with power diffused among groups that functioned more or less like autonomous nations. Among the autonomous national groups identified were the San people of Namibia and Botswana for whom decision-making required the face-to-face meeting of all adult males in the clan. In the Issa clan of Somalia, their practice of pastoral democracy was similar to the discourse of Jean Jacques Rousseau as described in the *Social Contract*.

Other less decentralized but still autonomous groups included the Maasai of Kenya/Tanzania, the Shilluk people of Sudan, the Swahili of East Africa, the Oyo Empire of Nigeria, the Mende people of Sierra Leone and the Zulu Empire of Southern Africa.[10] These latter groups were structurally more hierarchical and somewhat authoritarian. The governing order was top-down; passing from the authority of the ancestor to the edicts of the clan head. As in most ritually stratified traditional African political systems, the

---

7   G. Fortune, "The Contribution of Linguistics to Ethnohistory" in the Proceedings of the Tropical Africa History Conference of September 1960, Salisbury, 1962, p. 17.

8   Davidson, p. 35.

9   Peter Shraeder, *African Politics and Society: A Mosaic of Transformation* New York: Bedford/St. Martin Press, 2000, p.64-73.

10   Ibid.

ruler or clan-head "reigned but did not govern."[11]

The European introduction of the quasi-democratic Hobbesian model of an all-powerful Leviathan in Africa ran counter to the democratic imperatives of accountability. Term limit, which is constitutionally institutionalized in Western democracies, was an unthinkable proposition in Africa. In traditional African culture, the ruler of a nation, like the father of a family, is and should be ruler for life. Often referred to as the "father of the nation," he cannot be replaced or democratically voted out of office. At various lower levels of authority within the political institutions of Africa, the mere idea of challenging the authority of one's elder is absolutely unthinkable. Younger siblings have but high respect for their older siblings and are often expected to defer to the authority of the older sibling. The status of elder and leader are interchangeable, and there is the general belief that leadership requires wisdom, and wisdom only comes with age. So by virtue of being an elder or older sibling, one is expected to assume or play a leadership role. When the Western values of equality and competition are superimposed on a people whose traditional values are this different, there is bound to be total disorientation. The political disorientation that reigns in Africa today is explained by this reality.

Absence of a Democratic Culture

From the above discussion, we are led to come to the conclusion that Africa's inability to develop democratically may have to do with the lack of a democratic culture. Democracy in general requires a sense of accountability, transparency, tolerance, compromise, and the willingness to work across party lines. In other words, democracy is far more than just elections. It requires the rule of law, a free press, constitutional checks and balances, rotations in power, an independent judiciary, a nonpartisan civil service, a culture of openness, and a civil society. Power rotation and gracefully bowing out when defeated in elections adds dignity to the democratic process. Of course, bowing out gracefully here means congratulating your opponent even in the case of a closely contested election results. This was seen in the 2000 Presidential elections in the United States, where Al Gore rushed to congratulate George Bush even as the balloting was still being disputed in Florida. We saw it again in 2004, with John Kerry's rush to congratulate George Bush even as there were reported balloting inconsistencies in Ohio. And after a bitterly contested presidential primary campaign in 2008, we again saw a rather unusual show of conciliatory fence-mending between Barack Obama and Hillary Clinton, who went from disaffected political

---

11   Evans-Pritchard, E. E. *The Divine Kingship of the Shilluk of the Nilotic Sudan*, Cambridge: Cambridge University Press, 1948, p. 74.

rivals to campaigning together and eventually working together in the same administration. In a rare display of integrity and political modesty, Obama lavished his former opponent with the following praises:

> She's a leader who inspires millions of Americans with her strength, her courage and her commitment to the causes that brought us here tonight. Our party and our country are better off because of her, and I am a better candidate for having had the honor to compete with Hillary Rodham Clinton. America, this is our moment. This is our time - our time to turn the page on the policies of the past.[12]

A few days later, Obama again had this to say: weeks later, in an invitation for Clinton to join his Administration as Secretary of State,

> She possesses an extraordinary intelligence and toughness, and a remarkable work ethic. ... She is an American of tremendous stature who will have my complete confidence, who knows many of the world's leaders, who will command respect in every capital, and who will clearly have the ability to advance our interests around the world."[13]

Following an equally bitter general election campaign, Senator McCain's extension of congratulatory praises to Obama were both spontaneous and generous:

> A little while ago, I had the honor of calling Sen. Barack Obama to congratulate him. ... I urge all Americans ... I urge all Americans who supported me to join me in not just congratulating him, but offering our next president our goodwill and earnest effort to find ways to come together to find the necessary compromises to bridge our differences and help restore our prosperity, defend our security in a dangerous world, and leave our children and grandchildren a stronger, better country than we inherited. Whatever our differences, we are fellow Americans. And please believe me when I say

---

12   ABC News, June 4, 2008, Triumphant Obama praises Clinton in victory speech, (accessed 04/22/2018, http://www.abc.net.au/news/stories/2008/06/04/2265329.htm

13   MSNBC, Obama Names Clinton In National Security Team Rollout, (accessed 12/ 1/ 2014) http://www.msnbc.msn.com/id/27983003/

no association has ever meant more to me than that. Tonight — tonight, more than any night, I hold in my heart nothing but love for this country and for all its citizens, whether they supported me or Sen. Obama — whether they supported me or Sen. Obama. I wish Godspeed to the man who was my former opponent and will be my president.[14]

Remarks this spontaneous and graceful are virtually unthinkable in African politics. Obama actually went beyond these conciliatory remarks to tangibly invite members of the opposition party to serve in his cabinet. As in any country, one of the most important cabinet positions in the United States is the military. Obama, a Democrat, appointed Robert Gates, a Republican as his Secretary of Defense. Later in his administration, he appointed yet another Republican, Chuck Hagel, as his Secretary of Defense. In Africa, it is simply unthinkable that a president would appoint someone from an opposition party or rival ethnic group to such key government position.

In a quick flashback to elections that took place in Africa during the same period that Obama was elected, we see that in Nigeria, Olusegun Obasanjo attempted to amend the constitution in 2006 to remove term limits to allow himself stand reelection. In Kenya, Raila Odinga was cheated of victory by the incumbent, Mwai Kibaki in the presidential election of 2007. This provoked an uprising that led to the killings of some 500 to 1,000, and the displacement of as many as 200,000. The following year, in 2008, Morgan Tsvangirai scored a 47.3% victory over Robert Mugabe's 43.2% forced a runoff in the Zimbabwean elections. The runoff was foiled by growing threats of violence which forced Morgan Tsvangirai to drop out of a presidential election that he'd won in the first round.

Other historical examples of abuse and intransigence in the political culture of African rulers is seen in the brazen repeal of constitutional term limits. Burundi's Pierre Nkurunziza, Congo Republic's Denis Sassou Nguesso; Cameroon's Paul Biya; Rwanda's Paul Kagame are a sampling of African rulers who are guilty of such abuses.

How Freedom in Africa was Destroyed by the Imposition of European Rule

Freedom is at the very top of the foreign policy agenda of Western democracies. Colonialism was generally justified as a civilizing mission that would promote freedom, equality and prosperity. But the reality is that

---

14   *New York Times*, November 8, 2008, John McCain's Concession Speech, (accessed 3/3/2010) http://elections.nytimes.com/2008/results/president/speeches/mccain-concession-speech.html#

African societies were freer and more stable in pre-colonial times when the continent was made up mostly by tribe groups and stateless societies than it is today. Tribes in stateless societies generally have no central authority that placed restrictions on their civil liberties. What they have are council of elders and village assemblies. Kinship along with age and maturity provided law and order. The Pygmies of Central Africa, the Bushmen of South Africa, and the Fulani of Nigeria all used kinship to avoid centralized autocratic rule. Similarly, a system of checks and balances was instituted by the Nuer of Sudan, the Tiv and the Igbo of Nigeria, and the Bedouin of North Africa to guarantee freedom and individual liberties. Even when tribes were conquered by powerful kingdoms, they were afforded a certain amount of autonomy and independence.

European rule took away many of these freedoms. To prevent any form of organized opposition against colonial rule, the freedom of speech and assembly that Africans enjoyed prior to the arrival of Europeans was outlawed by colonial administrators. To preempt armed insurgencies, the right to bear arms was prohibited. The right of Africans to travel freely across tribal and regional boundaries was now heavily regulated and restricted by the colonizing powers. Imposed visa restrictions now made intra-African travel legally regulated. Even cross-border travel between members of the same clan was now regulated. To formally visit a relative who was forced by a colonially imposed boundary to now live on the other side of the border, one had to travel several hundred miles to the nation's capital to obtain a passport and a visa. An individual in Congo Brazzaville interested in visiting a relative in Congo Kinshasa had first to obtain government permission to leave Congo Brazzaville (an exit visa), and then a second permission (an entry visa) before he would be allowed to enter Congo Kinshasa. The same was true for an individual from Guinea Bissau who was interested in visiting a family member in Guinea Conakry. To obtain the visa, individuals were required to subject themselves to government interrogation. This, in every respect, was diminishing of the freedoms that Africans enjoyed prior to the imposition of European rule.

Prior to the advent of the oppressive rule that is in Africa today, coups directed at killing or ousting rulers were rare and often unthinkable. Why go through the trouble of overthrowing the ruler, when one was free to gather his supporters, move and resettle in any part of the continent? Many of the problems that post-colonial Africa has today are because they were not meant to be the nations that they are today. There is no better prescription for long term instability than the forced regrouping of people from competing ethnic groups into a fictionally created state. This is what was behind the Nigerian-Biafran War, the Rwanda Genocide, the Sudanese split, the Tuareg insurgency and the civil war in Darfur. Had the freedom that prevailed in pre-colonial Africa not been disrupted by colonialism and the European conceived modern state system, Africa would not have experienced these conflicts.

Africa's Failure to Adopt a Defined Ideology

In the quest for development, ideology provides a roadmap and the discipline that is needed to conscientiously follow that map. The absence of an ideological compass naturally means that the discipline or sense of purpose that allows society to follow an ideologically articulated path to development would be missing. The failure to articulate a new direction or ideology for Africa after it became independent is a major reason that contributes to the continent's inability to develop. With a clearly defined ideological roadmap, society would work to marshal the resources and the commitment that are needed to follow that roadmap. Without a clearly defined ideology, society would not know what direction to take.

Most regions of the world that have set and achieved development goals were guided by an ideological compass whose conception and formulation came from within. Africa's inability to follow a defined roadmap to sustainable economic development could partially be attributed to the lack of an internally developed political ideology. Without a realistic internal political ideology, Africa has had to rely on the wholesale import and unadulterated application of competing foreign ideologies. The most well-known of these were the communist ideology of the East and the capitalist ideology of the West. Experimentation with both ideologies in Africa came at a time when the East and the West were at daggers-drawn. Instead of becoming a place for the testing of African-conceived ideologies, Africa became a place for the testing of competing foreign ideologies. No doubt therefore that both ideologies failed to produce development in Africa.

In the meantime, the pervasiveness of tribalism in Africa has in many ways contributed to impeding the development of a unifying political ideology for Africa. In the absence of such a unifying ideology, tribalism then becomes the cue for making political choices. People want certainty in their lives, in their communities, and in their country. Nothing provides such certainty better than a candidate from one's tribe, ethnicity or region. A bad political agenda from a candidate who is from your tribe or region is preferable to a good political agenda from a candidate who is from a competing tribe or region. The dynamics of ideology and ethnicity in the West is however different. Here, because ideology more often than not transcends ethnicity, race, gender and region, political choices are based not on tribal or ethnic affinity, but on ideological affinity. This has particularly been the case in the U.S. In Africa, it is practically inconceivable that a presidential candidate would lose elections in his tribe, province or region. Yet, in the 2000 U.S.

presidential elections, this was exactly what happened to Al Gore – he lost in his home-state of Tennessee. The year before that, in an impeachment trial that was brought against President Bill Clinton, the most aggressive call for his impeachment and removal from office came from his home state of Arkansas. Had the decision to impeach and remove President Clinton been entirely in the hands the Arkansas congressional delegation, Clinton would have been impeached and removed from office. In almost every African country, lawmakers from a president's tribe or region are more likely to bring praises rather than charges against their presidential native son.

Failed Economic Experiments

Nowhere are Africa's failures more noticeable than in the inability to develop viable economic systems. Much of the misery in Africa is rooted in poor or failed economic reforms. Somehow, modern economic policies that work in the West - from consumer spending to deficit spending – do not seem to work in Africa. While a tax cut in the West most often produces economic stimulus, a similar tax cut in Africa would not produce the same result. For the African middle class, increased or growing disposable income is directed not at local consumption, but at the purchase of foreign consumer goods. Where the taste buds of the middle class are more attuned to foreign consumer goods than to domestic consumer goods, economic stimulus measures cannot produce the same results that such stimulus will produce in Western economies.

The global economic system, which started in pre-colonial times, imposed an international division of labor that forced Africa to specialize in the production of raw materials. At independence, as most other formerly colonized regions in the world worked to reform their economies, African states continued to depend on the monocrop economies they inherited from their colonizers. Today, more than half a century after gaining independence, most African countries continue to specialize in the production of raw materials. In some countries, oil, minerals and agricultural commodities generate as much as 90% in foreign earnings. Such disproportionate reliance on single commodities makes African economies vulnerable to fluctuations in international commodity prices.[15]

Aside from a few niche industries such as cut flowers which are airfreighted from Kenya and Ethiopia to buyers in Europe, African trade has not changed much since the end of colonial rule. The process today remains one where unprocessed raw materials go out and finished goods come in.

15 Nicholas van de Walle, African and the World Economy: Continued Marginalization and Re-engagement, in John W. Harbeson and Donald Rothchild, *Africa in World Politics*, Third Edition, Boulder, Colorado: Westview Press, 2000, pp. 266-266.

The trade imbalance is vividly illustrated by ships sent from Asia to pick up empty containers left at African ports. Within Africa itself it is difficult and costly to move goods. The continent has only a few railways, and many of them are in disrepair. Africa has nothing resembling an interstate or trans-continental highway system. Today, getting a container to the heart of Africa – say from the port city of Douala in Cameroon to the landlocked country of Chad still means a wait of up to six weeks at the port on arrival. Road-blocks, bribes, potholes and mud-drifts on the road along the way remain obstacles to economic activity across the continent. Indeed, according to a U.S. government report, it cost more to ship a ton of wheat from Mombasa in Kenya to Kampala in Uganda (two neighboring countries), than it does to ship the same ton of wheat from Chicago to Mombasa.[16]

Capitalism is an economic system that creates abundance. In Africa, however, it has failed to create abundance. Nigeria, for example, has since independence known nothing but the Western model of capitalist production. It is richly endowed with natural resources, and has for a long time been the largest oil producer in Africa, and the 5th largest oil producer in the world. This country that is first in Africa and fifth in the world in oil production, has inexplicably not been able to meet its own domestic oil needs. Annually, it imports almost 70% of its fuel needs, with power outages and long lines at gas stations a daily routine.[17]

Besides failing to diversify its economy at independence, Africa failed to make the investments in human capital that were necessary to produce development and economic growth. Africa's public sector instead became heavily involved in the private sector economy – providing the goods and services that would have been more efficiently provided by the private sector. The very government which is supposed to regulate private industry was itself a player in that industry. No doubt therefore that it found itself unable to effectively manage the development of the private sector. In becoming so heavily involved in the economy, both as a player and as a regulator, the public sector stood in the way of the ingenuity, the creativity and the industry of private citizens, stifling the development of the entrepreneurial skills that are necessary for economic development. The next section will look at some of the areas where entrepreneurial skills failed to develop because of an overly intrusive and unwarranted public sector involvement in the private sector.

---

16   *The Economist,* "Opportunity Knocks", October 9, 2008
17   December Green & Laura Luehrmann, *Comparative Politics of the Global South,* 4th Edition, Boulder, CO: Lynne Rienner Publishers, 2018, p. 184

Marketing through Marketing Boards

Nothing did more to sap the entrepreneurial spirit in Africa than the monopolistic practice of marketing through state-owned marketing boards. In stepping in to determine production quotas and fix market prices, not only did government marketing boards interfere with the efficiency of market forces, they helped sap the entrepreneurial spirit in the individual. Prices were determined not by demand and supply, but by bureaucratic officials. Farmers were paid lower prices than the prices their commodities earned in the international market. The very governments which frequently complained about the low prices that international commodity markets pay for Third World exports were in turn paying even lower prices to farmers who were the actual producers of these commodities. This explains why in most countries in Africa, the economic condition of rural farmers has seen no net improvement since independence. If anything, their condition has become worse. Farm earnings for most cash crops are lower today than they were in the 1960s. This was one factor that largely contributed to the collapse of African economies in the mid-1980s. African governments rushed to blame the international economy alone for the collapse. They however failed to extend the blame to their national marketing boards. The reality was that state-owned marketing boards had taken over and were doing to local producers what the colonial administration did to Africa. As a result, the most productive sector of the African economy was also now the lowest paid sector. Because African bureaucracies had joined in to become part of the chain that exploits African labor, the condition of the peasant farmer is much worse off today than it was in colonial times. With the income that is generated from the export of these commodities, the top echelons of African government employees frequently fly abroad for medical treatment at some of the most expensive medical facilities in the world. At the same time, the typical African farmer who generates this income cannot afford to fill a $5 medical prescription.

To say that Africa is a land of contrasts is an understatement. In almost every country in present day Africa, there are two separate worlds – divided, unequal and living side-by-side. One is a producer; and the other a consumer. One is modern and externally oriented, and the other is rural and internally oriented. One works an average of four hours a day, and the other an average of sixteen hours a day. The rural farm worker whose labor produces the commodities that earn foreign exchange for the country works from sunrise to sunset. In parts of Africa where the sun rises at 5:00 AM and sets at 6:00 PM, this adds up to a 13-hour workday. In Africa's modern sector which is run largely by state bureaucracies, the official work hour in most countries is set to start at 8:00 am. Frequently, it is not uncommon to see employees get to work at 9:00 or 10:00 am. By 12:00 noon, the routine in

French-speaking Africa is for employees to go home for a two to three-hour lunch break. Those who are able to return to work after lunch, generally return drunk or too exhausted to do any productive work.

As the efforts of the African public sector were directed at exploiting the rural peasant, no efforts were directed at facilitating the diversification in the modern sector of the economy. As a result, domestic self-sufficiency in Africa remains a pipe dream. For the basic amenities of modern life, such as stoves, refrigerators, television sets, and even vacations, the modern-oriented African continues to turn on the outside world. As a result, more capital has left Africa in the post-colonial era than it did at any time during the colonial period. The lack of growth and diversity in the local industry has contributed substantially in diminishing the domestic sources of tax revenues that are needed to build modern roads, highways, bridges and other public infrastructures. This partially explains why African governments are often forced to perpetually turn to international financial institutions for loans.

When such foreign loans are contracted, they are frequently used not in stimulating growth and diversification in the private sector, but in providing increased amenities to Africa's "consuming" public sector. Many of these amenities are not accessible to the rural peasant farmer. After more than half a century of independence, most peasant farmers still do not have access to electricity or television sets. With a disproportionately high amount of their farm revenue allocated to supporting the public sector and other government bureaucracies, the average African farmer cannot even afford treatment at the hospitals that are built by the loans that are obtained from the World Bank. As a result, impoverished Africans are often forced to resort to traditional medicine.

On the whole, African rulers see no need to invest in the development of modern health facilities at home, as they can afford to travel abroad for advanced medical care. There is therefore little concern for the deteriorating living conditions of the masses, even though the country's wealth is largely generated by these masses. Although the peasants and urban proletariats do work very hard to improve their living conditions, they have little or no power to influence the macroeconomic policies that would facilitate such improvement. As they grow into retirement age, the African bureaucrat is entitled to a pension, but the rural peasant farmer whose labor supported the bureaucrat's career gets nothing at retirement. Indeed, much of what African intellectuals claim colonial rule did wrong to Africa has in turn been done to the African masses by the African public sector.

Somehow, Africans have been made to believe that they cannot develop without bank loans. The reality however is that modernization or development does not come from banks; it comes from well thought out liberal policies. It was not IMF or World Bank loans that brought development to the West. Development came to the West from the ideas of liberal thinkers. Growing dependency on IMF and World Bank loans blinded Africans of the ability to think and come out with creative ideas to develop their economies. They may require mentally digging far deep below the surface, but there are obvious paths to development that do not require indebtedness or wholesale reliance on external resources.

The Production/Consumption Paradox in Africa

One of the most alarming paradoxes about Africa is that it consumes what it doesn't produce and produces what it doesn't consume. Africa produces cotton, but when Africans need textiles, or cotton swaps and cotton balls, they have to import it from foreign markets. Although Africa is the world's largest producer of cocoa, the mother of a hungry African baby has to wait for chocolate to be shipped in from Switzerland so she can feed that baby. Africa exports wood, but when Africans need a toothpick they have to wait for it to be shipped from China. It is a paradox that hails from the colonial distortion of African economies. In colonial times, African economies were for the most part transformed from subsistence economies to export-oriented economies. Much of the fertile farmland in Africa was taken over and transformed from the production of rice, corn, yams and plantains to the production of coffee, cocoa, rubber, and cotton. The typical coffee grower in Africa does not drink coffee, so coffee is produced primarily for export. If for some reason the export market refuses to buy, the coffee goes to waste. Imagine a scenario where some of the biggest industries in the U.S. or Europe are in the business of producing goods for which there is no demand at home. This is the reality that the economies of Africa are faced with. Across much of rural Africa, it is not uncommon to find under-nourished children in families that own plantations of coffee, tea, rubber or cocoa. Since these commodities are not readily sold in the domestic market and cannot be immediately converted into human or animal feed, whenever there is a fall in foreign demand, the harvest is stockpiled in warehouses, and sometimes left to rot away. This was the case in the 1980s when stockpiles of cocoa bean wasted away in Cote d'Ivoire, when world cocoa prices collapsed, and the country was unable to sell its harvest.

To meet the rapidly industrializing needs of Western economies, production in Africa was expanded to include the extraction of mineral and energy resources. It is generally acknowledged that without natural resources from Africa and the Americas, the Industrial Revolution would never have succeeded. The abundance of strategic minerals in Africa meant that equally a vast amount of African labor was going to be allocated to mineral production as they were to agricultural production. Minerals exported from Africa included copper, cobalt, diamond, gold, manganese, and uranium. Africa's lack of extraction and processing capacity meant that the production of these resources had very limited immediate impact in the local economy. So here were Africans producing what they could not consume. It wasn't until when the minerals were transformed into finished goods and re-exported to Africa, that Africans were able to buy. So, here again were Africans consuming what they could not produce. No doubt therefore that African economies remain stagnant.

At independence African states did little to restructure their economies. They failed to identify and plan for the production of goods and services that would meet domestic consumer needs. Even agricultural production was not redirected at meeting domestic nutritional needs. Just as Africans left the colonially imposed boundaries intact, they also left the colonially imposed economic structures intact. Africans continued the implementation of the colonial policies that allocated the most fertile farmlands to the production of commodities that went to satisfy demand in the West and failed to invest in production that would meet demand at home.

As extraction in Africa is directed at meeting foreign rather than domestic needs, so too are Africa's consumption habits. From clothing to automobile, healthcare, household items, travel and vacationing, Africans on the whole prefer the "foreign-made" over the "African-made." Political independence failed to wean Africans, particularly the African middle class, from Western tastes and Western lifestyles. Even for such basics as socks, tee-shirts and foot-ware, Africans have to import. In general, the average African would rather buy an imported used tee-shirt than a new tee-shirt that is made in Africa. It is a reality that raises pessimism for the economic future of the continent. Why would anyone want to invest in the production of goods and services at home when there is no domestic demand for those goods and services? This is a challenge that should have been addressed at independence. This failure to develop domestic economies in Africa allowed the former colonial powers – powers who were very reluctant to relinquish their hold on the continent in the first place – enough time to go home, regroup and come back first as neocolonialists, and today as globalizers.

Lack of Vision in African Leadership

Societies that have made remarkable strides in social and economic development are societies that were led by leaders with vision. Africa's inability to make such strides can be attributed to the lack of vision in its leadership. While most African leaders are bent on staying in office for the long term, they are not bent on developing long term visions for their countries. Many of the forces that contribute to economic development are frequently multifaceted, long term, and often unrelated. Unless a country's leadership is able to define and develop a vision that will place it on the path to development, the country may never achieve development. It is exactly because of the lack of strategic vision in African leaders that trade among African states is in most cases nonexistent. Even among neighboring states, African leaders have done little to promote commercial activity.

It has been demonstrated in other parts of the world that something as simple as a modern road infrastructure can grossly transform an economy and place it on the path to rapid development. The level of development that followed the construction of the European and American interstate systems were stratospheric. African leaders are yet to conceive, envision, and commit time, energy, and resources to similar infrastructural development. While Africans very much want to live the lifestyles that are lived in the West, their desires are not concomitantly accompanied by a guiding vision.

Trade is the most lucrative economic activity. It generates the most income and requires the least capital investment. In its most basic form, trade involves the simple transfer of assets from venues where there is high supply to venues where there is high demand. Other forms of revenue generation require heavy investments in machinery and capital equipment. The economy of almost every advanced country today has had to evolve from farming to industry to trade. The primary sources of revenues in Britain and the United States today, for example are in trade, services and IT know-how. This is why the two countries are among the strongest supporters of the trade policies of the World Trade Organization. As the global policeman for free trade, the WTO monitors and sanctions practices that interfere with trade. In the new world of free trade, trade benefits are enhanced largely by the value individual nations are able to add to traded goods. Unfortunately, it is a world in which Africa has neither the ability to extract the resources that are in its subsoil, nor the infrastructure to process, add value and transport them to the market.

Promoting Capitalism without Capital

Another one of Africa's dilemmas is the push to pursue a capitalist economy without capital. Pressure from the World Bank, the IMF and other Western institutions for Africa to restructure and adopt a market economy is tantamount to pushing Africa to pursue capitalism without capital. Capitalism is not an economic system that be imposed by external forces.

While mercantilist trade was among the principal forces that contributed to the development of capitalism in the West, in the past in most traditional African societies, these forces were seen as low and un-dignifying. Trade, or the buying and selling of goods and services, is an activity that was reserved either for landless commoners or for people from distant lands. Aristocrats and land owners did not engage in commercial activity. Materially self-sufficient, they did not see the need to travel to distant places to transact trade. For the typical land-owning African aristocrat, hunting, farming, craft and blacksmithing were leisurely professions that he exercised. He had nothing but disdain for the lowly profession of trade, which frequently involved traveling from village to village, and region to region to buy and resell. Even in the dignified professions of hunting, farming, craft making and blacksmithing, Africans who participated in them did so not for the market, but for sport, trophy, hobby and as rite of passage. On his day off, the hunter or farmer relaxed by crafting and sharpening his hunting and farming tools. If capital is the profit or surplus that derives from economic activity, we see in the economic life of the traditional African here that he was not involved in any activity that produced profit or capital; and if there is no activity that accumulates profits, there will be no capital and eventually no capitalism.

The expectations of modernization and capitalist development in Africa appear therefore overly ambitious. No region in the world, including the Western world, has been able to move from a subsistence economy into a capitalist economy without capital. But this is what is expected of Africa.

Among the recommendations frequently made by the World Bank and the IMF in their structural adjustment programs for Africa is a call for the privatization of state-owned industries. Critics who see the IMF and the World Bank as institutions of neocolonial rule see privatization as a euphemism for de-nationalization. Among the institutions' harshest critics is one of their former employees, Malawi's one-time President, Bingu wa Matharika, who angrily chastised the institutions in 2012, ordering them to "go to hell!"[18] Coming from a former World Bank employee, it gives reason to take a closer look at IMF and World Bank's policies.

The single most talked about flaw in IMF and World Bank policies is their "one-size fits all" approach. Like everything else, there are variations in economic conditions. Quite often, circumstances in each state are unique to that state. What works for Nigeria will probably not work for Kenya. Taking heed from the IMF, Nigeria's head of State in 2010 called for the privatization of the country's public utilities. Privatization makes sense only if there is balanced growth in the economy. Balanced growth produces full employment, and gainfully employed people can afford to pay their utility bills. So simply advising an African head of state to privatize his country's public utilities without first ensuring that there are sufficient employment opportunities to enable employees to pay their monthly bills can be a prescription that would lead to failure.

As much as the IMF and World Bank frequently called for the

18   *New African*, 01/04/2012 'I Am No Idiot!' Mutharika Tells Donors, (accessed 06/09/2016)
      http://thinkafricapress.com/malawi/hell-you-mutherika-tells-donors-leave-him-alone

privatization of government corporations, it often failed to assess the capacity of the African private sector to acquire and effectively run the privatized corporations. The rush to promote privatization in a region of the world that has no private capital and no private sector capacity was not only ill-conceived, it was seen as a veiled design to re-colonize Africa.

During their rule, colonial powers failed to develop a viable domestic private sector in Africa. At independence therefore, such services as electricity, water, telephone services, transportation and highway construction were taken over by government companies. Indeed, across much of Africa, it was common practice to the chagrin of the West, for newly independent governments to take over and run major economic investments such as public utilities. The West saw it as the "nationalization" (or seizing) of foreign investments. So, when African countries had liquidity problems and turned to the West for loans, the West often saw this as an opportunity to condition the loans on the privatization of the African economy. This insistence on privatization in countries which had no capital or developed private sector capacity was in many ways interpreted as the "de-nationalization" and "re-acquisition" of the Western investments that were nationalized at independence. That all of the former colonial powers are also World Bank and IMF shareholders, and that the two institutions are key advocates for privatization in Africa, one cannot help but see them as surrogates of neocolonial rule.

Not only is the private sector in Africa capital-poor, it does not have the money, the management or the technological know-how to buy and run costly government companies that are recommended for privatization. Private companies from the very Western countries that granted independence to Africa have such capital and such management know-how. With these assets in abundance, they were often able to rush back and buy state-owned investments at giveaway prices. In the face of such reality, it is hard not to see IMF and World Bank calls for privatization as a guise for the de-nationalization (or the taking back) of the Western companies that were taken over by African governments at independence. Privatization gave ownership of some of the most profitable industries in Africa (water, electricity, telephone services) away to foreign companies. Profits generated were generally repatriated to the West in their entirety, with not much left in the host country for investments in education, roads and healthcare.

Back in the early sixties, Guy Hunter, a British scholar who was generally in favor of free enterprise solutions to economic development warned that if Third World countries continued the unqualified encouragement of foreign private investment, a very high proportion of their economies will come under the control of foreign firms.[19] This is what is happening in Africa today. Thanks to the World Bank and the IMF, privatization and foreign loans have returned much of Africa into the neocolonial claws of the West. This may be why some of the most vociferous critiques of IMF and World Bank privatization programs prefer to refer to them as "piratization" rather than as privatization. Others see the World Bank and IMF as the heirs of the reins of colonial power - that is, institutions that have stepped in to indirectly continue the predatory and exploitative policies of the former colonial powers. This time around, it does appear that Africa's push for economic independence is not going to be as easy as the campaign it mounted in the 1960s for political independence. During the fight for political independence, the adversary was identifiably foreign. The names were Belgium, Britain, France, Italy, Portugal, Spain. Today, in a globalized economy, the adversary is faceless, and thus not readily identifiable. Not readily identifiable here means that liberating itself from the economic stranglehold that it finds itself in today is going to be a lot more difficult than the political liberation Africa achieved in the 1960s.

While the West has been actively pushing for privatization in Africa, it remains a historical fact that privatization and private property ownership is not foreign to Africa. In pre-colonial Africa, all property was privately owned. While land and landed assets in medieval Europe were owned and controlled mainly by feudal lords, in Africa land and landed assets were owned by individuals and families from all social backgrounds. Not even traditional rulers could lay claim or sovereign control on the landed assets that were privately owned by their subjects. With the colonization of Africa came the forcible seizure of privately-owned land. With the help of the British government, for example, Cecil Rhodes colonized and took over much of Southern Africa. And when European powers were forced by the decolonization process to give up their colonial holdings, they hurriedly put in place institutions and rulers that they trusted would stay behind and continue to be loyal to them. This was how rulers like Zaire's Mobutu, Uganda's Idi Amin, Central Africa's Bokassa, and Cameroon's Ahidjo were placed in power. In line with the colonial establishment, these leaders continued with the legacy of public ownership and public control that was instituted by European colonialism. Ironically, the same Western powers that forcibly ended Africa's tradition of private ownership are today advising Africa on the need to privatize.

19   Guy Hunter, *The New Societies of Tropical Africa*, Oxford, 1962, p. 186.

72

The Colonial Paradox

The controversy surrounding the imposition of colonial rule in Africa has been debated from different perspectives, but it has never been debated from an evolutionary/revolutionary perspective. We will here attempt to examine the institution of colonialism first from an evolutionary perspective, and then from a revolutionary viewpoint.

Looking at it as an evolution, it can be said that the foreign imposition of colonial rule enabled Africa to get integrated in the global system. As in the metaphorical "breaking of the egg to make an omelette," Africa's integration in the global system had to come with a price. The price was the dehumanizing exploitation of the continent's human and natural resources. However, without the forced integration of Africa into the global system, there is no saying where Africa would be today, and how the rest of the world would today perceive Africans.

On the basis of the preceding argument, while colonial rule may have been evolutionary, post-colonial rule in Africa has been somewhat devolutionary. Social conditions are much worse in some African countries today than they were under colonial rule. In most countries, the economic and social infrastructures (schools, hospitals, roads, etc.) that were left behind by European colonizers have fallen into disrepair. Despite abundant natural resources, African rulers have nothing to show in the form of social, political and economic progress. After more than a half century of independence and self-rule, the standard of living in Africa is characterized more by regress than by progress.

On the basis of the above facts, we are led to the realization that the greatest obstacle to development in Africa is the rule of African rulers. While the primary role of government in advanced democracies is to enforce the rule of law, the primary role of government in Africa is to enforce the rule of the ruler and those aspects of law that advance his personal interest. The ruling elite in much of Africa consider themselves exempt from the rule of law. Many do not pay income or import taxes, particularly those who are active members of the ruling party. This partially explains why the war against corruption in Africa has never been successful. Many of those who are involved in corruption are by virtue of status and ties to the ruling regime, immune from prosecution.

From a revolutionary perspective, it can also be argued that Africa's struggle and inability to find stability and focus can be attributed to the fact that its integration in the global system was revolutionary rather than evolutionary. While an evolution is deliberate change that comes with measured and manageable steps, a revolution is a radical social transformation that is carried out on a grand scale. Had Africa's integration in the global system come about as a result of gradual, measured and deliberate steps, the integration would possibly have been sustainable and easier to manage. But because the integration was imposed by external forces, it radically transformed Africa, displacing its political and socioeconomic system, redirecting them to serving the interests of Europe. It is a proposition that incontrovertibly obviates any postulation that sees colonialism as an evolutionary process. In every dimension, therefore, colonialism was a revolutionary affront on Africa.

Paradoxically, it had to take yet another revolution to end this revolutionary affront. The liberation struggle that were waged to free Africa from colonial rule were in many respects a counter-revolution. It was a counter-revolution that succeeded in getting rid of foreign occupation. It however did nothing to restructure and redirect Africa's economic and political institutions to the interest of Africans. Instead, it left in place and intact the colonial institutions and structures that were put in place by colonial occupiers. Independence did little to change or improve living conditions in Africa. The only thing that changed with independence were the faces of the exploiters. Instead of white European faces in Land Rovers, khaki shorts and safari hats, Africa was now ruled by black African faces that were in three-piece European suits, chauffeured limousines and secret foreign bank accounts. The new faces were quick to embrace the very bureaucratic structures that were used to exploit their continent. Using these inherited structures, they decided to leave intact the economic system that was in place in colonial times – producing the same items and marketing them to the same markets. The African producer remains politically and economically marginalized, and more than ever before, he remains increasingly exploited. If Africa has realized any change since becoming independent, it has been change for the worse.

Across the continent, the unemployment, poverty and mortality rates in Africa are much higher today than at any time in the past. The diasporization or rate at which Africans are fleeing Africa (an Africa that is ruled by Africans) to seek economic and political refuge abroad is much higher today than at any time in the past. Most of those who are migrating away from the continent are Africans who are in the most productive years of their lives.

As in the past, the destination of choice are the very markets where Africa's raw materials are marketed. On arrival, however, the fleeing Africans are sometimes surprised to discover that opportunities for employment are restricted by strict immigration laws. To survive, they are forced to seek job opportunities in the underground economy where they are overworked, underpaid and, like their predecessors who were forcibly abducted from the continent several hundred years earlier, exploited.

Over time, some are granted the legal right to work, and are able to find employment in the mainstream economy. And even with the legal right to work, they are likely to find employment only in jobs that are often not desired by citizens of the host countries. Others actually end up working in shops and factories that process raw materials that are imported from their homeland. In an interesting twist, the product of the labor of the African refugee is re-exported to the Africa that he ran away from. Thus, by constantly adapting and reinventing itself, capitalism continues to be able to extricate both human and material resources out of Africa, transforming them abroad and re-exporting them back to Africa. As in past centuries, Africans are continuing to fuel the global capitalist machinery that keeps Africa permanently in the hemmed periphery.

Why the Winds of Democracy Blew in from the East, Not from the West

In the early 1990s, the headlines of most international newspapers were about the winds of democracy that were blowing into Africa from the East. No one noticed the irony then. This is the Africa which had been under the physical influence of the West for close to a century – a West that defines itself as democratic and claims to be working to promote democracy around the world. So why did the winds of democracy blow into Africa from Eastern Europe and not from the democracies of Western Europe? There are several underlying reasons. Despite its global rivalry against the communist world, the West was always convinced that totalitarian regimes were in some respects more efficient at governing than democratic regimes. The Eastern bloc states were basically totalitarian regimes that passed for communist states. Communism, as defined by Karl Marx was a state in the evolution of human society which, if attained, will establish a classless society. Once a classless society is attained, there will be order and complete harmony, and there will no longer be any need for government. The one characteristic that was common to all the regimes in Eastern bloc states was that they were all government controlled. Had Karl Marx come back to life during the "communist" era of the Eastern bloc states, he would not have classified any of them as communist. They did not in any form or shape meet the litmus test of a Marxist state. But what was true about them was that their rule was effective, albeit, oppressive. It enforced order – in the very manner that European powers enforced it in Africa in colonial times. Like the Eastern European version of communism, colonialism was exploitative. And any system that exploits is ipso facto intolerant of dissent. This is why colonial powers did not introduce democracy in Africa. It is intolerant of dissent. Had they introduced it in Africa, it would have made their predatory mission difficult. The West was not in Africa to promote equality. This explains why the winds of democracy did not and could never have blown into Africa from the West.

After the Second World War, the minority regime in South Africa campaigned to get the backing of the West by portraying itself as a bulwark against communism. Like the iron curtain in the East, South Africa became the self-professed apartheid curtain in the South. It was a curtain that found an excuse to keep blacks and whites apart, keeping the black citizens of South Africa so visibly oppressed, it atrophied the political and economic potential of black South Africans. As communism persisted, the imaginary fear of the East block "iron curtain" was used as a pretext to keep the apartheid curtain in place. When the winds of freedom that blew out of Perestroika finally brought down the Berlin Wall, the minority regime in South Africa could no longer convincingly evoke the fictional fear of communism to deny democratic reform in South Africa. Thus, as the iron curtain collapsed in Eastern Europe, it produced winds of freedom that blew to Africa and caused the collapse of apartheid and various other non-democratic one-party regimes. Thus, the paradox about the winds of democracy blowing in from the East.

The Euphemism of Africa as a Continent of "Developing Nations"

The general description of Africa as "developing nations" is a euphemism that is both condescending and misleading. In the first 50 years of Africa's independence the reality on the ground was that Africa was not developing; it was "under-developing." Continent-wide, there were very few signs of progress towards development. Year after year, what one saw was political instability, economic decline and a downward spiral towards civil war, anarchy and underdevelopment. Somalia, Rwanda, Guinea Bissau, Darfur, and the Central African Republic, were all illustrations of that downward spiral. All indexes of political and socioeconomic performance for the continent, from life expectancy to GDP to political stability, reveal that living conditions were better under colonial rule than under post-colonial rule. If Africa's past was materially better off than its present, then it will be appropriate to see the region not as "developing nations" but as "under-developing nations." Even the most ardent critique of colonialism would admit that on balance, more development took place in Africa in colonial times than in the post-colonial era. Despite its horrors, colonialism was a period when Africa's modern bureaucratic institutions, educational institutions, hospitals, communications and transportation infrastructures were planted. These developments enabled Africa to be linked to the outside world – albeit in a subordinate status. And during that period, the economic performance of such sub-Saharan nations like Ghana, Kenya, Nigeria, and Uganda was higher than the performance of such East Asian nations like South Korea, Malaysia, and Thailand. However, by 2003, while the GDP per capita of Kenya was $405, Ghana $258, Uganda $227, and Nigeria $495, the GDP per capita of South Korea was $10,243, Malaysia $3,701, and Thailand $1,888.

If the colonizing powers had their way, colonial rule in Africa would have actually lasted longer. Somehow, the devastation of World War II emasculated Europe and diminished its ability to effectively continue the administration of its African colonies. African nationalists saw here an opportunity and took advantage of it. They began a campaign for independence. In some countries, the campaign and transition to independence was peaceful. In others, it was bloody. Taking a quick look back, one would recall that European powers had marketed their colonization of Africa as a "civilizing mission." If this were a genuinely "civilizing mission", and had Europeans treated Africans civilly, Africans would have, instead of mounting a campaign for independence, mounted a campaign for European powers to continue their "goodwill" civilizing mission. Basically, it was the harsh, repressive and predatory treatment disguised as a civilizing mission that forced Africans to mobilize and campaign against colonial rule.

Western Europe occupied Africa from 1884-1980, with the stated goal of preparing Africa for independence. In reality, the real goal was the exploitation of Africa. A popular anecdote in Africa goes that, when the European first came to Africa, he came with a bible in one hand and a gun in the other. He invited Africans to close their eyes so they could pray together. By the time Africans opened their eyes, a gun was pointing at them, their land was gone, and they were left holding the bible. Africans have been holding the bible ever since then. Today, it is a region with the fastest growth of the Christian faith in the world.

Given Africa's inability to manage development, one cannot help but ponder if Africa's independence came too soon. Was Africa ready for the independence and self-rule at the time it sought it? Does Africa have the ability to efficiently manage a modern economy? Can Africa compete in the new global economy? And finally, "does Africa have the 'will' to develop?" It is difficult to find "feel good" answers to these questions. However, in the chapters that follow, we are going to attempt to address some of these rather mortifying questions. Given the realities that are present in Africa today, our findings are not always going to be pleasing. But a physician has the ethical duty to report to his patient the diagnosis. Africa is a patient with a chronic disease. Her diagnosis may not be pleasing to report, but it is our moral duty to report it. Much of Africa is not "developing." Neither is it "emerging." It is "under-developing." It is only by telling it like it is – without cloaking them in euphemisms) – that our patient would be compelled to take the measures that are necessary to effectively manage his condition.

To illustrate that Africa's economy is under-developing rather than developing, one needs but to travel out of Africa for a brief period. On return, one is more likely to find an increase in the number and size of potholes on streets and highways. Buildings, including state buildings, will either be in decay or in disrepair. In every respect, these are countries that are "under-developing", not developing. On the other hand, travel out of a Western country for a brief period; on your return you would likely see new infrastructural developments. Resurfaced highways expanded airport concourses and runways, new shopping centers. This is development that should be taking place in developing countries. The phrase "developing-countries" is actually a more suiting description of advanced countries where socioeconomic conditions are constantly improving, than African countries where conditions are constantly deteriorating.

From a broader cross-national perspective, to look at how far Africa has under-developed since independence, one needs but to look at the changes that have occurred in other parts of the world within the same time period. It was in the 1960s that a vast majority of African states won independence, took charge and became masters of their own destiny. At about the same time, sending a man to the moon was still a wish in the minds of American political leaders. The president of the United States then, John F. Kennedy, expressed this as wish, rhetorically promising to put a man on the moon before the end of the decade. Eight years later, the political rhetoric became an accomplished reality. The mission was actually completed two years before the end of ten-year period that Kennedy cited in his speech. In line with the classic adage that says, "where there is a will there is a way", Americans had the will, and the way was created. Africa's inability to develop has more to do with the lack of "will" than to the lack of resources.

The will that should have paved the way for development in Africa was overtaken by "the personal," and squandered away into personal greed, corruption, and myopia. Africa's native sons have in the end contributed more to the under-development of Africa than the "foreign sons" that colonized Africa. The euphemism that describes the states of Africa as "developing countries" gave Africa the fallacious belief that their countries were making progress. The reality on the ground told a completely different story. Up to the first half century of their independence and self-rule, Africa was in reality "under-developing," not developing.

Chapter 5

Could Africa be Saying No to Modernity?

This is a question that has never been asked about Africa, but a question that needs to be asked. Vast amounts of resources have been invested to develop and modernize Africa. But never once has anyone sought to ask if Africa has the ability to manage modernity. It is a question that is undoubtedly going to stir the ire of diehard Africanists. But the frequency of electrical blackouts, the inability to extract and domestically process their abundant natural resources and the lack of a culture of preventive mainte-nance all seem to reveal a patent inability to manage modernity. It is only through an introspective self-examination and self-criticism that society can diagnose, and work to correct its failures. Modernity is not a finishing line or an end that societies attain and then keep their arms folded. It is a continuous pursuit. It is fluid, flux and constantly changing. It generates unanticipated challenges, and managing such challenges requires partici-pation, transparency, research and development, and a societal sense of creativity, innovation and an ability to foresee and develop solutions to challenges before they occur. It is verifiably true that transparency, partici-pation, research and development, creativity and innovation are not values that are dear to the hearts of the managerial class in Africa. Not much is done in anticipation of unforeseen or upcoming challenges. A society that is not managed in anticipation of possible challenges cannot be in the position to harness and process modernity. This is why it is appropriate to question Africa's ability to manage modernity.

After more than half a century of independence and self-rule, blaming everyone but Africans for Africa's inability to develop can no longer be an acceptable excuse. That the continent with the richest endowment of natural resources is at the same time the poorest continent in the world demands questions and answers that must go beyond any acts of commission and omission that were committed by Africans and non-Africans alike. Blaming a specific African leader for his country's woes implies that things would be better if that leader is replaced. And blaming colonialism for the underde-velopment of Africa would mean that ridding Africa of colonialism would bring accelerated development to Africa. But this has not been the case.

New regimes that come to power in Africa promising to make life better always end up doing as bad, if not worse, than their predecessors. This has been the case in Cameroon, in Cote d'Ivoire, Nigeria, Libya, Kenya, Uganda, and the Democratic Republic of Congo. The high expectations that accompanied the inauguration of the new leaders of these countries soon fizzled into exasperation. In almost every case, not only did economic conditions become worse, social conditions deteriorated and eventually degenerated into factional political violence. In some countries, there was a nostalgic longing for the return of the departed leader.

In cases where indigenous leaders replaced colonial powers, a similar trend was noticed. When Guinea's Sekou Touré severed neo-colonial ties with France, and when Zimbabwe's guerilla forces defeated the Rhodesian government, it brought hope that life was henceforth going to get better. In a classic show of Guinean nationalist pride, Sekou Touré stated in a public address to his fellow citizens that "We prefer freedom in poverty over riches in slavery" (*Nous préférons la liberté dans la pauvreté a l'opulence dans l'esclavage.*"[1] Unfortunately, as was the case in countries where the first promotion of nationalist leaders was replaced by a newer generation of leaders, political and economic conditions also deteriorated. In Guinea, retributive sanctions by the French produced such deterioration in the Guinean economy, it took its toll on the health of the once proud and defiant nationalist founder of independent Guinea. Worsening economic conditions in Zimbabwe under the rule of President Robert Mugabe led to popular uprisings, with much of the frustrations directed at white farmers. In other countries, worsening socioeconomic conditions forced some Africans to start wondering if the acquisition of Africa's independence had been premature. While life under colonial rule was harsh and oppressive, living conditions in Africa after a half-century of self-rule drove Africans into such desperation that there was a nostalgic yearning in some circles for a return to colonial rule. In close conversations among elderly Africans who experienced life in colonial and post-colonial times, it is not uncommon to hear many say that things were better in colonial times. Of course, younger Africans cannot make a similar comparison. They were not alive in colonial times. All they know and have experienced is rule by African leaders. Given the rate at which many of them have fled the continent and emigrated to live in other parts of the world, one can but conclude that they too would have preferred life under colonial rule.

The "organized" inability to eliminate human suffering and improve living conditions undoubtedly translates to the inability to manage modernity.

1   Video: *Sekou Toure à Paris*, Bolibana Productions, Africa Productions, 1999.

Modernity is a process that has been successfully realized in other parts of the world. The blueprint is out there. Realizing it in Africa does not require reinventing the wheel. That with its abundant natural resources Africa has not been able to do so forces one to ponder if Africa has the ability to manage modernity.

The significance of this question cannot be fully understood unless the reader has actually had the experience of living in Africa and dealing directly with the various institutions that provide basic services to the public. There is no denying that various African countries have invested substantially in building airports, highways, schools, hospitals, electricity generating plants, telephone services and other modern infrastructures. The blueprints for these infrastructures are generally similar to blueprints for similar infrastructures in advanced countries. When new, they meet the standards and quality of similar infrastructures that are found in advanced countries. But no sooner are these infrastructures put into use than they are left to crumble and go into disrepair. Could Africa's inability to provide maintenance and upkeep for costly capital investments very well be an indication of its inability to manage modernity? I will leave this to the reader to ponder.

One needs but to look at the airline industry. With growing the *diasporazation* of Africans, it is potentially one of the most lucrative industries in the world. Yet, Nigerians, Ghanaians, Cameroonians and other Africans in the diaspora who want to travel to Africa frequently have to fly on foreign owned airlines. After more than a half century of independence, these African countries have proven themselves capable of establishing and managing consistent and sustainable flight route to the United States, the world's largest travel destination. Yet, all the knowledge that makes for a successful airline company – from the technology to the management know-how – has already been developed, tested and proven, and is out there for the taking. Out of Africa's 54 countries, only a handful – Cape Verde, Egypt, Ethiopia, Kenya and South Africa - have established successful flight routes to the United States. This gives us reason to ponder if Africa actually has the ability to manage modernity.

Try using a public toilet at an airport or anywhere else in Africa, one would find that the bathroom facility is either out of service or simply too filthy for human use. Even when in service, there is a good probability that there will be no toilet paper or running water. If all else is in place, there is a strong likelihood that sanitary conditions inside would be repellent.

In other areas of social comportment, unless compelled to stand in line, the typical African would want to rush to be served ahead of the person that is ahead in line. In some cases, a service provider would skip clients who are ahead in line to serve a friend or a relative in the back on the queue. Of even greater privilege are public officials, particularly officers in uniform.

The "first-come, first-serve" discipline that is exercised in developed countries is replaced in Africa by "last-come, first-serve friend, family member or uniformed officer."

Driving through an African city, one is likely going to find the roads and the driving conditions terrifying. Besides negotiating around potholes, drivers must also struggle to avoid crowds of pedestrians (and occasionally herds of cattle) that share highways with automobiles. Even though more walking than driving takes place in African cities, roads are built with no provision for pedestrian walkways. Most intersections have no traffic lights. Even if they do, they are seldom respected. The few traffic lights that are in place are frequently in disrepair. Often, typical rush hour traffic in a typical African city looks very much like herded cattle stampeding in every direction. Often there are no lanes, and in the rare cases where there are lanes, most drivers do not respect them. Most roads and highways that are currently being constructed in many African countries today are roads that were condemned in the United States as dangerous and unsafe more than a century ago. Not only do they not have shoulders, they do not have pedestrian crossings. In this modern era, any people that has the ability to manage modernity should know that modern roads come with shoulders and with pedestrian crossings.

Managing modernity requires a culture of "preventive maintenance." Here too, Africa is lacking equally. Here, the general dictum in most African countries is that "if it ain't broke, don't fix it." And usually when it breaks, it often takes forever to fix. Air conditioning is a modern amenity. Nowhere is it most needed than in the perennially hot climates of tropical Africa. At most ports of entry to the continent, it is not uncommon to find airports with no air-conditioners, or with air-conditioners that have been in disrepair for months, if not years. Unless a street or highway is besieged with axle-breaking potholes, it will not be patched. While the capitals of most African countries may be adorned with modern-looking story buildings, it is not uncommon to find the elevators in many of these buildings in disrepair. Government budgets often do not budget for the routine maintenance of new and existing infrastructures. Yet, whenever a foreign head of state is scheduled to visit, there is a mad rush to repair streets, highways, and buildings along the path that the foreign dignitary is going to travel through.

Almost every African country has a ministry of town planning or urban development. Yet, very little urban planning takes place in Africa. There are often no street names or signs, and no house numbers or street addresses. As a result, in most African countries home mail delivery does not exist. The inability to provide for such basics does not only pose doubt on Africa's ability to manage modernity, it reinforces the myth that Africa does not have the suffix, "mental", that comes in the word "development". All it takes to give names to streets and to place numbers on houses is simply a mindset – a modern mindset. Apparently, in much of Africa this simple mindset is not there. This is why we cannot help but doubt if Africa has the ability to manage modernity.

As a result of this lack of the ability to manage modernity, Africans are losing out on one of the most profitable industries in modern times – the home delivery industry. Countries whose infrastructures are developed to facilitate home delivery derive tremendous profits from the growth and global expansion of services in the home delivery industry, from DHL to Fedex, UPS, and Pizza restaurants. That Africa has not been able to develop a modern infrastructure that would allow it earn a share of the profits that are generated by such globalization-related industries leads us to ponder if Africa could actually be saying "No" to modernity.[2]

This question is pondered in *Resistance to Modernization in Africa*, by Giordano Sivini. Written from a first-person account as a 25-year foreign aid consultant in Africa, Sivini laments the degree to which foreign aid to Africa goes to waste. Governments which receive aid are interested not so much in promoting development, but in advancing their personal self-interest.[3]

Modernity is change in social and cultural conditions that is brought about by the wholesale transformation of society. It involves the embrace of the scientific – the tested and the proven. It discards superstition. What makes the hold on modernity in Africa tenuous may have to do with the fact that it is externally driven. Throughout much of the advanced industrial world, modernity is internally driven. It is also evolutionary rather than revolutionary. In Africa, it is externally driven and revolutionary. Because it is external and revolutionary, there seems to be an unconscious effort by Africans to resist it. It would appear that some societies simply do not fit the development model.

Modernity requires giving up the old, the known, the familiar and embracing the new, the tested, and the proven. This includes deviating from established social norms. Implicitly, such deviation comes by confronting and challenging the status quo. Modernity also requires the development of a creative and freethinking mind. The mind that produces the creativity that advances society is more readily found in frontier societies than in traditional societies. The challenges of frontier societies are new and unfamiliar, prompting the mind to probe deeper for solutions. In traditional societies, the challenges are old and familiar, thereby requiring effortless solutions.

---

2   Similar questions have been raised elsewhere: See Axelle Kabou, *Et Si l'Afrique Refusait le Développement?*, Editions L'Harmattan, Paris, France, 1991.

3   Giordano Sivini, *Resistance to Modernization in Africa*, Translated by Joan Krakover Hall, Brunswick, NJ: Transaction Publishers, 2007.

The tendency to conform is therefore greater in the latter than in the former.

Geophysicists theorize that the world started out as one massive landmass. Over time, the landmass splintered and began to gradually drift away. Africa, the piece of the continental landmass that stayed put as its sibling pieces drifted away has since then stayed unchanged. Over time, inhabitants of the landmass that drifted away realized substantial progress. While inhabitants of the landmass that shifted north and became the European continent have been engaged in a constant quest to explore and conquer nature scientifically, residents of the landmass that stayed put on the African continent held on steadfastly to tradition, making little social, economic, or scientific progress. In looking back at the degree and pace of modernization that has been realized on the landmasses that drifted away, one cannot help but ponder why similar progress has not occurred in Africa. The simple answer is that in choosing to stay put, Africa, its inhabitants and landmass, may actually be saying no to modernity. Unlike inhabitants of the landmasses that drifted away from the initial splintering of the global landmass, Africa's inhabitants have never had the experience of being a frontier society. Many of the challenges that the continental Africans face are addressed not by searching for scientific solutions, but by accommodating and turning either to tradition or to spirituality.

Africans are generally lulled into believing that there is a reason for everything that happens, and that nothing in life happens by accident. Indeed, the word "accident" does not exist in the languages of most African countries. For them, every loss or disaster has a spiritual cause. Things that cannot be changed are attributed to the will of God. Even among educated Africans, there is the fear of deviating from traditional norms. For society to modernize, it must be willing to challenge and/or give up tradition. This has not been the case in Africa.

Prior to being brought into the global economic system, Africa was politically, economically, and socially self-sufficient. Life was simple and familiar, and happiness was measured not by material wealth, but by spiritual and communal harmony. Africans lived in total harmony with nature. They took from their environment only that which was needed for subsistence. Economic activity was directed at providing sustenance and sustainability to both the family and the environment. Despite its abundance, wildlife was hunted not for the market, but for family consumption. Wood was harvested not for export, but as a source of energy. Palm-wine was tapped from life trees, and when the tapper was done collecting the juice, the trees were allowed to continue their growth, just as African families continued theirs. Because of the vast abundance of natural resources, economic competition was not necessary. Neither was there a need for the frantic accumulation of wealth. The customary virtues of cooperation and communal living produced disdain for members of the community who sought to individually advance their self-interest. To this day, the word "economics" and the phrase "economic development" do not exist in most African languages.

It is obvious that the forced integration of Africa with the West has brought nothing but confusion and disorder. In a world where cooperation and communal living have been replaced by competition and individualism, Africa appears unable to adapt. That the life of the average African is today characterized by hardship is not just an indication that modernization efforts in Africa have failed, it is an indication that Africa may be saying no to modernization.

Saying no to modernization is not unique to Africa. There are examples of peoples in other parts of the world who have refused to modernize, and who have shown nothing but disdain to modern values and lifestyles. Among them are Pacific Islanders, the Amish, the Maasai of East Africa, the Pigmies of Central Africa, the Bushmen of Southern Africa, Amazon Basin Indian tribes, the *Rebelados* of Cape Verde, and the Sarks of Great Britain. Curiously, some of these people have come to gain the respect and admiration of people who live modern lifestyles. The case of the Amish is uniquely interesting here; so let us take a brief look at it.

Living in the heartland of the most capitalist and most advanced country in the world, the Amish have not only succeeded in maintaining an ascetic lifestyle, they have succeeded in shunning the trappings of modernity that so ubiquitously surround them. While most people around the world are yearning to live the modern lifestyle that most Americans live, the Amish who live in America have nothing but abject disdain for a modern lifestyle. Though physically living in America, the Amish culturally believe that they are not of America. For their tenacity and steadfastness, they have succeeded in gaining the respect of much of the world. Any forcible attempt to modernize them is likely going to produce a backlash similar to the backlash against modernity that we see in Africa today.

The Amish have largely succeeded in convincing the world to leave them alone. In so doing, they have been able to maintain some degree of exoticism. Drawn by curiosity, tourists come from all over the world to see the Amish way of life. It is exoticism that is similar to the exoticism that characterized life in Africa prior to European colonization. Without colonization and forced adulteration of African traditional values, Africans would probably have remained as exotic, and the culture of its people a cause of fascination, not denigration. As with the Amish, Africa would today be a favorite destination for tourists and tourist revenues. Already self-sufficient in pre-colonial times, it would have become even more so with the additional resources that will be generated by tourism. We will be taking a closer look at the Amish later, but for now, let's examine the missing link in Africa's futile effort to modernize.

Identifying the Missing Link

In Europe, modernity started first as an intellectual process – a process commonly referred to as the Renaissance. It was then followed by the Industrial Revolution. The Renaissance challenged traditional patterns of thinking, forcing people to begin questioning the status quo. The status quo at the time included religious orthodoxy and superstitious beliefs. Challenged by Isaac Newton, Copernicus and other early scientists, science and reason soon grew to replace myth and religion. Then came the Industrial Revolution, where machine tools replaced hand tools as instruments of production and innovation. With the Industrial Revolution came mass production, the demand for raw materials and the quest for markets. From philosophers to inventors and discoverers, all of the forces that challenged the old order were homegrown and internal to Europe. The forces and ideas that stood up and challenged the entrenched oligarchy of medieval times were all European.

An element of intra-European rivalry was also instrumental in the push that transformed European society in medieval times. It forced competing European powers to look beyond Europe for colonial and material resources that would increase their national capabilities and give them a competitive edge. As the push became increasingly competitive, investments were made in the development of intellectual, military, and commercial skills. The investments translated into technological advances. The advances led to the Industrial Revolution in Britain. The rest of Europe soon caught up. Subsequent transoceanic competitive challenges extended the benefits of Europe's technological advances to the United States. Because traditional African culture is characterized more by cooperation rather than by competition, Africans have not been able to make the same advances that Europeans have made. In other words, had Western culture been characterized by cooperation rather than by competition, it may never have achieved the level of modernization that it has today.

In our quest to identify the missing link in Africa's inability to harness development, the absence of a competitive culture may very well be it. Socially and culturally, Africans are more prone to cooperating than to competing. In much of Africa, rivalry and competition, along with self-interest are disdained and frowned upon. But these are the values that are celebrated in the West, and values that were instrumental in transforming Western societies into modern societies. Where there is no push to advance self-interest or compete to outperform others, there will be incentive to develop the skills and tools that enhance individual and group performance.

Nothing spurs modernization and technological advances than warfare. The history of Europe is in essence the history intra-European warfare.

Military threats that came from hostile neighboring states gave Europe the impetus and urgent need to develop and modernize their societies. Thanks to the abundance of land and landed resources, warfare in this degree did not exist in Africa. Without threats of war from neighboring states, the impetus and urgent need to modernize was simply not there.

Try Modernizing the Amish

Among the justifications for the colonial conquest of Africa was the concept of a "civilizing mission." This concept could be interpreted as an indication that the West was more concerned about the development and modernization of Africa than Africans themselves. Prior to interfacing with the West, Africa's economic needs were simple. Like the Amish, African societies were organized around subsistence living, and there was economic self-sufficiency. With the forced introduction of colonial rule, Africans were forced to abandon their subsistence way of life and adopt market economies. This may have contributed to the disorientation that we see in Africa today. If similar reforms are forcibly imposed on the Amish, there is no doubt they too will become permanently disoriented.

Because the Amish were left intact, they have unlike Africans been able to maintain a peaceful, stable and self-sufficient society. The Amish peacefully resist any policies that attempt to fragment their community and promote self-interest. They refuse to own and use automobiles, electricity, computers and other modern amenities. They see such amenities as spiritually corrupting. They have since the 16th century been waging a stubborn but persistent struggle to remain separate and distinct in what Donald Kraybill describes as a legacy of dissent, separation from the world, along with the virtues of humility, simplicity, and self-denial.[4] The legacy is founded on the biblical teachings that warn in Romans 12:2 that "Be not conformed to this world," and in Corinthians 6:17, that "wherefor come out from among them and be ye separate, saith the Lord..."

The four most important values for the Amish are self-denial, humility, meekness, and obedience.[5] The Amish avoid all social changes that increase interaction with the world, or that fragment the community and accent individual achievement. This explains why they refuse to own cars or use technology that undermine community values. The Amish refuse to study the sciences and other disciplines that promote critical or abstract thinking. Their rejection of television and other forms of mass media insulates them from the temptations of modern life. "The practice of endogamy, the use of

4   Donald Kraybill and Marc Olshan, *The Amish Struggle with Modernity*, Hanover, NH: University Press of New England, 1994, p. 6.)
5   Kraybill, p. 7.

the dialect, the prohibition on membership in public organizations, the taboo on political involvement, and the rejection of mass media are among many of the factors that help to preserve the cultural boundaries that separate the Amish from the winds of pluralism."[6] It would be impossible to attempt to modernize a people who have no use for self-improvement seminars, self-actualization workshops, and "no books on positive thinking or how to get smart." Yet, Marc Olshan and Kimberly Schmidt think that "in some ways the Amish are more liberated than those who feel compelled to excel at whatever the latest expert dictates, to conform to the latest fashion, or to ponder the legitimacy of every cause."[7]

Unlike their European forebears who were persecuted for their religious beliefs, the Amish in North America are able to practice their religion without fear of persecution. Thanks to the constitutional guarantees of religious freedom, no Amish in the United States or elsewhere in the New World has been executed or forced to emigrate because of their religious faith. Those who refuse to serve in the military out of religious convictions are given the option to perform alternative services. Thus, besides shielding them from such non-communal values as individualism, pride, arrogance and selfishness, the faith of the Amish shields them from the influences of outside authority.

While the Amish church provides the main shield that prevents its members from straying into the cesspools of worldliness, no such shield is present in Africa. Colonialism, along with other Western influences, was largely successful in striping Africa of a protective shield. In the push to modernize Africa, its religion and traditional values were forcibly replaced by Western religious and cultural values. Unable to fully master the new values that were imposed on them, and having given up many of the traditional values that provided harmony and stability in society, Africans would become locked in a perplexing mist of inertia that persists to this day.

Relatively, Africans like the Amish were a happier people prior to being hounded by the push to modernize. And despite the many centuries of Western influence, much of Africa, particularly rural Africa, does appear to have more in common with the Amish than it has with the West. Like Africans, Amish society is defined and held together by communal values. Collective wellbeing transcends claims of individual rights. While the belief in the West is that happiness rises as individual freedom expands, the Amish, like Africans, believe that true happiness comes not from unfettered individualism but from belonging to the community.

---

6   Kraybill, p. 27.
7   Marc Olshan and Kimberly Schmidt, in Donald Kraybill and Marc Olshan, *The Amish Struggle with Modernity,* Hanover, NH: University Press of New England, 1994.

A 1985 joint survey of some 400 richest Americans and the Maasai of East Africa by the University of Illinois and University of Pennsylvania researchers ranked the Americans and the Maasais all as equally satisfied in the study's satisfaction and wellbeing measure. Like the Amish, the Maasai are a traditional people who live in huts that are roofed with cow dung, and do not care about electricity or indoor plumbing. What was most revealing about the study was that economic development and personal income do not account for their happiness.[8]

Whatever is thought of the Amish, there is no denying that they have waged a successful challenge against modernity. No other civilization located in the heart of the world's most industrialized society and surrounded by the trappings of modern life can remain so faithfully attached to its culture and traditions for this long. In a rather direct and unflinching manner, the Amish have succeeded in saying no to modernity. In accepting, yet failing to fully embrace the culture of modernity, Africa could in its own very ambivalent manner be saying no to modernity. That efforts at modernizing Africa have in most cases succeeded but in destabilizing the continent, raises the probability that Africans may be unconsciously saying "No" to modernity.

---

8   Elizabeth MacDonald, "Money, Happiness and The Pursuit of Both," *Forbes Magazine*, February 14, 2006.

Chapter 6

Assessing the Performance of Internal Influences

> In Africa, corrupt and self-interested state elites are part of the development problem
> rather than part of the solution.
>
> Robert Jackson[1]

In a popular classic on Africa titled, *How Europe Underdeveloped Africa*, Walter Rodney accuses Europe of creating the conditions that produced under-development in Africa. In this chapter, I argue that external forces alone cannot be held responsible for the continent's beleaguered status. African leaders who inherited the reins of power from Europeans have done as much, if not more harm to Africa. Indeed, post-independent African rulers have done so much harm to Africa that if a sequel to Walter Rodney's famous book is written today, its title could very well be *How Africa Underdeveloped Africa*.

Walter Rodney's charge was, among other things, based on the fact that during the European colonization of Africa, the resources that should have been directed to the development of Africa were directed to the development of Europe. Africans who inherited the reins of power from the departing colonial powers have gone on to exercise what can be aptly referred to as "internal colonialism." They have revealed a new reality, and that reality is that colonial predation is not the exclusive preserve of external powers.

Former Kenyan Prime Minister and head of government, Raila Odinga openly warned against the use of "colonialism as a scapegoat for Africa's poor governance," accusing post-independence African leaders of betraying their people and shifting the blame to former colonial powers. Noting that the constant colonialism blame game was simply an excuse used by corrupt leaders to cover up for their incompetence, he argued that "50 years since many African nations attained independence, we cannot continue blaming the colonialists for our problems. Since the 1990s, a clear consensus has emerged both within and outside Africa that the problems the continent

---

1   Robert Jackson, *International Relations*, London: Oxford University Press, 1999, p. 205.

faces have to do with the way it is governed today"[2]

The number of years that Africa was under colonial rule is almost equal to the number of years the continent has been independent. Just as the continent was plundered under colonial rule, the cycle was repeated at independence. Under the leadership of post-independent African rulers, more Africans are actually fleeing the continent today than they did in colonial times. As will be seen in later chapters, the hope of every young African is to run away from Africa; and in their attempt to do so, many of them are dying in the Sahara Desert and the Mediterranean sea struggling to get to Europe – the very continent Africans blame for colonizing them. With overall human conditions much worse in Africa today than they were under colonial rule, it would be proper to hold post-independence African leaders responsible for the continent's failure. Despite the economic exploitation and political deprivation that took place under colonial rule, Africa was debt-free. Today, while Africa is politically free, it is debt ridden. Using the World Bank and the IMF as a quick fix for their corrupt and mismanaged economies, post-independent African rulers worked to drive the continent into a debt bondage that could in many ways be seen as a new form of slavery. Designed to lock Africa into a vicious cycle of debt and poverty, loans obtained from international financial institutions came with conditions that were deleterious to sustainable economic development.

Despite this deleterious impact, African rulers continued to see the World Bank and the IMF loans as quick fixes for their misconceived and mismanaged policies. In response to the growing demands for loans, the World Bank and the IMF require African states to pursue free market policies. This included a requirement that they remove protectionist policies that protected their infant industries. This requirement essentially extinguished Africa's infant industries, stagnating and in most cases atrophying industrial development. Compounding this aggressive push for free market reforms was the vicious cycle of debt. It outrightly asphyxiated economic development. Douglas Web laments that "resources connected with debt repayments still flow from the South to the north, away from the development of preventive healthcare services, while privatization of those very same state services often means that poor people cannot afford to access them even where they exist. Although some debt cancellation has happened, the burden of servicing debt continues seriously to hamper the abilities of African countries to respond to the challenges of development. Zambia in 2002 spent 30% on debt repayment than it did on healthcare, while the government of Malawi allocated

---

2   Shortwave Radio Africa, April 30, 2011, Colonialism – a Scapegoat for Africa's Poor Governance, (accessed, 02/08/2013), http://www.swradioafrica.com/pages/odingaad-dress290411.htm (Accessed 9/4/2018)

$2.40 on healthcare and $5 on debt repayment. Half of the countries that received debt relief (13 out of 26) in 2002, still spent more on debt than on public health."[3] That a continent that has the richest endowment of natural wealth is at the same time the poorest continent in the world is a paradox that no modern economist has been able to satisfactorily explain. Unless this paradox is satisfactorily addressed, any form of debt relief would only lead to another cycle of debt.

For obvious reasons, the billions of dollars that Africa obtained in foreign loans produced no gains for the common person. Interest payment on the loans alone deprived average Africans of access to basic healthcare, education, food and clean water, as priority was given to loan repayment than to economic development. This has contributed to the forced emigration of Africa's youth from the continent. If the rate at which Africans are emigrating from the continent today continues, not before long the continent will lose as many people as it did during the trans-Atlantic slave abductions. Using U.S. immigration data from 1990 to 2005, Sam Roberts reported in a February 21, 2005 *New York Times* article that more Africans are entering the U.S. today, than in the days of slavery. As many as 50,000 come in annually – a figure higher than during any of the peak years of the Middle Passage.[4]

As hard as it may be to admit it, many of Africa's current problems are self-inflicted. They are self-inflicted by the very persons who, in their youth, faulted the West for Africa's problems. By both commission and omission African leaders are responsible for Africa's failures. If performance in the public sector is measured by the prevalence of stability and public welfare, then African leaders have in every measure failed. If they were CEOs of private corporations, their corporations would all have gone bankrupt, and many of them would likely be indicted for malfeasance. So how do we explain why many of them are still in power? Using the monopoly powers that are inherent in totalitarian political systems, they successfully stripped their citizens of the right to effective participation in the electoral process. As soon as independence was achieved, the idea that the independence was for all Africans quietly disappeared. The multiparty democracies that were spelled out in the founding constitutions of most African states soon turned into one-party dictatorships. In countries where voting was allowed, the masses could only vote for one party. Through institutionalized greed and corruption, a privileged few reserved for themselves a disproportionate share

---

3   Douglas Web, "Legitimate Actors? The Future Roles for NGOs Against HIV/AIDS in Sub-Sahara Africa," in Poku, Nana K. & Alan Whiteside, The Political Economy of AIDS in Africa, England: Ashgate Publishers, 2004, p. 21.

4   Sam Roberts, More Africans Enter U.S. Than in Days of Slavery, www.nytimes. com/2005/02/21/nyregion/21africa/html?ex=1109653200&en=c164ab867f6bf987 &ei=5070 (Accessed 9/4/2018)

of society's wealth. On the whole, Africans who fought for independence were not allowed to participate in the spoils of independence.

Before, during, and immediately after independence, the blames directed at the West held them responsible for the deplorable economic conditions that colonial rule left behind in Africa. A whole new school of thought - the dependency school - was founded and directed at the study of the link between the development of the West and the underdevelopment of the Third World. Inspired largely by socialist philosophy, the school was highly critical of Western thought and Western models of development. The school's primary thesis was that the development of the West was realized at the expense of the Third World. Frantz Fanon, Andre Gunder Frank, Samir Amin, and Immanuel Wallerstein were among the main proponents of this school of thought.

Today, after witnessing the performance of African leaders after more than half a century of self-rule, activists of the dependency school suddenly became silent. Many seem to now hold Africa rather than Europe responsible for under-developing Africa. In the words of the Guinean scholar, Carlos Lopes, "one can no longer blame the colonial settler for all Africa's ills."[5] Even Zimbabwean Vice President, Simon Muzenda, in an opening address to OUA foreign ministers in 1997 admitted that the violent and derelict state of much of Africa was "partly of our own creation," and went on to add that "lack of justice, fairness and openness in governing has kindled many uprisings."[6]

That economic conditions in some African states are much worse today than they were during the colonial and pre-colonial eras, the West can no longer be held solely responsible. In 1972, for example, Ghana's per capita GDP was higher than South Korea's ($310 vs. $300). Twenty years later, in 1992, Korea's per capita GDP had risen to $6790, while Ghana's stagnated at $450.[7] The GDP per capita in the Democratic Republic of Congo – geographically Africa's largest country - was actually 50% higher at independence in 1960 than it is today." Ranked the world's poorest country, only 9% of Congolese have even intermittent access to electricity.[8] By the first decade of the 21st century, after fifty years of independence and self-rule, eighteen of the world's poorest countries by GDP per capita were in Africa. With a few exceptions, there is little hope that the situation will improve in the next half century.

5   Carlos Lopes, *Guinea Bissau: From Struggle to Independent Statehood*, Boulder, Colorado, Westview Press, 1987, p. 168.
6   Deutsche PresseAgentur, Sunday, June 1, 1997
7   W. Phillips Shively, *Comparative Governance*, New York, McGraw Hill Publishers, 1997, p. 89.
8   *The Economist*, November 26, 2011.

An unbiased look at Africa's performance in precolonial, colonial and post-colonial history would reveal that most everything that is wrong with Africa, from corruption, to famine, hunger, poverty, civil war, lack of water and healthcare, is man-made. Corrupt officials at all levels of society bleed money from the economy, personalizing the collective resources of the people, stealing and resorting to civil wars to fuel personal ambitions. While some find ways to redirect foreign aid to private interests, others find ways to tax their countries' domestic industries into bankruptcy.

The very leaders who just two generations ago were castigating Europeans for oppressing and ignominiously humiliating Africans are today perpetrating these very indignities on Africans. While colonial rule bowed to internal and external pressure and came to an end, there seems to be no end in sight for African rulers, as they remain insensitive and intransigent to internal and external pressure, and bent on maintaining life, and in some cases, dynastic presidencies. This has denied younger generations of Africans their turn at governing their countries. It is this usurpation that largely contributed to the forced exile and vast *diasporazation* of Africans across the Western world. Contributions that younger generation of Africans should have made to the development of the continent is now directed to the development of the very West that was once accused of causing underdevelopment in Africa. On the whole, whatever the views of the current generation of African intellectuals is, it is no longer aligned with the arguments of the dependency school. It is directed squarely at decrying the excesses of contemporary African rulers.

The Quest for Self-Aggrandizement

The quest for self-aggrandizement among African leaders is irresistible. Responsible for the mismanagement and poor governance that Africa is known for is this quest. It is a quest that is a lot stronger than the quest to advance the national interest. While the mission of public officials in advanced democracies is to serve the people, the mission of public officials in Africa is to be served by the people. In a continent where as many as 70% of the population is unemployed and subsisting on less than one dollar a day, African rulers have arrogated to themselves a reputation for profligacy, ostentation, corruption, and petty self-indulgence. On the whole, the leaders are driven not by how rich and powerful their nations can become, but by how rich and powerful they can individually become.

For the typical African head of state, self-aggrandizement is a greater priority than national development. When faced with the choice of directing the nation's last penny to creating job opportunities for the country's youth or to providing for personal security, the typical African head of state will invest in providing for his personal security. As funds are directed at building presidential palaces, purchasing presidential jets, and raising the salaries of presidential guards, cuts are being made in school and healthcare budgets, public infrastructures, and skills training.

The most scandalous case of self-aggrandizement in Africa was that of Cote d'Ivoire's head of state, Houphouet Boigny. After ruling the country for life, as he was aging and getting closer to the end of his life, he decided to direct vast sums of the country's wealth to the development of a modern city in his hometown in Yamoussoukro. The development included a $3 billion Basilica that he built and offered to the Catholic Church as a personal gift. At the time it was inaugurated, the Basilica was reportedly the biggest church in the world – bigger than Saint Peter's Basilica in Rome. At the time work started on the Basilica, his country's national debt stood at $7 billion. If this was a leader who was interested in national development, he obviously would have invested in building schools, healthcare facilities, and skills training centers that would grow the national economy. The construction of the Basilica was seen by many of Boigny's critics as an effort to buy his way into heaven. But while the construction of a church for God on earth may have bought President Boigny entry to heaven, what it left behind in the country was a devastating civil war. Like most of his African counterparts, Houphouet Boigny was not concerned about his legacy. In the words of Louis XV, "after me all hell can break loose" ("*après moi, le deluge*[9]"). And all hell did break loose in Cote d'Ivoire.

A similar policy was carried out in Cameroon in the 1980s, when Paul Biya became president. On assuming power, Biya redirected the country's national revenues to growing his personal wealth. He built a hospital in Baden-Baden Germany, a presidential palace in his village and an international airport on the road leading to his village. Prior to the construction of the airport, international flights landed at an international airport in the country's economic capital in Douala. The country's airline, Cameroon Airline, provided domestic shuttle services to international arrivals at the Douala airport. When the construction of the new international airport close to the president's place of birth was completed, he signed a decree obligating all international flights to start using the airport. This meant that all international flights to Cameroon had to make two landings and two takeoffs - one at the new airport at the president's region of birth, and one in Douala. The two international airports were a mere 30 minutes apart. Finding the policy both costly and unsafe, British Airways, Lufthansa, and

---

9   A premonition of impending political and social collapse attributed to Madame de Pompadour, the mistress of Louis XV." http://www.phrases.org.uk/bulletin_board/3/messages/14.html and From Le Mot Juste edited by John Buchanon-Brown & others (Vintage Books).

Swiss Air, all decided to discontinue flights to Cameroon. Thousands of jobs were lost. The country's domestic airlines, CamAir, whose market niche had been in domestic and regional flights was forced into bankruptcy. This again caused the loss of thousands of jobs. In the president's quest for self-aggrandizement, the rest of the country was forced to pay the price.

Other cases of African rulers whose quest for self-aggrandizement was stronger than the quest for national development include Zimbabwe's Robert Mugabe, who took a country that was the food basket of Southern Africa and turned it into a basket case; Zaire's Mobutu Sese Seko, whose greed and quest for self-aggrandizement got him to leave behind nothing but devastation and unending wars in the world's most mineral endowed country. Then there is the case of Gambia's absolute ruler, who insisted on being addressed "His Excellency President Professor Dr. Al-Haji Yahya Jammeh," while declaring among other things that he had a cure for AIDS and was with the help of Allah going to rule his country for one billion years.[10]

In no country has the quest for self-aggrandizement contributed to as much destruction as in Angola. After a successful liberation struggle against Portuguese rule, the factional leaders in the war of independence re-engaged in a fratricidal warfare that was far bloodier than the war for independence. Despite UN supervised elections that were declared fair and transparent, and despite an offer of vice presidency to the party that would lose the elections, Jonas Savimbi, leader of the party which lost, chose to return to fighting, refusing to settle for nothing less than the presidential palace. The war raged on, causing the loss of hundreds of thousands of more lives. It was not until he was killed in battle on February 22, 2002, that the war finally came to an end. Elsewhere in Africa, Liberia's Samuel Doe, Nigeria's Abacha were met with a similar fate – they were all assassinated because of their political intransigence and quest for self-aggrandizement. Liberia's Charles Taylor and Cote d'Ivoire's Laurent Gbagbo luckily avoided a similar fate.

The typical African ruler is defined by Machiavelli in the unsolicited advice he gives in his book *The Prince*. In it he says it is better for a ruler to be feared than to be loved. Expounding on this, the French writer, Andre Blancet observe that the typical African head of state is "venerated and protected by his Negro and white entourage as if he is a living Buddha, the object of an adulation which he has never sought but which is lavished on him by official and unofficial people."[11] Mindful of this adulation, and interested in sustaining the aura, a disproportionate quantity of national

---

10   BBC News, 12/12/2011, Gambia's Yahya Jammeh ready for 'billion-year' rule, http://www.bbc.co.uk/news/world-africa-16148458 (accessed 12/15/2011)

11   Andre Blancet, in Gwendolen M. Carter (ed.) *African One-Party States*, New York, 1962, p. 275.

resources is often allocated to personal exaltation, presidential security and other aspects of propaganda that are directed at preserving power and at preventing potential challenges to presidential power. In what Davidson describes as "nest-featherers," African leaders come to power not with the goal of working for their country, but to "find ways to convert public revenue into personal income."[12]

As poor as the African continent is, the personal wealth of its average ruler is by far higher than the personal wealth of the rulers of advanced industrial countries. In Rene Dumont's interpretation, "independence has meant taking the place of the whites and enjoying the privileges, often exorbitant, hitherto accorded to 'colonials.'"[13] These privileges include disproportionately high salaries, presidential palaces, presidential jets, government paid overseas medical care, personal body guards and chauffeured Mercedes cars. Given that their personal standard of living is higher than the standard of living enjoyed in the advanced industrial countries of the West, African rulers see no urgency in working to provide services that will improve the welfare of their citizens. Why build and equip a hospital or health center in Africa when you can be shuttled out in a personal jet to Europe or North America for first rate medical care? Why build or repair collapsing highways when your primary means of transportation are private jets and helicopters? And why keep schools, colleges, and universities funded when none of your children attends school in the country? Rather than fix their educational systems, most African leaders prefer to enroll their children in private schools in Europe and North America. The same is true with healthcare. African rulers prefer to be evacuated abroad for medical treatment than to invest in the development of medical facilities at home.

Universities are the incubators of the science and technologies that have enabled the West to lead the world, yet African rulers have been known to close down universities in their countries, whenever students demonstrate against their policies. The managers of the Western banks where African leaders frequently go to hide their stolen wealth were educated at schools and universities that were funded and kept open, even in cases where students at these institutions organized public demonstrations against their governments. Most other ideas and theories of development, from road construction to manufacturing, agriculture and healthcare come from well-funded and well-managed educational institutions. The American and European medical facilities that African leaders frequently go to get treatment from are run by professionals that were trained and educated at universities. African rulers would today have nowhere to go for quality healthcare or for the education

12 Davidson p. 111.
13 Davidson, p. 135

of their children, had governments in these regions shut down their institutions of learning in response to student demonstrations.

Looking at other parts of the Third World, projections are that by 2050, China and India will account for nearly half the world's gross domestic product. How did two nations that were at par with Africa in the 1960s make such great strides? Diana Farrell of McKinsey *Global Institute and Insight* thinks that it was through sustained investments in higher education. Chinese and Indian universities are educating and graduating engineers at an unprecedented rate – with 10% of Chinese and 25% of India's graduates with degrees in engineering.[14]

Thanks to investments in education, India has carved out a niche, popularized and given new meaning to the word outsourcing. It is a niche that benefits not just the Indian private sector, it benefits its public sector. Units of the Indian military that are specially trained in computer programming compete with private sector companies for contracts in data entry. This added a whole new dimension to the posture of competition in the rapidly globalizing international economy. The line between strictly military and strictly economic functions (which modern economists believe should be driven by the private sector) was not only narrowing, it was increasingly becoming flux. While the military is among some of the most highly institutionalized institutions in Africa, African countries are yet to find an income generating niche for their militaries.

Like their counterparts in China and India, one would expect African leaders with genuine interest in national development to work in nurturing rather than in shutting down their institutions of higher education. The global search for the cheap and talented workforce that made China and India attractive destinations for outsourcing and other foreign investments, could have very well-made Africa attractive, if only its leaders made similar investments in higher education. Besides the economic benefits that derive from investments in education, there are cultural and social benefits. It is through education that culture is celebrated, propagated and preserved. While Africans take tremendous pride in their culture, African leaders have failed to establish institutions that will propagate and make their culture sustainable.

For a continent that is awash in archeological treasures, no indigenous efforts have been directed at cultivating and/or investing in the research that will explore the rare findings that bring fame, national pride and foreign investments. Blinded by the pursuit of self-interest, African rulers see no need to establish educational policies that will promote development

14   Diana Farrell, India Outsmarts China, http://www.foreignpolicy.com/story/cms.php?story_id=3348&print=1 (Accessed 9/4/2018)

in these areas. That Africa is the oldest continent is a truism that even the most ardent detractor of Afrocentricism cannot refute. It is also a fact which educated Africans take pride in. Yet it is a fact that has been established not by Africans but by non-Africans. As culturally rich as Africa is, most of the modern archaeological discoveries of Africa's great past have been made and continue to be made by non-Africans.

In the early years of his presidency, Zaire's Mobutu Sese Seko sought to gratify his ambitions for self-aggrandizement by financing the construction of a space rocket in the interior of the Zairian rainforest. At the time, university students in Zaire were organizing nationwide demonstrations against Mobutu's government. Mobutu responded to the uprisings by ordering a shutdown of the University of Kinshasa – the very university that would have produced the intellectual skills that were needed to operate his ambitious space rocket project. Eventually, the rocket project collapsed, and the hundreds of millions of dollars invested in it went to waste.

Later, towards the end of his presidency, when Mobutu was diagnosed with prostate cancer, there were no healthcare facilities in Zaire that were equipped to treat him. As a result, he had to fly to Europe for treatment. His personal wealth, estimated in the billions of dollars, was far greater than the amount of money that may have been used in the construction of the European hospital that treated him. Had he been interested in national development, he very well could have built a similar hospital in his country. Had Mobutu made such an investment, his prostate cancer treatment would have taken place in the comfort of his home. His fellow citizens will benefit, and citizens of neighboring countries would be flying to Congo/Zaire for advanced medical treatment. This likely would have made Congo/ Zaire the medical capital of Africa. And in the long run, instead of being a net recipient of aid and foreign assistance, Zaire could very well be a donor of foreign aid.

Unfortunately, the myopic quest for self-aggrandizement turned a country that would have otherwise been one of the richest countries in Africa, into one of the poorest.

In the twilight of his rule, Mobutu's presidential budget was actually 90% of the country's national budget. Official corruption became so rampant that on May 20, 1976 Mobutu subtly prodded members of his governing cabinet with the slogan "*yibana mayele*" ("steal, but steal cleverly"). The World Bank, IMF and other international underwriters of Mobutu's loans were obviously aware of this public endorsement of corruption. They however continued to grant him new loans.

As indicated above, during the Cold War, the West relied heavily on Zaire for the rare strategic minerals of its subsoil. The U.S. in particular desperately wanted to gain access and monopoly control of these minerals. Given how desperately America wanted to gain access to Zaire's mineral resources, if Mobutu had been interested in his country's national development and approached the U.S. for help, America very well could have built a highway network that would have crisscrossed Zaire from North to South and East to West. But because Mobutu was driven more by the quest for self-aggrandizement than the quest for national development, he never saw road development in his country as a priority.

In their quest for self-aggrandizement, African rulers in the first half century of independence gave themselves monopoly control over television broadcasting. Instead of using television as a free market platform for linking consumers to suppliers, creating product awareness and helping promote economic growth, it was used as a medium for propaganda. Viewers were often restricted to one government-controlled channel, and it was a channel that sang raises of the head of state every day, and as it marketed the agenda of the ruling political party.

The monopolistic control the state had on television left domestic businesses with very restricted advertisement outlets. Had the light bulb been invented in Africa, it would have taken a very long time for African consumers to find out about it. And if the politically appointed manager of a national television station had a choice between broadcasting a paid commercial that would earn the station millions of dollars and broadcasting a propaganda piece on the president, he would pass on the commercial.

Africa Presidential Dynasties

As with medieval monarchs, most African rulers today believe that their right to govern is a divine right. This myth is reinforced by a culture of sycophancy which adulates and deifies rulers as demigods. When so deified, it becomes difficult for these rulers to want to step down at the end of their term, to go back to living like regular citizens. This is why violations and repeals of presidential term limits in Africa has become an epidemic. Until forced by circumstances beyond their control, the typical African head of state would find a way to remain in power for life. Some actually go beyond seeing themselves as life presidents to seeing their presidencies as dynasties. Among them was Gabon's Omar Bongo, who ruled his country for 43 years, and upon his death in 2009, the throne was passed down to his son, Ali Bongo. Four years earlier, following the death of the Togolese President Gnassingbé Eyadéma on February 5, 2005, the presidency too was passed down to his son Faure Gnassingbé. Following the assassination of the president of Equatorial Guinea, Macias Nguema, in 1979, his nephew Teodoro Obiang Nguema Mbazogo took over and established yet another dynasty. In Northern Africa, it was exactly because Zine el-Abidine Ben Ali of Tunisia, Egypt's Hosni Mubarak, Libya's Muammar Gaddafi, and Algeria's Abdelaziz Bouteflika tried to run their countries like personal dynasties that their citizens mobilized in what was referred to as the Arab Spring to overthrow them. Prior to his bloody ouster in 2011, Muammar Gaddafi who had ruled Libya for more than 40 years was actually preparing to hand power down to his son.

Part of the strategy to violate constitutional term limits and remain in power for as long as they want is to buy the silence of policymakers in Western capitals by paying money to lobbyists and public relations firms. Between 2004 and 2007, the President of Equatorial Guinea, Obiang Nguema, paid Cassidy and Associates, a prominent Washington, D.C. lobbying and communications firm, $120,000 per month to promote his image in the United States. And up until March 2011, he again paid former Special Counsel to the Clinton Administration, Lanny J. Davis, a million dollars every year to help market and cleanse his image in the West.[15] In 2002, Uganda hired Hill & Knowlton, a prominent public relations company to invalidate criticism of the country's atrocious human rights record. During the same period, there was an effort by Sudan's $530,000 attempt to hire the public relations firm C/R International to organize visits to Sudan for congressional staffers to show that Sudan was cooperating in the war against terrorism. And just before Cameroon's October 2004 elections, the President of Cameroon, Paul Biya, paid $400,000 to Patton Boggs to market Cameroon's image to Congress, to the World Bank, the IMF and the Overseas Private Investment Corporation. In the aftermath of the disputed presidential elections in Cote d'Ivoire in 2010, the incumbent, Laurent Gbagbo hired two former Clinton Cabinet officials, Michael Espy and Lanny J. Davis to work in convincing the U.S. Government and the rest of the international community that Gbagbo was the duly elected president of Cote d'Ivoire. In an attempt to deflect criticisms, Davis, who was former chief counsel to President Clinton, indicated that he viewed himself not as an advocate but as a "conveyor belt" to pass information to the U.S. Government. For his duties, he was placed on a monthly salary of $100,000, with an upfront payment of $300,000. After a mere ten days of work, Davis submitted a letter of resignation to Laurent Gbagbo, citing among other things that Gbagbo had refused to accept a phone call from President Barack Obama. The $300,000 payment would therefore be payment for ten days of work.[16]

In a 2009 message addressed to Secretary of State Hillary Clinton captioned "The Easy Way to Rob a(n African) Bank, U.S. Ambassador to Cameroon Janet Garvey indicated that then Gabonese President, Omar Bongo

---

15   http://www.nytimes.com/2011/05/31/world/africa/31guinea.html?_r=1 (accessed August 31, 2011)

16   Helene Cooper & Eric Lichtblau, *New York Times*, DEC. 22, 2010, American Lobbyist Work for Ivorian Leader, http://www.nytimes.com/2010/12/23/world/africa/23coast. html (Accessed 9/4/2018).

ordered the transfer of $36 million to fund the presidential campaigns of French presidents. He was in the habit of financing both right-wing and left-wing parties, but frequently gave more money to right wing parties. Among the candidates to whom he gave money were Nicolas Sarkozy, Jacques Chirac, Francois Mitterrand, and Valery Giscard d'Estaing. Bongo's largesse made him the favorite African head of state among French politicians.[17]

Ranking the Priorities of African Leaders

As the typical African leader is more interested in self-aggrandizement than in national development, he accordingly sees self-preservation as his number one priority. That self-preservation ranks at the top of the priorities of African leaders come as no surprise. Much of the money that African governments spend is spent on the security forces that provide protection to the president. As discussed above, in the last days of his presidency, Zaire's Mobutu allocated as much as 90% of his country's national budget to providing for his personal security. In the 1990s and early 2000s, the presidents of Cameroon and Guinea passed decrees granting higher pay to their militaries. This raised the incomes of some non-commissioned officers above that of lawyers, medical doctors and engineers. The educational attainment of the average military recruit in Africa is 12th grade. That doctors, lawyers and engineers who have spent several years in school are paid less than individuals with only a 12th grade education is in many ways a disincentive to education and hard work. Yet education and hard work are exactly the values that are needed to develop an underdeveloped country.

That the security of African rulers is prized higher than national economic development can be seen in the degree to which resources are allocated to the social control of citizens. In Francophone Africa, the most important document citizens are required to carry at all times is a national identity card. Money that should otherwise be used in building schools, roads and hospitals is used in the employment of a large police force to monitor compliance. Identity cards bear the name, date and place of birth; names of parents and in some cases, tribe of origin of the bearer. It was one of the identifying tools that made it easy for the perpetrators of the Rwandan genocide to readily identify their victims. Such distinguishing identities as "Tutsi" and "Hutu" were visibly marked on the cards.

Just as the police was used in colonial times to enforce the will of the colonizer, the military and police forces in post-colonial Africa are used by African rulers today to impose their will. "In many cases, the control of the police has merely changed hands from one authoritarian government to

---

17 www.ufppc.org/.../10102-news-cable-funds-diverted-to-chirac-a-sarkozy-from-bank-controlled-by-african-dictator-bongo.html (Accessed 9/4/2018)

another ... Many African leaders have been able to continue in the colonial tradition of using the police for political ends. These have included the use of the police to oppress and intimidate political opponents and dissidents, trade unionists, university lecturers and students; and to control the working class generally.[18]

Next to the quest for self-preservation and self-aggrandizement is the head of state's allegiance to the foreign power that backs him. In African states that are yet to embrace democracy, the head of state is there not to serve the national interest, but to serve the interest of the foreign power that enabled his rise to power. To maintain power therefore, he has no choice but to place the interest of that foreign power above his country's national interest. Failure to do that could mean more than the loss of power; it could mean the loss of his life through a foreign sponsored military coup. This was what happened to Burkina Faso's Thomas Sankara. Seen as a threat to French interests in the country, the French had him replaced in a palace coup by Blaise Compaore, a candidate that would more readily give allegiance to France and French interests.

Because the allegiance of many African heads of states is directed externally rather than internally, their personal assets are equally often kept outside the country. They bank, vacation and shop outside the country. Most Francophone African heads of states who leave office, (and they seldom do), often move to live abroad. This was the case with Cameroon's President Ahmadou Ahidjo, Central Africa's Jean-Bédel Bokassa, and Senegal's first two heads of state, Senghor and Abdou Diouf. They all moved to live in France. Some of them do not have to wait to retire to move to live in Europe. Cameroon's president, Paul Biya, frequently spent more time in Europe than in his country.

Overall, a careful study of the history of post-colonial Africa produces one confounding finding: an African leader who is good for Africa is bad for Europe, and a leader who is bad for Europe is good for Africa. Congo's Patrice Lumumba, Cape Verde's Amilcar Cabral, Burkina Faso's Thomas Sankara, Cameroon's Um Nyobe and Libya's Muamar Ghaddafi, Cote d'Ivoire's Laurent Gbagbo were all bad for Europe and had to be eliminated. Years after their assassination, these nationalist leaders remain popular across much of Africa. In some countries, they have acquired the status of folk heroes. In others, they are considered martyrs.

On the other hand, because they were good for the West and bad for their countries, Congo's Mobutu Sese Seko, Central Africa's Jean-Bédel Bokassa, Burkina Faso's Blaise Comproare, Cameroon's Paul Biya, Togo's

---

18   B. Cole, Post-Colonial Systems, in R.I. Mawby, ed, *Policing Across the World: Issues for the Twenty-first Century*, London, UCL Press, 1999, p. 98

Eyadema I & II, and Gabon's Bongo I & II, all put in power by the West, were allowed to stay in power as long as they remained good and faithful. As reward for their lifetime of faithfulness to French interests, France made sure that Gabon and Togo's rulers were succeeded by their sons. Hence, Gabon's Bongo II and Togo's Eyadema II.

Next to the allegiance extended to their foreign patrons, the typical African head of state shows allegiance to his tribe or ethnic group. This is the group and place in the country where he feels most at home. As a child of that tribe, he shares a common bond with them. If he came to office through elections, it is obvious that the highest percentage of the votes that elected him came from members of his tribe. Since ethnic affinity is generally stronger than national affinity, presidential security is often disproportionately composed of members of the president's ethnic group. A president who is from Texas would, for example, make sure that almost all his bodyguards or security detail come from Texas. Because of a strong sense of distrust, most African presidents would rather contract out their security detail to a foreign security force than recruit his security from a different tribe in the country. With this option, goes hundreds of millions of dollars in payment and thousands of employment opportunities to foreign security forces.

Next to the allegiance the head of state gives to his tribe is the allegiance he gives to his province or region of origin. While the inner-core of the president's immediate staff is often made up of members of his village or immediate tribe, the outer core is made up of people from his region or province. A high percentage of his qualified staff, particularly those who are hired on merit comes from here. At this level, the pool is large enough to find people who are both qualified and loyal. It is from his region of birth that he will appoint individuals to fill key cabinet positions that require presidential trust and confidentiality. In terms of the distribution of national resources, African heads of states have the tradition of allocating a disproportionately high percentage of national resources to their region of origin. When northerners were in power in Nigeria, for example, they lobbied to have Nigeria's capital relocated from Lagos to Abuja. Above, we saw that when Cameroon's President, Paul Biya, came to power, he relocated the international airport to his region, and ordered international carriers to use that airport. The most infamous of all was Cote d'Ivoire's President, Houphouet Boigny who as we saw above, built a Basilica in his place of birth.

Finally, in our ranking of the priorities of African rulers, national interest ranks lowest. It is only after all of the other interests have been taken care of that remaining resources can be directed to national interest. That national interest and national development is the lowest in the priorities of most African heads of states can be seen in the redirection of foreign loans that are intended for national development into offshore private accounts.

In addition, when one compares the length of time it takes to repair a pothole on a public highway to the length of time it takes to respond to a security threat against the president, one readily sees that what is in the public or national interest is not a priority for African rulers. While a threat to presidential security would generally be responded to within hours, it can take months, if not years to repair a pothole on a public highway. Even though African rulers take pride and often rush to claim credit when their youths excel in international athletic competitions, government contributions to these achievements are often minimal. The skills that we see in Africans who play in professional leagues in Europe and elsewhere are skills that were developed playing on dirt roads, narrow alleys and muddy/dusty corridors in Africa. But for China which has since the end of the Cold War gone on a building spree, constructing football stadiums across Africa, youth in many African countries would still be training and playing on makeshift muddy terrains. That after 50 years of independence, most African countries still depend on foreign engineers and technical experts for the construction of such basic development infrastructures as roads, bridges, highways, airports, water, electricity and even sports stadium reveals how low national development is on the priority list of most African rulers.

Ironically, despite massive investments in the security sector in Africa (large militaries and police forces), the average African remains insecure. To build a house, a typical middle class African needs to budget for two houses – first a budget for the house, and secondly a budget to build a security fence around the house. Elsewhere in the world, the responsibility of providing security and protecting citizens in their homes is government's. But because African governments are more concerned with protecting the president and his regime than in protecting citizens, the burden of protecting one's life, one's home and property becomes that of the individual. Because security in Africa means the security of the regime, the police are often more readily available to respond aggressively to a rally or public demonstration (particularly one organized by an opposition political party) than to a home invasion or break-in. For state security forces, political rallies, including peaceful rallies, are often seen as a greater threat than criminal acts that are directed at private citizens. The most common police response to the report of an armed robbery or home invasion is that they do not have a vehicle. And even when a vehicle is available, they will say they do not have fuel in the vehicle. They do not give a similar excuse when there is a public demonstration against a given government policy. Here, truckloads of armed police officers will rush in to monitor and possibly crackdown on the demonstrators. In a growing number of areas in Africa, crime victims frustrated by the lack of police action are sometimes forced to resort to lynching and other forms of vigilantism.

Missing a National Will

The literature on failed states is restricted to the study of countries whose governments have collapsed or are centrally too weak to extend their reach into the periphery. It would be proper to revise and expand the literature to include states which are unable or unwilling to effectively provide public security to their citizens. In other words, the literature on failed states needs to go beyond the study of countries such as Somalia, Guinea and Charles Taylor's Liberia, to the study of countries such as Nigeria, Chad, Cameroon, Guinea and Central Africa Republic, where armed robbery is rampant, police response ineffective, and where building a house often requires budgeting for two houses – the house, and a fence around the house.

National development requires more than money or physical resources. It requires selflessness, will power, a vision and an ideological roadmap. These are values that are in very limited supply in Africa. Countries such as Israel, Japan, Cuba, Korea, Singapore and Taiwan started out with very limited natural resources. But with the right vision, with determination and willpower, they were able to make tremendous strides in a very short time. This leads us to the rather intriguing hypothesis that development is more readily achieved in resource-poor countries than in resource-rich countries. One does not need to go beyond a cursory study to see that almost everywhere around the world resource-poor nations experience more rapid economic development than resource-rich nations. National will does seem to play an important role here. Resource poor Korea has it; resource rich Zimbabwe does not. What Zimbabwe has in natural resources (gold, diamond, rich soil), Korea had in national will. Bent on preventing a repeat of the humiliation that it suffered from Japanese occupation in World War II, Korea mobilized its rather limited natural resources and embarked on the pursuit of national economic development. It saw Japan as an economic competitor rather than as a former colonial master. Within a couple of decades, Korea was able to transform itself from a net importer into a net exporter of consumer goods. Today, Korea is self-sufficient in the civilian and military technologies that it needs to run its economy. Close to fifty years after gaining independence, Africa continues to depend on the outside world for the supply of basic consumer goods. Had Africa developed the will and the vision that it needed to pull itself out of underdevelopment, it certainly would be in a position to meet its demand for basic consumer goods. That national interest ranks lowest on the priority of African heads of states explains why Africa remains underdeveloped.

The Psychological Mindset of Corruption in Africa

In every index of good economic performance, Africa ranks dead last. However, in the index of corrupt regimes, Africa is a gold medalist. If one can point a finger at the one single most important barrier to development in Africa, it will have to be corruption. One excuse frequently given to explain away corruption is that corruption occurs because wages are low. The reality however is the most corrupt class in Africa are not low wage earners; it is the wealthy – heads of states, government ministers, government officials, bureaucrats and the police. From Nigeria's Abacha to Cameroon's Paul Biya and Zaire's Mobutu we saw people who did not seem to have had enough even after they became multi-billionaires. That anyone in the Third World can possibly spend a billion dollars in their lifetime is unrealistic. Yet, the selfish quest to transform the national treasury into a personal treasury found no limits among these corrupt rulers. Just as they are corrupt, so too is their bureaucracies. Incapacitated by the lack of a moral compass, these leaders were not in the position to elicit anti-corrupt behavior in their subordinates. As a result, corruption became endemic across much of Africa.

But what exactly is the mindset of a corrupt official? In political systems where tribal affinities are stronger than national affinity, and where patronage rather than merit determines upward mobility, people generally tend to wager their bets with the tribe rather than with the nation. The appointment of a minister from a given tribe brings joy and jubilation to everyone in that tribe. The appointee is seen as the broker or medium through whom resources will be sent to the tribe. Just as members of Congress in the United States are expected to bring home the pork, the minister is expected to bring home jobs, schools, roads, and healthcare facilities. But unlike in the U.S., these resources are obtained not by logrolling or legislative budgetary deal-making, they are obtained by misappropriation and by giving sycophantic allegiance to the head of state.

Across much of French-speaking Africa, corruption is justified by a metaphor that says a goat grazes where it is tethered (*la chèvre brute là où elle est attachée*). This is an unusual but brazen rationalization of corruption. A public official who fails to enrich himself or his clan through corruption or misappropriation while in office is often ridiculed, despised and sometimes ostracized my members of that clan. For well-intended officials who started out wanting to stay clear of corruption, the pressure can sometimes be overwhelming.

For most government bureaucrats, the tribe is not only their place of origin, it is a place where they would eventually go back to at the end of their careers. A public official who sends resources and opportunities back home to his clan and clans-people will receive a hero's welcome when he retires and returns to the village. As indicated above, failure to provide such services could mean rejection and ostracism at retirement. In Africa and in much of the Third World, the gravitational force of the clan and tribe still remains too strong to allow for the selfless pursuit of national interest.

What if Barack Obama, Bill Gates, Steve Jobs and Ted Turner Were Born in Africa?

No society has exclusive monopoly in talent or intellectual ability. While all societies are endowed with intellect and creative talent, what makes the difference is how that talent is incubated and nurtured. From a little-known community organizer, Barack Obama rose to become president of the United States. And from humble middle-class backgrounds, Bill Gates, Warren Buffet, Sam Walton, Steve Jobs and Ted Turner, among others, used their talents to produce achievements that benefited millions of people. What if any of these people were born in Africa? The answer is obvious. Obama will either be in jail or killed for daring to declare his intention to run for president. At best, his candidacy will be challenged by a supposedly "independent electoral commission" on the grounds that one of Obama's parents was not an African.

As for Gates, Jobs and Turner, and other technology entrepreneurs, they will all be imprisoned for inventing technologies and technological gadgets that threaten state security and the president's monopoly over information. After witnessing such social media outlets as Twitter and Facebook bring down governments in Tunisia, Egypt, and Libya, not too many African rulers would want to see a young person with the talents to develop similar technologies emerge in their society. Another possible fate for Obama, Gates, Jobs and Turner could very possibly have been life as child soldiers, fighting in oversize tee-shirts under the command of a warlord in Liberia, Sierra Leone, Sudan, Cameroon, Democratic Republic of Congo and the Central African Republic. The probability that any one of them will reach puberty without getting killed will be low. And should any one of them manage and reach puberty, they likely will be mentally and physically incapacitated. If born in any of the countries where AIDS was rampant, none of them would have lived to see their 40th birthday. There are hundreds of potential Barack Obamas, Bill Gates and Steve Jobs in Africa, but the African environment makes it impossible for them to maximize their potential. Sam Walton, the founder of the largest private sector company in the United States would have been taxed into bankruptcy, particularly if he were affiliated with an opposition party. Up until the early 1990s, it was difficult if not impossible for entrepreneurs in most African countries to be granted government licenses to operate television or radio stations. Thus, had Ted Turner been born in Africa, he never would have had the opportunity to realize his dream of a 24-hour news network. Political institutions in Africa are designed to frustrate rather than to nurture or foster creativity and entrepreneurial potential.

What if Computers and the Internet Were Invented in Africa?

One of the greatest technological achievements of the 20th century was the invention of the Internet and computer information systems. It is a revolution that has transformed the world in ways previously unimagined. The revolution is not so much in the invention of the technologies themselves, but in the democratization of the use of these technologies. Had the Internet been developed in Africa, the global liberalization of its use would never have occurred. As the West seeks to democratize every new invention and every new idea, African rulers by and large find ways to maintain monopoly control over inventions and ideas that can potentially empower their populations.

The internet was developed during the Cold War as a secret means of maintaining communications in the event of the breakout of World War III. At the end of the Cold War, the U.S. government moved to liberalize its use nationally and internationally. The liberalization was facilitated by an earlier liberalization of the telecommunications industry in the early 1980s. With the breakup of AT&T and the birth of the "Baby Bells," the growth of the telecommunications industry took off at an unprecedented pace. So when it came time for the Internet to hit the consumer market, multiple telecommunication highways were already in place to accommodate the new technology. Instantaneously, it created an unprecedented boom in the U.S. economy. Between 1990 and 2000, more jobs and more wealth were created in the U.S. than was created in all of Africa throughout the first half century of its independence. So had the Internet been invented in Africa therefore, it would have permanently been kept as a state secret. Even if government leaders know that liberalizing it will produce millions of jobs and billions of dollars, as long as self-preservation and self-aggrandizement remained the primary goals of government, they still will prefer to keep a tight grip on it.

For the first half century of its independence, the telephone, television, electricity and various utility services in Africa were virtual state-controlled monopolies. Throughout this period, these industries whose Western counterparts produced remarkably high profits produced but deficits in African parastatals. Despite the fact that phone service in Africa generated more revenues per capita than phone service in the advanced industrial countries of the West, government-owned telephone providers failed to see this revenue potential. For them, phone service was seen not as a profit generating business, but as a service that was to be granted as a favor to cronies, to party faithfuls, and to those who were prepared to pay a bribe.

Electoral Fraud and the Paradox of Pro-Independence Referendums

Referendums were one of the institutional processes that were used to legitimize the transition from colonial rule to independence in some African countries. Among those charged with supervising, processing and proclaiming the results of referendums were colonial administrators – many of whom were politically opposed to granting independence to Africa. No one stood to lose more from the independence of Africa than the colonial administrators who supervised the referendums. They were in a position to rig the results of the referendums to deny independence to their colonies independence. Yet, in almost every case, colonial administrators counted, and fairly proclaimed the results in favor of pro-independence movements. Given Africa's knack for rigging elections, were these administrators African, they likely would have rigged the elections to deny Africans their vote for independence.

African heads of states were among many of the observers who were actively supporting Obama in the 2008 U.S. presidential elections. Had there been a near attempt at manipulating the results of the election to deny Obama victory, African rulers would have been among the first to cry foul. Yet, these same rulers are regularly in the business of rigging elections to deny victory to opposition candidates. There are many potential Obamas in Africa who have not been allowed to freely participate in the political life of their countries.

What we see from Table 6.1 is that in after more than half a century of independence, only 15 or 27% of the countries in Africa are democratic; 13 or 24% are semi-democratic; and 27 or 50% are non-democratic. By every measure, this is a disappointing performance. It is a disappointing performance not just for Africa, it is a disappointing performance for the West. This is a region whose modern governance structures were designed by the West; and since becoming independent, it has continued to remain anchored to the West economically, politically and culturally. Such anchoring meant that the West had leverage that it could exercise on African governments to carry out the political reforms that will lead to democratic development in Africa. In failing to exercise this leverage, the West made Africa's failure the West's failure.

Table 6.1. Status of Democracy in Africa at the Half Century Mark

Democratic (15)	Partially Democratic (13)	Undemocratic (25)
Benin	Camoros	Algeria
Botswana	Congo (Brazzaville)	Angola
Cape Verde	Gabon	Burkina Faso
Ghana	Eritrea	Burundi
Liberia	Ethiopia	Cameroon
Malawi	Kenya	Central African Rep
Mauritius	Lesotho	Chad
Mozambique	Madagascar	Congo (DR)
Namibia	Mali	Cote D'Ivoire
Nigeria	Morocco	Djibouti
Sao Tome	Sierra Leone	Egypt
Senegal	Swaziland	Equatorial Guinea
Seychelles	Tanzania	Gambia
South Africa		Guinea
Zambia		Guinea Bissau
		Libya
		Mauritania
		Niger
		Rwanda
		Somalia
		Sudan
		Togo
		Tunisia
		Uganda
		Zimbabwe

Classification Criteria:

- Democratic: Successfully conducted two peaceful transfers of presidential power in the last three elections.
- Quasi-Democratic: Periodic elections but no prospects of transfer of presidential power.
- Non-Democratic: Entrenched presidential powers. Results of presidential elections are readily predictable.

A Performance Appraisal of Self-Rule in Africa

Nation-states exist to promote the security and welfare of their citizens. They work to establish conditions that are favorable for social order, human dignity and self-actualization. It was the realization that these conditions could never be fully realized under foreign rule that got African nationalist movements to mobilize and campaign for independence. The campaign succeeded, and Africans won the right to govern themselves. So after half a century of independence, how well has African rule contributed to the realization of social order, human dignity and self-actualization? Freedom House, a Washington, D. C. based nongovernmental organization conducts annual ratings that measure the democratic performance of countries around the world. From 1972 when the study began to the mid-2000s, none of the African countries in Freedom House's annual reports met the conditions of a fully democratic state. Even with the democratic reforms that swept through Africa in the 1990s, most still did not fulfill the conditions that qualify them as democracies. We therefore need to go beyond Freedom House's ratings to take our own score on Africa's post-independence performance.

To take score, we have to look at comparative data over various intervals and over similarly situated regions. The scores will have to compare social and economic performance in colonial times against performance today. In his study of Africa, Nicolas van de Walle found that during the colonial period that ran from the 1850s to the early 1960s, Africa accounted for more than 5% of total world trade. However, since gaining independence, Africa's share of world trade has been on the decline. In 2010, it accounted for a mere 2%. Indeed, between 1980 and 1995, a time period when almost 100% of Africa was independent and under self-rule, Africa's share of world trade was stagnant at 0.9%. During the same period, the growth rates of similar regions of the Third World – from Latin America to Southeast Asia ranged from 6.6% to 17.8%. What went wrong? In addition to some of the reasons already discussed, such as the greater quest for self-aggrandizement and the lack of visionary leadership, we can add political instability, civil wars, the absence of inter-African trade, and the failure to diversify the African economy. Economic diversification and increased trade among African nations are policies that good or visionary leadership could have long adopted. But in a region where the quest for self-aggrandizement is much greater than the quest for national interest, developing a vision that goes beyond self-interest is a far cry.

When oppression under colonial rule is compared to oppression in post-colonial Africa, the performance record of African leaders is about as alarming, if not more so, than the record of colonial rulers. While human suffering in colonial Africa was in the hands of foreign occupiers, human suffering in post-colonial Africa has been in the hands of fellow Africans. Given what we know about the human rights record of African heads of states, we cannot help but ponder what would have been the plight of Nelson Mandela had he been the citizen of a country that was governed by a black African. Would he have come out of prison alive; and would he have gone on to become president? To answer this question, one needs but to look at what happened to Patrice Lumumba, to Moshood Abiola and many of the tens of thousands of opposition leaders that disappeared or were summarily executed for calling for fairness in the democratic process.

The very African countries that were decrying the injustices of the apartheid regime in South Africa were themselves carrying out worse injustices in their own countries. The Organization of African Unity which lobbied hard for sanctions against the apartheid regime in South Africa made no effort to denounce or demand sanctions against the oppressive police states that proliferated Africa in the post-independent era. While the former apartheid regime in South Africa can point to the sophisticated economic infrastructure that it built with proceeds from the sale of South Africa's natural resources, most African rulers cannot say what they did with proceeds for the sale of their countries' natural resources. While much of the national wealth of most African dictatorships was directed away into secret foreign bank accounts, much of South Africa's wealth was used to build an economic infrastructure that rivals that of any advanced industrial nation. Any Californian driving on South Africa's highway system would at every turn feel at home. On healthcare, patients in South Africa can receive treatment for such serious health problems as cancer, lung disease, heart and kidney transplant at home in South Africa. In the rest of tropical Africa, such treatment is simply not available. When top government officials need treatment for any of such diseases, they are evacuated to European or American hospitals for treatment. Even for a tropical disease such as malaria, African rulers frequently have travel to the temperate regions of Europe and North America to seek medical treatment.

African leaders who stash away their nation's wealth in foreign bank accounts often fail to realize that greater wealth can actually be generated by investing the money at home. Banks are in business to sell money. Money is deposited in banks is loaned out to businesses. Some of these businesses are multinational corporations that do business in Africa. In the 1990s, the Botswana and Nigerian stock markets grew at an average rate of 80 – 100%. European and North American stock markets grew at a 5 – 12% rate. This pushes us to ponder why any African leader would want to deposit his loot in foreign banks, when investing it at home will yield exponential growth.

Nowhere is hard currency in much greater need than in the developing economies of the Third World. Heads of states who stash away billions in foreign private bank account appear to be cheating themselves of potential high earnings at home. James Boyce and Léonce Ndikumana of the University of Massachusetts estimate that between 1970 and 2004, capital flight from 40 sub-Saharan African countries stood at $607 billion. That this is about three times more than the $227 billion foreign debt that the continent owes, ought to have made Africa a net creditor to the outside the world, rather than a net debtor. Despite the growing transparency that has been produced by recent democratic reforms, capital flight from Africa continues at the rate of $20 billion to $28 billion a year. What is most bothersome is the fact that while the assets are in private/personal bank accounts, the liability from the foreign loans that provided these funds remains a public debt that is owed and will have to be paid by present and future African governments.[19] In a continent with high unemployment and abundant natural resources waiting to be processed into finished goods, it is hard to understand how anyone would not know what to do with billions of dollars? Simply investing it to build factories, hospitals, schools and other job creating industries can potentially yield more returns than the low interest rates that are paid by foreign banks. That African rulers would not make such investments in their own countries, it would appear that they themselves have no confidence in the countries that they govern.

The white minority government that ruled South Africa up until 1994 was made up entirely of people whose roots were traceable to Europe. As Africans of European descent, one would have thought they would be the ones to see and trust Europe as a safer place to invest or hide their wealth, particularly given the instability and uncertainty that was characteristic of apartheid South Africa. Since gaining independence, South Africa has been about as unstable, if not more so, than most of the other countries on the continent. Despite the instability, South African rulers (unlike their counterparts in other African countries) invested their wealth at home in South Africa. The investments led to the development of infrastructures that enabled South Africa to emerge as an economic powerhouse on the continent.

An index that is seldom used to measure economic performance is the emigration/immigration index. It is an index that can be used to measure population flows in and out of a given country or region. If the net inflow is higher than the net outflow, it will be presumed that the economy of a country or region is performing well. If the net outflow is higher than the net inflow, the economy is presumed to be performing poorly. Economic conditions in Africa have been characterized by the latter since independence. As we are going to see in the next chapter, the rate of emigration from Africa today is alarmingly high. While the analysis in next the chapter faults the West for hemorrhaging Africa, here we are going to examine how African governments have contributed to that hemorrhaging.

As indicated above, more Africans are entering the United States today than at any time during the slave trade. Analysis from data produced by the 2000 U.S. Census reveals that since 1990, more Africans – as many as 50,000 annually – have entered the United States voluntarily than the total who were disembarked in chains before the 1807 ban in the trans-Atlantic abduction.[20]

The numbers reflect legal immigrants only. It is assumed that the number

---

19   Paul Redfern, The East African (Nairobi), 12 October 2008.
20   Sam Roberts, www.nytimes.com/2005/02/21/nyregion/21africa/html?ex=1109653200 &en=c164ab867fbf987&ei=5070 (Accessed 9/4/2018)

of illegal immigrants, estimated somewhere in the "multiple of at least four,"[21] dwarfs legal immigrants. An even greater number of Africans are immigrating to Europe. Those who are unable to obtain entry visas still find ways to enter Europe by whatever means necessary. Some try to enter in makeshift boats. Traveling from as far away as the Gulf of Guinea, some have dared to trek across the Sahara Desert. Many have found untimely and agonizing deaths in the Sahara Desert, some have endured slavery and torture in Libya, and many have died at sea.

In 2007, 47 African migrants died of hunger and thirst trying to cross into Spain.[22] Five years before that, the swollen corpse of 37 would-be illegal immigrants were discovered off the shores of southern Spain. Their over-crowded makeshift boat, or *patera*, was unprepared for the strong currents and rapidly changing weather conditions along the Strait of Gibraltar. In the previous 20 years, more than 80,000 Africans died trying to get to Europe by sea.[23] And between 1995 and 2015, approximately 25,000 Africans lost their lives trying to cross the Mediterranean Sea to Europe. In 2014, alone some 200,000 migrants, including 15,000 unaccompanied children, sailed across the Mediterranean. These figures do not include the 140,000 people, including 22,700 minors that were rescued at sea and brought to Sicily and southern Italy.[24]

Almost all of the victims are youths who are in the most productive years of their lives. The most heart wrenching of the deaths was that of Gambian national team goalkeeper, Fatiman Jawara, who died November 2, 2016 trying to cross the Mediterranean to Europe. A goalkeeper in soccer is the equivalent of a quarterback in American football. In almost every country in the world, athletes who defend their countries at international sporting competitions are considered national heroes. But here was a young athlete, her demonstration of patriotism to her country of birth, the country was unable to create conditions that would help her earn a living.[25]

In a continent that badly needs development, youths are resources that, if trained and armed with the right skills will make contributions that lead to economic takeoff in Africa. Paradoxically, as African youths are fleeing

---

21 Ibid.

22 BBC, November 6, 2007, African migrants die in Atlantic, http://news.bbc.co.uk/2/hi/africa/7081700.stm (Accessed 9/4/2018)

23 BBC, 09/10/2008, From shipwreck to solidarity, http://news.bbc.co.uk/2/hi/africa/7586597.stm.

24 African Immigrants Risk it All in the Mediterranean Sea, http://news.yahoo.com/photos/african-migrants-risk-all-in-the-mediterranean-sea-slideshow/ (Accessed 9/4/2018)

25 Kevin Sieff, *The Washington Post*, 11/4/2016, She was Gambia's Star Goalkeeper, Yet she Died as yet another drowned migrant in the Mediterranean, (accessed 07/14/2018) https://www.washingtonpost.com/news/worldviews/wp/2016/11/04/a-gambian-soccer-star-becomes-the-tragic-face-of-this-years-migrant-deaths-in-the-mediterranean/?tid=a_inl

the continent, escaping unemployment and lack of opportunities, Chinese youths are flowing in to take advantage of opportunities in Africa. Ushering them in are African rulers who have found in China a convenient alternative to the West. Convenient in that, unlike with the West, its loans and investments in Africa come without structural adjustment preconditions. In addition, Chinese trade with Africa comes with the added flexibility of permitting Africans to repay with raw materials. In a continent where hard currency is hard to come by, Africans saw this as welcome relief. In the meantime, the Chinese youths who are emigrating to Africa are not doing so on their own. They are doing it with the aid and backing of the Chinese government. Apparently, the Chinese government sees in Africa what African governments do see – an abundance of economic opportunities. They train and empower their youths with the skills that are needed to take advantage of the opportunities. The Chinese emigrants who are sent to francophone Africa come in speaking French, and the ones sent to Anglophone and Lusophone Africa come in speaking English and Portuguese. More astonishing are the ones who are sent to Cape Verde. They go in speaking Cape Verdean creole – the most widely spoken language in the country.

What this says is that Chinese emigration to Africa is based on a planned and well thought out policy that involves the Chinese government and Chinese youths interested in going out to take advantage of opportunities that are out there in the world. The role of the government here is to simply identify the opportunities and help the youth develop the skills that would enable them to succeed. If African governments did the same thing in their countries, the opportunities that are opening up on the continent would be opening up for African youths and not for Chinese youths. Africa's youth will have no reason to want to emigrate to distant lands to search of opportunities.

That African leaders have failed to highlight or express concern over the mass deaths at sea and in the Sahara Desert gives reason to believe that they acquiesce to the mass exodus of the continent's youths. Apparently, the solution to their mismanagement of Africa's economies is to allow the continent's youths to silently emigrate. If this were not the case, one would expect African governments to raise alarm or do something tangible to address the crisis. At the continent-wide policy-making level, not even the African Union has made any effort to stem the mass exodus of the continent's youths.

If these youths were migrating to neighboring African countries, the risk of accidental death would probably not be as imminent. But then, the chances for an African to find employment in a neighboring African country are sometimes a lot more difficult than in Europe or North America. For most African countries, the record for the past half century has been one of hostility to immigrants from other parts of Africa. National policies are directed at expulsing rather than at welcoming human talent from other parts of the continent. Even with the skills of a Bill Gates, it is hard for a Nigerian to find official employment in Gabon, or for a Ghanaian to be employed in the Democratic Republic of Congo. The same is true for a Cameroonian who wants to work in neighboring Equatorial Guinea, or for a Kenyan who is interesting in working in neighboring Uganda.

Intellectuals provide the theoretical insights that define the paths to political and socioeconomic development in modern society. But for obvious political reasons, African rulers see the ability of intellectuals to expose their shortcomings as a threat. Unlike the military general who is duty-bound to obey and serve with honor and respect, the intellectual is not bound by oath. Denied intellectual freedom in their countries of birth, most African intellectuals have been forced to emigrate to other parts of the world. This has produced a brain-drain crisis of epic proportions. Across the continent, there is an acute shortage of professionals of all backgrounds – from university Professors to medical doctors, teachers, engineers, nurses and pharmacists.

Increasingly, several African countries have more doctors serving abroad than at home. For every doctor in Liberia, there are two working abroad. A study conducted by the Center for Global Development in Washington found that the loss of doctors often went hand-in-hand with political instability, economic stagnation and civil strife. Among the receiving countries examined were the UK, the US, France, Canada, Australia, Portugal, Spain, Belgium and South Africa. Among the countries that saw more than half their doctors leave were Angola, the Democratic Republic of Congo, Guinea-Bissau, Liberia, Mozambique, Rwanda and Sierra Leone. What many of these countries have in common is that they all experienced civil wars in the 1990s. By early 2000 they all had lost most of their doctors to foreign countries. In Mozambique, as many as 7% of doctors left the country, Angola 70%; Ghana 56%, Kenya 51%, Rwanda 43%, Sudan 1%, and Niger 9%.[26]

How African Leaders Try to Justify their Poor Performance

In an effort to explain away their poor performance, African rulers generally tend to play the blame game. When asked why they have not been able to perform as well as their counterparts in other parts of the world, they give the excuse that African states are only a few decades young, and so their mistakes can be tolerated. Some argue that African states are performing at the same level that Western states performed when they were in their first half century of independence. Prior to the independence of most Western countries, there were not too many "self-made" successful nation-states out

---

26   BBC, 01/10/2008, Africa 'being drained of doctors', http://news.bbc.co.uk/go/pr/fr/-/2/hi/health/7178978.stm (Accessed 9/4/2018)

there that provided a roadmap or blueprint for the successful management of the affairs of a sovereign state. The newly independent countries therefore had to learn the art of modern governance by trial and error. Today, there are many successful countries out there. Modeling any one of them will make Africa achieve in less time what it took the West to achieve. For African rulers to make the claim that their mistakes should be tolerated because they are still young nations is a claim that does not hold sway.

Mistakes are unintended actions that are made without malicious intent. Much of what obstructed development in Africa in the past half century were not unintended actions. They were deliberate acts of commission motivated by greed and selfishness. Even if one were to accept the excuse that these were mistakes, the mistakes would be excusable for the first generation of African post-independent African rulers, who we can say were ill-prepared and inexperience in the art of governing. Whatever mistakes may have been made by the first generation of African leaders, those mistakes should have served as a learning experience for the second generation. The second generation of African leaders that came to power in the 1980s were mostly educated and trained in Western societies, where the art of governance had been perfected and carried out in the general interest of the public. This means that unlike many of their first-generation predecessors, the second generation of African leadership was actually exposed to both the theory and practice of good governance. On return home to Africa, some had the privilege of incubating either as civil servants or as cabinet officials prior to becoming national leaders. So youthful indiscretion, or the argument that the mistakes of African states can be excused because they are still in their infancy is not a good enough excuse.

At independence, the first generation of African leaders frequently sought to increase their domestic popularity by blaming Africa's social and economic ills on colonialism and by pointing to the threat of neocolonialism. At the same time, these very critiques of the colonial order were partnering with the very neocolonialists to exploit Africa's economic resources. Rhetorically, no African ruler was harsher at criticizing the West than Mobutu Sese Seko of Zaire. In an open tirade against Western values, he passed a law banning the use of Western names. Yet, worse than his neocolonial partners, Mobutu and his cronies looted the country's fabulous wealth, and transformed it into one of the poorest countries on planet earth. Just as Mobutu and other members of the first generation of African leadership were quick to blame colonialism and neocolonialism for Africa's ills, today's generation in turn blames the first generation of African leaders for the misguided start they gave the continent.

But what seems to be true about the failures of the first generation of African leaders is that they were placed in power by the departing European colonialists not because they had leadership abilities, but because they were subservient and nonthreatening to the interests of the departing colonial powers. Mobutu was of course more subservient and nonthreatening to Western interests than Lumumba was. And when it came to leadership skills, Lumumba was by far a lot more qualified to lead his country than Mobutu was. But qualification or good leadership was not what the departing Europeans wanted for Africa. They wanted a faithful custodian who would serve their neocolonial interests. Mobutu perfectly fit the profile.

The second generation of post-independence African rulers were in turn equally given power because of their subservience and sycophancy to the first generation of African heads of states. As second in command to Anwar Sadat, Hosni Mubarak was unusually subservient and sycophantic. At the death of Sadat, he was seen as a candidate best suited to continuing Sadat's legacy. It was equally because of his subservience and sycophancy that Paul Biya of Cameroon was picked to succeed the country's president, Ahmadou Ahidjo in 1982. Similar traits – subservience and sycophancy – played a role in the selection of Kenya's Arab Moi as Jomo Kenyatta successor. In short, good leadership was not a trait that colonial rulers and first-generation African heads of states wanted in their successors. What they wanted to see in those to whom they would hand over power were subservience, obedience, and continuity of the status quo. If there is one undergirding explanation for the lack of effective leadership in Africa, this is it.

Could Africa be Ripe for Re-colonization?

For more than five hundred years – that is half a millennium – Africa has been a net supplier of labor and raw material resources to the outside world. Since gaining independence, nothing has happened to change this relationship. That Africa has been a "net supplier" of labor and raw materials to the outside world comes across as a positive, but the reality however is that the "net" here does not translate into net gain for Africa. The net supplier of a product in the market ought to in return receive a net profit. A country or continent that exports more than it imports should in economic terms have a trade surplus. But this is not what has happened to Africa. Africa has throughout its trading history with the outside world had, and continues to have a trade deficit. The deficit is caused by a variety of factors. By design and by default, the unwritten rules of international trade have assigned Africa to the exclusive production and supply of raw materials. Raw material production comes with no value added. So even as net suppliers, producers of raw materials cannot earn enough to give them the purchasing power that is needed to become a major player in the global economy. In addition, reliance on mono-crop or single product economies does enable conditions that will lead to sustainable development and economic self-sufficiency.

All combined, these factors make Africa economically more vulnerable to today than at any time since the end of colonial rule. Current foreign investment trends are once again suggestive of a renewed scramble for Africa.[27] For the first time in a long time, the views of late Libyan President, Muammar Gaddafi, an ardent critique of foreign exploitation in Africa, were seconded by French Farm Minister, Bruno LeMaire. They both saw the frantic rush by rich countries to acquire farmland in Africa as both predatory and feudalistic.[28] Working through local intermediaries, foreign companies from advanced and emerging economies moved to purchase vast tracts of farmland across Africa. In the brief three-year period between 2008 and 2011, as much as 60 million hectares – an area about the size of France – was acquired by foreign companies for use in growing food for export and for guaranteed security in bio-fuels production.[29] In Sudan, South Korea acquired 1.7 million acres of land that was going to be used for wheat production. The United Arab Emirates acquired 1,033,000 acres for corn, alfalfa, wheat, potatoes and beans production. In Tanzania, Saudi Arabia negotiated to buy 1.2 million acres of farmland. Another Saudi purchase by the billionaire Sheikh Mohammed al-Amoudi acquired half a million hectares of fertile farmland in Ethiopia, and was expected to invest as much as $2 billion to grow rice, wheat, vegetables and flowers for export to the Saudi market.[30] In South Sudan, as much as 9% of the country's farmland was negotiated and sold away by a Texas-based firm - Nile Trading and Development - even before the country was independent. In Cape Verde, the scramble for land by European real estate developers has priced land out of the reach of the average Cape Verdean citizen in such places as Boa Vista, Sal and San Vincente.

Other buyers included the International Finance Corporation (IFC) - the

27   Padraig Carmody, *The New Scramble for Africa*, 2nd edition, Boston: Polity Publishers, 2016

28   Africa: Stop Acquisition of Farmland in Continent' – Gaddafi, November 20, 2009 allafrica. com/stories/200911201127.html; See also, "Is There Such a Thing as Agro-Imperialism?" by Andrew Rice, 11/16/09; http://www.nytimes.com/2009/11/22/magazine/22land-t. html?pagewanted=1&_r=1&ref=africa; "Millions facing famine in Ethiopia as rains fail" 08/30/09; http://www.independent.co.uk/news/world/africa/millions-facing-famine-in-ethiopia-as-rains-fail-1779376.html. (Accessed 9/4/2018)

29   International Business Times, Western Investors Buying Up African Farming Properties In "Land Grab": Report, http://m.ibtimes.com/africa-food-farms-land-grab-us-europe-hedge-funds-159663.html (Accessed 08/20/2011).

30   Frank McDonald, *The Irish Times*, June 22, 2011, Petition calls for halt to new 'land grab' in Africa; http://www.irishtimes.com/newspaper/world/2011/0622/1224299382733.html (accessed 08/20/2011); See also, Jim Lane, ActionAid reports that biofuels production for EU will add 100 million to hunger rolls. http://biofuelsdigest.com/bdigest/2010/02/15/actionaid-reports-that-biofuels-production-for-eu-will-add-100-million-to-hunger-rolls/ (Accessed 08/20/2011)

commercial investment arm of the World Bank; the Blackstone Group; Deutsche Bank; Goldman & Sachs and Dexion Capital; and South Korea's industrial conglomerate, Daewoo, which in July 2008, leased 1.3 million hectare in Madagascar, about half of the island's territory, to cultivate maize and palm oil.[31] A British investment firm, the Cru Investment Management, projected earnings of as much as 30% for its agricultural fund's investments in Malawi.[32]

Triggering the land acquisitions were the 2008 global food shortages that caused domestic unrest in many countries around the world. For the buyers, what makes Africa attractive is the ready willingness of African governments to sell, and the fact that only about 14% of the continent's productive agricultural farmland is currently cultivated. Among the willing sellers was the notorious Sudanese warlord, Paulino Matip, who signed a lease agreement in 2008 with Phillippe Heilberg, CEO of the New York-based investment fund Jarch Capital.[33]

The case of South Sudan needs a much closer look, for even before it achieved independence in July 2011, as much as 9% of the country's farmland had been purchased by foreign interests in shady deals. One of the deals, as published in a March 2011 Norwegian People's Aid report involved the Texas-based firm, Nile Trading and Development Inc. (NTD), and Mukaya Payam Cooperative which, in March 2008 signed to lease away 600,000 hectares for $25,000, with the option of later including another 400,0000 hectares - the largest in pre-independent land deal in the country. Representing the seller was an obscure "Paramount Chief" of the Mukaya community. The sale granted NTD full legal rights to natural resource exploitation on the land, including but not limited to:

- Farming
- Timber and forestry exploitation
- carbon credits from timber on the leased land
- cultivation of biofuel crops (jatropha plant and palm oil trees)
- explore and exploit subsoil minerals, petroleum, natural gas, and other hydrocarbon resources for both local and export markets
- engage in power generation activities on the leased land
- right to sublease any portion or all of the leased land or to sublicense any right to undertake activities on the leased land to third parties

---

31 Stephen Leahy, China, Korea, Saudi Arabia Lead Global Land Rush To Buy Farmland In Other Countries, http://stephenleahy.net/2009/05/11/china-korea-saudi-arabia-lead-global-land-rush-to-buy-farmland-in-other-countries/ (Accessed 9/4/2018)

32 Julio Godoy, Africa: The Second Scramble for Africa Starts, 20 April 2009; http://allafrica.com/stories/printable/200904201447.html (Accessed 9/4/2018)

33 http://sudanwatch.blogspot.com/2009/01/former-wall-street-banker-philippe.html

In addition, Mukaya Cooperative was asked to state in writing that it will not oppose any of NTD's activities on the leased land and will cooperate with the company in all efforts to obtain more concessions from the soon-to-be independent government of South Sudan.[34]

As with the deals that opened up Africa for slavery and for colonial occupation, current land deals are as shady. Concluded mainly between foreign scramblers and corrupt African leaders, they go beyond speculative land acquisitions to a replay of the deceitful and predatory practices that were used by slave merchants and colonial settlers of the likes of Cecil Rhodes. Then, illiterate chiefs along the West African coast were coaxed and lulled into signing treaties in languages they did not read. The treaties stated that the chiefs had legally and willfully transferred over ownership of Africa's human and landed properties to the European buyers. While times have change, the deceitful predatory tactics do not seem to have change.

A 2011 report by *The Oakland Institute*, a US environmental think tank, revealed that the same regulatory failures that allowed financial firms to drive the international economy into global recession in 2008 were again resurfacing in Africa in the form of permissive, speculative land acquisition. Titled, *Understanding Land Investment Deals in Africa*, the report focused on claims that Harvard, Vanderbilt and other American universities with large endowment funds had invested heavily in African land with the expectation of making huge returns. For the authors of the report, this new scramble for Africa had the long-term potential of "creating insecurity in the global food system that could be a much bigger threat than terrorism."[35]

Given the two cataclysmic experiences that Africa has had with the outside world – slavery and colonialism - one would expect the continent's rulers to adopt measures that will help prevent a repeat. But African leaders have done nothing to prevent the continent from ever again falling prey to the outside world. Instead, Africa continues to depend on the very external forces that brought devastation to the continent. In April 2012, Nigeria's Central Bank Chief, Chukuma Soludo warned that Africa's "future is once again on the table, and it is Europe that holds the ace. Unlike the Berlin Conference of 1884-1885 which balkanized Africa among 13 European powers as guaranteed sources of raw materials and market, the current contraption under the Economic Partnership Agreements (EPAs) spearheaded from Brussels is a modern-day equivalent of the Berlin Conference." [36]

---

34 *Pambazuka News,* Understanding land investment deals in Africa: Nile Trading and Development, Inc. in South Sudan,(Accessed July 10, 2010).

35 Understanding Land Investment Deals in Africa, http://www.abovetopsecret.com/forum/thread714536/pg1 (Accessed 08/20/2011)

36 Africa: From Berlin to Brussels - Will Europe Underdevelop Africa Again? http://allafrica.com/stories/201203191099.html (Accessed April 5, 2012).

Sharing the Blame for Africa's Failure with the Citizens of Africa

On the internal dimension, while the lion's share for Africa's failures falls primarily on African leaders, African citizens to a certain extend do share in the blame. Nowhere is the dictum "people deserve the government they have" more fitting than in Africa. Across much of Africa, there is a pervasive cult of adulation and sycophancy, along with a general tendency to condescend, impress and curry favor from those in power. While the role of government in the West is to serve the people, in Africa, the general belief is that the people should serve their leaders. It is thus not uncommon to hear Africans refer to their rulers as "His Excellency;" "His Majesty;" "the Messiah;" "the Great One;" or "father of the nation." When individuals consumed by the cult of mediocrity are exalted and lavished with such praises, they are misled into believing that their right to govern is divine. Rulers intent on staying in power for life often use such flattering adulations to say they are simply honoring the will of the people. With so much adulation and exaltation, African presidents just do not see how they can step down from office and go back into being ordinary citizens. In worshipping and in deferring to leaders who have mismanaged and bankrupted their economies, African citizens share in the blame for the continent's failures.

In two famous quotes by the famous American abolitionist, Frederick Douglas he warns that 1) "power concedes nothing without demand;" 2) "The limits of tyrants are prescribed by the endurance of those whom they oppress." Concurring these warnings, Franz Wright cautions that "if we stand silent because we fear the government, we will have the government that we fear." Along the same lines, speaking on the necessity of sacrifice, one of America's founding fathers, Benjamin Franklin, hinted that "those who would give up essential Liberty to purchase a little temporary Safety deserve neither Liberty nor Safety."[37]

Change and progress demand sacrifice. From what they have demonstrated so far, Africans have demonstrated that they are not ready to make the sacrifice. If Europeans were as acquiescent to their rulers as Africans are to theirs, the Magna Carta, the American Revolution, the French and the Russian revolutions would never have happened. Europeans would still be under the rule of monarchs, and the United States will still be under the rule of the British monarchy.

Besides their sycophantic support for unworthy leaders, ordinary Africans can also be blamed for their inability to respect time. When an African event is scheduled for 6:00 PM, Africans will not get there till 9:00 PM. It is a habit that has become so generally accepted that it has earned for itself derogatory acronyms such as BMT (Black Man Time) and AMT for (African

---

37   Benjamin Franklin's motto in the "Historical Review of Pennsylvania" (1759). [1]

Mean Time). While this may be seen as a laughing matter, the quest for modernization is not. Development and modernization cannot take place without respect for time. The ability and the discipline to manage time is the first evidence of the ability to manage modernity. Modern life revolves around, and modernization cannot be realized in cultures that do not honor time. While development requires both tangible and intangible inputs, it is intangibles such as respect for time that work to actually produce the habits that generally place countries on the path to development. Countries that fail to honor the timely principles of time will ultimately fail to master the complex intricacies of development.

Being on time is as important for social events as it is for the organized processes that go into modern assembly line production. A machine or production part that is not delivered in time could mean a complete halt in the chained processes that spin that assembly line. Such a halt can cause losses that would lead to bankruptcy, business failure and possible decline in national productivity. The challenge for policy-makers is to rethink and redefine a new approach to addressing Africa's problems, including paying attention to such non-tangibles as time. If focusing on material resources has not succeeded in bringing development to Africa, then it may be time for Africans to focus on such intangibles as time and time management.

Basically, development is a mental process. When deconstructed, the word "developmental" becomes two words – "develop" and "mental." Hidden in the suffix is the realization that development requires a mental state of mind. With this understanding, underdevelopment can be seen not so much as a physical endeavor, but as it is a mental one. A mental-less mind can never achieve development. Thus, the key to understanding what has perennially remained elusive to Africa's quest for development is in the suffix "mental."

As indicated above, time is the principle around which development and modernity revolve. Mastering development comes with the ability to manage time. Any civilization that does not master time will never be able to master development. On top of the ability to master time is the need to develop a probing mind. A probing or inquiring mind constantly seeks to challenge the status quo. Culturally, Africans are yet to develop a probing mind. As a mental process, development cannot be entirely imported. Importing physical and material resources that have been conceived and invented somewhere else cannot lead to sustainable development. To achieve sustainable development, it is necessary to begin by domestically developing the mental processes that produce development. Ultimately, the processes that are going to produce sustainable development in Africa are going to come from Africans. It is only by seeing development as a mental process that Africans can effectively begin to take the measures that are necessary to achieve sustainable development.

What Africa's Driving Culture can Teach us About African Political Culture

A quiet observation of driving habits in Africa will reveal that most Africans do not respect traffic lights. A culture that shows no respect for traffic rules will show no respect for democratic rules. Like the presidency, the highway is a public space. Both are regulated by written rules – one by a written constitution and the other by a written driving code. While the constitution provides conditions for acceding to the presidency, presidential terms limits and conditions for leaving office, the driving code provides conditions for obtaining driver's licenses and rules for driving on the highway. Anyone who has visited or driven an automobile in Africa would admit that at intersections, Africans on the whole do not respect traffic rules. It is rare to see a driver yield the right of way to a driver who has the right to cross first at an intersection.

Stop signs are seldom available, and when available, they are seldom respected. Frequent blackouts make traffic lights unreliable and risky, and so roundabouts are the preferred architectures of intersections. At such roundabouts, all drivers try to force through at the same time, with no one willing to yield the right of way. This failure to yield the right of way at road intersections is very similar to a president who fails to yield power at the end of his term or following the loss of an election. At intersections with traffic lights, it is not uncommon to see drivers violate or force through when the light is red. This is not different from the practice of African rulers who rig elections and violate term limits. If there is a lesson here, it is that disrespect for driving rules translates to disrespect for democratic rules. In cultures where traffic rules are respected, drivers will even at midnight stop at a red light, including red lights on isolated country roads.

Ironically, aggressive drivers – drivers who drive fast and have the habit of violating and forcing themselves through red traffic lights – often tend to gain greater admiration from the passengers that are in their cars, than drivers who drive cautiously and honor driving rules. There is a parallel to this in African political culture. Politicians who are most admired by their supporters are politicians who rig elections, who refuse to yield when they lose elections, or who refuse to step down at the end of their term. Commonly referred to as "Africa's strongmen," they in every way have the same attributes as drivers who violate traffic rules. Just as a driver who respects traffic rules is generally seen by his passengers as weak, timid, and incompetent, a political leader who respects election results or constitutional term limits is seen by his supporters as weak, timid and incompetent.

While every attempt to violate the constitution and extend presidential term limits in Africa has been condemned abroad, it has been applauded at home – mainly by supporters of the president. In 2015 alone, there were constitutional amendments in Congo and in Rwanda to abolish term limits which allowed the incumbent presidents to run for reelection. A few years before that, within the same region, similar constitutional amendments extended the rule of Chad's Idriss Deby and Cameroon's Paul Biya. Mwai Kibaki's refusal to cede defeat in the 2007 presidential elections in Kenya despite overwhelming evidence that he had lost to Raila Odinga, is very much reminiscent of an African driver's refusal to yield the right of way at an intersection.

The Perception of Politics as a Matter of Life and Death in Africa

In the zero-sum all-or-nothing nature of politics in Africa, the rules are that "if you are not with me, then you are against me." Members of the opposition party as seen not as rivals or competitors, but as enemies – enemies that must be eliminated by every means necessary. In the run up to the 2007 presidential elections, former Nigerian President, Olusegun Obasanjo publicly declared that elections were *a matter of life or death*.[38] In Zimbabwe, the same degree of intransigence was captured in the Chisona expression, *poritikisi ihondo*, or politics as war. Call it Machiavellian on the African political scene, but this is the level of intransigence that defines the political culture in Africa. This intransigence went deadly in Cameroon in 1992 when Paul Biya used his military to deny victory to his challenger, John Fru Ndi, and in 1993 when Moshood Abiola, winner of Nigeria's 1993 presidential elections was imprisoned and later assassinated along with his wife; and in Kenya in December 2007 when the disputed presidential elections between Mwai Kibaki and Raila Odinga degenerated into a bloodbath that was described by the American Undersecretary of State for African Affairs, Jendayi Frazer as "ethnic cleansing."[39] Political intransigence was again seen in the 2010 presidential election in Cote d'Ivoire, where both the incumbent Laurent Gbagbo and the challenger Alassane Ouattara claimed victory. Neither accepted to cede or yield defeat, preferring instead to launch the nation into a bloody civil war.

By and large, democracy is based on the rule of law. In a political system where the rules are changed at the whim of the ruler, where the goalpost keeps getting pushed further and further away, democracy cannot flourish. Could the Machiavellian ideal of winning by every means necessary be an indication that political development in Africa today is where political development in the West was in medieval times? An adequate response to this question would be a potential subject for another book. For now, it is

---

38   Obasanjo in his New Book Says he Planted Moles in his VP's Camp, http://www.thisdaylive. com/articles/obasanjo-in-new-book-says-he-planted-moles-in-his-vp-s-camp/196244/;

39   US Envoy: Kenya Violence is Ethnic Cleansing, http://www.msnbc.msn.com/id/22908642/

sufficient to say that the political mindset that made Machiavelli's book, *The Prince*, a bestseller in Medieval Europe is noticeably present in the political culture of Africa today. Our challenge ultimately is to figure out how to tame it. It is by taming it that African political culture can be leapfrogged into the 21st century.

Frustrated and willing to do something about the anachronism of African political culture, Sudanese communications magnate, Mohamad Ibrahim, established a foundation that gave African heads of states financial incentives for exercising good governance, and for respect of constitutional term limits. Established in 2006, the foundation offers a prize that recognizes achievement in African leadership and provides a practical way in which African leaders can build positive legacies.

With a $5 million initial payment, plus $200,000 a year for life, the prize is believed to be the world's largest for public service. It exceeds the $1.3 million that is paid to Nobel Peace Prize recipients.[40] Eligible recipients are African heads of states who have delivered security, health, education and economic development to their citizens, and who gracefully stepped down at the end their term of office. An index, "The Ibrahim Index of African Governance" is used to evaluate performance. The five categories evaluated in the index include: 1) safety and security, 2) rule of law, transparency and corruption, 3) participation and human rights, 4) sustainable economic opportunity, 5) human development. The prize's first recipient was the former president of Mozambique, Joaquim Chissano.

Conclusion

After almost half a century of independence and self-rule, the world has had time to compare and contrast the performance of Africa under colonial rule and Africa under African rule. While idealism may bring us to accept that the dignity of self-rule (even in poverty) is far preferable to the indignities of foreign rule (even in prosperity), the reality on the ground in Africa today challenges such idealism. Because of greed and political mismanagement, Africa has lost and continues to lose much of its abled labor force to the outside world. For an African, the inability to live in his country of birth means the loss of a birthright. Today, pointing a finger of blame at former colonial powers is no longer a good enough excuse. After more than half a century of independence and self-rule, it is time African leaders accept responsibility for their failures. The promise of independence was for African leaders to take control of the destiny of Africa and make life better for Africans. African leaders have failed to keep that promise. Across

40   Ibrahim Index of African Governance, (accessed 3/9/2013) http://www.moibrahimfoundation.org.

the continent, there has been no noticeable gain in standards of living. In failing to place the interest of the nations they were sworn in to serve ahead of personal interest, African heads of states have betrayed their citizens. The political calculations of African policy-makers are directed more at promoting the self-interest than at promoting the public interest.[41] If modernization is a universal aspiration, then when put in perspective, we would see that the pace of modernization realized in Africa under colonial rule was more substantial than what has been realized under African rule.

Devastated and humiliated in World War II, China and Korea developed a stronger determination to recapture and regain their dignities at the end of the war. Through discipline and hard work, they both succeeded in developing their economies and regaining their lost pride.

Africa has the potential to do the same. But it needs to make the sacrifice that is necessary. The technological transformation that is currently taking place in the world today presents an unprecedented opportunity for Africa to leapfrog and catch up with the developed world.

The more devastating a peoples' past experience, the more motivating it ought to be. All in all, the unmaking of Africa's man-made misery is going to require not just an understanding of what has gone wrong, but a genuine show of goodwill and an avowed commitment to promoting a culture that will work in promoting the greatest good for the greatest number.

---

41 Robert H. Bates, *Markets and States in Tropical Africa: The Political Basis of Agricultural policies* Berkeley: University of California Press, 1981. See also *Rural Responses to Industrialization: A Study of Village Zambia*, New Haven: Yale University Press, 1976.

Chapter 7

Assessing the Performance of External Influences

> The states of Africa reflect the preferences of the colonial powers.
>
> Henry Kissinger[1]

> The Europeans came and assumed command of African history; and the solutions they found were solutions for themselves, not for Africans.
>
> Basil Davidson[2]

What lasting effect did the imposition of the modern nation-state system have on Africa? On balance, was colonialism a net benefit or a net loss for Africa? What have been the consequences of adopting foreign development ideologies? These are some of the questions that keep current scholarship on Africa sleepless, and therefore questions that we are going to attempt to address in this chapters. To be sure, there are no easy answers. If there were, social scientists would have by now been out of business.

The European Colonial Legacy

Colonialism forcibly imposed Western values and institutions on Africa. These values left scars that currently contribute to the instability reigns on the continent today. A January 15, 2011 *New York Times* article by the iconic Nigerian novelist, Chinua Achebe, decried the lasting damage that the European scramble for Africa did to Africa. In his words, "That controversial gathering of the leading European powers, which precipitated the 'scramble for Africa,' we all know took place without African consultation or representation. It created new boundaries in ancient kingdoms, and nation-states resulting in disjointed, inexplicable, tension-prone countries today."[3] With the notable exception of "settler colonies" such as Kenya, South Africa and Southern Rhodesia, colonial regimes did little to promote domestic economic

---

1   Henry Kissinger, interviewed on the Charlie Rose Show, NPR, June 15, 2007.
2   Basil Davidson, *Africa in History: Themes*, New York: Macmillan, 1974, p. 17.
3   The New York Times, January 15, 2011, http://www.brown.edu/conference/achebe-colloquium/

development. For colonial regimes, their central economic imperative was to avoid a drain in the treasury of the metropolis. This meant that the colonies had to pay their own way. For the colonizing power, the top agenda was to raise revenue. This was often achieved by capitalizing in an area of production that supported the colonial regime's economy and concurrently generated profits for the metropolis.

Independence was expected to bring respite. Instead, it transformed Africa from a colonial appendage to proxy battlefields for superpower rivalry. Governed by puppet regimes, the allegiance of the continent's rulers remained unshakably shackled to the outside world. Today, the legacy of colonialism remains visibly present. It continues to shape the course of politics and economics in Africa. "For better or worse, although Europe no longer rules over much of the earth, it has left (it) with the legacy of the state..."[4] Developed in Europe after countless lives lost in conflict, the state system was forcibly imposed on Africa even though cultural and historical conditions on the continent were radically different. The borders, economic structures, and political systems left by the colonial powers created the foundations for the challenges that were going to permanently haunt the newly independent African states. Lingering linguistic, cultural and trade ties to former colonial regimes continue to influence life throughout Africa. In his analysis of the causal factors of democracy, the political scientist Robert Dahl (1971) hinted that historical and external factors do need to be taken into account.[5] Among the historical and external factors that influenced the design and shaping of the current political institutions in Africa was European colonialism.

For obvious reasons, the rule that is in post-colonial Africa today is very much similar to the rule that was in Africa colonial Africa. It is despotic, it is top-down, it is oppressive. This is undeniably a direct legacy of European colonialism. In failing to plant the seeds for good governance, Europe set Africa up for failure. This should lead us to see Africa's failures as Europe's failures. All of the institutions that are in place in Africa today, from state structures to electoral processes, and even the names and boundaries of countries and cities were put in place by the West. Some of the names reflect the raw materials and natural resources that initially attracted Europeans to the continent. They included the Gold Coast for today's Ghana, the Slave Coast for Nigeria, Ivory Coast for Cote d'Ivoire, the Grain Coast for Senegal, and *camarão* (Portuguese for shrimp) for Cameroon. Northern and Southern Rhodesia (today's Zambia and Zimbabwe) were both named after Cecil

---

4   Patrick O'Neal, *Essentials of Comparative Politics*, New York: W.W. Norton & Co, 2004, p. 35
5   Robert Dahl, *Polyarchy*, Chapter 1, New Haven, CT: Yale University Press, 1971

Rhodes, the European explorer who forcibly occupied and plundered the region in the 19th century. The capital of the Democratic Republic of Congo (DRC) was named after yet another European plunderer, King Leopold of Belgium, and Congo Brazzaville's capital named after the French explorer, Brazza. On achieving independence, there was hope that life was going to get better for the citizens of these countries. Instead, Zimbabwe's Mugabe and the DRC's Mobutu turned out to be as brutish as Cecil Rhodes and King Leopold's

The borders that were imposed by colonial authorities showed no concern to existing regional or cultural harmony. Groups that were previously homogenous were balkanized up and regrouped with groups and regions with whom they had nothing in common. The permanent state of conflict that Somalia finds itself in today has more to do with European colonial policies than with internal differences. Here is a country that was, prior to European rule, culturally and geographically homogeneous. By the end of the rule, this one-time homogeneous nation was now a country that was arbitrarily factionalized into four different territories with competing sovereignties – Djibouti, Kenya, Ethiopia and Somaliland. It was this factionalism that is responsible for the perennial state of warfare that we see in Somalia.

Instability as a Legacy of Colonial Rule

That many of Africa's crises are found in those areas of Africa that were established and directly influenced by the West (governments, urbanized areas, etc.) provides a direct cause and effect relationship to instability as a legacy of European rule in Africa. We should understand that it was not so much colonialism per se, but the arbitrariness with which colonialism was administered that is the root cause of the instability that Africa faces today. Had Africa been colonized by a single foreign power, and had it been colonized along the defined ethnic populations with the intention of protecting the cultural homogeneity of those populations, the continent would be a lot more stable today. Like it or not, a continent that was divided up and colonized by as many as eight competing foreign powers cannot be guaranteed a stable future. Africa would have since recovered from the trauma of colonial predation had the colonizing powers simply taken away the natural resources and left without attempting to change boundaries, the culture, the politics and the indigenous religions.

Behind every stable and prosperous economy, there is a guiding ideology. Colonialism went a long way to sapping Africa's ability to develop a guiding ideology. The views of America's founding fathers, which included democracy and free trade, provided a defining ideology that has led to the rise of the United States to superpower status. And despite the untold suffering that it caused, China's cultural revolution produced a guiding ideology that led to the rise of China as a global economic powerhouse. Had European colonial powers left African cultural and political institutions intact, it too could have gone through an awakening moment that would have produced a guiding ideology for the continent. Lulled by colonialism into believing that there was only one path to modernization - the Western path – Africans were denied the opportunity to produce an ideology and a visionary roadmap to guide their quest for development. Why bother digging deep into your thoughts to come up with a vision when the colonizer has convinced you that your values and culture do not matter? In essence, colonialism was a stampede on the harmony that existed among Africans in pre-colonial Africa. It left Africa with new boundaries that demarcated not just African states but European colonies.[6] Indeed, the primary reason why Africa remains politically unstable today is because it was literally scrambled up by its architects at the 1884 Berlin conference. In Berlin, competing European powers met to decide from a distance, thousands of miles away, the economic and geopolitical fate of Africa. Paradoxically, the very Berlin that organized and presided over the split of Africa in 1884 was itself split up in 1945. For more than sixty years, it remained divided between East and West, Communist and capitalist ideologies. Germany was forced to experience firsthand the harm what the imposition of an arbitrary boundary by external powers can do to a once homogeneous people. As soon it was realized that a divided Germany cannot maximize its potential, it dismantled the boundary and negotiated a return to one Germany. Curiously, when Berlin was reunited sixty years later in 1990, development took off. Despite the potential economies of scale to be derived, the thoughts of uniting Africa remain to this day a remote idea.

Europe's destabilizing policies in Africa have not gone without criticism by some of the West's most highly revered statesmen. In Thomas Jefferson's original draft of the Declaration of Independence, he lodged the following indictment against Britain's King George III:

> He has waged cruel war against human nature itself, violating its most sacred rights to life and liberty in the persons of a distant people who never offended him, captivating and carrying them into slavery in another hemisphere, or to incur miserable death in their transportation there thither ... Determined to keep open a market where MEN should be bought and sold, he has prostituted his negative (veto) for suppressing every legislative attempt to prohibit or restrain

6   Joseph Gugler and William Flanagan, *Urbanization and Social Change in West Africa*, London: Cambridge University Press, 1978, p. 25.)

this execrable commerce.[7]

One would think that a tirade this excoriating, is the work of some radical black nationalist of the likes of W.E.B Dubois, Nat Turner, Malcolm X, or Marcus Garvey. Yet the revolutionary tirade is that of one of America's founding fathers. These angry references to the enslavement of Africans were however edited out of the final draft of the American Declaration of Independence, out of concern that it could infuriate and possibly polarize the revolutionary war effort.

Even after Africa became independent, European powers continued to work to make sure that the regimes and the institutions they left behind remained ideologically pro-West. For half a century, billions of dollars were spent to prevent Communist Russia and Socialist China from extending their influence to the continent. In refusing to let Africa at least consider alternative worldviews, the West denied Africa the opportunity to determine what foreign values were going to best align with its indigenous values in the search for the most appropriate path to development.

After arbitrarily imposing geographic boundaries that transformed Africa into a patchwork of ungovernable states, colonial powers went on to use the principle of national sovereignty to turn a blind eye to the domestic abuses of their client states. These arbitrarily drawn boundaries contributed and continue to contribute the instability that has produced ethnic crises across much Africa, including the ethnic crises that led to fratricidal bloodshed in Rwanda and Somalia. The ethnic animosity that triggered the Rwandan genocide could have been mitigated had colonial rule worked to de-emphasize ethnic or tribal identities. But guided by the well thought out principle of divide-and-rule, colonial powers knew that identifying Africans along tribal or ethnic lines will deter the development of any veneer of nationalist sentiments that could be mobilized and directed against the colonial enterprise. For Europe, "so long as drastic cleavages existed to separate distinct tribes and ethnic groups within Africa, it was unlikely that energy would be directed towards expelling the colonizing powers."[8] In other words, highlighting physical and ethnic differences to remind Africans that they did not belong together meant that they were less likely going to unite and rise up against the interests of colonial powers. Caroline Elkins illustrates this in her study of British colonial policy in Kenya:

---

7   John Hope Franklin and Alfred A. Moss Jr. *From Slavery to Freedom: A History of African Americans*, 7th edition, New York: McGraw-Hill, 19994, p.71. Philip A. Klinkner, *The Unsteady March: The Rise and Decline of Racial Equality in America*, Chicago: University of Chicago Press, 1999, p. 16

8   Edward J. Dodson, *Third World Problems: A Post-Colonial Legacy?* www.coperativeindividualism.org.dodson_third_world_problems.html (accessed June 12, 2000)

if you're looking for the origins of Kenya's ethnic tensions, look to its colonial past. Far from leaving behind democratic institutions and cultures, Britain bequeathed to its former colonies corrupted and corruptible governments. Colonial officials hand-picked political successors as they left in the wake of World War II, lavishing political and economic favors on their protégés. This process created elites whose power extended into the post-colonial era. Added to this was a distinctly colonial view of the rule of law, which saw the British leave behind legal systems that facilitated tyranny, oppression and poverty rather than open, accountable government. And compounding these legacies was Britain's famous imperial policy of "divide and rule," playing one side off another, which often turned fluid groups of individuals into immutable ethnic units, much like Kenya's Luo and Kikuyu today. In many former colonies, the British picked favorites from among these newly solidified ethnic groups and left others out in the cold. We are often told that age-old tribal hatreds drive today's conflicts in Africa. In fact, both ethnic conflict and its attendant grievances are colonial phenomena.[9]

Not only did the strategy work well in colonial Rwanda, it carried over to the post-independence era. African governments adopted the use of personal national identity cards. But instead of using them to identify citizens nationally, they were used to serve as daily political reminders of primordial ethnic affinities. Officially, a Rwandan was a Hutu or a Tutsi because it says so in his identity card. Had the identity provided in that card simply identified the bearer as a Rwandan, it would have created doubts in the mind of anyone who may be out to single the bearer out for persecution or discriminatory treatment. Whatever physical differences may have existed between the Tutsis and the Hutus, the differences were exacerbated by the ethnic identities that Rwandans were obligated to reveal in their government-issued "national" identity cards. As the result of a divide-and-rule colonial legacy that identified Africans along tribal lines, a domestic strife that should have remained a low-level conflict quickly degenerated into a genocidal war. The architects of the legacy, the former colonial powers watched indifferently from a distance, failing to intervene in time to stop it. Rwanda in 1994 was

---

9   Caroline Elkins, Divide and Rule: What's Tearing Kenya Apart? History, for One Thing Sunday, January 6, 2008; B03, http://www.washingtonpost.com/....html, http://www.kalenjin.net/newsite/index.php?option=com_content&view=article&id=914:whats-tearing-kenya-apart-history-for-one-thing (accessed 7/3/2008).

the apotheoses of the feeling that Africa does not count. Even the Catholic Church which universally proselytizes the message of brotherly love failed to speak out for Rwanda. The U.S. media was fixated on the O. J. Simpson trial and paid virtually no attention to the bloodletting in Rwanda.

Belgian colonial authorities actually went through the painstaking effort of highlighting racial differences between the Hutus and the Tutsis. Hutus and Tutsis have the same skin color, so the distinguishing differences that made the Tutsis easily identifiable during the genocide were based not on skin color but on racial classifications developed by Belgian researchers in the colonial era. The classifications alleged that the Tutsis had physical features that were very much similar to European physical features. It was probably the first time in modern history that a black race was physically likened to the white race. Advanced at a time when white supremacy was used as one of the psychological justifications for slavery and for the imposition of European colonial rule on Africa, this was alarmingly illogical. Charles Caldwell, Joshua Nott and other 19th century apologists of polygenesis – the view that the races evolved from different genes – must be turning around in their graves.[10]

But in reality, likening the Tutsis to the white European may have had more to do with Belgium's need for an internal ally. What better way was there to maintain power and control than to play the classic card of *divide-and-rule*? In this game, what was important was temperament and not physical features. Colonial powers generally adopted a strategy that allowed them to co-opt and ally with ethnic groups whose temperament was friendly and nonthreatening. Tribes that were seen as threatening to European interests were often ostracized, blackballed, blacklisted. Had the Hutus been temperamentally welcoming and accepting of Belgian rule, they probably would have been selected as the model ethnic group and granted privileges at independence.

Ironically, the predatory practices of colonial rule were in direct conflict with the values and principles of the European Enlightenment. Among the values promoted by the Enlightenment were inalienable rights to life, liberty and the pursuit of happiness. Prior to the extension of European rule to Africa, these values were promoted as universal rights. In colonizing Africa, the European heirs to the Enlightenment affirmatively chose to deprive Africans of these rights.

We are informed by Western anthropologists and historians that prior

---

10   Joshua C. Knot & George R. Gliddon, eds, *Types of Mankind or Ethnological Researches,* 7th edition, Philadelphia: Lippincott, Grambot, 1885, pp 67, 71, 77; Philip A. Kinkner, *The Unsteady March: The Rise and Decline of Racial Inequality in America,* Chicago: University of Chicago Press, 1997. P. 32.

to the European colonization of Africa, the continent was politically stable, wealthy, self-sufficient. The West had the option to build on the traditional institutions it met in place; it chose instead to out rightly dismiss as primitive the cultural and traditional values that had governed Africa for hundreds, if not thousands, of years. In most cases, the powers that were exercised by traditional African rulers prior to the coming of European colonizers were forcibly stripped and transferred over to colonially appointed bureaucrats. While practicing democracy at home in Europe, the colonizers were aggressively promoting autocracy in Africa. Traditional rulers who refused to subject themselves to the rule of the European colonizer were deposed, assassinated or forced into exile. The stable, simple life that Africans enjoyed prior to the coming of European colonizers was now replaced by repressive exploitation. Under European rule, life suddenly became harsh, brutish and short. The instability that we see in Africa today is without doubt traceable back to this era. And because vices are quicker to learn than virtues, Africans were quick to learn the autocratic ways of the European colonizer. Imperialism is inherently predatory. The predatory practices of Nigeria's Abacha, Sudan's Al-Bashir, Zaire's Mobutu, and Zimbabwe's Mugabe, were all manifestations of the imperial institutions that Europe established in Africa. Psychology teaches us that a child who is raised in an abusive home will grow up to become an abusive parent. Denial of civil liberties, denial of political rights, intolerance and violent repression - all learned behavior from colonial administrators – would go on to become acceptable political behavior across Africa. This is indisputably the legacy of European colonizers.

That most of the crises in Africa are particularly noticeable in the areas of Africa that were directly influenced by the West (governance, modernization, urbanization, finance) produces a direct link to imperialism and its legacy. Not only did Europe fail to build on the stability that it met in Africa, it failed to safeguard the indigenous political institutions that guaranteed Africa's stability in the past. Any architect who destroys the foundation that has kept a building sturdy for several thousand years does have some explaining to give if the new foundation he builds fails to hold up.

That Africa was created in the image of the West is seen in the fact that Africa, like the West, became a male dominant society. All of the leaders to whom the departing colonial powers handed over power were male. From then and up to the first two generations of post-independent African heads of states, not a single female was head of state. It was not until by the middle of the first century of independence that Africa had its first female head of state – Liberia's Sirleaf Johnson. Meanwhile, prior to the imposition of Western rule, Africa had had the experience of female rulers. Among them were Queen Nzingha of Angola, whose monarchy negotiated and established diplomatic ties with Portugal from 1582 to 1663; Queen Amina of Zaria, who introduced iron helmets and chain mails to the armies of Zaria in 1588; Queen Nandi of Zululand; Queen Nehanda of Zimbabwe; Queen Makeda of Sheba; Queen Adelaide of South Africa; Queen Cleopatra of Egypt; the Nubian Queen Tiye of Egypt; and Queen Hatshepsut of Antiquity.

As the French adopted the concept of *mission civilizatrice* or civilizing mission to provide morally self-vindicating justification for the imposition of French rule in Africa, the British adopted the all too self-deprecating notion of "the white man's burden." Article VI of the 1885 Act of Berlin read: "In the name of the almighty God, All the Powers exercising sovereign rights, or having influence in the said territories undertake to watch over the preservation of the native races, and the amelioration of the moral and material conditions of their existence."[11] One would expect an article that is solemnly prefaced with the phrase "almighty God" to be given the most meticulous attention. But a careful assessment of the political and economic performance of European powers in Africa will show that they failed to live up to the meaning of their declaration. Africa would be a lot more stable and prosperous today had Europe simply introduced in Africa the same democratic rule it had at home in Europe.

European powers left behind a governing system and a governing class that was bound to produce failed states. Designed in the interest of the colonizing powers rather than in the interest of Africans, the departing European powers made sure the African leaders to whom they handed power were individuals they trusted will continue their legacy. At independence, the allegiance of most African leaders was naturally directed externally rather than internally.

That the political systems of Africa were not designed in the interest of Africans can be seen from the caliber of leaders that were left in place by the departing colonial powers. Not only had these leaders been carefully vetted and found to be subservient, they had served in the colonial administrations either as bureaucrats or as military officers. Some, like the former Central African Emperor Jean-Bédel Bokassa, who had only an 8th grade education, barely knew what democracy was, much less the complexities of managing a modern economy. While the philosophy that guided democratic rule at home in Europe was Rousseau's social contract, in Africa the philosophy that guided colonial and post-colonial rule was, and remains, de Gaulle's *l'etat c'est moi* (I am the state). Even economic institutions that should have been left in the private sector came under the political control of the colonial government. At independence, the heir to the departed colonial rulers

---

11   Matthew Craven; Between law and history: the Berlin Conference of 1884-1885 and the logic of free trade, *London Review of International Law*, Volume 3, Issue 1, 1 March 2015, Pages 31–59

brought all of it – the public and the private sector – under his personal political control. Both in theory and in practice, the ultimate expression of the democratic state is through self-determination. As much as the West exalts the values of democracy, the state system Europe bequeath Africa was undemocratic.

In his book *The Black Man's Burden: Africa and the Curse of the Nation-State*, Basil Davidson laments the colonial legacy's asphyxiation of post-independence governance in Africa. "For African freedom fighters, mostly schooled in Western ways, could only imagine an African future inspired by the very West whose shackles they sought to break. Even the language of their discourse was derived from the West. Thus, they turned their backs on whatever might have proved useful and usable from their own African heritage. The creation of nation-states, like the Janus-faced nature of nationalism itself, proved, in the event, to be not so much liberating as suffocating. The state, Davidson argues, became a monster, its ever-inflating bureaucracy enrolled in the service of a particular family or ethnic group or tribe or alliance of tribes."[12]

Had democracy been introduced in the West the way it was introduced in the Africa, Western society would probably be as dysfunctional as Africa is today. Not only did the institution of democracy in the West evolve from the bottom up, it was gradual, accommodating and piecemeal. The British in particular, allowed their experimentation with democratic institutions to evolve from the bottom-up, alongside their long-standing traditional institutions. To accommodate the liberal aspirations of elective government, a House of Commons and an elected Prime Minister were established to function alongside such traditional institutions as the Monarchy and the House of Lords. Over time, democracy gradually and steadily grew to gain the acceptance of even the most conservative of British traditionalists. The British model could have very well worked in Africa alongside the traditional rulers that European colonizers met in place.

Frantz Fanon's emphatic argument that "there is no new entity born of colonialism" is heralded by the British writer, Basil Davidson, who indicates that while many people need a renewal of their civilization, none so obviously and urgently need it more than the people of the underdeveloped world. But "what colonialism, imperialism, capitalism may or may not have achieved, one thing is certain about them. They have utterly failed to raise those structures – whether social or moral, political or economic – upon which the deprived peoples, the abused peoples, the 'underdeveloped' peoples as they are sometimes if odiously called, can carry themselves into a

---

12   Basil Davidosn, *The Black Man's Burden: Africa and the Curse of the Nation-State*: New York: Times Books/Random House, 1992

new civilization capable of standing and evolving on its own foundations."[13]

Even if the European view that its mission in Africa was to promote democracy and modern civilization were true, then this would have been a mission that would have radically revolutionized Africa. Democracy and modernization did not come about through a revolutionary process. That these values can be summarily transplanted from one culture and society to another could only have but been wishful thinking. Yet, when Europe set out to allegedly introduce modernity in Africa, it worked first to destroy the long and stable tradition on which Africa's political, religious and historical foundations were built. Stripping Africa of the proven traditions that had kept the continent stable and in harmony for thousands of years has led to the instability we see on the continent today.

If only the colonizing powers had left the traditional governance structures they met in place intact, Africa would be a lot more stable today. The same can be said about Africa's integration into the global economy. Had this integration come about through trade rather than through enslavement and colonial conquest, development in Africa would have been more sustainable. Trade would have produced a lasting mutual profit for both parties. In a written brief to the London Missionary Society, the Scottish explorer, David Livingstone, informed Europe that the two essential investments that were necessary to produce equality between Europeans and Africans were trade and conversion into Christianity.[14] Had Europe heeded this advice and moved to promote trade between the two peoples, it would have produced an outcome that would have been a win-win outcome for both regions. It was Europe's push for a win-lose policy that is behind Africa's inability to develop a sustainable political system.

How European Colonialism Stripped Africa of its Culture and Identity

Colonial rule undeniably stripped Africa of the identity and cultural values that produce stability. Culture, religion and tradition have historically interacted to temperate human excesses. Confucian culture, for example, sees a natural harmony of mutual obligations between leaders and followers. Here, leaders are expected to be modest in their personal demands and fair and balanced in their policy-making.[15] Like Confucius, African culture in pre-colonial times went beyond the emphasis of fairness and balance to stressing the transcendental. It was a culture that on the whole believed in

---

13 Basil Davidson, in Gerard Ghaliand, *Armed in Africa,* New York: Monthly Review Press, 1969, p. ix.
14 Basil Davidson, *Africa: A Voyage of Discovery* – Episode 5
15 W. Phillips Shively, p. 91.

the omnipotence and omnipresence of God. Africans believe that there was an all-knowing God out there who will identify and punish transgressors, even if society is not able to identify and convict him. With this in mind, "guilty persons would voluntarily identify themselves as responsible for wrongdoing without waiting for the system to do so, and they would come forward even if others were unable to identify them. The belief of those faithful to the native system leads to increased control, thus avoiding much crime and deviance."[16] Not only did these beliefs moderate human conduct, they served as deterrent to deviant behavior. With the imposition of Western values and institutions, control by tradition has been replaced with control by the police, and the fear of the omnipresence of the supernatural has been replaced by the Western notion that one is presumed innocent until detected and proven guilty.[17]

As Europe took upon itself the responsibility to build Africa in its image, it began by condemning and supplanting the core foundations of African value. To build a stable society, we cannot start by condemning the social, cultural and religious values that have kept that society stable for thousands of years. While the religious and cultural values of other colonized peoples (for example, Bangladesh, India, Pakistan) were left in place, Africa's cultural and religious values were systematically eliminated. Even something as basic and as personal as first names were forcibly replaced by Western first names – a policy that colonial rule did not carry out in Asia.

Traditional African rituals were condemned as pagan practices and those who carried them out were frequently persecuted. So too was the playing of the African drum in church. African drums are made of wood and leather – all-natural materials. The very church that preaches that all things in nature were made by God was quick to condemn drums and drumming as pagan instruments. Ironically, as European missionaries were persecuting Africans for using drums that were made of God-created natural materials, they were at the same time importing drums that were made of plastic and other artificial materials for use in high schools as marching bands. This was the extent to which Europe was willing to go to strip Africa of its culture.

Be it in Africa or in the Diaspora, Africans and peoples of African descent are among the most spiritual of humans. No people call on God and attribute more to God than people of African descent. In good times and in bad

16 Nonso Okereafezeke, Political Challenges in Indigenizing Justice in Post-British Nigeria, in Charles B. Fields and Richter H. Moore, Jr., *Comparative and International Criminal Justice*, Long Gove, IL: Waveland Press, 2005, p. 344.

17 S.I. Oli, "A Dichomatization: Crime and Criminality among Traditional and Christianized Igbo: in Sulton, A.T., ed. *African-American Perspectives on Crime Causation, Criminal Justice Administration and Crime Prevention*, Englewood, CO: Sulton Books, 1994, p. 26.

times, they attribute every achievement and every obstacle to God. In the United States, for example, seldom does an African American award winner make a speech without praising or giving thanks to God and to his or her mother. Obviously, this is not a trait acquired from the Christian West. For the Europeans to come to Africa and say that the God that Africans worshipped was but a pagan god was the utmost expression of bigotry and religious chauvinism.

Lamenting this irony, an African Christian pastor pondered: "Is Europe still Christian or heathen? If we had power enough to communicate ourselves to Europe we would advise them not to call themselves 'Christendom' but 'Europeandom' Therefore the life of the three combined bodies (missionaries, government, companies) is all together cheaty, too thefty, too mockery. Instead of 'give' they say 'take away from.'"[18]

A non-Christian visiting the Catholic Church for the first time would very likely interpret the ritual that accompanies the holy sacrament as a pagan ritual. Candle burning, kneeling and performing the sign of the cross, the sprinkling of holy water, reciting the catechism, the beatitudes, and the Lord's Prayer are not un-similar to some of the rituals that Western missionaries persecuted Africans for performing. Had European missionaries taken time out to carefully study African religious practices, not only would they have found dialectic commonalities between African and European religious practices, they very well may have discovered that African religious practices were fully in sync with Christian religious practices.

Such syncretism is today witnessed across the Atlantic on the Portuguese colony of Brazil. Here, the Catholic Church tolerated African religious traditions, allowing them to be integrated with traditional Catholic mass services. The African drums that the Catholic Church once banned on the continent were welcomed here. Before long, the merging of the two forms of worship produced syncretic synergies that soon became a global sensation. Today, the Catholic Church is liveliest in Brazil. The spiritual stability produced by the symbiotic relationship has translated into social, political, and economic stability – conditions that are absent in Africa. That Brazil, a society that was built largely by slave labor is a lot more stable and prosperous than Africa, the difference here may have to do with the fact that while Africa was stripped of the foundations of its religious traditions, in Brazil the tenets of African religion were nurtured, syncretized, and used as an integral part of religious worship.

Any society that is stripped of its indigenous culture, including its religious traditions, is bound to lose the moral and spiritual compass that is integral to moral rectitude and social stability. Psychologically, spiritually,

18   G. Shepperson and T. Price, *Independent Africa*, Edinburgh, 1958, p. 163.

and morally, Africa today has lost much of the indigenous spiritual and historical values on which stable and harmonious societies are built. Africa's unsuccessful attempts to embrace modern governance systems can actually be attributed to the fact that it is attempting to build modernity over insufficiently mastered foreign (European) values. Because the duration of colonial rule was just long enough to disrupt indigenous African values, but not long enough to enable a good mastery of the new introduced values, it left behind a cultural and institutional vacuum that now poses a challenge to Africa's development. No people have ever modernized in a sociocultural vacuum. This, in the main explains why Africa remains hemmed in.

Human Rights Abuses as a Legacy of Colonial Rule

The imposition of European rule in Africa came with untold human suffering and undue destruction of the social fabric. Yet, it was possible to establish Western values in Africa without the undue and unnecessary destruction of the general fabric of traditional Africa. In the late 1800s King Leopold of Belgium colonized the territory that is presently referred to today as the Democratic Republic of Congo. The sheer destructiveness of the methods employed were mind-boggling. They went beyond the dismantling of African traditional and religious values, to the use of forced labor, firearms, torture, and genocide. In 23 years of his reign, as many as ten million Congolese were murdered. This represented about twice the population of the colonizing power, Belgium, and about half the population of Congo at the time. Ransacking and carting away Congo's natural resources was not enough. Leopold's mining foremen carried out a ruthless campaign of maiming and chopping off the limps of innocent Africans – men, women and children included. The limbs of indigenous Africans were frequently chopped off and presented to Belgian authorities as proof that Belgian foremen on the field were doing a good job pushing Africans into increased productivity. The hidden machinations of King Leopold are revealed in a letter he wrote to Belgian missionaries in 1883:

Reverend, Fathers and Dear Compatriots,

The task that is given to fulfill is very delicate and requires much tact. You will go certainly to evangelize, but your evangelization must inspire above all Belgium interests. Your principal objective in our mission in the Congo is never to teach the niggers to know God, this they know already. They speak and submit to a Mungu, one Nzambi, one Nzakomba, and what else I don't know. They know that to kill, to sleep with someone else's wife, to lie and to insult is bad. Have courage to admit it; you are not going to teach them what they know already. Your essential role is to facilitate the task of administrators and industrials, which means you will go to interpret the gospel in the way it will be the best to protect your interests in that part of the world. For these things, you have to keep watch on dis-interesting our savages from the richness that is plenty in their underground.[19]

Though by no measure close to King Leopold's genocide, the methods used by German colonial administrators to impose their rule in Africa were almost as atrocious. When the African leader of the Gogo people in East Africa made an offer of peaceful talks with the German invaders, Carl Peters, he responded instead with a fury of wholesale pillaging, plundering, and bloodletting of local Africans.[20]

The British historian, Basil Davidson, believes that Africa could have survived all of the genocide, destruction, slavery and bloodletting but "for the economic intervention of the invaders."[21] By this, Davidson is saying that the most enduring harm colonialism may have caused in Africa was the destruction of its economic base. By systematically dispossessing Africans of their land, a subsistence economy was transformed into a dependent economy, and owners of prime agricultural farmlands were transformed into landless migrant laborers. In regions of Africa where Europeans settled, there was an immediate drive to carve out large regions of fertile lands within which Africans could no longer farm or live, except as laborers. Well known examples included South Africa, Zimbabwe, Kenya, and Algeria. During the Apartheid regime in South Africa, the majority-black population which made up 87% of the population was forced to live on 13% of the land – much of it barren. In Algeria, prior to the coming of the French, most of the country's fertile lands was used in the production of grain that was used for domestic consumption. These lands were seized by French colonialists and transformed into vineyards. It did not matter to the French that Algerian cultural and religious norms forbade the production, sale, and consumption of alcohol. The same colonial power that was promoting Christianity in sub-Sahara Africa and accusing them of paganistic rituals was here promoting the production of alcohol in a country whose religious values saw the consumption of alcohol as a paganistic practice reserved for infidels. It is obvious that colonial rule was on a self-declared mission to destroy every traditional value that it met

---

19   http://docslide.us/documents/letter-leopold-ii-to-colonial-missionaries.html (Accessed 03/15/2016).
20   Davidson, p. 38-42.
21   Davidson, p. 39.

in Africa. In Algeria, the expropriation of farmland rendered more than half a million Algerian families landless and unemployed. Many were forced to become wage-earners in the very European plantations that confiscated their lands. Even the African who would rather not work for the European expropriator of his land had no choice. All adult citizens were forced to pay taxes, and the only accepted currency the currency imposed by the colonial ruler. It was only by joining the wage economy that they could earn the meager wages that were needed to pay the mandated taxes. Thus, whether they liked it or not, all adults were forced to work. The alternative for not paying taxes was prison sentence.

Prior to the coming of Europeans, traditional subsistence economies met the overall needs of Africans. Chronic famine of the type that is common in Africa today was unknown. That a continent that was self-sufficient and self-sustaining in the past is now unable to feed itself, can only but be attributed to the deliberate measures that European colonial powers took to dismantle and transform Africa's traditional economy into an economy that produced not for Africans but for Europeans. This explains why much of what is produced in Africa is not consumed in Africa, and much of what is consumed in Africa is not produced in Africa. Western reporters are often blamed for reporting mainly negative stories on Africa. But in keeping with the "truth in reporting" ethics of their profession, their reporting accurately reflects the everyday reality that is lived in Africa. What may be missing at the end of their news reports is a concluding statement that says, "the realities that I just reported are part of the legacy that European powers left behind in Africa." The forced transformation of any landed people into a landless people anywhere in the world would inevitably lead to the crises that African is experiencing.

Perceptions of the Modern State System in Africa

Europeans came in on a supposedly "civilizing mission," and instead of instituting a governance system that was civilized and enhancing to individual and group freedoms, they forcible imposed centralized police states that robbed Africans of their dignity, autonomy and the freedom to govern themselves at the decentralized clan and tribal levels that defined precolonial political structures.

Today, the typical state in Africa is in reality a multinational state. Much of precolonial Africa was composed of stateless nations. With colonial conquest came the forced imposition of the modern state system. The fragile and failing states that we see in Africa today are fragile and failing because they were created not from the bottom-up, but from the top-down. The state of Nigeria was established not by the member nations which make up Nigeria (the Hausas, Ibos, Yorubas and others), but by Britain. This explains why ethnic affinity in Nigeria is stronger than national affinity. It is also the reason why in Somalia greater allegiance is given to the clan than to the central Somali state.

In Somalia as elsewhere in Africa, the modern state system in Africa is seen a supranational institution that was superimposed on the various independent and self-sufficing clans that were in place prior to the forcible imposition of European rule. The state as a concept implies order. Instead of producing order in Africa, the modern state system produced challenges to order. Many of Africa's ills – from warlordism to poverty, corruption and irredentism - are attempts at rejecting this supranational institution. J. Peter Pham notes that as much as in Iraq, the Somali state is "a modern invention ... in which disparate clans and regions have long been held together by brute force."[22]

Following the collapse of the modern state system in Somalia, the outside world rushed to describe Somalia as a failed state. Somalis however do not see themselves as a failed state. Indeed, what the international community referred to in the 1990s as warlords were actually clan and tribal rulers fighting to reclaim the precolonial clan self-rule that governed them prior to the forced imposition of the centralized modern state. Prior to the European imposition of the supranational state structure, Somalia was governed by clan heads. Government rule was direct, personal and close to the people. With the introduction of the modern state system came a sense of alienation and estrangement. Citizens now saw themselves governed by a complex mix of commoners that are called president, parliamentarian, bureaucrat. For the president and parliamentarian who now made governing policies, their right to rule was determined not by birth, but by a ballot. For a traditional society accustomed to the belief that rulers are born, not elected, the idea of casting pieces of papers called "ballots" into a box to select leaders was laughable. The Somali Civil War can therefore be seen as an organized and determined effort to get rid of this rather alienating modern state system and return the country to the clan rule that kept Somalia stable and self-sufficient prior to European colonization. While the outside world saw Somalia as a failed state, Somali clans saw the fight to rid themselves of a national government as victorious struggle. In other words, Somali clans want the central state in Somalia to fail.

Somalis genuinely believe that social stability and group wellbeing is better guaranteed under clan rule than under a centralized modern state system. A quick comparison of social conditions in Somalia, which has since the early 1990s been largely under clan rule, and the Democratic Republic

---

22 Pham, J. Peter. "Resurrecting Somalia." *The National Interest*, January 12, 2007: http://www.nationalinterest.org/Article.aspx?id=13434

of Congo (DRC), which is currently under centralized national rule will help shed some light to the Somali viewpoint. Both countries have experienced protracted civil wars, so we are here comparing apples to apples. In Somalia where the state completely failed and where there was no effective national government, the crime rate, including sexual assault against women actually declined. In the Democratic Republic of Congo, however, a country that has a national government and functioning state, the rate of sexual assault on women went up. One would have expected more cases of sexual assault against women in Somalia where there is no central government. That the rate of sexual assaults in Somalia is lower than in the Democratic Republic of Congo gives some credence to the Somali belief that security and wellbeing were better guaranteed under decentralized/clan rule than under the centralized rule of the Eurocentric state structure that we see in the Democratic Republic of Congo today.

Looking at it from another perspective, we can argue that while the traditional chiefs and kings that ruled precolonial DRC were displaced by appointed government bureaucrats in colonial and post-colonial times, Somalia somehow still had clan leaders and local clan courts working to enforce law and order. For them, such a decentralized governance structure is seen as a more effective deterrence to rapists than the centralized structure that European colonial powers imposed on them.

For Somalia as for most of Africa, not only is the modern state system abstract, it is restraining. It is restraining of the rights and freedoms that Africans had prior to the superimposition of the new Eurocentric state system. As indicated above, prior to the imposition of the modern state system, government rule was personal. Citizens knew their rulers and their rulers knew their subjects. They spoke the same language and practiced the same customs. Then came the modern state, with a ruler and a collection of elected and appointed officials, some of whom were from different and possibly competing clans. The officials lived and governed from a national capital that is both distant and impersonal. Monopoly of power and the coercive law enforcement that is inherent in the Eurocentric state system further adds to the perception that the new state system is restraining. Thus, with respect to Somalia, what the West sees as anarchy or failed state, Somalis see as freedom from a system that forcibly transferred power away from their traditional rulers to a distant, abstract and impersonal supranational system that is called "the state."

The lessons to take home from the Somali civil war are that: 1) no lasting solution to the country's problems can be imposed from the top-down; 2) the ultimate breakthrough in a fratricidal civil war comes not from the use of hard power, but from the use of soft power. Eventually, the solution to Somali problems will have to come from the Somalis themselves. Unlike the central state system that was imposed from the top-down, the Somalis will have the opportunity to establish a government that has the imprint and backing of internal stakeholders such as clan heads and warlords.

No one is more critical of the disruptive legacy of European colonialism in Africa than Sheila McCoy, who argues in *The African Paradox: The Tribalist Implications of the Colonial Paradox* that:

> Colonialism has played a crucial role in the underdevelopment and decay of the nations of sub-Sahara Africa... Colonial nations, it has been shown, made an effort to protect their own interests and national security by creating within Africa a patchwork of nation-states that seemed to have been drawn without consideration for existing cultural and linguistic patterns of settlement... These boundaries were, in all likelihood, intended to provoke intra-continental conflict... Colonizing powers understood that there is always the potential for conflict when imperialistic missions are undertaken. But if the powerless and conquered peoples can be made to fight among themselves, they are considerably less likely to turn their collective efforts against their oppressors. Such was the reasoning of colonial powers... Therefore, it is apparent that European colonialism most certainly contributed to the fact that African nations lag behind most others in terms of development.[23]

McCoy goes on to say that "one could cite countless examples of tribal conflicts that have been generated by the divisions that continue to be maintained today. These struggles have had so much of an effect on the underdevelopment of African nations as a result of the economic limitations imposed by colonialism."[24]

National authority is necessary in the building and maintenance of a nation-state, but national authority from colonial times to present day Africa has not always served the interest of Africans. Some national governments were outrightly hostile to the interests of their citizens. To prevent the "Somali syndrome," therefore, national leaders in Africa today will need to work to bring government closer to their citizens. This certainly will help prevent a nostalgic re-embrace of the clan rule that governed Africa prior to the forcible imposition of the modern state system.

---

23   Shiela McCoy, The African Paradox: The Tribalist Implications of the Colonial Paradox: www.drake.edu.artsci.PolSci/ssjrnl/2001.mccoy.html (accessed 8/3/202)
24   Ibid

Reckoning with Five Hundred Years of Hemorrhaging

In chapter five, we made brief mention of the brain-drain crisis that has caused and continues to cause the loss of Africa's youth and intellectual talent to emigration. We lamented the fact that African rulers see their intellectual resources not as assets, but as a potential threat to their rule. The loss of African skills to the outside world is not just a contemporary phenomenon; it is a phenomenon that has been going on for more than 500 years. African scholars frequently point to the ongoing brain-drain as one of the main reasons why, since gaining independence, Africa has not been able to get back on its feet. Millions of African intellectuals, including PhDs, MDs, engineers, lawyers, pharmacists, nurses, entrepreneurs, school-teachers are living and working outside the African continent. Any region of the world that hemorrhages this much in human talent will find it difficult, if not impossible to develop economically.

Today, the loss of Africa's human capital to the outside world has gone beyond brain-draining to what can be appropriately described as brain hemorrhaging. No one seems to know how to stop it. The abolition of slavery in the 19th century gave some hope that the hemorrhaging had stopped. Not before long, slavery was replaced with colonial rule. And as soon as new human capital re-developed in Africa, the outside world quickly snatched it away and the hemorrhaging started all over again. As Africa begins the second half of its first century of independence and self-rule, a growing number of its scientists and healthcare professionals are abandoning the continent and emigrating to live and work outside the continent. It is a trend not much different from the involuntary emigration that forcibly removed Africans from the continent during the slave era. Indeed, throughout five hundred years of Africa's interaction with the outside world, there has been a continuous one-directional outflow of its human and material resources. No other continent can suffer this much hemorrhaging for this long and still have any life left.

Hypothetically, had aliens somehow landed on the shores of the United States and abducted and taken away such great minds as George Washington, Thomas Jefferson, Abraham Lincoln, Alexander Bell, Andrew Carnegie, Albert Einstein, Henry Ford, the Wright Brothers, Bill Gates, Steve Jobs, Jeff Bezos, Franklin Roosevelt, Martin Luther King, or Barack Obama, it is doubtful that America would be the paragon of stability and prosperity that it is today. Such abductions would certainly have deprived America of the creative talents that have contributed to making it a great nation. But this is exactly what the outside world did to Africa. It stripped Africa of the human and material resources that could and would have made historic political and scientific contributions to the continent's development. Scientists who study human reproduction inform us that our genes are passed down from

150

our forebears. On the basis of this scientific assumption one can argue that in forcibly abducting and taking away the forebears of Washington Carver, Charles Drew, Martin Luther King, Frederick Douglas, W.E.B. Dubois out of Africa, Africa was deprived of the lasting contributions that these creative geniuses would have made to the development of Africa. As elaborated above, should some foreign power (in Africa's case, they were several powers) invade the U.S. today and forcibly take away a good percentage of its healthy 18 to 40-year olds, it will certainly have an adverse impact on the American economy both now and in years to come.

The hemorrhaging of Africa continues to this day not just from brain-drain, but in various forms of marketable talents. Besides the more than 30% professionals that leave the continent every year[25], African athletes who excel in international competitions are often lured and taken away by professional leagues in the wealthier countries of the north. Following Akeem Olajuwon's basketball performance in the early 1980s, a bevy of basketball recruiters descended on Africa in search of six and seven feet-tall potential basketball players. At the end of every Olympic or World Cup soccer competition, African countries are raided by recruiters from the wealthier countries of the north, in search of athletic talent to take back home to Europe, Asia and North America. Unlike in earlier times when they came to launch slave raids, this time they are coming with checkbooks. If after every international competition the likes of Lebron James, Michael Jordan, and Tiger Woods are recruited and taken away by much wealthier countries, it would be difficult to develop an industry of professional sports in the United States. Besides the human aspect, equally devastating to Africa's development is the material aspect.

Back to our fable with the aliens, imagine that aliens descend on the United States and find Fort Knox, where America's gold reserves are stored; Texas and Alaska, where America has its oil reserves; Florida, where America's citrus fruits are grown; Silicon Valley, where America's advanced technologies are developed; and Detroit where America manufactures its automobiles. They take control of these resources and redirect them to producing goods that are consumed primarily by the alien homeland. Profits generated are repatriated to the alien homeland. Should the governor of any of the states where these resources are located attempt to restrict or interfere with the interests of the aliens, he is eliminated by a coup organized through the covert action of alien intelligence services. While this scenario may depict what a hypothetical alien civilization could do to America and to America's economy, it is actually a reality that Africa has experienced and continues to experience.

---

25 *International Herald Tribune*, 10/18/01, p.7.

On the often-asked question that how could a continent that is so richly endowed with natural resources also be the poorest continent in the world, an appropriate answer would be that much of Africa's vital natural resources are neither owned nor controlled by Africans. Just as hypothetical aliens took over and redirected America's farmlands to producing for alien consumption, the most fertile farmlands in Africa are used not for production that feeds Africa, but for production that feeds the outside world.

Could Colonialism Have been Slavery by Another Name?

To address this question, let's begin by taking a quick glance at the characteristics of the two institutions – slavery and colonialism. Common to both institutions were ownership, forced labor, and master-servant relationship. With colonialism, the European enjoyed even greater ownership. Not only did he not own the individuals who provided him with cheap labor, he owned the land, the minerals and the raw materials. With chattel slavery, he had to pay to purchase the slave, and was responsible for providing for the slave's welfare.

Whether exploited in one's native land or shipped away to be exploited in a distant land, it all adds to slavery. This makes slavery and colonialism two sides of the same coin. Whether it was the callous maiming of Congolese indigenes by the Belgians, or the lynching of African Americans in the American South, colonialism was as much slavery as slavery was colonialism. Comparing the two systems in Africa, a Portuguese government official actually wrote that colonialism in Angola was "in some ways worse than slavery. Under slavery, after all, the native is bought as an animal: his owner prefers him to remain as fit as a horse or an ox. Yet here (in Africa) the native is not bought - he is hired from the state, although he is called a free man. And his employer cares little if he sickens or dies, once he is working, because when he sickens or dies his employer will simply ask for another."[26]

Equally common to both slavery and colonial rule was the use of forced labor. Although the practice was most dehumanizing in the Central African colonies of Angola and Congo, forced labor was a practice common to all colonial powers. Even the Boer settlers of South Africa were "accustomed to regarding Africans as natural slaves."[27] The same Europeans who were forcibly shipping Africans as slave labor to the New World also controlled the economies of Africa, where they instituted forced labor. Just as they depended on slave labor in the New World, they depended on forced labor in colonial Africa.

The question then is that, if these two terribly dehumanizing institutions

---

26   Basil Davidson, *The African Awakening*, London, 1955, p. 204.
27   Davidson, 2004, p. 41.

had the same impact, why then was one abandoned in favor of the other? Why would a country such as Britain, whose parliament mounted a relentless campaign for an international ban against slavery and whose navy patrolled the high seas to police the ban, take part in the colonial enterprise? Why would France, whose national motto celebrated, *"liberté, fraternité, égalité"* (liberty, fraternity, equality) take part in an enterprise that denied *liberté, fraternité* and *égalité* to Africans? Britain, France and other European powers were aware of the genocidal atrocity that King Leopold carried out against the people of Congo. Why did Britain, the country that found the inhumanity of slavery so abhorrent that it enforced a ban against, refuse to act to stop an even more abhorrent acts of inhumanity in Congo? The answer may have to do with the historical rivalry that existed among European nations at the time. As Basil Davidson puts it, the European had been conditioned by centuries of internecine competition to seizing and expropriating whatever was not hers, wherever she could find it. It was evidenced in her occupation of Africa, the Americas and Australia.[28] Among European states, there has always been the latent fear of falling behind or of being overtaken by other European rivals. This was not the case in precolonial Africa where relations among sovereignties were characterized more by a culture of cooperation than by a culture of competition. Small monarchies coexisted side by side with large monarchies, without fear or concern of annexation or invasion. The large Ashanti, Bakongo, Yoruba, Zulu kingdoms could very well have expanded their kingdoms by conquering and ruling over the smaller clans that were on their peripheries. They however did not. Had they done so, they possibly would have developed an aggressive and expansionist spirit that would have been similar to the spirit of rivalry and competition that reigned in Europe. This would no doubt have made the task of the European colonizer difficult.

Although China is credited with inventing the gunpowder (one of the primary instruments used in Western imperial expansion) and was until the fifteenth century more technologically advanced than much of the rest of the world, it expressed no imperial ambitions in Africa. Apparently, the absence of the element of internal rivalry and competition, along with its abundant domestic wealth caused China to become somewhat complacent. Like the large and rich kingdoms of Africa, China was territorially so vast and so wealthy that it saw no need for the discovery and colonization of territories and resources in distant lands. Had China been a resource-poor state, and had it had a history of intra-regional rivalry, it certainly would have aggressively gone foraging for wealth in distant parts of the world. China would have no doubt colonized Africa long before Europeans got there, and

---

28 Davidson, 2004, p. 58

World War I would have likely broken out between China and Europe rather than between Germany and the rest of imperial Europe.

The first historical account of diplomatic contact between Africa and China was in 1421-1422. Among the prized items that were sent as gifts to the Chinese Emperor were a giraffe, a zebra, and an oryx.[29] Described by the Chinese press as a "celestial horse," the giraffe was welcomed by the Chinese Emperor in a stately ceremony. China was not tempted by the abundance of the "celestial horses" and Africa's other natural resources to move in and colonize the continent. Following a similar exchange of gifts between the Portuguese king and Queen Nzinga of the Bakongos (today's Angola) in the 15th century, the king of Portugal moved to authorize the enslavement and trans-Atlantic shipment of Angolans to the New World. A relationship that started out friendly, equal and diplomatic was soon turned into a relationship of prey and predator.

Despite the handful of empires that were in pre-colonial Africa, the political system in much of the rest of the continent remained decentralized and autonomous. Africans were essentially governed by clan heads, village and tribal chiefs. Largely a subsistence economy, and absent major security threats, they had no need for a bureaucracy or a standing army. Not having a standing army, a bureaucracy or a centralized political system meant that Africans were not in a position to quickly mobilize to defend themselves against slave raiders and colonial invaders. A decentralized and autonomous political system also meant that a covetous foreign enemy could come in initially as a friend and before long, morph into an occupier. This was exactly the strategy that Europeans used in Africa.

The question that begs for an answer here is that why did a relationship that started out equal and friendly quickly turn into a relationship of colonized and colonizer? Here once more, the element of intra-continental rivalry and competition provides a basis for our analysis. Had the Portuguese not rushed to lay claim on Angola, some other European country would have done it. Had China had regional competitors, and had it been a nation with no natural resources, she too could have done exactly what the competing European nations did – move to lay claim and colonial control over the region of Africa that gave her the "celestial horse" in 1415. Such control could possibly have evolved into an institution of slavery, with Africans enslaved and taken away to China rather than to the Americas – assuming of course that China was a wilderness and there was need for their labor there.

Whether it was carried out by the Chinese or by Europeans, colonialism

---

29   New World Encyclopaedia: Zheng He, http://www.newworldencyclopedia.org/entry/ Zheng_He (accessed December 18, 2011). http://www.blackjadeworld.com/article2_2. html (accessed December 18, 2011)

and slavery did not need to be as dehumanizing and as militaristic as it was. The brutality and inhumanity with which Belgium's King Leopold and Britain's Cecil Rhodes administered their colonial enterprises in Africa was totally unwarranted. The dictatorship that characterized governance in postcolonial Africa was undoubtedly a legacy of the political culture that was instituted by European colonial rule. As Mobutu continued with King Leopold's genocidal rule in the Congo, Mugabe provided continuity to Cecil Rhodes' brutish rule in Southern Africa. In all, Zimbabwe's Robert Mugabe, Zaire's Mubutu, Uganda's Idi Amin, Central Africa's Jean-Bedel Bokassa and Cameroon's Biya were diligent students of the European colonizer. Their atrocities were textbook replicas of Cecil Rhodes' and King Leopold's atrocities. Had European colonial rulers instilled a culture of democracy and humanism in Africa, it could have served as a model of good governance for the Mugabes, the Mobutus, the Amins, the Bokassas and the Biyas. As much as the West taunts the ideals of democracy today, when it controlled Africa and had the opportunity to implement these ideals, it failed to do so. Today, it is the first to criticize African rulers for not implementing democratic ideals.

At independence, Africans were for the first time faced with managing a new set of institutions and a new form of governance for which they had no prior exposure. Within the first few years of their establishment, the institutions disintegrated and Africans fell back to the oppressive forms of governance they were exposed to by European colonizers. In a rather concerted manner, almost every country on the continent abandoned multiparty rule and embraced one-party dictatorships. Today, as we decry the lack of a democratic culture in Africa, we must go further and decry the absence of democratic culture in colonial times, and the intolerance of the British, Belgian and French to such a culture when they governed Africa. Had colonialism, which was justified by European powers as a "civilizing mission," introduced the ideals of democracy in Africa, these ideals would have made it impossible for Nigeria's Abacha, Uganda's Idi Amin, Central Africa's Bokassa, Congo/Zaire's Mobutu, Zimbabwe's Mugabe and other African despots to come to power.

Even as these despots came to power, and despite their abuses, they continued to receive support and honorary endorsement from Western institutions that really ought to have known better. Edinburgh University, one of Britain's top universities, was one of such institutions. In 1984 it awarded an honorary degree to Zimbabwe's Robert Mugabe, only to vote in June 2007, 23 years later, to revoke it.[30] The decision to grant Mugabe the degree was actually made two years earlier, in 1982, when Mugabe had

---

30 *The Guardian*, Edinburgh leads moves to axe Mugabe honours, http://www.theguardian.com/world/2007/jun/07/highereducation.zimbabwe (Accessed 12/8/2015)

only been in power for two years. Honorary degrees are generally granted only after a careful and systematic assessment of a nominee's long-time track record or life's work. Mugabe came to office in 1980, which means he had only been in office for two years. Why had Edinburgh University been in a rush to grant Mugabe an honorary degree? What track record had he established in two years that made the university think that he deserved an honorary degree? Zimbabwe was one of Britain's major client state. How could one of Britain's best universities not have been aware of human rights abuses that the Mugabe regime had committed in that country? That Edinburgh University turned around 23 years later to revoke the degree raises a host of questions that directly impugn on the reputation of the university and on the honorary degree granting process. Was the honorary degree revoked because the abuses Mugabe committed between 1984 and 2007 were more directly against British interests? And would the expropriation of farmland from white farmers be included in those abuses? When juxtaposed, which abuses were more egregious – the pre-1982 human rights abuses that included the taking away of human lives or the post-1984 human rights abuses that included the seizure of farmlands?

At yet another Western institution of higher education, this time an institution across the Atlantic, a similar decision was made to grant Robert Mugabe an honorary degree. Awarded in 1986 by the university of Massachusetts Amherst, the University too later voted on June 12, 2008 to rescind it.[31]

Colonized by Democracies, Totalitarian by Rule

Culturally and historically, Africa was ruled for many years by kings, chiefs and clan heads. For the continent as a whole therefore, democracy is a relatively new concept. Indeed, for many, Western institutions of democracy remain an abstraction. It was not until in the early 1960s, and again the early 1990s that African states began genuine attempts at adopting multi-party democratic reforms. Prior to that, almost all of them were autocratic one-party states. During the Cold War, the two superpowers worked actively against the democratization of Africa. Concerned with the promotion of their interests and the imposition of their ideology, they provided material support to African leaders that autocratically defended these interests. It is thus a continent that has gone from a tradition of rule by monarchies, to rule by imperial autocracies, to rule by post-colonial autocracies. This makes Africa's experiment with democracy an experiment by "trial and error." Trial and error here means the lack of prior experience. More often

---

31 University World News, US: Massachusetts revokes Mugabe's honorary degree, http://www.universityworldnews.com/article.php?story=20080620090158659 (Accessed 12/8/2015)

than not, experiments that are done by trial and error (that is, with no prior experience) end up failing. No doubt therefore that the democratic attempts in Africa has so far been a failure.

At the wake of the independence of African states, there was optimism among Western liberal scholars that if African economic and political structures were modeled after Western systems, this would lead to rapid economic development. What these scholars failed to realize was that what the departing colonial powers left behind at independence were political and economic structures that were modeled after the autocratic systems of the Soviet-leaning Eastern bloc states. This was why when the Soviet Union and the Eastern bloc one-party dictatorships collapsed in the early 1990s, the shock waves sent Africa's one-party dictatorships collapsing too. Indeed, it was not until after the collapse of the Soviet Union that the winds of change swept through Africa, igniting a vocal civil society that was determined to push for democratic reforms.

On looking back, a fundamental question that remains unanswered about Africa is that why were political systems that were designed and put in place by the West end up looking more like the state-controlled totalitarian systems of the Eastern bloc states? In the fifty yearlong East/West rivalry, the objective of each side was to have Africa shaped in their ideological image. Throughout the colonial period, the West had direct control of Africa for close to a century. Had the West used this period to develop democratic rule and free market economies in Africa, it would not have had to face-off with the Communist East in an ideological Cold War campaign to win the hearts of Africans.

The reality historically is that the institutions that govern Africa today were virtual makeshift institutions that were hurriedly put in place on the eve of Europe's departure from the continent. In many ways, they were put in place as an afterthought. At independence, Africans were made to rely on strong leaders rather than on strong institutions because the departing colonial powers needed strong men to continue their legacy in promoting autocratic order (and not democracy). Dictators such as Zaire's Mobutu Sese Seko, Uganda's Idi Amin, Central Africa's Bendel Bokassa, Cameroon's Ahmadou Ahidjo and Paul Biya, Gabon's Omar Bongo, Burkina Faso's Blaise Compaore, and Egypt's Hosni Mubarak were put in power not so much because of their ability to govern, but because of their ability to tame the population, forcibly instill order, and ruthlessly deal with potential threats against the interests of the departed colonial powers. Under colonial rule, elected legislatures or presidencies were unknown. Because they were established as an afterthought, the institutions were weak, and because they were weak, they quickly gave way to the cultivation of personality cults. Had colonial rule been democratic and had its institutions been established early on, not only would they have had time to better prepare Africans for independence, it would have been difficult, if not impossible, for Africa's strong men to take advantage of these institutions.

Expressing his distaste for African dictators, United States President Barack Obama pointedly asserted during his first official visit to Africa in 2010 that "Africa doesn't need strongmen, it needs strong institutions."[32] Barely two years after Obama's call for strong institutions, in a stark reminder of the resilience of the stranglehold that strongman rule has had on the continent, two of Africa's strongmen, Muammar Gaddafi and Laurent Gbagbo, sought unsuccessfully to reassert their strongmen rule. This may have been an indication that Obama's call for "strong institutions" may have come a little bit too late. It is a call that should have come in colonial times, when Europeans were on the ground in Africa, building the legacy that now influences governance on the continent today.

At independence, what Africa needed was the full-scale embrace of liberalism. Unfortunately, colonial rule did little to prepare and place Africa on this path. In Africa, European colonial powers made sure that Africans were not exposed to John Locke's ideas of equality, natural rights and consent of the governed. In the administration of their African colonies, they adopted the Hobbesian model of an all-powerful Leviathan. Not knowing any better, it was the form of government that African rulers rushed to embrace at independence. No doubt therefore that the continent is characterized more by "strong men" rather than by "strong institutions." Had Africans been as exposed to Locke's ideas as colonial Americans were, they too would have undoubtedly gone on to build "strong institutions" just as was the case in the United States.

The values that Africa inherited from its European colonizers – harsh authoritarianism, state ownership, and absence of the rule of law – guided its post-colonial governance structures. This disregard for the rule of law began in colonial times, when colonial administrators made it known that native Africans had no legal rights that deserved to be respected. Instead of providing security and combating crime, the colonial police assisted the state in seizing land and provided the force needed to enforce the property rights of minority white settlers.[33] Not only were many of the resources that were owned and controlled by colonial powers forcibly seized in disregard of the due process rights of property owners, the institutionalized system of forced labor again forced the expropriated property owners to work for

---

32   White House Press Release, Remarks by the President to the Ghanaian Parliament, July 11, 2009, https://www.whitehouse.gov/the-press-office/remarks-president-ghanaian-parliament; (accessed 8/14/2011)

33   Mbaku, J. and Kimennyi M., Rent Seeking and Policing in Africa, *Indian Journal of Social Science* 8(3):225-250.

their colonial expropriators. If this is the legal order that Africans inherited from the colonial administration, it is no wonder therefore that at independence, they did not know any better. Looking back, it is hard to think that the political institutions that are in Africa today were actually put in place by the democratic governments of the West. Why would a democratic parent produce an offspring that has no identifiable democratic trait? In African culture, when a child fails, society wants to know who the parent of that child is. And when a child succeeds, there is curiosity over who the parent of the child is. Since we are dealing here with the failure of Africa, our task is to find out who the colonial parents are, and have them share blame for the continent's weak, fragile and failing states.

For many critiques of European colonial rule in Africa, African political systems were purposefully designed to be centralized and authoritarian. Only by so structuring Africa would it best serve the economic and political interests of the European colonizer. When it comes to efficiency in governing, social scientists overwhelmingly point to the centralized one-party regimes that were established by the Soviet Union and its Eastern bloc states. By virtue of their colonial ties, African states were at independence considered European satellite states. It is hard to understand why a Western world that was fighting to prevent communism from gaining grounds in Africa would at the same time allow its satellite states on the continent to adopt totalitarian one-party political structures. Such a contradiction puts to serious doubt current Western rhetorical concerns about promoting democracy in Africa. During the fifty-year ideological rivalry between the East and the West over whose political system was better for the Third World, Europe and the United States had a golden opportunity to push for the institution of genuine democracy in Africa. They failed to do so. As a result, the winds of the democratic reforms that ended the state-controlled one-party systems in Africa wounded up coming from the totalitarian East rather than from the democratic West.

The state-controlled one-party systems that came to power in Africa in the 1960s were not much different from the state-controlled one-party states that came to power in Cuba in 1960. While the West aggressively campaigned against Cuba's one-party state, it acquiesced, propped and actively promoted political and economic ties with Africa's one-party states. The most incomprehensible was Western support for Mobutu's one-party fascist state in Zaire. Here, the West masterminded a coup that forcibly removed the country's democratically elected government (the government of Patrice Lumumba), replacing it with a corrupt fascist dictator. This for a long time ended aspirations of democratic rule in the Democratic Republic of Congo. On assuming power, Mobutu faithfully maintained ties with the West, while actively disparaging Western culture and Western dress codes.

On return from a state visit to China in the early 1970s, Mobutu passed a law banning the baptism of children, Western names, Western-style attires, including ties for men and pants for women.[34] He set the example himself by getting rid of his own Western first name, Joseph; leaving him only with his African names – Mobutu Sese Seko Koko Ngbendu Wa Za Banga. Men who were caught wearing Western suits and women caught wearing pants or Western dresses were jailed.

On November 30, 1973, Mobutu confiscated all foreign businesses by nationalizing the private sector.[35] Despite his anti-Western conduct, Mobutu remained actively courted, supported and protected by Western powers. This was certainly a succinct expression of Lord Palmerston's assertion that in international affairs there are no permanent friends or allies, there are only permanent interests.[36] Culturally, Castro never campaigned against Western names or Western dress codes, so some could say that Mobutu was actually more anti-West than Cuba's Fidel Castro. Yet, as the West was actively campaigning to get rid of Cuba's Fidel Castro, it was actively supporting Congo/Zaire's Mobutu.

The relationship between the collapse of the Eastern bloc states and the beginning of democratic reforms in Africa remains so far unclear. What is clear however is that when future historians shall sit down to retrace the source of modern democracy in Africa, it is probable that they will trace it not so much to the West, but to the collapse of communist bloc states. In the era of the African wars for independence and freedom, the most sympathetic supporters were not from the freedom-loving Western bloc states, they were the communist-leaning Eastern bloc states. They went beyond verbal criticism of European colonial rule in Africa to providing material and diplomatic support to African struggle for freedom. Western democracies worked aggressively to deny Africa these freedoms. For example, up until the early 1990s, the West was opposed to democracy and majority rule in South Africa. Before that, the United States was opposed to the independence of Angola, Mozambique, Cape Verde and Guinea Bissau. The West went as far as to provide NATO's support to Portugal, as Portugal was fighting to deny independence to Cape Verde and Guinea Bissau – two tiny countries in Africa that were simply demanding to be allowed the right to enjoy the

34 Mobutu Sese Seko Biography, (accessed 11/2/2016) http://www.imdb.com/name/
    nm0782891/bio
35 Alex Thomson, *An Introduction to African Politics*, 3rd edition, New York: Routledge,
    2011, p. 95
36 Erik Gartzke and Alex Weisiger, *Permanent Friends, Dynamic Difference and the Demo-
    cratic Peace, International* Relations Quarterly, International Studies Quarterly (2012)
    1–15

very freedom that is enjoyed in the West.[37]

In South and Southern Africa, the West refused to give support to countries that were fighting for freedom and democracy. The military and logistical support the anti-apartheid movement received came not from the West, but from Eastern bloc states. The West actively allied with, and provided strategic military support (in violation of UN sanctions) to the fascist Apartheid regime that was opposed to freedom and democratic rule in South Africa. The support included technical assistance to South Africa's nuclear weapons program – assistance that violated the nuclear non-proliferation treaty. It took a determined and relentless grassroots campaign (marches, letter-writing, public demonstrations, hunger strikes, and civil disobedience) for the West to finally agree to withdraw its public and private investments in Apartheid South Africa.

Following the collapse of the Apartheid regime, attempts by the United States to compel South Africa's first democratically elected President, Nelson Mandela, to disassociate himself from Cuba and Libya met with spontaneous rebuff from the legendary freedom fighter. Mandela publicly gave credit to Cuba and Libya for helping provide his country with the support that eventually brought freedom to South Africa.

Colonialism's Failure to Establish a Civil Society

That the winds of democracy came not from the West but from the East has cast a cloud of doubt on Western pretensions over the promotion of freedom and democracy as a foreign policy priority. The precondition for effective democratic governance is a civil society. The most damaging legacy of colonial rule in Africa was the creation of the state (the formal institutions of power within the African political system) without the creation of a countervailing civil society. John W. Harbeson believes that civil society constitutes the "missing key" in the building of viable democratic institutions in Africa.[38] The reality is that, beyond the pacifying institutions of Christian missionaries, it was not in the interest of the West to promote the establishment civil society in Africa. As institutions that preached the virtues of obedience, submission, and delayed gratification for the hereafter, churches and various missionary institutions were there not to serve the interest of the oppressed but to advance the agenda of the oppressor. Actually, the people who needed religious teaching were the people who were using inhumane means to covet and take by force, that which did not belong to them. The party which needed conversion into the Christian

---

37 Adriano Moreira, *Portugal's Stand in Africa*, New York, 1962, p. vi.
38 John W. Harbeson, Donald Rothchild, and Naomi Chazan, eds., *Civil Society and the State in Africa*, Boulder: Lynne Rienner, 1994, p. 1.

teachings of "love thy neighbor as thyself" were not Africans but the people who brazenly violated the 10th commandment's edict against coveting thy neighbor's house.

Colonialism's Failure to Establish Markets for European Manufactures

The two driving forces behind the European colonization of Africa were the quest for markets for raw materials and for European manufactures. While Europe succeeded in securing Africa as a market for the supply of raw materials, it failed to see Africa as a potential market for the sale of its manufactures. It failed because its colonial policies were based uniquely on a zero sum calculus. Compared to its European counterparts, the U.S. adopted a mutually beneficial strategy with the developing economies that were under its hegemony. In Taiwan, South Korea, Indonesia, Singapore, and the Philippines, the U.S. promoted the development of an economic middle class that today serves not only as a market for U.S. manufactures, but as off-shore producers of goods and services for the American market. Taking advantage of labor rates in Asia and Latin America, the U.S. developed off-shore industries for the manufacture and sale of consumer goods. This contributed to the creation of the S.E. Asian Tigers. Not only do these satellite regions serve as processors of American consumer goods, they also serve as markets for the sale of these goods. Following in the American model is China's careful stratification of its trade policies in Africa. China sees Africa not just as a source of raw materials, but as a promising market for its manufactures.

Britain, France, Spain and Portugal's colonial policies failed to establish an industrial base in Africa. Even at the height of rising labor costs in Europe, some of which produced economic recessions, European states did not consider moving their labor-intensive industries to Africa to take advantage of the region's cheap labor. While much of America's clothing and footwear were as early as in the 1970s produced at offshore factories in Latin America and Asia, Europe continued to have its basic consumer goods produced in Europe. Not only did Europe fail to build factories for the processing of European consumer goods in Africa, it refused even to allow for the semi-processing of Africa's raw materials on the continent. As a result, much of Africa's raw materials, including bulk items such as timber, are to this day extracted and exported in their raw form - robbing Africans of basic employment opportunities.

Had Europeans directed their *mission civilizatrice* not solely at exploiting Africa, but at also developing a viable economic middle class in Africa, the economies of both Africa and Europe would be better off today. Today, the African middle class is both too small and too impoverished to constitute

162

a sizeable market for European manufactures. This left a void that China has stepped in to fill. Quick to see Africa as market for raw materials and for consumer goods, it today provides consumer goods that are cheap and readily affordable to Africans. Apparently, Europe's win/lose colonial strategy has undoubtedly returned to hurt Europe's competitiveness in the African market.

The Deleterious Role of International Financial Institutions

The record of international financial institutions in Africa is not impressive. As a precondition to receiving loans from international financial institutions, the IMF and the World Bank frequently recommend reductions in force, which translates to layoffs in the civil service. On the view that the private sector is more efficient in the allocation of resources, African governments were often advised to allow market forces determine the management of their economies. What this view failed to make clear was that colonial rule left behind no viable private sector in Africa. In a region where illiteracy and unemployment are high, capital and entrepreneurship lacking, any prescription for privatization is misguided and irresponsible. World Bank and IMF recommendations for the privatization of African economies failed to explain why many institutions in the West, such as healthcare, education, welfare and old age pension are largely run by the public sector.

The one-size-fits-all prescription frequently failed to take into account the multiplying effect that civil service layoffs has on African families. Despite the push for modernization, the everyday life of Africans remains deeply rooted in the extended family tradition. Within a single extended African family, several generations are dependent on the income of an employed civil servant. From immediate parents and grandparents who may depend on the income of the civil servant for medical care, to uncles and aunts who may need help in replacing a roof on their house, to nephews, nieces and possibly grandchildren, whose school fees are paid from the civil servant's salary. The civil servant's education itself may have been paid for by an aunt, an uncle or some other extended family member.

That the IMF and World Bank frequently called for the downsizing of the African public sector meant that they saw the public sector as an obstacle to development. Yet, the loans that these institutions grant to Africa were often granted to the public sector. And what do public sector administrators do with the money? In the best-case scenario, the money is directed at further expanding the public sector. In the worst-case scenario, the money makes an immediate U-turn back into secret bank accounts in the West. That the World Bank and the IMF would stress the importance of private sector-driven development, while in the meantime disbursing loans to the African public sector, utterly smacks of hypocrisy. Equally hypocritical is the policy of granting additional loans to governments who are too impoverished to continue making interest payments on existing loans. In a hearing before the U.S. Senate Committee on Foreign Relations in May 2004, Jeffrey Winters, a professor at Northwestern University, argued that the World Bank had participated in the corruption of roughly $100 billion of its loan funds intended for development.[39] Granting additional loans to bankrupted governments just so that they could continue to make interest payments on defaulted loans is a policy similar to serving more drinks to an alcoholic who is buying drinks on credit; or giving more drugs to a drug addict who is buying the drugs on credit. Neither more money to government officials nor more drugs to a drug addict can help get them out of their self-destructive spiral. If anything, it perpetuates the problem.

The intentions of international financial institutions will always remain suspect as long as they continue to see the "fat" in mismanaged African states only in terms of a large civil service. Because the foreign imposition of structural adjustment plans directly conflicts with the legitimate needs of social forces, the question frequently asked by critics of IMF and World Bank policies is that "why is the common person the first to be eliminated whenever a structural adjustment is called for in Third World governments?" That these institutions are frequently reluctant to call for reductions in military spending, private presidential airplanes, government luxury spending and other forms of ostentatious living triggers the perception that they are enemies of the common man and friends of wasteful government spending. In "The Road to Tahrir," Ty McCormick traces the roots of the 2011 Egyptian Revolution to "bad economic advice - and the crony capitalism it left behind. He argues that the seeds of Mubarak's eventual downfall were planted in a 1990s IMF imposed structural adjustment plan, where Mubarak was asked to cut government services, liberalize interest rates, and undertake an ambitious privatization program." The impact of reform on employment was so pernicious, in fact, that Stella, Egypt's local beer, and Coca Cola were the only two cases where privatization led to an increase in the number of jobs."[40]

If the IMF and the World Bank think that structures in Africa need adjusting, they should start by recognizing that the flaws in the structures are flaws that are attributable to the colonial powers that conceived them. Had the initial political structures that were handed down by Europe been properly structured, structural adjustment programs would not be necessary

---

39 The Wall Street Journal, March 21, 2009; http://online.wsj.com/article/SB123758895999200083.html?KE... (accessed 02/18/2017)

40 Ty McCormick, The Road to Tahrir, http://www.foreignpolicy.com/articles/2011/08/18/the_road_to_tahrir (accessed August 20, 2011).

in post-independent Africa today.

Cabinet ministers in several African countries where the per capita income is among the lowest in the world are upon appointment, entitled to government paid and chauffeured Mercedes cars, free housing, government-paid first-class travel abroad, and free medical care in costly foreign hospitals. The president is entitled to multiple presidential palaces, private jets, private helicopters, and a personal budget whose figures are often kept as a national secret. In much of Francophone Africa, the official drink at state banquets is imported French wine and French champagne. The cost of just one bottle of champagne could be about a week's pay for an entry level government employee. Yet, IMF officials are quicker at calling for the elimination of employment for lowly paid civil servants than for the elimination of such luxury spending.

In spite of their taste for the good things, the development of an appropriate public infrastructure has never been a priority for most African governments. Among other things, African highways are among the most dangerous in the world. The highways that most countries in Africa are currently building are highways that were condemned and eliminated a hundred years ago in most Western countries as unsafe. In countries where the official vehicles assigned to public officials are luxury cars, one would expect to find well maintained luxury highways. Instead, one finds roads that go unmaintained and unrepaired for years. Across much of the continent, potholes and dirt roads are a common sight. Africa does not produce motor spare parts, so frequent vehicle breakdowns means frequent transfers of Africa's hard currency to auto-parts producing countries. The cost of one spare part for a government-owned luxury vehicle can easily exceed a year's income for a mid-level African civil servant.

In the early years of independence, the French economist, Rene Dumont was among the critics of Africa's misplaced priorities. He lamented that "independence has meant taking the place of the whites and enjoying the privileges, often exorbitant, hitherto accorded to colonials. To high salaries there are now often added villas splendidly furnished; or even palaces for ministers, the whole of their upkeep paid for by the budget...To the Peugeot 403s there followed, after independence, the Chevrolets of Abidjan and the Mercedes of Yaoundé, Cameroon - often renewed after six months, something that makes ordinary folk grind their teeth."[41] Lamenting the glaring disparities that were immediately visible when Africans came to power in his country, a Cameroonian villager stated in despair that "Independence is not for us, it is for the people in the towns."[42]

---

41 Rene Dumont, *L'Afrique noire est mal partie*, Paris, 1962, p. 34.
42 Davidson, p. 135

As institutions that advise Africa on economic and financial matters, the World Bank and IMF are very well aware private capital is not available in Africa. Yet, they frequently called for the privatization of state-owned enterprises. Privatization would be an appropriate remedy if Africans had the capital and the management know-how to buy and run privatized companies. But such a call in countries where there is no viable private sector can be seen as guise for the re-colonization of Africa. Almost all major state-owned companies that were privatized on the advice of the World Bank and the International Monetary Fund were bought by foreign corporations. Profits generated by these companies are generally sent back home to shareholders. As a result, not much is left behind that can be invested in the construction of the highways, schools and hospitals that will help develop Africa.

Experience has shown that loans granted to governments do little to promote growth in the private sector. If anything, they contribute to strengthening the predatory capacity of the public sector. Often, the money is used to hire more police and military personnel, create more government ministries and expand regulatory bureaucracies and eventually delay the further privatization of existing public enterprises. Thus, instead of granting loans to the African public sector the World Bank and the IMF provided funding and management training to private sector entrepreneurs, the African private sector would be in a position to purchase privatized government corporations.

It takes more than IMF and World Bank loans to develop a nation-state. It takes human as well as material resources. In the absence of human capacity and good governance, IMF and World Bank money alone will not produce development in Africa. Yet structural adjustment programs have never included programs to help reverse the brain-drain that has depleted Africa of its human capital. While Africa needs about one million new scientists and engineers a year to help address its current development needs, only about 20,000 are currently working on the continent. At the dawn of the 21st century, there were more African-born scientists and engineers working in the United States than in Africa. More than two thousand Nigerian physicians practiced medicine in the United States. The city of Chicago alone had more Sierra Leonean medical doctors than the country of Sierra Leone.[43] Despite this, Home Office figures in Britain show that 17,620 African doctors and nurses joined the National Health Service (NHS) in 2007. While NHS trusts are banned from actively trying to recruit from Africa, nothing prevents health professionals from leaving the continent to find

---

43   Interview given to the BBC by Nigerian-born Computer Scientist, Emeagwali, programmer of the world's fastest computer, at 3.1 billion calculations per second, in June 1999.

employment elsewhere.[44] Substantial financial investments go into training pilots and other aviation technicians, only for them to run off with the skills and experience to work in countries outside of Africa. Sadly, Africa gets no compensation from the receiving countries. To make up for the lost skills, Africa again has to spend hundreds of millions of dollars to replace these skilled professionals.[45]

Finding ways to bring back home the many African intellectuals that are making contributions to development in other parts of the world is a responsibility that ought to be assumed by international financial institutions that have given themselves the mandate of promoting structural adjustment in Africa. Just as "gentrification" provided American professionals incentives to move back to help revitalize American inner cities in the 1980s, a similar program that works to bring back African intellectuals from the diaspora can help stem and possibly reverse the brain drain. Not only will the returnees bring back the education, skills and work experience they have acquired in other parts of the world, they will be returning to provide the creative and innovative talents that are essential for development. More importantly, they will be in a position to serve as mentors and as role models to younger generations of Africans. This is a program that can be funded and facilitated by international financial institutions.

Depending on individual African countries alone to reverse the national brain-drain by bringing back their citizens who are in the diaspora, they will never do it. Most African rulers see intellectuals and the diaspora community, as potential "troublemakers." They are concerned that if allowed to return, the returnees will swell the ranks of opposition parties and civil society organizations that frequently mobilize to push for change. The change that nondemocratic African rulers are most dreadful of is change that has to do with respect for the rule of law, political transparency and term limits. The only hope for the establishment of a program that will encourage the return of Africans from the diaspora would therefore have to be international financial institutions. If institutions such as IMF and the World Bank are genuinely committed to promoting the "structural adjustments" that will produce lasting economic transformation in Africa, they will need to place the repatriation of the African diaspora at the top of their proposed structural adjustment policies for Africa.

Following the above observations, we are ultimately led to ponder why World Bank and the IMF structural adjustment directives do not include

---

44 BBC News, Africa 'being drained of doctors', http://news.bbc.co.uk/go/pr/fr/-/2/hi/health/7178978.stm (accessed 2/4/2010).

45 Dagnachew Teklu, African Aviation Strangled by Brain Drain, The Daily Monitor (Addis Ababa), September 7, 2005.

recommendations for promoting intra-African trade. Nowhere in IMF structural adjustment programs would one see a recommendation for the export and sale of Senegalese peanuts to Ethiopia, Malian cotton to South Africa or Cameroonian bananas to Somalia. Cameroon and Nigeria are neighbors but there is very little official trade between the two countries. The bulk of trade and commercial activity that exists between Nigeria and the French-speaking countries in the region is largely conducted as contraband.

It is by giving priority to intra-African trade over extra-continental trade that Africa would in the long run be able to achieve sustainable development. Just as the bulk of America's trade is done with its North American neighbors, and Europe's with its European members, Africa needs to work in opening up more trading ties with its African neighbors than with its former colonial powers. Africa represents 15% of the world's population, but its 2010 contribution to global trade stood at only 3.4%. Intra-African trade remains equally minimal, at less than 10% of total trade in 2010. Without intra-European trade, not only will Europe's economy stagnate, the European continent will not be in a position to compete effectively at the global level. Similarly, to effectively compete in the global level, Africa will have to "globalize" regionally and continentally before it can aspire to globalizing globally. And for Africa to globalize continentally, efforts have to be directed at removing the existing physical and bureaucratic barriers that make trade between neighboring states impossible.

That much of the economic activity in Africa remains focused on the export of raw materials and the import of finished or processed goods explains why Africans have not been unable to promote intra-African trade. Countries that produce the same basket of goods cannot trade. Since most countries on the continent produce nearly the same raw materials, they cannot import from one another. So without a push to diversify their economies, the quest to promote intra-African trade will remain wishful thinking.

Conclusion

There is no denying that modern democracy is a legacy of the West. Politically, it is a value that has since the age of the Greek City States defined the West to the outside world. Indeed, democracy and republicanism in the West developed as a result of revolutionary challenges against European monarchies. The writings of John Locke, Thomas Hobbes, and Jean-Jacques Rousseau popularized the philosophies of natural rights and human equality. These ideas inspired the American and French revolutions. Mobilized by the slogan that "all men are created equal," Americans freed themselves from the exploitative rule of the British monarchy in 1776. A few years later, in 1789, the French were inspired by the same ideals to rid themselves of the kleptocratic rule of the French monarchy. Yet less than 98 years after the American Revolution and less than 85 years after the French Revolution, European powers imposed on Africa the very tyrannical rule that they fought so valiantly to dismantle on their continent.

Europe's colonial legacy in Africa is one of authoritarian rule and forced labor. It is a legacy that was continued so very well by Europe's African heirs. The first and second generation of post-independent African leaders were a textbook embodiment of the political and administrative rule that Europe instituted in Africa. Nowhere was this so more openly admitted than at a press conference in Paris where the Cameroonian President, Paul Biya stated to the French media that *"je suis le plus mieux élève de President François Mitterrand,"* (I am the best pupil of President Francois Mitterrand).[46] Not only was his rule at home highly centralized and driven by a personality cult, his rule promoted a kleptocratic machinery that was very much reminiscent of the exploitative rule of Louis XIV.

Finally, if poverty and corruption are external statistical indicators of underdevelopment, then it would not be improper to say that the World Bank and the IMF have been active contributors to underdevelopment in Africa. In continually granting loans to regimes that they knew were patently corrupt, these institutions were manifestly contributing to the underdevelopment rather than to the development of Africa. And in promoting structural adjustment programs that called for reductions in government spending on education, healthcare and other vital areas of basic human development, these two global institutions must have known that such policies to produce underdevelopment, poverty and chronic debt. At inception, structural adjustment programs were designed not so much to end poverty or produce debt-free economies, they were designed to place African economies in a perennial state of indebtedness – very much like the long-term debt that credit card companies aggressively marketed to college freshmen in the 1980s. Even if unemployment and the poverty rate were at 80%, as long as African countries were able to continue to make interest payments on World Bank and IMF loans, these economies were according to these institutions doing fine.

---

46 Peter W. Vakunta, Upstation Mountain Club, Manufacturing the Illusion of Freedom, http://www.postnewsline.com/2010/07/manufacturing-the-illusion-of-freedom.html ?cid=6a00d8341c824e53ef0147e3630e71970b (accessed 11/02/2008).

Chapter 8

Reordering the African Public Sector

We face neither East nor West: we face forward.

Kwame Nkrumah[1]

When spider webs unite they can capture a lion.

An Ethiopian Proverb

The global economy is at such critical crossroads today that unless Africa is politically and economically re-ordered, Africans are not going to be able to take advantage of the opportunities that are emerging from the growing globalization of the international system. By re-ordering, we mean restructuring Africa politically and economically, so it can take advantage of the opportunities that the global economy has to offer. It can no longer be business as usual. To stem the tide of missteps that Africa has made in the past, Africa must be re-ordered. But where does the re-ordering begin? And what exactly should be re-ordered? In this chapter, we are going to explore the various reforms that must be carried out if Africa is to catch up with the rest of the world.

Re-ordering Africa is ultimately going to have to begin with political reforms. In the final analysis, Nkrumah was right – "give me political power and everything else will fall into place." This mantra was as true in the 1960s as it is today. In advocating for the primacy of political power, what Nkrumah meant was that Africa should first be allowed the sovereign right to determine its political destiny. In modern governmental systems, the ultimate measure of political independence is self-determination, and the ultimate expression of self-determination is by referendum. A referendum is the most direct and indisputable way in determining the democratic will of an electorate. Once determined, the will provides legitimacy. And legitimacy is the incontrovertible guarantor of domestic stability. Had a referendum been organized at independence to give Africans the option to redraw their

---

1   Kwame Nkrumah 1900–72 Ghanaian statesman, Prime Minister 1957–60, President 1960–6: conference speech, Accra, 7 April 1960; *Axioms of Kwame Nkrumah* (1967)

national boundaries, it certainly would have produced a different map and different ethnic groupings in Africa – a map and ethnic groupings that is self-determined by Africans, not Berlin. The legitimacy that would have resulted from such a politically self-determined re-ordering would have helped reduced the irredentist uprisings that have since independence stood in the way of stability and development in Africa. The world would have obviously avoided the million lives that were lost in the Nigeria-Biafra War, the 800,000 deaths that were reported in the Rwandan genocide, and the more than 6 million deaths that occurred in the Congolese civil war.

Ethnicity and political rivalry were primarily responsible for the civil crises that devastated Nigeria in 1965 and Rwanda in 1994. While peace and stability were finally imposed by military force, the internal political systems in Nigeria, Congo and Rwanda remain to this day, precarious and highly fragile. Domestic ethnic relations continue to be characterized by mutual suspicion. Absent a sense of trust, it is going to be impossible to produce the conditions that will lead to national unity and lasting stability across Africa.

Building Africa from the Bottom-Up

There are basically two development models: the bureaucratic/top-down model, and the self-determined/bottom-up model. The latter is sustainable, and the former is not. The model that was imposed on Africa was the former. No doubt therefore that development in Africa remains unsustainable.

A stable political system is reminiscent of a house that is built from the bottom-up. For Africa to achieve the stability that will lead to lasting development, it does need to be built from the bottom-up. As indicated in the preceding chapters, almost all of the political systems in Africa were built from the top-down. National governments in Africa are virtual foreign structures that were hurriedly imposed on Africans. As a result, these governments lack domestic legitimacy. In emphasizing this point, Crawford Young points out that "the ephemeral independence constitutions mostly failed to survive because they were wooden copies of metropolitan institutions. Liberal institutions, if they are to survive, they need to be rooted in domestic cultural heritage."[2]

In the same vein, J. Peter Pham points out that in Sub-Saharan Africa "the most formidable obstacle to stability, the rule of law, development, democracy, and the other goods we in the West take for granted has been neither poverty nor any other material factor." Rather, it has been the questionable legitimacy of the state itself, legitimacy being understood not as a normative judgment about juridical right or moral virtue but in the social

---

2   Crawford Young, in Jennifer A. Widner, ed., *Economic Change and Political Liberaliza-tion in Sub-Sahara Africa*, The Johns Hopkins University Press, 1994, p. 245.

and political sense of whether or not the structures of a given polity have evolved endogenously within a society and its institutions can claim some historical continuity.[3] While Africa has a rich social, cultural, and political past, the structure and processes of modern African states are not rooted in that rich heritage. Instead, modern African states and their borders are legacies of colonial rule, emerging directly from the often, arbitrary ways that the great powers delineated their respective spheres of influence. The survival of these artifices has been contingent not so much on internal legitimacy (by and large non-existent) but on international recognition. Without any organic ties such as shared language, culture, and history binding them to a historic nation-state, many post-colonial rulers use the "sovereignty" awarded them to pillage national resources, while resorting to human rights abuses to prevent protests from those that are excluded from the spoils.[4]

Democracy calls for self-determination. In a genuinely democratic state, Africa's various ethnic groups should be allowed to "self-determine" how to organize themselves politically and territorially. If Africans were allowed to exercise self-determination at independence, the Hutus and the Tutsis would probably have voted to have separate sovereignties. The Ibos, the Yorubas, the Hausas, and various other ethnic groups in Nigeria would probably never have voted to belong together under one sovereign state. Not only are these various groups ethnically, religiously and historically different, they all have a long and proud heritage that predates colonial rule. In Nigeria, it is about as difficult to subject a Hausa to the rule of an Ibo, as it is to subject Mecca to the rule of the Vatican. Forcing Ibos, Yorubas, and Hausas to live together under one rule is like forcing India, Pakistan, and Bangladesh to live under the same rule. There couldn't have been a better prescription for instability in Africa than forcing rival and distinctly heterogeneous ethnic groups to live together under one sovereign rule.

Challenges to the legitimacy of the current state system in Africa come primarily from the fact that they were imported and superimposed from the top, with total disregard to Africa's cultural and historical differences. Africans had no say in the design and adoption of the institutions that now govern them. However, it would be different if this top-down imposition of foreign rule were the work of one colonial power. That is to say, had Africa been colonized by one European power, as was the case with Britain's colonization of Canada, India and the United States, the top-down imposition of sovereignty would have worked as it did in Canada, India and the United States, and the continent would probably be a lot more stable today. But Africa was colonized by as many as eight competing foreign powers.

---

3   J. Peter Pham, http://worlddefensereview.com/pham011708.shtml
4   ibid.

Obviously, it is easier to run a self-determined government than to run a government that is imposed by foreign powers from the top-down. As indicated in previous chapters, the primary reason why the American union has remained stable and successful is because it was self-determined and restructured from the bottom-up by its member-states. Had the political system in the United States been forcibly imposed from the top-down by Britain, it would have been as dysfunctional as African states are today. Even states as small as Delaware with a population of a mere 58,000 people at independence were allowed to exercise the right to self-determination. As a whole, for all of the founding member states of the American union, the decision to join the union was self-determined. It came from the bottom-up. This of course meant that the federal government was a creation of the individual states. Similarly, had the various ethnic populations in Africa been allowed to vote to form their national or federal governments, this certainly could have led to lasting political stability.

African states are, in reality, an amalgamation of multiple nations that were forcibly regrouped together by the tyranny of colonialism. The average African nation-state is made up of some 20 separate nations. Some states, such as Cameroon and Nigeria, had as many as 250 distinct ethnic groups that were autonomous and self-governing prior to the imposition of colonial rule. In colonial times and again at independence, Africa was denied recognition of the various autonomous nations that were within its European carved borders. It was this denial of recognition that is largely responsible for the persistence of irredentism in Africa today. Stability cannot flourish in an environment where recognition is denied nations that have been around for thousands of years. This was the case in Mali, where the Tuaregs sought to reclaim their long-lost sovereignty in a 2012 insurgency. It was also the case in the Horn of Africa when Eritrea and Ethiopia, two nations that were separate and autonomous prior to European colonization, were forcibly integrated by colonial rule, robbing them of self-determination. In a bitter war of secession that went on for decades, Eritrea finally won the right to self-determination and became an independent (but regrettably autocratic) state. Afraid that Eritrea's secession was going to open up a breakaway Pandora Box for other nations within the Ethiopian state, the government of Ethiopia organized a general referendum that gave the various ethnic nations within Ethiopia an opportunity to exercise self-determination by voting to become part of the modern nation-state of Ethiopia. A union that is formed by referendum or self-determined will of its constituent members has the potential to enjoy long term stability than a union that is decreed or imposed from the top-down.

Not only were the states in Africa established from the top-down, they were established with total disregard for the various sovereign nations and nationalities that existed prior to European colonization. Because these internal nations were not allowed to have a say in the establishment of the modern states that now exercise power over them, they see the authority of these states as illegitimate. It is this perception of illegitimacy that is largely responsible for the instability that reigns across Africa today. So far, only one governing constitution in Africa - the Ethiopian Constitution - addresses this concern. Unlike the constitutions of other countries in the continent, the Constitution of Ethiopia is grounded on a preamble that reads "We, the Nations, Nationalities, and Peoples of Ethiopia."[5] Whereas other nations are more likely to see constitutional clauses that acknowledge and grants recognition to the nations and nationalities within a state as potentially destabilizing, Ethiopians saw it as a potential building block for legitimacy. Not only does Ethiopia acknowledge the sovereignties of the various nations that are within its borders, it grants these nations "the unrestricted right to self-determination up to secession." This means that any nation within the state of Ethiopia has the constitutional right to secede whenever it feels that its "national" interests are no longer being fully realized within the union.

Besides the right to secession, the various nations that make up Ethiopia are granted the right to self-government, and the right to speak, write, and develop their own language, promote their culture, and preserve their unique heritage. At first glance, one would think that such a loose and liberal granting of rights is a potential prescription for instability. That a sense of statehood can develop in a society in which the right to secession and self-rule is guaranteed in the constitution is, for many, inconceivable. As potentially destabilizing as this may be, it is a model that appears to have promise for Africa. Yet, it is the refusal of these guarantees that has historically been behind the push for secession.

Almost every African country has more than one identifiable internal nation or ethnic group whose roots as an autonomous, self-governing population is traceable to pre-colonial times. Most of them have experienced and continue to experience political instability. Burundi and Rwanda are two neighboring states whose domestic political makeup is characterized more by uncertainties than by certainties. The ethnic asymmetry that was left behind by colonial rule in both states remains a potential incubator for instability. Colonialism provided these states with no democratic platform for the peaceful handling of this asymmetry. Had European colonial rule left behind a democratic tradition in Rwanda, the Rwandan genocide would never have happened, as the political frustrations of the Hutus would have been directed not at exterminating the Tutsis but at the ballot box.

---

5   Worldwide Constitutions, (accessed 8/12/206) http://www.concourt.am/armenian/
     legal_resources/world_constitutions/constit/ethiopia/ethiop-e.htm

To really understand the Rwandan genocide, one should imagine a political arrangement in which the Germans and the Polish are forced by some external power to live together under one sovereign rule. Even though the Poles are a demographic minority, a Polish national is made president of this Germano-Polish state. His governing policies grant economic and political privileges exclusively to the Poles. Because the source of his political power is foreign, the Polish President remains impervious to the domestic demands of ethnic Germans. There is no guessing the blood-letting that would result from such an arrangement. It would certainly make the Rwanda genocide look like child play. Like everyone else, Europeans hate to be ruled by people who are not of their ethnic background, especially if the rule is ironfisted and exercised by a member of a minority ethnic group. Yet, this was the political arrangement that was established in Africa on the eve of the departure of European colonial powers.

So far, none of the measures that have been taken by the international community to reinstate normalcy in Rwanda effectively guarantees against future civil wars. The union that forces the Hutus and Tutsis to continue to live together under one centralized state was not a voluntarily concluded union. It is a union that has once again been imposed from the top-down. It is only when these two ethnic groups are guaranteed the right to self-determination and the freedom to secede would they want to voluntarily vote to form a union that would govern them. As indicated above, it is when the right to secede is guaranteed, that states will more likely vote to form larger unions. In other words, the most effective guarantees against secession are not so much laws or military threats against secession, but laws that guarantee the right and the freedom to secede. The ethnic tensions that continue to fester between the Hutus and Tutsis in Rwanda and in Burundi are motivated not so much by hatred for each other, but by the denial of the right to self-determination and ethnic sovereign autonomy.

The Case of Nigeria

The nation of Nigeria is an incongruous federation of some 250 heterogeneous ethnic groups. It is one nation that is delicately held together by a complex web of internal and external stakeholders. Nowhere are the differences among Nigerians more noticeable than in their cultural and religious lifestyles. The North is predominantly Muslim, paternalistic, and polygamous; while the East is mostly Christian, monogamous and individually independent, and the West, Christian, monogamous and culturally communal. With such inherent sociocultural differences, the exercise of democratic rule can be quite a challenge. Because of the demographic advantage that derives from a polygamous culture, in a one-person/one-vote democracy, there is the likelihood that the president will most likely always come from the North – assuming all northerners decide to always vote for northern candidates. This is not a political outcome that would be readily welcomed by Nigerians from other regions of the country.

In the mid-1960s, Nigeria fought a bloody civil war in a futile attempt to reorder its complex political order. It was a reordering that would have caused the splintering of Nigeria into two or more states. Nigeria's external stakeholders (Britain, the US and even the USSR) resisted the splinter. Since then, Nigerians remain compelled to live together under one state, established from the top-down, with a very low sense of national identity. As a matter of urgency, Nigeria would rank at the top of the countries in Africa whose political systems call for a reordering.

Culturally, religiously, and linguistically, the Hausas, Ibos and Yorubas are distinct nations of peoples within the modern state of Nigeria. Prior to the forcible imposition of colonial rule, some of the nations within Nigeria actually had organized political and administrative structures that rivaled the political structures of some European states. To force these nations to live under one state without duly recognizing their status as nations and their rights to self-determination is an ominous prescription for long term political instability. As indicated above, the secessionist war would never have occurred had the various nations within the state of Nigeria been given recognition, along with a constitutionally guaranteed Ethiopia-like right to secession. Reordering Nigeria along the lines of the Ethiopian model would require the conduct of a national referendum in which Nigerians will be given the choice to vote to either stay together, or splinter into separate states formed along ethnic lines. Should they vote to stay united, we will have a Nigeria that is self-determined, legitimized by the electoral will, and created from the bottom-up. People will more readily accept the legitimacy of a political institution that is created with their consent than one that is forcibly imposed on them. The primary objective of a referendum is to establish such legitimacy. And should the citizens of the various nations within Nigeria vote against staying together, then such a democratically expressed will should be honored. The ultimate goal here ought not to be a united Nigeria at any cost. The ultimate goal should be political order. The disintegration of Nigeria restructuring into stable/friendly states is certainly preferable to a united but unstable Nigeria. If there is perception that under the present national arrangement Nigeria is ungovernable, then any other form of political arrangement should be preferable to the continuous impo- sition of a union from the top-down.

Ultimately, voluntary rather than forced unions could eventually be negotiated once the disintegrated nations have established and fully con- solidated sovereignties within their respective national jurisdictions. Such unions could take the form of federations or confederations.

Reordering the African Public Sector

The greatest obstacle to growth and prosperity in Africa in the past half century has by every measure been the public sector. It is large, bloated, predatory and self-preserving. We are reminded by the teachings of Socrates that government is best when it is small and closest to the people. The structure of governments in post-colonial Africa is anything but small. In the quest for self-preservation, resources are directed at preserving and at expanding bureaucratic self-interests, rather than at providing for the common good. Jealously concerned with monopolizing the power that was inherited from European colonial powers, African governments went on to become virtual monopolies. Many saw the development of the private sector as a potential threat to their monopolistic power and worked to discourage its development. In seeking to provide both public and private services, African governments became inefficient and corrupt in both. Governments frequently rushed to bailout public companies that went bankrupt. Before long, the governments themselves were running budgetary deficits that equally brought them into bankruptcy. To stay afloat, they sought bailout by turning to the World Bank and other international financial institutions. The African debt crisis was directly linked to loans that were granted to support a bloated and poorly managed government sector. The vicious debt cycle could have been avoided had IMF and World Bank loans been directed at growing the African private sector rather than at growing the African public sector.

The violation of the second principle of efficient government has meant that governmental systems in Africa do not only distance themselves from their people, they also appear to be indifferent to their needs. Most countries in Africa have centralized national governments, with the seat of power located at a distant capital. The human tendency for the monopoly and control of power has meant that administrative power is jealously guarded at the national headquarters and all decisions made from there. Even in matters of local interest, local and provincial civil servants must seek permission or authority from the national government. A local administrator will not authorize the replacement of a local street sign unless approval is obtained from the national capital. In French speaking Africa, for example, the authority to hire local staff, including receptionists and janitors, must come from the national capital.

Unless there is a total reordering of Africa's political institutions, such inefficiencies will continue. Western philosophy specifically demands that the branch of government that makes our laws – as opposed to the branch that enforces or interprets them – should be the most powerful. African legislative bodies are anything but powerful. Given that most of its members are handpicked and/or elected in rigged elections, they naturally owe allegiance to the president or the party leader. Their role as lawmakers therefore is simply to rubber-stamp decisions of the head of state or party head. The power of the head of state is used not so much to protect the weak from the strong as Thomas Hobbes would want, but to prey on the weak. Most African governments provide no constitutional protections for their masses. Though written in the constitution, civil rights and civil liberties remain abstract concepts. At the same time, there are few constitutional limits on presidential powers, and whatever limits there are, they are seldom respected by the president. Frequently, the president exercises more powers than are provided in the constitution. Vis-a-vis the legislative and the judiciary, the balance of power disproportionately favors the president, making it impossible for the other branches to effectively check and balance the executive.

Any reordering of the political institutions in Africa therefore would require a total reconfiguration of this imbalance of power. The Hobbesian model of an all-powerful ruler will have to be replaced by the Lockean model that shifts the balance of power in favor of the legislative branch of government.[6] The powers of appropriation and appointment that are currently exercised by the president will have to shift to the legislature. Africa's inability to achieve sustainable development is directly attributable to mismanagement and the misappropriation of state funds. Currently, public officials who manage state resources are appointed by the president and remain accountable to him alone. Because the president frequently misappropriates state funds himself, he often lacks the moral high ground to take disciplinary action against his appointees. Shifting these powers to the legislature should transfer the accountability of state officials from the president to lawmakers. It is to the people that accountability for the management of public resources is owed, not to the president or the executive. As the peoples' representatives, legislators can better carry out this function.

A political reordering that shifts power away from the president to the legislature should guarantee against the instability that often results from military coups. Frequently, it is the accumulation of absolute power in one person that makes individual heads of states the envy and target of military coups. Just as bank robbers say they rob banks because that's where money is, heads of states are the targets of coup plotters because that's where the power is. Once power is transferred or shifted away from the individual person at the presidency to the collegial body at the national legislature, it reduces the temptation to militarily target the president. Not only would such a reordering make African rulers more secure, it will no longer be necessary to spend vast sums of money to maintain a large and

---

6   Constitutional Rights Foundation: Bill of Rights in Action, http://www.crf-usa.org/bill-of-rights-in-action/bria-20-2-c-hobbes-locke-montesquieu-and-rousseau-on-government. html (accessed September 6, 2018).

costly presidential security.

In most of the non-democracies in Africa, the president determines his salary, and not even parliament is allowed to know how much he earns. In some oil producing countries, parliamentarians are not even allowed to know how much the country receives in oil revenues. A political reordering that shifts the balance of power away from the president to the legislature should instill a culture of transparency and accountability and put an end to such secrecy. Once it is made the most powerful branch of government, the legislature will be able to place a cap on the president's salary and on his spending powers. The motivation to run for president ought not to be income but love for country and the ability to serve. Thus, in setting a cap on how much the head of state can earn, it should be a cap that minimizes the role of income as an incentive. The ability to serve would have to be determined by achievements in previous endeavors. A possible yardstick could be entrepreneurial achievements or proven leadership experiences in international organizations. Experience has shown that success in one endeavor is transferable to other endeavors. For example, after successfully serving as Secretary General of the United Nations, the late Koffi Annan should have been presumed qualified to serve as president in his native country. And after founding and successfully running the mobile communications company, Celtel, the telecommunications entrepreneur, Mo Ibrahim, should be presumed qualified to serve as president of his country of birth, Sudan.

The most stable and successful countries of the world are countries that are run like businesses. An entrepreneur that has succeeded in turning failed or bankrupt businesses into successful businesses should, if elected to the presidency, be able to turn a failing or bankrupt country around into a stable and prosperous country. Businesses are all about generating revenues. Governments ought to be pursuing a similar mission – the mission of generating public goods through the efficient management of government services. In Africa the difference is that while the entrepreneur achieves his mission by placing corporate interest ahead of personal interest, the African head of state too often places personal interest ahead of national interest.

If the African public sector could be reordered to benefit from the infusion of entrepreneurial or private sector leadership skills, it could also be reordered to benefit from the leadership of women. It was not until 2005 that Africa's first female head of state, Ellen Sirleaf-Johnson, was elected in Liberia; and in 2012 that the second female, Joyce Banda, came to power in Malawi. A brief look at the devastating records of their male predecessor - Liberia's Charles Taylor and Malawi's Bingu wa Mutharika - could only but assure the world that women can provide better leadership. The remedy for Africa's economic and political crises may actually lie in the election of more females as heads of states. There are no definitive studies on whether women are better at governing than men, but in the African context, popular wisdom shows that women can be better trusted than men.

By and large, men have so far been inept in the management of the public trust. To put it bluntly, men have failed Africa. In more than half a century of controlling power, men failed to pull Africa out of underdevelopment. This should lead us to conclusively posit that political failure in Africa has been the failure of male leadership. It would therefore be appropriate for men to accept defeat, gracefully step aside, and allow women to give it a try. While it may be true that African regimes are ethnically heterogeneous and complex to govern, there is ample historical evidence that women are more skilled at managing complex situations than their male counterparts. Just as entrepreneurial skills can be readily transferred from the private sector to the public sector, the experiences of women in the management of complex situations in other areas of life can be readily transferred to the management of the complexities of public life.

Recklessness in male leadership is most noticeable in the practice of stealing and hiding away national funds in foreign bank accounts. This is reminiscent of a male head of household who, on pay day, goes away and squanders the family's income on gambling and alcohol. Women on the whole cannot allow themselves to be driven by such reckless debauchery. Unlike their male counterparts, women on payday will more likely use their income to provide for the family than in gambling or drinking. It is on the basis of this virtue that the slogan, "educate a woman and you'll educate the whole village" is grounded. As president, a woman would less likely be tempted to steal and hide her country's wealth away in foreign banks. Instead of a luxury villa in some offshore location, she would rather spend that money at home. If we think of home here as a metaphor for country, then what this means is that a woman would rather spend to her country's wealth in educating and developing the skills that develop her country than hide it away in a secret foreign bank account. If it is thus clear that women are more honest managers of the national wealth, then having them lead Africa should lead to the development of the continent.

Going Beyond Election Monitoring to Election Administering

A common trigger for political instability in Africa is the maladministration of the electoral process. Repeated reforms, including reforms that created independent electoral commissions have failed to end the claims and counter-claims of victory that both sides always make whenever election results are proclaimed. Even with the presence of international monitors, there were claims and counter-claims of victory in the 2007 presidential elections in Kenya between Mwai Kibaki and Raila Odinga. Other presidential elections with disputed results included Robert Mugabe and Morgan

Tsvangirai in Zimbabwe in 2008; Goodluck Johnathan and Muhammadu Buhari in 2011; Gbagbo and Outtara in Cote d'Ivoire in 2011; Paul Biya and Fru Ndi in Cameroon in 1992 and 2011; Joseph Kabila and Étienne Tshisekedi in the DRC in 2012; and Abdoulaye Wade and Macky Sall in Senegal in 2012. So far, election monitoring by international teams of observers have failed to prevent post-election disputes. Our modest proposal here would be to go beyond election monitoring to actually having foreign or international bodies administer political elections across Africa. So in place of domestic independent electoral commissions, teams of administrators from East Africa would be brought in to administer elections in countries in West Africa, and teams from Southern Africa brought in to administer elections in Northern Africa; and vice versa. Having election administering bodies all come from Africa should avoid potential charges of neocolonial interference. The sense of neutrality that a foreign-elections administering team brings should help legitimize election results. This legitimacy will help prevent the bloody confrontations that usually break out whenever election results are proclaimed in Africa.

So far, African countries have no objection to letting foreign coaches, some of whom are actually from Europe and other regions outside Africa administer their national football teams. They should hopefully have no objection to letting in neutral teams from other regions of Africa conduct and administer their national elections. Indeed, compared to sports teams, the stakes in national politics are a lot higher; thus, a greater need for impartiality and fair play. Since impartiality cannot be found domestically, it is necessary to look externally. As with the neutrality that a good referee brings to a high stakes sporting event, foreign election commissions can bring the fairness and legitimacy that is needed in African national politics.

Conditioning National Sovereignty on Good Governance

All states, good and bad, lay claim to the international law principle of non-interference in the internal affairs of sovereign states. They use sovereignty as a shield and as immunity against foreign intervention. Rogue states frequently hide behind this shield to commit human rights abuses. Hamstrung by the principle, the international community is often powerless in the face of even the most egregious human rights abuses. Often, to override the principle, the legal authority of the UN is required. The process is slow and can often be vetoed by any of the permanent members of the UN Security Council. This renders victims of brutal regimes helpless and the inaction of the international community inexcusable. As much as there is need for the continuous respect of the principle of national sovereignty, there is equal need for the principle to be conditioned on good governance. To do so, it may be necessary to begin by redefining national sovereignty not as right, but as a privilege. Only states that respect the rule of law and do not violate the human rights of their citizens should be allowed to enjoy the right of non-interference in their internal affairs. Conditioning sovereignty on good governance would allow the international community to intervene in time to prevent such gross human rights atrocities as were witnessed in the post-Cold War era in Cambodia, Syria, Libya, Bosnia, Rwanda, Darfur, Zimbabwe and Burundi.

Transitioning African Democracy through Benevolent Dictators

On the whole, Africans are culturally authoritarian. Authoritarianism is found not just in the rulers who govern Africa, it is institutionally rooted in all levels of the African society – from the family to schools, worship places, traditional rulers, and various social organizations. It is difficult, if not impossible, for a culture this old and deep rooted in authoritarianism to transition directly into democracy. This could be seen with the democratic reforms that were adopted across Africa in the early 1990s. In less than ten years, there was a gradual but determined effort by the continent's entrenched oligarchs to roll back the reforms. Presidential term limits that were constitutionally instituted in the early 1990s had by the late 1990s been abolished by politically maneuvered amendments to constitution. The "breeze of democracy" that the African masses were briefly exposed to in the early 1990s had by the end of the decade been transformed into life presidencies and presidential dynasties. To have imagined in the first place that an authoritarian culture that is several thousand years old could have been reformed by a simple parliamentary act legalizing multiparty democracies was naive. With this failed attempt at democratic reforms in Africa, we are forced to reexamine how the resilience of authoritarianism in Africa can be used as prelude to sustainable democracy in Africa.

In all societies, there are some ingrained social and cultural habits that must be authoritatively corrected before democracy can take root. These include indiscipline, bribery and corruption, nepotism, and laxity. In the case of Africa, we may want to add tribalism and the traditional order. Democracy is a new order. Any effort to adopt it while still holding on to the old order would not work. In all, any transition to democracy that leaves the above habits intact will spell doom. This is the doom that most African democracies have been forced to experience in their first half century of independence. To avoid such a doom, an intermediary stage is needed in the transition from authoritarian rule to democratic rule. It is a stage that would have to go through the rule of yet another authoritarian rule – but this time the rule of a benevolent dictator. Democracy cannot stamp out indiscipline, corruption and laxity. If anything, in a democratic environment indiscipline can only but get worse. The role of the benevolent dictator here is that he would work to stamp out those habits that are antithetical to the democratic culture. Laxity, corruption, indiscipline, and other pathologically ingrained habits are better tamed by the rigors of autocracy than by the liberties of democracy. The most important right that is guaranteed by democracy is freedom. But it is well known that freedom without discipline would lead to disorder. Autocratic rigor is thus needed to cultivate and by necessity forcibly instill the ethics and sense of civic responsibility that are necessary for the smooth and efficient exercise of democratic governance. The international system has scores of political systems that transited through autocratic rule to become vibrant democracies. Among them are Germany, Singapore, South Korea. But for the ruthless rule of South Korea's General Pak Chung Hee, and Singapore's Lee Kuan Yew, these two countries will not be celebrated today as models of democracy in Southeast Asia. The same is true for Germany. Decades of autocratic rule under Bismarck and Hitler culminated in a foreign occupation that transited Germany into a democratic society with one of the most disciplined and law-abiding citizens in the world. For democracy in Africa to be sustainable, it may have to transition through similar autocratic rule.

There are in the main two types of dictators – the absolute dictator and the benevolent dictator. Both are intolerant of dissent and intolerant of challenges to their rule, but the absolute dictator is generally more ruthless and narcissistic. For him, power is an end; and he will use every means necessary to acquire and keep it. He will let nothing stand in his way. All other interests, including national interests are secondary. To guarantee against any interference with his power, he has absolute control of the country's security forces. The national media sings his praises daily, and his portrait is ubiquitously displayed in offices and in public places.[7] Among some of sub-Sahara Africa's well-known absolute dictators were Uganda's Idi Amin, Central Africa Republic's Jean-Bédel Bokassa, Zaire's Mobuto Sese Seko, Equatorial Guinea's Teodoro Obiang Nguema, Zimbabwe's Robert Mugabe, Sudan's Omar al Bashir, Malawi's Hastings Kamuzu Banda, Cameroon's Paul Biya, and Gambia's self-absorbed Yahya Jammeh, who during his reign, actually insisted to be called "His Excellency Sheikh Professor Alhaji Dr. Yahya Abdul-Azziz Jemus Junkung Jammeh. Driven more by narcissism than by national interest, these absolute dictators did more to hold their countries back than to move them forward. It wouldn't be an exaggeration to refer to them as "domestic neocolonial rulers." When their accomplishments are compared to what colonial rule accomplished in Africa, one readily sees

---

7   *New York Times*, Adam Nositer, U.S. Engages With an Iron Leader in Equatorial Guinea; http://www.nytimes.com/2011/05/31/world/africa/31guinea.html?_r=1 (accessed August 31, 2011)

that colonial rule actually accomplished more in Africa than these absolute dictators did.

Benevolent dictators on the other hand are driven more by a strong quest for national development. Not as narcissistic as the absolute dictator, he believes however that he and only he alone has the unique vision and mission to provide the leadership that will bring national unity and national prominence. He aggressively invests in such major infrastructural developments as roads, bridges, dams and highways. He personally supervises these projects and works to create jobs and promote full employment. Discipline, honesty and hard work are the watchwords of his administration. He works to stamp out all veneers of greed, corruption, tribalism, nepotism and cronyism. Among some of Africa's well-known benevolent dictators were Ghana's Jerry Rawlings, Rwanda's Paul Kagame, Burkina Faso's Thomas Sankara, Guinea's Sekou Toure, and Cameroon's Ahmadou Ahidjo. Plato actually believes that the best form of government actually comes from such benevolent dictators, which he calls philosopher king. One distinct difference between the absolute dictator and the benevolent dictator is that the absolute dictator's narcissistic impulses drive him to lay claim to such undeserved titles as Emperor, Marshall, or General or Professor, as we saw here above with Gambia's Yahya Jammeh, while the benevolent dictator in most cases maintains the rank or title he had prior to acquiring power. For example, on gaining power, Jean-Bédel Bokassa suddenly went from a man who had the rank of an army sergeant in the French army to crown himself emperor, while Idi Amin went from an infantry Sergeant to a General, and Mobutu Sese Seko from a civilian newspaper reporter to a military Field Marshall. In the meantime, Lt. Rawlings, Captain Sankara and General Kagame, all of them benevolent dictators, maintained the military ranks they had prior to becoming presidents.

Democracy is inherently chaotic. For it to function smoothly, it requires tolerance, self-discipline and a sense of moderation. If the transition from a non-democratic society to a democratic society is direct and immediate, it likely will carry over and potentially exacerbate much of the indiscipline and intolerance that is characteristic of non-democracies. It is exactly for this reason that many of the new democracies that were launched in Africa in the early 1990s failed. For democracy to be sustainable, it first needs to transit through an intermediary stage - a stage that I will here call "the rule of a benevolent dictator." For any people that are not used to the culture of free, open and transparent electoral practice that is part of the democratic governance, it would need to take a strict but cuddling leader to forcibly instill these values.

For illustrative purposes, two of Africa's benevolent dictators come to mind. The first is former Ghanaian President, Jerry Rawlings, who came to power by military coup in 1979 and again in 1981. Upon coming to power, he immediately declared an open war against corruption. The execution of the "war" was ruthless. All public servants, including ministers, who were found guilty of corruption were sentenced to death and executed by firing squad. Among his detractors, Rawlings' harsh rule earned him the reputation of a dictator; but for the masses, he was a populist. Initially leftist leaning, Rawlings established workers' councils and instituted production benchmarks and price controls. Over time, the policies afforded Ghana relative political and economic stability, though at some cost to civil liberties and human rights. He however maintained his reputation as an honest and patriotic leader. In 1991, on the advice of the World Bank and the IMF, Rawlings agreed to liberalize the Ghanaian economy. The winds of democracy that were blowing across Africa at the time also forced him to open up the political process for multiparty competition. He established a political party - the National Democratic Congress - and in November 1992, he was elected president. Reelected in 1996, Rawlings finally retired from politics in 2001. Today, Ghana remains one of the most stable and prosperous democracies in Africa. Inspired by this democratic accomplishment, United States President Barack Obama chose the country as the destination of his first official visit to Africa in 2010. Credit for this democratic accomplishment undeniably goes to Jerry Rawlings, whose benevolent dictatorial rule forcibly instilled the values that transformed Ghana from a corrupt and mismanaged society to a disciplined and stable democracy.

Our second example of a benevolent dictator is Rwanda's Paul Kagame. On assuming power in the aftermath of the Rwandan Genocide, Paul Kagame, went on to govern the country with stern authority. Internally, he did not hesitate to use force to muzzle out domestic challengers. Externally, he frequently silenced his critics by reminding them of their failure to prevent the 1994 Genocide. In working with lobbyists in Western capitals, Kagame succeeded in cultivating an image that portrayed him not as a dictator, but as a hero and visionary. Under his leadership, Rwanda was ranked the number one country with the most women in parliament.[8] He was singularly credited with providing the leadership that brought national reconciliation and healing to post-genocide Rwanda. Merely one decade after the genocidal war, this country that had every reason to fail re-emerged as a beacon of stability in Africa. Economically, Rwanda is seen as one of the most attractive destinations for foreign investment on the continent. Guided by the policy that believes Rwanda needs "freedom to market itself around the world," Paul Kagame worked to create conditions that allowed Rwandans

---

8   Women in National Parliaments; http://www.ipu.org/womn-e/classif/htm (accessed 4/12/2012).

to develop a sense of self-reliance, expressing his preference for trade and investment over foreign aid. To achieve this, he established a simplified tax code, transparency in government, and respect for the rule of law. In just one year, Rwanda's ranking among countries with the "ease of doing business" moved from 143rd in 2008 to 67th. It even outranked the United States in the "ease of paying taxes," taking the 59th position, as the US took the 61st place. Among the major foreign companies that rushed to invest in Rwanda was the American electric and utility group, Contour Global. Between 2004 and 2010, the country's economy grew at an average of 8.8%.[9] Kagame personally courted Costco, the American warehouse club chain and Starbucks to invest in Rwanda. Using his personal ties to the CEOs of these companies, he got them to make Rwandan coffee the primary bean for their stores' brand. Starbucks went on to open a coffee-farmer support center in Rwanda.[10]

Adopting well thought-out macroeconomic policies, Kagame's regime went beyond endorsing a privatization program to establishing a special economic zone to attract foreign investment. He established a Rwanda Development Bank charged with funding a fiber-optic broadband network. Infrastructural planning and development included the construction of a US$300 million conference center with the goal of transforming Rwanda into a conference destination; a planned new airport and increased hotel rooms to accommodate the nearly US$100 million that Rwanda attracts every year in business tourism. Infrastructural development goes beyond the national capital, to developing a national highway system that links Rwanda to Burundi, to the Democratic Republic of Congo, and to Tanzania. Rwanda was the only country in Africa that designed an architectural plan of what it would like its national capital to look like 50 years from now. Called *Kigali 2050? The Audacious and Green(ish) Master Plan*, the plan included restored ecosystems and every thinkable sustainability feature - from walk-ability, to bicycling, to recycling to green jobs. The plan even includes a provision to compensate people who will be displaced.[11] In a continent where the rights of average citizens are seldom respected, this is unusual.

To attract foreign skills and entrepreneurial talent, Rwanda adopted an open immigration policy; and to develop domestic talent, the government promotes free schooling for children aged 12 to 15. A German consulting

9   Anne Jolis, "Rwanda - A Supply-Sider in East Africa," *Wall Street Journal,* April 24, 2010: A11.

10 *The East African,* "Why some small African nations are beautiful and what they can teach the 'ugly' ones." http://www.theeastafrican.co.ke/news/Why+some+small+African+nat ions+are+beautiful/-/2558/1206702/-/6x4nfa/-/index.html Accessed July 30, 2011

11 Nick Aster, Rwanda, a Sustainable Singapore of Africa? http://www.triplepundit. com/2011/11/rwanda-singapore-africs-sustainable/ (Accessed November 8th, 2011).

firm was brought in to open up German-type vocational technical colleges. Writing for the international press, an analyst at the Russia-based investment bank, Renaissance Capital, indicated in April 2011 that the level of development he saw in Rwanda, from visa-free travel, to a well-functioning airport, a reassuring police presence, working streetlights, low-crime and a good road network, "provided for the greatest positive shock of his professional career." Comparing Rwanda to Singapore, he said he saw "clear evidence of forward planning and a strategy for the country" that was reminiscent of the visionary policies that transformed Singapore from an impoverished third world country in the 1960s to a celebrated Asian tiger by the 2000s.[12] The Russian banker was not alone in his observations. At the end of 2010, the World Bank's 2010 Doing Business survey again ranked Rwanda Africa's best country to do business.[13] That year alone, 6,000 companies were registered in Rwanda. Addressing a class on competitiveness at the Harvard Business School in 2013, Kagame was modest about his country's accomplishments: "Every day we are looking forward to see what will make a difference for us. The story of social economic transformation in Rwanda is real. We lifted one million people out of poverty in past five years."[14]

These are achievements that are often credited to liberal democracies. Yet, Kagame's Rwanda was by no stretch of imagination a democracy. As with most African countries, Rwanda under Kagame was a dictatorship. But because his rule brought growth and prosperity that was universally acclaimed, he could aptly be described as a benevolent dictator.

In an October 19, 2011 Foreign Policy article entitled "The Cleanest Place in Africa," David Dagan argues that in a country where the populace is not educated enough to make the right political choices, a benevolent dictator who knows what's good for his country can be far more beneficial than a democrat. He cites Frederick the Great of Prussia's reign, whose authoritarian rule transformed Prussia into one of the rapidly industrialized nations in the 18th and 19th centuries. Juxtaposing that with the 1930s democratic Germany that elected Hitler as its ruler, he points with regret to the harm that a rush to democracy can cause. Dagan compares Kagame to Frederick the Great and Napoleon - two of Europe's benevolent dictators

---

12 The Singapore of Africa? Rwanda's ambition to become the Singapore of Africa is succeeding, according to a recent report by Renaissance Capital, http://www.howwemadeitinafrica.com/the-singapore-of-africa/9210/?utm_source=feedburner&utm_medium=email&utm_campaign=Feed%3A+HowWeMadeItInAfrica+%28How+We+Made+It+In+Africa%29 (accessed 04/12/2011)

13 The World Bank Report, Doing Business 2011, http://www.doingbusiness.org/reports/doing-business/doing-business-2011

14 *The New Times*, Zipline to start assembling drones in Rwanda, http://www.newtimes.co.rw/news/index.php?i=15294&a=64824&icon=Results&id=2 (accessed October 30, 2013)

who catapulted their respective nations into prosperous modern states. In the case of Rwanda, indignation and pent up anger from its genocidal past were still too present in the minds of Rwandans that an accelerated transition to pluralist democracy could have likely led to factionalism and retributive violence.[15]

As with most dictators, Kagame's heroic image came at the cost of civil liberties. Kagame governed with an iron fist. In June 2010, Peter Erlinder, law professor at William Mitchell College of Law in St. Paul, Minnesota was arrested by the Kagame regime and charged with "denying" the genocide. In a lecture given in Arusha, Tanzania, the professor had simply stated that it was inaccurate to blame the Rwandan genocide on one side.[16] Later that same year, Kagame vigorously refuted a 2010 UN Report that accused Rwanda of war crimes in eastern Congo. In his early years in power, the Kagame government imposed harsh sentences of 12 and 33 years on two opposition journalists charged with insulting the president and spreading false rumors. They included former president Pasteur Bizimungu, former prime minister Faustin Twagiramungu, former speaker of parliament Joseph Sebarenzi, and Paul Rusesabagina, the hotel manager whose heroic action during the genocidal war was produced into the movie, *Hotel Rwanda*. In January 2011, the Kagame regime convicted and issued severe sentences to four of the President's former collaborators, including his Chief of Staff and former Ambassador to the U.S., Theogene Rudasingwa; his former Prosecutor General and Vice President of the Supreme Court, Gerald Gahima; his former Director of External Security Services, Colonel Patrick Karegeya; and his former Army Chief of Staff, General Kayumba Nyamwasa. The latter survived an assassination attempt in South Africa in 2010. All four of them were sentenced from 20 to 24 years on terrorist charges, threats against state security, undermining pubic order, promoting ethnic divisions and insulting the president. But what the four had actually done was issue a "Rwanda Briefing" in which they denounced Kagame's rule and called for a change of course for their homeland. In the Briefing, Kagame was described as "a callous and reckless leader," motivated by "greed for absolute power." The Brief asserted that there was "more to Rwanda and Paul Kagame than new buildings, clean streets, and efficient government ... Rwanda is essentially a hardline, one-party, secretive police state with a façade of democracy." Concerned about national harmony, they urged the President to convene a

15 David Dagan, "The Cleanest Place in Africa," Foreign Policy, October 19, 2011. http://navalwarcollege.blackboard.com/webapps/portal/frameset.jsp?tab_tab_group_id=_2_1&url=%2Fwebapps%2Fblackboard%2Fexecute%2Flauncher%3Ftype%3DCourse%26id%3D_4930_1%26url%3D (accessed 3/3/2012)

16 Fox News, Rwanda to Charge US Lawyer with genocide denial, (accessed 2/2/18) http://www.foxnews.com/world/2010/10/21/rwanda-charge-lawyer-genocide-denial/

"genuine, inclusive, unconditional and comprehensive national dialogue" with the aim of creating a new "national partnership government."[17]

The four genuinely believed that opening up the political space was the best way to prevent another genocide. Kagame's regime on the other hand contended that opening up too much political space would unleash unfettered claims to civil liberties, and such claims could rekindle new forms of ethnic hatred and possibly provoke another genocide. Throughout his presidency, he was frequently accused of ruthlessness and intolerance. By accusing and having the opposition jailed for stirring up ethnic hatred, he was able to effectively bar them from running against him in the 2010 presidential. This allowed him to win the August 2010 election with 93% of the vote. The Obama Administration condemned Kagame for suppressing political participation and indicated that it did not regard the regime a democracy.

Kagame's supporters however had but high praises for him. Among them was former British Prime Minister, Tony Blair, who developed close friendly ties with Kagame, referring to him as a "visionary leader," and indicating that he was "a believer in and supporter of Paul Kagame." Concurring with Blair, former U.S. President Bill Clinton also referred to Kagame as "one of the greatest leaders of our time."[18] In 2008, Blair's NGO, the *Africa Governance Initiative*, inaugurated its first project in Rwanda, with staff placement in high government offices, such as the president's policy-making divisions, the prime minister's office, the cabinet secretariat and development boards, to serve as moderating voices in government policy-making.

Economically, the Kagame regime worked to tame inflation, stabilize the currency and provide universal healthcare. Socially, it carried out an educational campaign that provided universal education, and a clean-up campaign known as *umuganda*, where everyone in the community takes part once a month in liter removal and community beautification. Rwandans must have their *umuganda* participation certified on a card by local officials. Without that, they can be denied services at government offices, and/or held to pay a fine of 10,000 frs, or US$20. Top government officials are not exempt from participating in the clean-up campaign. President Kagame himself, along with his Uganda counterpart, Yoweri Museveni was witnessed cleaning up a Kigali neighborhood in preparation for the construction of a school building. David Dagan thus argues that while Rwanda may be "a budding

---

17 *The Guardian*, Stephen Kinzer, Kagame's authoritarian turn risks Rwanda's future, (accessed 5/2/2016); http://www.guardian.co.uk/commentisfree/cifamerica/2011/jan/27/rwanda-freedom-of-speech

18 *The Guardian*, Tony Blair defends support for Rwandan leader Paul Kagame; (accessed 3/2/15) http://www.guardian.co.uk/world/2010/dec/31/tony-blair-rwanda-paul-kagame

police state, it's also a stunning African success story."[19] Between 2000 and 2010, Rwanda had one of the ten fastest growing economies in the world.

Nick Aster admits that the country ranks near the bottom of the barrel for freedom of the press, making vocal criticism of the Kagame regime a delicate affair. In a rather blissful attempt to compare Rwanda to Singapore, he indicates however that despite the simmering political discontent, Rwanda went from the worst place on earth to Africa's crown jewel of stability and economic growth in less than 20 years. Aster raises the following rather thought-provoking question: "Must a certain amount of command and control be expected in a country coming out of genocide, eager to re-join the civilized world on a tight time line?"[20]

We are forced by this question to reflect on the following rather perplexing axiom: As long as the king is a good man, we probably can do without democracy in the short run. Supporters of benevolent dictators would gladly welcome such an axiom. But then, democracy represents the general will of all the people, and not just the will of supporters of the benevolent dictator. This is why the rule of the benevolent dictator should and must be restricted mainly to the transitional stage of democracy. For the transition to democracy to be fully achieved, the dictator and his regime must either voluntarily relinquish power or be forced to do so. When Ghana's Jerry Rawlings voluntarily did so, and when South Korea's Chung Hee forced to do so, it led to the flourishing of democracy in both countries.

Expanding the Civil Society in Africa

No matter how well sophisticated the public sector is, unless there is a large and dynamic civil society, governmental institutions alone cannot effectively perform the much-needed function of checks and balances that are needed to run a democracy. Without the free press that America enjoys, along with an independent judiciary, and a powerful legislature, Nixon would never have been held accountable for the 1972 Watergate scandal. In Africa where the president commands the military, dictates to the supreme court, and controls the legislature, no domestic political institution can dare criticize, much less compel a reigning president to release tapes that contain self-incriminating information.

If efficiency, transparency, democratic accountability are to be realized in Africa, efforts must be invested in expanding the civil society. The dynamism

19   David Dagan, "The Cleanest Place in Africa," Foreign Policy, October 19, 2011.
http://navalwarcollege.blackboard.com/webapps/portal/frameset.jsp?tab_tab_group_id=_
2_1&url=%2Fwebapps%2Fblackboard%2Fexecute%2Flauncher%3Ftype%3DCourse%2
6id%3D_4930_1%26url%3D
20   Nick Aster, Rwanda, a Sustainable Singapore of Africa? http://www.triplepundit.
com/2011/11/rwanda-singapore-africs-sustainable/ Accessed November 8th, 2011

of American democracy is not so much in the handful of political parties that participate in electoral politics, but in the various civil society organizations and interest groups that work year-round to aggregate interest around topics of concern for society. No modern democracy can function without a plurality of competing interest groups. Yet, political systems in Africa for the past half century have been characterized by the total absence of civil society and issue-related interest groups. Democracy flourishes where there are no restrictions on pluralism or political participation. African governments therefore need to go beyond legalizing political parties, to permitting the establishment of civil society organizations and interest groups.

Let's take labor unions for example. If the purpose of democracy is to improve the wellbeing of citizens, then the purpose is in sync with the agenda of labor unions. Initially organized in Western countries during the Industrial Revolution, labor unions were instrumental in pushing for the democratization of the workplace. Experiences gained from organizing the democratization of the workplace were later transferred to helping democratize the larger political society. Unionization in Africa can similarly play the dual role of fostering democratization in the workplace and democratization in the larger society. Thus, strategies that have succeeded in producing improved working conditions in the workplace can equally succeed in producing improved political conditions in the larger society.

Making the Private Sector More Attractive than the Public Sector

While the dream of the typical American who is interested in making money is to become a business CEO, the dream of the typical African interested in making money is to become a governor or government minister. And while it is more common for lawyers in the United States to quit their public sector employment for better paying opportunities in the private sector, in Africa the reverse is true. Lawyers who are interested in making money generally prefer public sector employment.

A reordering of the African public sector is going to require a shift in the balance of power between the public sector and the private sector. It requires making the private sector pecuniary more attractive than the public sector. Currently, the fastest route to wealth and prestige in Africa is through government employment. The wealth obtained comes not from hard work, but from corruption and thievery. This brings to fore one of Africa's most ironic contradictions: The public sector of the African economy is the least productive, yet it is the most lucrative. Africa, in its first half century of independence and self-rule was consuming more than it was producing. While much of that consumption took place in the public sector, the consumption did not always go to benefit the public sector. If it did, then Africa would today have some of the most sophisticated public infrastructures among nation states. But because much of the public consumption benefited private interests rather than the public interest, Africa remains a continent with the least developed infrastructures. The lack of infrastructure has been largely responsible for the inability of African economies to take off.

Box 8.1: African Corruption in Comparative Perspective – An Anecdote

Asian governments have often been more effective than their African counterparts in part because they are less corrupt. By Western standards, Asia has huge amounts of corruption, but for the most part graft there is just another cost of doing business. In Africa, it often prevents business from being done at all. The following anecdote is a frequent staple in African social circles:

An African government official, on a visit with a friend and fellow government official in Asia could not hold back his admiration for the official's beautiful home and opulent life style. The Asian explained his wealth with a wink toward his "cut": "You see that highway out there? Fifteen percent!"

In return, the Asian travels to Africa to visit with his African counterpart. While there, he finds out that the African official was living just as lavishly. Asked how he had achieved such prosperity? The African pointed outside, saying: "You see that highway out there?"

"No," the Asian said, peering helplessly out the window.

The lesson in the anecdote in Box 8.1 is that corruption in Africa is a winner-take-all transaction. No doubt therefore that most democratic elections in Africa always end up in bloody clashes. For the African public official, 15% is obviously not good enough. He must get all of it – all 100% of the public funds budgeted for development. There is no better illustration for how "Africa underdeveloped Africa."

The difference between corruption in Africa and corruption in Asia does have something to do with the degree to which African traditional values were rigorously supplanted by European colonialism. Social values in most societies are wedged on long held traditional values. While the social values of Asia and other colonized regions were preserved, in Africa the values were steadily supplanted. To a large extent, social mores in Asia are still influenced by Confucius and Buddhism. In Africa, the religious values that held the continent together prior to the imposition of European rule no longer exist in the modern sector that governs Africa.

For the current trend to change, the bulk of investment and consumption spending in Africa would need to be directed away from the public sector and into the private sector. It is in the private sector that the fiscal revenues that run government are generated. It is in this sector therefore that the bulk of national resources ought to be invested. For this to happen, international lending agencies will need to stop partnering with African governments and begin partnering with the African private sector.

More MBAs and Less MPAs

The modernization process in the advanced countries of the West started out in the private sector. Over time, as the process of modernization became increasingly complex, Western societies established business schools to develop the expertise that was needed to manage the private sector economy. While the development efforts pursued in Africa are directed at modernizing Africa along the lines of the West, the bulk of Africa's resources are directed not so much at the development of private sector skills, but at developing public sector talent. If development is going to be realized in Africa, it will have to begin with a shift in emphasis on the skills and talents that are in demand in the private sector. What is in demand in the private sector are the management and entrepreneurial skills that are taught in business schools. The most well-known program where entrepreneurial and private sector managerial skills are developed are in master's in business administration (MBA) programs. In market-driven economies, the management talent most demanded is the MBA. MBAs are managers whose performance is driven by the bottom line and by a quest for efficiency. So for Africa to place itself on the path to economic development, it will have to start educating and producing more MBAs (master's in business administration) and less MPAs (master's in public administration). Given the inefficiencies that are characteristic of all sectors of the African economy today, it would be appropriate to say that the continent's investments in education so far have not only been wasted, they have been misdirected at growing a public sector that has today become bloated and unproductive. A typical Western entrepreneur sees Africa primarily in terms of the continent's resource potential and business profits. A typical African administrator or public official sees Africa primarily in terms of turf, power and authority. This needs to change.

Education

Before we conclude this section on the reordering of the African public sector, it is necessary to examine the role of education. Education is the flashlight that lights up the path to modernization. It was education - or what historians commonly refer to as the enlightenment – that provided the spark that traced the path that transformed the West from a feudal society to a modern society. A similar enlightenment is needed in Africa. At independence in the 1960s, and again at the proclamation of the New World Order in the early 1990s, there was euphoria among *afro-optimists* intellectual circles that the African enlightenment was here. A series of academic conferences were organized to examine and celebrate the phenomenon. By the mid-1990s, the euphoria had flickered into pessimism.

Despite the array of Africa's shortcomings, the shortage of intellectual talent is not one of them. Africans can be faulted for everything else, but they cannot be faulted for the lack of intellectual prowess. But as in everything else, Africa's rich intellectual potential remains untapped, under-utilized and misdirected. The curriculum of study in most African countries is to a large extend directed at the development of skills that do not immediately meet Africa's development needs. At independence, educational programs in Africa were designed not to the development of the technical skills that were needed to pull the continent out of underdevelopment, but to the study of the humanities, the classics and religion. Schools in Africa churned out intellectuals who knew more about European history than average European citizens. The average bible student in Africa was better versed in the teachings of the bible than the average Christian in Europe. Because the school curriculum failed to develop the practical skills that were needed for Africa's development, Africa has not been able to transfer the continent's abundant natural resources into material wellbeing for its citizens.

The path to development in America began not with emphasis on Western classics, but with emphasis on agricultural and mechanical studies. As early as in 1862, the Morrill Land Grant Act funded the establishment of A & M universities that were directed at the development of the agricultural and mechanical skills that were needed to transform the country's abundant natural resources into finished goods and material wellbeing for American citizens. So far, in the educational programs of most African states, there is no direct link between education and economic development. If Africa is to modernize and achieve economic development, it would need to adopt an educational curriculum that goes from kindergarten to industry (K to I). This would require redesigning educational curriculums with industry in mind. Employers – from small companies to large industries – will have to work closely with schools and colleges in identifying job skills that are needed in industries, and design curriculums of study that lead to the development of those skills. Through work-study programs, institutions of higher education will enable students to develop readily marketable employment and entrepreneurial skills. Thus, in place of an educational system that prepares students to become job applicants and employees, Africa would need to establish an educational system that prepares students to become employers and job creators. This will require developing a "project-oriented curriculum" – a curriculum that goes beyond the study of the classics to developing skills in the design and transformation of such basic raw materials as bamboo into chopsticks, sand into solar panels, cocoa into chocolate, copper bullion into finished copper products, and raw rubber into bicycle and automobile tires. The granting of paper diplomas or degrees at educational institutions will be conditioned on the successful development of marketable products. Upon completion of studies, students interested in entrepreneurship will be granted start-up capital that will enable them to go into producing and marketing the products they developed while in school. The student's "thesis-defense committee" – that is, the committee which certified the student for graduation – will after the student's graduation continue to work as an advisory board for the student. Responsibility for the success or failure of the project will be shared by both the student and the board. Instructors will be forced to become more effective teachers if they are made to understand that their responsibility as teachers does not end when their students graduate. They have the responsibility to continue to work to get the student to succeed in the real world. And when the student succeeds in the real world, the teacher who now serves on the graduated student's corporate board, will share in the success.

With such reforms in the educational system, not only will students be graduating from educational institutions and going into business for themselves, they will be creating jobs and employment opportunities for others.

There is no better place to invest in the processing of Africa's natural resources than on college and university campuses, where talent and creativity are in abundance and eager to take on new and innovative challenges. In a continent where institutions of education are under-funded and where students have no money to pay for their studies, combining work and study can only but be a win-win. Student-manufactured goods will be marketed locally and/or exported to foreign markets, with the proceeds going into tuition, room-and-board, school supplies, and other educational expenses.

Adopting the Two-Year Community College System

In the long haul, sustainable development in Africa is going to come not from the transfer of technology, but from the domestic development of technology. The most appropriate and formal environment for developing such technology is at vocational institutions that are similar to the two-year community college system that is in the United States. Informally, however, vocational education does need to begin at the pre-K level, with kindergarten kids exposed to the design and inner workings of the mechanical and electronic toys they play with at home and at day-care centers. By the time the kids turn 18, community colleges will provide an environment for them to transform the know-how that they have acquired in the mounting and dismantling of electronic and mechanical gadgets into the formal skills that can be used in the design and fabrication of machines that can address the technology deficit in Africa.

It is only after lower order needs have been met that individuals will strive to satisfy higher order needs. The skills that will be acquired from

196

technical community colleges should help Africans meet such immediate low order needs as food, clothing, shelter and security. Africans cannot begin to produce high tech equipment unless they have mastered the production of low tech equipment. It is only after mastering the production of bicycles that one can move up to acquire the skills that are necessary to produce motorcycles and automobiles. Honda, Suzuki and Kia automobile companies are good examples of this technological progression. They all started out as cycle manufacturers.

Africa's immediate needs at independence were not the high order needs of the arts and humanities, but the low order needs of roads, bridges, farm machineries and healthcare facilities. The establishment of liberal arts universities in Africa at independence was thus incongruent to this hierarchy of needs. At independence, Africans needed to develop skills that were needed to build bicycles and farm plows. Instead, universities established at independence were universities that allowed them to master European history and Shakespearean literature. Today, the same African who reads Shakespeare with the flare of a British aristocrat and handles himself with the elegance of a Parisian is, when called upon, unable to produce lemonade when given a lemon, or replace a spare tire on his $150,000 Mercedes car. Africa is the only continent where the most productive scientists and engineers are given promotions that remove them away from their labs or fieldwork onto air-conditioned offices where they are assigned responsibilities that have no immediate connection to their engineering or scientific skills. It was the rush to provide for higher-order needs at the expense of lower-order needs that is largely responsible for African's inability to pull itself out of underdevelopment.

Although Africans make costly investments in the purchase and acquisition of new inventions, they seldom make investments in the development of the talents that are needed to adapt those inventions to local conditions. As a result, many of the technological equipment purchased by Africa generally serve only a fraction of their lifespan. A machine that is built for a given lifespan in Europe or North America ends up lasting just a fraction of the time in Africa. No doubt therefore that most African economies are often caught in a vicious cycle of indebtedness.

If properly conceived, local community colleges can develop the skills that will invent and/or adapt imported technologies to local needs. With the knowledge and understanding of local conditions, graduates of these institutions will be better placed to redesign machines that were initially designed from processing wheat into flour into machines that can process the African yam or cassava into flour.

Chapter 9

Reordering the African Private Sector

> We, in Africa, cannot continue travelling the worn path of limited success of being
> exporters of raw materials. Our problems require that we think outside of the box.
>
> Ghanaian President, Nana Akufo–Addo

In the colonial era, the public and private sectors were controlled exclusively by colonial powers. At independence, the control of both sectors was handed over to the newly independent African governments. These governments established government corporations and charged them with providing the various goods and services that are best provided by private sector companies. The inexperience and inefficiencies of these corporations were hidden by the monopoly protections that sheltered them from competition. It sometimes took months, and even years, for these government-run corporations to fill orders for customers who applied and were willing to pay for services such as utilities. The budgetary deficits that resulted from such mismanagement were made up for by yearly government subsidies. When African governments ran into financial strains and were no longer able to subsidize their parastatals, the International Monetary Fund and other international financial institutions stepped in to recommend a reordering of state enterprises with the imposition of the all too well-known structural adjustment plan (SAP). As seen above, the plan's recommendations generally called for the privatization of government enterprises.

While privatization may be a sound prescription, it failed to take cognizance of the fact that the African private sector did not have the necessary capital and expertise needed to buy and manage government corporations. In a region where the bulk of the population has no capital to invest, the call for privatization was indirectly a call for the neocolonial reacquisition of the corporations that colonial powers handed over to the newly independent African governments on the eve of their departure. As seen in Chapter 4, the call for privatization was essentially a call for the denationalization or return of the economic assets that Africa inherited at independence to corporations from countries that controlled those assets in colonial times. Foreign corporations alone had the management and financial capital to purchase those government enterprises that were privatized on the advice of the IMF. Once acquired, the bulk of the profits generated are repatriated to corporate shareholders – most of whom are outside Africa – with nothing left behind in the host countries for reinvestment.

In many ways, privatization may have actually contributed to making corruption anonymous and faceless in Africa. In the first decades of independence, for example, roads and highways were built by government agencies such as public works departments (PWD). When a pothole or a bridge needed repairs, a PWD crew was dispatched and the repairs were immediately taken care of. If the work was not properly done, the director of the public works department was directly held accountable. With public works contracted out to the private sector, highway construction and maintenance have not only become faceless, they have become corrupt. Today, when a pothole or structural defect is noticed on a local highway, the government administrator simply submits a report to the public works ministry at the national capital. The ministry in turn submits a report to the presidency. The process can sometimes take months, if not years. Once the report on the pothole is approved for funding, a call for bids is published, inviting the public to tender for contracts.

To have a shot at winning a bid, a contractor would have to either be a relative to the minister or an active supporter of the ruling party. In either case, there is a tacit understanding that the contractor would have to give the minister or someone in the ministerial hierarchy a cut before the contract is awarded. The cut can go from 10% to as much as 30%. To make up for the cut, the contractor will have to either inflate the cost or cut down on the quality of the work to be performed. If the contract was for the construction of an 8 feet thick highway, for example, the contractor will make it 4 feet and still obtain certification from the ministry that the project was dutifully performed. In the meantime, it remains a fact that the African entrepreneur or private sector contractor does not have the capital, the capital equipment or technological know-how to execute the major infrastructural projects that produce development. Such projects are usually contracted out to foreign contractors. This meant that privatization virtually returned Africa's fate to the very forces that were ejected from the continent at independence.

If such a fate is to be avoided, then structural adjustment plans would have to be directed more at the development of the African private sector than at the re-Berlinization of Africa's public assets. In the next paragraphs, we are going to identify some of the strategies that, if adopted, could lead to the development of a viable private sector in Africa. But before we get there, I would like to state that just as Africa's raw materials are there for the taking by the West, Western technology is equally there for the taking by Africa. Those who imitate, initiate; and those who initiate, innovate. Africa does not need to reinvent the wheel. Much of what the continent needs for its development has already been invented. From indoor plumbing to health-care, communications and transportation, the blueprints are all out there.

On governance reforms, there are no copyright laws against the copying or wholesale adoption of the governing constitutions of western democra-cies. African diplomats who represent their countries in the West ought to have, as primary responsibility, the acquisition of the governance, economic and technological secrets of their host countries. Diplomatic representation is in reality an official license to spy. It is an opportunity for diplomats to officially obtain and share with the home country the new ideas, inventions and innovations that are taking place in their host country. It is a well-known fact that the Industrial Revolution began in Britain. One of the reasons why it quickly spread to other countries in the West was because foreign diplomats in Britain communicated the secrets of what was going on in Britain back to their home governments. This is exactly what today's African diplomats who are serving in developed countries should be doing. Monitoring the new inventions and innovations that are taking place in their host countries and communicating the secrets back home can be instrumental in helping Africa catch up economically with the more advanced countries. For the Ghanaian or Ivorian diplomats in Switzerland, their first line of duty should be the collection of information on how their principal export commodity, cocoa, is processed from the bean through to chocolate. And for Zambian diplomats in China, they should be monitoring the various manufacturing processes that copper ore goes through to become finished copper products.

Obtaining Western secrets on how Africa's raw minerals are processed or transformed into finished goods can do more to bring development to the continent than any amount of foreign aid that Africa receives. The same is true with Africans who are privileged to study in the West. Their primary goal should be to acquire and take back home with them, the secrets that have given the West a technological edge over the rest of the world.

Replacing Africa's Drinking Houses with Reading Houses

Traveling across Africa, one is more apt to run into more drinking houses than into reading houses. On virtually every street corner or alley-way in most African countries, there is a drinking house. But finding a library, a museum or reading house can be near impossible. It is not uncommon to hear comedians of all racial backgrounds remark derisively that the best place to hide something of value from a black person is to put it inside a book. In Africa, it is not just a laughing matter, it is a living fact. Most Africans at formal institutions of education are dutiful readers of assigned classroom materials. But once outside of this formal environment, the aver-age African loses the reading habit. Whereas across much of the Western world libraries and reading clubs are found in almost every city, in Africa libraries and reading clubs are among the rarest organizations on the continent. Of course, where there is no reading culture, there is no reason to invest in libraries or bookstores. What is found in abundance in Africa are dancing and drinking houses. Not only are bars and drinking places noisy and distracting, they deny Africa the quiet time that would otherwise be invested in reading. Cultures that do not read do not reflect, and cultures that do not reflect do not invent or innovate. Invention and innovation are the foundations of development. The lack of development in Africa can be directly linked to the lack of a reading and research culture in Africa. If Africa wishes to pull itself out of underdevelopment, it will have to begin by transforming its drinking culture into a reading culture. Public and private resources would have to be directed away from the promotion of drinking and dancing houses to the promotion of reading houses, research labs, museums and think-tanks. No nation has ever transformed itself from a traditional society into a modern society without substantial investments in research and development. And no nation can embark on research and development if it does not have a reading culture.

Investing in Research & Development

The essential elements of modernization and growth are research and development (R&D). The reordering of the private sector in Africa is going to require considerable investments in R&D. Research and development enables the relentless pursuit of innovation, and innovation leads to the development of new product lines. In some cases, R&D is driven by material dissatisfaction with the quality of existing products, or by a relentless quest for a new and improved way of producing existing goods and services. Any product, no matter how perfect, can be perfected or improved upon through R&D.

Much of the advances that contribute to the modernization process come from investments in R&D. Here, as in other areas, Africa seriously lags behind. Policy-makers in most African countries are yet to see the importance of investing in research and development. This partly explains why the continent remains underdeveloped. It is impossible for sustainable development to be achieved unless considerable time and resources are invested in research and development. It is only when technology is developed locally and adapted to local needs that sustainable development can be achieved. If Africa is interested in realizing such development, it would need to start by investing substantially in research and development.

Through research and development, local talent can be brought to develop and produce goods and services that are most appropriately suited for local needs. Existing products can be improved upon and/or adapted to suit unique local conditions. From such improvements and adaptations, ideas for new products will be born. Ultimately, an African country that is a net importer of technology today could, at some future time, become a net exporter of technology. It is a model that has been successfully implemented by other countries around the world. It was through committed investments in research and development that countries such as Japan, China, Hong Kong, South Korea, Taiwan and Brazil were transformed from net importers of technology to net exporters.

Besides the technological improvements that result from investments in research and development, there are many other potential gains. As the only continent that produces much of what it does not consume and consumes much of what it does not produce, unless Africa develops technologies that are adapted to the realities of the African environment, sustainable development will continue to evade Africa. Only through research and development can such a paradox be addressed.

Practically, to get started, each African country could begin by identifying industries that it is interested in developing and/or innovating. Among some of the lucrative industries that can be targeted are education, healthcare, food processing, transportation, telecommunications, farming, and beverages. These are industries that span a broad sector of every economy - developed or underdeveloped. No country can achieve sustainable development without growing these industries. Any African country that introduces research and development in these industries would potentially be placing itself on the launching path to sustainable growth and development.

There is an abundance of tropical fruits and fruit choices in Africa, yet frequently what one readily finds are imported sodas and various foreign concoctions of sugar and color with little nutritional value. Even though Africa grows and exports substantial quantities of tea to the rest of the world, anyone traveling to Africa expecting to drink iced tea will be disappointed. In other words, iced tea is rare in Africa, and most Africans have never actually seen or tasted the drink. Yet, this is a tropically hot continent, and a continent where drinking is a favorite past time. The welcome tradition in almost every home is an invitation to share a drink. While the market for fresh drinks is there, Africa has not made the necessary R&D investments that are needed to grow this highly lucrative industry. The same is true with alcohol beverages. Beer and hard liquor are heavily consumed in Africa. As with soft drinks, no effort has been made to develop and market alcohol beverages using local ingredients. If anything, the production and distribution of local liquor is prohibited. Such criminalization was instituted in colonial times to protect liquor imported from Europe against local competition. That fifty years after independence African rulers continue to enforce laws that criminalize aspects of their domestic economy is a vivid illustration of the numbing spell that perpetuates dependency and stagnation in Africa.

While indigenous know-how may be in abundance in Africa, visionary leadership is woefully lacking. All that a visionary leader would need to do would be to identify and bring together the country's best minds in one discipline such as chemistry. Together with a team of traditional brewers, the chemists will work in formulating and perfecting the various brands of local beverages that can be sold locally and abroad.

Besides promoting research and development in beverages, Africa has the potential of becoming one of the world's best suppliers of spring water. In many of the highly developed countries of the world, industrialization has created a rather costly pollution problem. Acid rain, for example, directly results from industrial pollution. It is a problem that has affected and continues to affect the air, the water, and the subsoil. To remove these pollutants, drinking water has to go through a rather costly purification process. Africa remains a continent whose environment, particularly its underground, has not yet been too negatively impacted by industrial or environmental pollution. In the increasingly competitive global economy, this is the one area where Africa can turn its underdevelopment to an advantage. Because of its low level of industrialization, Africa does not have the problem of acid rain. With an environment that is still relatively pristine, its spring water should be among the purest in the world. In the multi-billion-dollar spring water industry, Africa can, with the right investment, carve out a niche for itself.

Sex is another one of Africa's favorite pastimes. In almost every African community, particularly in the exclusive circle of men, there are frequent talks about herbs and chewable nuts that have aphrodisiac powers. Long before the West came up with Viagra, Africa could have long developed its own version of the aphrodisiac. But because Africa does not invest in R&D, it has had to lose out on the hundreds of billions of dollars that aphrodisiacs generate for the West. Beyond aphrodisiacs, much of Africa's healing secrets have disappeared for lack of research and development. As the older generation dies out, and as logging depletes Africa of the thousands of years old medicinal herbs that were protected by the rainforest, the world is left with no documented records of the healing powers of many of Africa's plants.

Salvaging what may still be left of medicinal plants in Africa's ecosystem is however not too late. With the right leadership, a team of biologists, chemists, traditional herbalists and modern medical practitioners can be brought together to work in documenting and processing Africa's current and past knowledge in healthcare into a modern pharmaceutical industry. It is only by making such investments that the healthcare system in Africa can aspire to someday becoming self-sufficient. Eventually, Africa could in the future be transformed from a net importer of pharmaceutical drugs to a net exporter.

With its designation as the world's oldest continent, Africa is an archeo-logical gold mine. Yet, Africans allocate no resources to the study of this very fascinating field. Even at Africa's institutions of higher learning, the curriculum seldom includes the study of archeology, anthropology, and other disciplines that study living conditions in Africa in antiquity. Because of the lack of investments in R&D at institutions of higher learning in Africa, Africans interested in the study of Africa's cultural past often have to travel outside of Africa to do so. Yet, it is to Africa that scholars from all over the world go to excavate and study the fascinating relics of our human origins. It is the one area in which the returns on investment can go beyond aca-demic fame. Not only would the discovery of a rare fossil produce unusual publicity, it can provide a tremendous boost for Africa's tourism industry. For an extraordinarily spectacular discovery, entertainment industries such as Hollywood, with their massive financial resources, could be encouraged to visit and produce movies in Africa.

Ultimately, investing in research and development can help Africa iden-tify and focus on the production of those goods and service for which it has the highest comparative advantage. It is only then that Africa would be able to carve out a niche for itself in the increasingly competitive global economy.

Catching up with the Rest the World in the Home Delivery Industry

Globally, home delivery is a multibillion-dollar industry. With the glo-balization of the international economy, it has become one of the fastest growing industries in the world. It generates record profits for countries that invested in the development of the appropriate modern infrastructure. As with all other industries, Africa has completely fallen behind the home delivery industry as a result of the lack of the appropriate infrastructure. If Africa aspires to someday become part of this industry, it may have to start by tearing down and completely rebuilding its urban infrastructure. Socially and financially, this is a costly proposition, but it is a proposition that would pay off in the long run. A good economy demands a good infra-structure and a good infrastructure is a necessary precondition for a good economy. The home delivery industry is so lucrative, Africa cannot afford to deny itself participation in it. DHL, Fedex, and UPS and other multination-als that currently have a presence on the continent manage daily to wade through the costly structural inefficiencies. But if Africa ever hopes to cash in on similar home delivery businesses, including such other businesses as pizza delivery, home internet services and home emergency services, town and city planners will have to work to make sure that all streets are named and house numbered. Without these infrastructures, modern technologies such as the GPS, and lifesaving emergency services that are triggered by 911 calls may never have applications in Africa.

Identifying a Niche

If Africa hopes to become a player in the rapidly globalizing and highly competitive international economy, it would have to start by identifying a niche and capitalizing on that niche. It is a strategy that has historically worked for all nations that have come from behind – from Switzerland to Germany to Japan to Korea and China. What makes these nation players in the highly competitive global economy are the niches that they have carved out for themselves. To pull itself out of underdevelopment, it too will need to find a niche.

The importance of identifying and capitalizing on a niche was first proposed by classical economists Adam Smith and David Ricardo when they theorized in the 17th century that as nations specialize in the production of goods and services for which they have a natural or comparative advantage, it leads to increased efficiency and increased output. Specialization and trade have since been seen as the fastest means to accumulating national wealth. In today's highly competitive global economy, specialization requires finding a niche and developing the skills and resources that are necessary to capitalize on that niche. Since gaining independence, Africans have failed to re-identify and re-develop such a niche. They continue to occupy the economic niche that was defined and imposed on them in colonial times. It was a niche that restricted them to the production of raw materials. Even though there is no market on the continent of Africa for rubber, cocoa or coffee, Africans at independence continued to produce rubber, coffee and cocoa. With the growing globalization of the international economy, Africa can no longer suffice itself in this role. As other economies have evolved from agriculture to manufacturing to service to information technology, Africa needs to begin examining how it too can move up from its role as mono-crop raw material producers and carve out a new niche for itself in the highly competitive global economy. In most cases, identifying a niche does not necessarily require much in start-up capital. The following are a sampling of ideas for niches that Africa can capitalize on.

Swissing Africa

One of the areas where Africa is most lacking is in the provision of services. From hotel to travel to maintenance and repairs, Africa lags far behind the rest of the world. Africa is a vast continent, with tremendous opportunities in the service industry. In the travel industry alone, the first country in Africa that is able to develop the human capacity that enables her to capitalize on this niche and gain a reputation for quality service will experience rapid growth and development. An African airline that can demonstrate through consistency and timeliness that it is able to provide quality service will undoubtedly gain control of the air travel market in Africa.

Although Switzerland is one of the smallest countries in Europe, it succeeded very early on in identifying and capitalizing on a niche that has placed it on the global map as a nation that excels in perfection. Globally, the name Swiss has come to mean timeliness, perfection and quality. Because the quality of Swiss banking is unrivaled, African leaders see it as a safe haven for their loot. But Swiss quality did not just happen. It came from discipline and hard work. Universally, the values that shape the mind that produces development include a sense of hard work, dignity in work, efficient time management, savings, delayed gratification, material success, individualism, asceticism, trust, honesty and persistence. Any African country that can invest in the development of these values would, with time, possibly become the Switzerland of Africa.

Mayo-Instituting Africa

According to the World Health Organization's 2017 annual report, malaria is among the top ten biggest killers in Africa.[1] Malaria has been around for as long as Africa has been around. Today, it is the biggest killer on the continent. If the disease's morbidity rate were this high in pre-colonial Africa as it is today, it well could have wiped out the continent's population. That the population of Africa - the oldest continent in the world - has not gone extinct, it very well could be that prior to the development of modern medicine, Africans had a more effective way of preventing malaria-related deaths. But because colonial rule dismissed offhand everything that was African, modern society may have missed out on the traditional remedies that were used in the treatment of malaria in pre-colonial Africa. In focusing too much on modern medicine to address the malaria epidemic in Africa, the international community may have failed to look at Africa's past for a possible cure.

Today, health and healthcare remain an essential development goal for all societies, developed as well as underdeveloped. As long as humans are alive, there will always be demand for healthcare services. Nowhere is there greater need for quality healthcare than in Africa. Any African country that identifies and develops the resources that fill this niche will not go wrong.

In the United States, the Mayo Institute created a niche by distinguishing itself as a premier reference clinic in the healthcare industry. Among its frequent patients are Africans – most of them heads of states and cabinet ministers. They go there for treatment because of the clinic's renowned

---

1   https://www.iflscience.com/health-and-medicine/hivaid-is-no-longer-the-biggest-killer-in-africa/ (Accessed 9/9/2018).

207

reputation for quality. Even though the clinic has limited specialty in tropical medicine, some patients come there to seek treatment for tropical diseases. In the absence of a medical facility of comparable quality in Africa, it remains the place of choice for the African elite.

There is sufficient wealth in Africa to build clinics that would rival Mayo and other Western clinics. If some of that wealth can be directed to building hybrid medical facilities that, like China's hybrid healthcare system, combine modern and traditional medicines, not only would it treat Africans, it could actually attract patients from other continents.

Silicon-Valleying Africa

Recent breakthroughs in software and engineering technologies have democratize and brought the development of intellectual capital within everyone's reach, including Africans. Today, generating the capital that would allow underdeveloped countries to catch up with the rest of the world now appears much easier than at any time in the past. In the past, countries which needed to catch up with the more advanced countries of the world needed vast amounts of capital investments to build the factories and industries that will produce development. The world now lives in an age where rapid economic growth is driven more by investments in software development and information technologies than in costly industrial factories. This has been proven by the experiences of India and South Korea. Though a third world country, India, in a very short time rose to become one of the world's most computer literate country. Today, India generates about as much income from its IT investments as it does from its investments in heavy industries. The same is true for South Korea.

If appropriately directed, Africa's investments can realize similar gains. Our information based post-modernist era presents an unprecedented opportunity for Africa. "Plug African schools into the global network, and for the first time, students will gain unlimited access to the shared knowledge of the world."[2] It is an era where investments in brain power can leapfrog and produce more rapid development than investments in financial, military or industrial power. It is those African countries that are able to direct their resources into the development of the intellectual capacity or brain power that is needed to produce such technologies that are going to be able to compete with the West.

Despite skepticism from many fronts, in the 1990s the American computer giant Hewlett Packard was of the opinion that one of the ways out for Africa was for Africa to invest in the development of skills that would take advantage of the revolution in information technology. Describing the

2   Boston Globe, July 22, 2001.

idea as "World E-Inclusion," Hewlett Packard invested millions of dollars promoting the idea that World E-Inclusion was going to give Africa and the rest the Third World "... its best chance of catching up with the rest of the world, by transforming itself from a pre-industrial society directly to an information-based economy." With financial contributions from Japan, the World Bank and the UN, governments of the seven leading industrial nations formed the "Digital Opportunity Task Force" in 2000 to do a feasibility study of the idea. [3]

Privatizing Highways

Physically, the most noticeable sign of underdevelopment in Africa are in its highways. After a half century of independence, many of the highways in much of sub-Sahara Africa remain dirt roads. In the rainy season, these highways become muddy and difficult to drive on. A trip that should take one hour on a normal highway would on these roads take a whole day. In some cases, commercial transporters refuse to transport female passengers in rainy seasons out of concern that women will not be as helpful as men when the vehicle gets stock in mud and needs to be pushed out. In the dry season, the muddy highways become dusty highways. Almost everything along the highway - from passengers to vehicles and houses - becomes dusty and dirty. If there are records on how many Africans die from lung cancer, many of those deaths will most likely be attributed to the heavy pollution that is caused by dusty highways.

As deplorable as the highway system in Africa is, wealthy Africans do not mind driving their $100,000 luxury vehicles on them. In a continent whose underdevelopment is attributed to the lack of financial resources, the number of people who own luxury vehicles is amazing. Many of these people are public sector employees. While Africans complain about the lack of money to build public highways, they somehow have money to buy luxury vehicles.

One strategy to developing highway infrastructures in Africa would be to promote the concept of "adopt a highway" – an idea that will entice wealthy Africans to contribute in the construction of highways in their countries. Conceived in the United States during the recession of the 1980, it is a concept that invites private citizens to pay for the repair of portions of a highway, in return for public recognition. The recognition comes from having the donor's name carved or imprinted on a public monument. The experiment proved so successful that by the 2000s, Canada, New Zealand,

Puerto Rico and 49 states in the United States had adopted it.[4] Cash-strapped local governments were able to provide for highway maintenance by simply indulging their citizens' ego for recognition. Nowhere does the ego have a greater craving for recognition than in Africa. It is all too uncommon to see Africa's elite at public ceremonies doling out series of paper money to dancers and other celebrants. A program that invites these elite to adopt portions of highways in return for public recognition can potentially generate substantial sums of money.

Toll highways provide another possible funding option to African countries that cannot come up with the financial capital that is needed to develop roads and highways. It may in some cases require leasing out the construction and management of highways to private developers. The developers will be invited to build and collect toll on the highways for the number of years that it would take to recover their investments. At the end of the lease, the ownership of the highways would then be transferred over to the government. It is a development option whose outcome should benefit everyone. Without having to spend money, African governments can end up owning a network of roads and public highways debt-free – thus avoiding the debt trap that has burdened Africa since independent. African citizens will enjoy the luxury of driving on highways that do not hurt their health or produce severe wear and tear on their vehicles. Finally, shareholders of the companies that build the toll roads will, besides the profits realized in their investments, gain some degree of satisfaction in the realization that they made a contribution to the development of Africa. An all-round win-win for all.

Floridaing Africa

Warm weather is one of Africa's untapped natural resources. Like everything else, it is a resource that Africans have not actively marketed. The potential for long term returns for any investment that is directed at the study of how other warm regions in the world market this resource is tremendous. Marketing techniques used in regions such as Florida, Hawaii, the Caribbean, and Southern Europe can be successfully duplicated in Africa.

As the populations of countries in the temperate regions of the world age, more and more people in these regions are going to want to retire to regions with warm climates. It is a demographic reality that could provide a lucrative niche for Africa. But before any country could aspire to taking advantage of such a niche, it first would need to work in developing key areas of its economy. To attract the retiree population, Africa will need to bring its healthcare system up to par with standards that retirees in temperate

---

4   Texas Department of Transportation, Year 1 Annual Report, http://www.dot.state.tx.us/trv/aah/history.htm (accessed 8/16/2011)

regions are accustomed to. A retiree from Sweden or Minnesota who chooses to spend his winter seasons in Africa should be able to have access to the same quality medical facilities that he or she is used to back home.

Investing in Tourism

Tourism is a multibillion-dollar industry. While Africa may be richly endowed with natural resources, tourism has as much a potential in generating hard currency. Yet, tourism remains one of Africa's most underdeveloped and untapped industry. As with everything else in Africa, its development is neglected. In much of Africa, including countries that have tourism ministries, there are no GPS or roadmaps, no tourist brochures, and no rest areas or toilets along major highways. For directions, a tourist is at the mercy of a taxi driver. For toilet or bathroom relieve, it is culturally acceptable for African males and females to park their car along the highway and dash behind the bushes for a quick ease up. Apparently, African governments seem to see nothing wrong with this. If they did, they would have since done something to correct it. Most African ministers know that in developed economies, major highways come with rest areas and bathroom facilities. Providing roadmaps and rest areas with bathrooms facilities is the most elementary investment any country that is interested in promoting tourism can make.

As with paid toll roads, African governments that do not want to go through the World Bank for loans can contract with private developers to build rest areas that include bathrooms and mini-shopping centers along major national highways. The developers will be granted an exclusive license to produce and sell tourism paraphernalia and collect fees from travelers who use the facilities. Up until their investments are recovered, the developers will be exempt from paying sales taxes.

Wildlife once added to the exoticism that attracted distant travelers (tourists and explorers) to Africa. Some of this exoticism has been taken away and caged in foreign zoos. Species of wildlife that were once plentiful and naturally at home in Africa are now either extinct or found elsewhere outside of Africa. Tourist income that once flowed to Africa from the outside world now flows to the foreign zoos that now house Africa's wildlife. Other than Kenya and South Africa, there is very little in Africa to draw in wildlife tourists. Why travel thousands of miles to see wildlife or African art in Africa, when they can see the animals and the artifacts in their local zoos and local museums?

While some of the African wildlife and artwork found in Western museums may have been acquired legally, much of it was looted in the colonial era. American zoos pay as much as $1 million to lease pandas from the government of China. Should the panda give birth while in an American zoo, the zoo is required to pay China another $600,000 as lease payment for the newborn.[5] Most biologists would agree that the chimpanzee is more exotic and thus a lot more valuable than the panda, as it is genetically similar to humans. Indeed, long before manned space crafts were sent to space, an African chimpanzee from Cameroon was sent on one of NASA's experimental space missions.[6] If the world had to pay to lease the thousands of African Chimpanzees that are in its zoos and labs, it would have been in the hundreds of millions of dollars. This is how much Africa has lost in tourism revenue as the result of foreign exploitation. Much more important is the fact that all animals have an ecological purpose that cannot be performed in the zoo. Taking wildlife away from their natural habitat does not only hurt Africa, it hurts the ecological balance that is indispensable to global environmental sustainability.

This has permanently robbed the continent of a major source of income. Just as the Lincoln and Washington monuments generate tourism revenue for the U.S., L'Ouvre and the Eiffel Tower for France, and Stone Hench for Britain, African wildlife and African artifacts should be kept and protected in Africa to generate tourism revenue for Africa.

Other potential areas for developing and promoting tourism in Africa are national festivals. Here, each African country will need to invest in the organization of annual festivals. Nothing attracts foreign tourists in Brazil like annual carnivals. The classic African novel, *Things Fall Apart*, recounts with spellbound detail, the splendor of the pre-colonial tradition of yam festivals that brought thousands of participants together each year in Nigeria's Iboland. The potential for similar festivals today to generate revenues from foreign and domestic tourists can be astronomical. Almost every African country has a festival of some kind that can be developed into a national festival and marketed globally. In partnership with commercial airlines and travel agencies, African governments can attract foreign group tours.

Equal effort will need to be invested in the promotion of domestic tourism. No people are more ignorant of the various regions within their countries and continent than Africans. Wealthy Africans generally prefer to vacation in Europe or North America. African governments can change this by encouraging and facilitating domestic and intra-continental tourism. Making it easy for the residents of coastal regions to vacation in the interior regions of the country, and for those in the interior to vacation in the coastal regions can lead to new knowledge and a renewed sense of national pride. Continentally, instead of vacationing in London or in Paris, West Africans

5   Panda "Rent" to Hire, US Zoo Says; http://news.nationalgeographic.com/news/2006/03/0313_060313_pandas.html (accessed 2/14/2016)

6   Ham, the First Chimp in Space, (accessed 4/2/2018) http://www.savethechimps.org/the-chimps-history/ham-space-chimp/; http://www.spacechimps.com/theirstory.html

would be encouraged to vacation in East Africa; Egyptians in South Africa and South Africans in Egypt. Cruise ships sailing along African coastlines, with port calls along major coastal cities, should be a gold mine for the tourism industry.

As a potential tourist attraction, the islands of Cape Verde, Equatorial Guinea or Sao Tome are so strategically located that if properly developed, they could become lucrative theme parks very much like Disneyland or casinos similar to Las Vegas and Atlantic City. Such attractions will undoubtedly redirect to Africa the many Africans that regularly travel to amusement parks in Europe and North America for vacation. The hundreds of thousands of jobs that will be generated from amusement parks, hotels, casinos, transportation, food service, private security, and various other forms of entertainment will go a long way to addressing Africa's chronic unemployment problem.

Museums are a tremendous tourist attraction. In spite of Africa's rich history and artistic talent, most cities in Africa do not have museums. A foreign tourist who hopes to see museum holdings of an artistic, historical or sporting activity that he or she may have read about will go back disappointed. Despite its pride as the football capital of Africa, Cameroon has no football or soccer museum that celebrates its legendary achievements. While Graceland generates millions of dollars from tourists who come from all over the world to visit Elvis Presley hometown, no such attractions exists to attract foreign tourists interested in visiting the birthplaces of such legendary African musical artists as Manu Dibango, Rochereau, Nico Mbarga, Fela Ransom-Kuti, or Miriam Makeba. Tourism can help turn African economies around only if Africans make the commonsense investments that promote their countries to foreign and domestic tourists.

Not only does a country like Cameroon need a soccer or football museum, it needs to use soccer to sell much of what the country produces. As the first country in Africa to win the hearts of world soccer fans, Cameroon became a soccer Cinderella of sorts, after defeating Argentina, Brazil and Italy on the world stage. Since 1990, Cameroon has become a household name in the world of soccer. Capitalism is partly about capitalizing on opportunities. Soccer provided a niche for Cameroon, but Cameroon somehow failed to capitalize on that niche. Cameroon could have done wonders for its tourism industry by simply adopting a slogan as simple as *"Cameroon - the Soccer Capital of Africa."* Roger Milla was for African football what Michael Jordan was for American basketball. But while Michael Jordan's name was used to brand and market products that generated hundreds of millions of dollars, African businesses failed to capitalize on Roger Milla's athletic fame in marketing of its consumer products. Not a single African product was marketed with Roger Milla's name. In Cameroon, the most that the country did was to give Milla a desk in an office and the title of "Football Ambassador." Just as

Europe and North American use sports to sell everything from automobiles to household appliances, Cameroon and other African countries could be using soccer, and the fame of such soccer stars to market their consumer goods. On supermarket shelves that are frequented by soccer fans, a bag of Cameroon coffee that has the picture of the Cameroon national soccer team would most likely outsell other brands of coffee. A soccer ball that carries Roger Milla's name or picture, or a ball that is stamped that says "Made in Cameroon," would possibly outsell soccer balls produced in other parts of the world.

Interfacing Africa with Europe

Politically and economically, Europe does need to work to anchor Africa to Europe. Just as the United States has since the proclamation of the Monroe Doctrine laid hegemonic claim over Latin America, Europe, by de facto for a long time laid hegemonic claims over Africa. Looking back at the performance of the two hegemonies, we see that while the United States influence in Latin America did sometimes lead to disturbing outcomes, it eventually led to political stability and economic prosperity. The same cannot be said about Europe's hegemonic influence in Africa.

From the onset, the goal of the United States was the promotion of democracy and economic development in Latin America. In the process, it was confronted with the threat of communism. So to this goal was added to the rather daunting task of combating communism. It required tremendous investments in time and resources. The United States had the will. It carried on steadfastly and, with time it succeeded in accomplishing all three of its defined goals. It overcame communism. It facilitated the institution of democratic reforms. And it promoted economic growth. Today, almost all of Latin America is democratic and free of communism. It became so economically stable, the United States began considering using its hegemonic influence to bring all of Latin America into the ambit of the North American Free Trade Agreement. In America's economic relationship with its satellite states, it frequently sought to promote win/win policies. It did so by helping develop a middle class in countries that fell within its hegemonic zone of influence. Also known as the consumer class, this middle class has expanded and is now in a position to begin supporting the American economy by buying goods and services that are produced by American manufacturers – from automobiles to computers, food, music, movies etc.

Across the Atlantic, instead of promoting win/win policies, Europe's exploitation of Africa has been regrettably one-directional. Besides the search for raw materials, the other motivating goal behind the imperialist expansion of Europe was the search for markets. The Industrial Revolution produced a surplus in production that was beyond the consumption capacity of the European market. As Europe set out to discover foreign outlets for its manufactures, it found in Africa the potential for new markets. In the process, it was blinded by the abundance of the natural resources it found in Africa and failed to develop Africa as a market for the sale of European industrial manufactures. Developing such a market would have meant promoting policies that would grow the African middle class. Today, as most advanced industrial economies are increasingly gaining market share within their respective economic zones of influence, Europe is increasingly losing market share. Japan and China control a commanding share of the Asian market, while the United States controls a commanding share of the Latin American market. In the meantime, Europe is getting increasingly squeezed out of these markets as it competes globally and regionally. Had Europe invested in developing an economic middle class in Africa, it would today be an economic giant in its own right, with control of a consumer market that stretches from northern Europe to southern Africa.

Hoping that it is not too late, if Europe is interested in regaining a dominant position in the world, it would need to work to interface with Africa. Despite the successful integration of the European Union, the economy of the Union is not going to be able to guarantee Europe the level of economic growth that Europe will need to compete effectively in the new global economy. Without the cultivation of new foreign markets, manufacturing industries within the current EU zone may not have enough outlets for the sale of their manufactures. It is exactly the quest for a larger market that gave the United States the insight to begin envisioning a NAFTA that is going to go from Canada to Argentina. Europe does need to start thinking along the same lines – a bi-continental common market that will extend from Iceland to South Africa. Developing such a market will of course require extending the Euro zone to Africa. As Europe brings a stable currency into the union, Africa will bring a stable supply of minerals and raw materials.

Developing African Think-Tanks

Development results not just from a wealth of material and financial resources, but from a wealth of ideas. As the incubator of many of the ideas that produce change, the mind is the single most important natural resource. While ideas may be intangible, they make a far much greater contribution to social change than material resources. If the mind is the incubator of ideas, then think-tanks are the nurseries in which these ideas are harnessed, nurtured and passed on to policy-makers. There is a plethora of such nurseries in advanced societies. For solutions to many of society's problems – civilian or military - Western nations often turn to think-tanks. In Africa, they turn to senile heads of states. The outcome speaks for itself: while countries with think-tanks are developing and prospering, Africa remains underdeveloped.

In the one, millions of minds are constantly at work, working to come up with new and innovative ideas. In the other, one person alone, the head of state, determines and dictates what he thinks is good for the country.

As African states begrudgingly implemented World Bank and IMF policies that were imposed on them in the 1980s and 1990s, they were not in a position to come up with counter or alternative policy choices. Obviously, African governments ought to be more informed about their domestic economic conditions than faraway ivory tower economists at the World Bank or the IMF. But because they generally do not get input from think-tanks, Africans are not in a position to come up with alternative policy choices to IMF proposed structural adjustment plans.

Because think-tanks are nurseries of ideas, they can only thrive in environments where there is tolerance for freedom of expression and freedom of thought. The absence of freedom in Africa explains why ideas are in very short supply. It is stifling to creativity and other potential generators of ideas when one individual (such as the head of state) thinks that he alone knows what is best for the country. Until Africa sees think-tanks as a resource that will facilitate its development goals, all of the efforts directed at the pursuit of development will remain misguided.

This was exactly what happened to the now defunct Union of Soviet Republics. The Soviet regime was openly hostile to individual rights and liberties. Soviet Citizens were not allowed to think independently, and therefore no one had the freedom or courage to come up with ideas that were contrary to the state's policy positions. Across all sectors of society, creativity was stifled, leading to the eventual implosion of the empire. In the United States where free-thinking and individual liberties were promoted, and which depended on private citizens and organized think-tanks for ideas, the political system prevailed. There is no better illustration of the virtues of a free society.

Much more than foreign aid and World Bank loans, the two most essential values for sustainable development are freedom and creativity. Freedom inspires creativity, and creativity is fodder for development. Authoritarianism and dictatorship in Africa have shackled the freedoms that were supposed to produce the creativity that would have led to the development on the continent. After successfully stifling the values that produce development, African dictators turned the World Bank and IMF for financial assistance. Without the right set of values, the hundreds of billions of dollars that the Marshall Plan invested in Europe would never have led to the successful reconstruction of Europe. The same is true for Africa.

It is certainly cheaper to promote development through the promotion of liberty than through the pyramid of revolving debts that the international financial institutions sell to Africa. If African rulers are truly interested in achieving development, they first must be prepared to open up their societies to free thinking. Ideas produced either by individuals or by think-tanks can do more for growth and development than all other forms of foreign derived resources.

Universities are a natural setting for thought and reflection. This is where the most insightful minds in society come together. Unfortunately, this oasis of ideas is among Africa's most underutilized resource. Seldom do African governments turn to their institutions of higher education for ideas or solutions. Establishing an atmosphere of open discussion and debate, including debates that are critical of the government is not a sign of weakness, it is a sign of political maturity.

Making Absolute Freedom a Precondition for Development

There is a strong correlation between poverty and human freedom.[7] Africa is poor because it is not free. A review of the Heritage Foundation's Index of Economic Freedom (IEF)[8] reveals that of some 40 Sub-Saharan nations studied, none has an IEF score of "free."[9]

The reverse is true for Hong Kong and Singapore. Former British colonies, both have among the world's highest population densities (3rd and 4th, respectively), and neither have appreciable natural resources or arable land. A final common thread for both countries is their degree of economic freedom. According to the IEF, Hong Kong and Singapore rank 1st and 2nd, respectively placing them among the freest economies. What then are their per capita GDPs? Hong Kong ranks 6th in the world at $38,127, and Singapore ranks 17th at $32,866.[10]

In Africa, countries that have improved their economic status and moved up to middle income status have done so mainly by first extending democratic freedom to their citizens. They include Mauritius, Botswana, South Africa, Namibia, Tunisia, and Cape Verde.[11] These countries are doing better because they are free. This would explain why the outspoken Ghanaian-American economist, George Ayittey, argues that "Africa is poor because she is not free."[12] It is only under guarantees of absolute liberty that modernization can properly flourish. It is true that when people are given the liberty to do whatever they want with their lives, some will fail and some will succeed.

7   Index of Economic Freedom, http://www.heritage.org/index/) (accessed 4/22/2009
8   ibid
9   ibid
10   Taxi,   Design   in   Progress,   http://designtaxi.com/article/100054/
     Design-in-Progress-Hong-Kong/
11   The Economist Intelligence Unit, January 28, 2008, http://www.viewswire.com/index.
     asp?layout=VWArticleVW3&article_id=82987593
12   Ayitteh, George, *Defeating Dictators: Fighting Tyranny in Africa and Around the World*,
     New York: Palgrave Macmillan, 2011

In the long run, those that succeed will inspire others, and even those that fail will learn from their failure.

The concept of unfettered freedom does sound abstract. Yet in the real world there are cases where it has been successfully experimented. At one of the most highly sought-after schools in the United States, Sudbury Valley School in Massachusetts, students are given complete freedom to do whatever they want, including the option to come or not to come to class, or to do or not to do their homework. When students come to class, they are free to choose what they want to learn. If a student chooses to spend all day playing, exercising, dancing, drawing or playing a musical instrument, the student is free to do so. As unconventional as this is, parents are competing to enroll their children at the school, and there is a long waiting list.[13]

Creativity and innovation cannot take place in an oppressed or deprived environment. Inventive spirits can only thrive and flourish in a free environment. The creativity that gave the world rhythm & blues, soul, jazz, funk, rock and roll came from the minds of the African-Americans who fled the oppressive south and to the free north. Africans that are interested in developing wealthy and prosperous economies must start first by granting freedom to their citizens.

Instituting a Three-Shift Workday

The workday in most African countries is limited to eight hours. In much of French-speaking Africa, the lunch break goes from noon to 2:30 pm. During these two-and-a-half hours period, workers spend time eating, drinking or sleeping. In the African public sector, workers on the whole seldom put in eight hours. Where work is scheduled to begin at 8:00 am, some workers come in at 9:00 am. By 11:30 am, some are already leaving work, with excuses that range from going to pick up their children from school, to going to visit an aunt or uncle at the hospital, to going to attend the funeral of a friend or family member.

If any region of the world should be putting in more hours of work and working hardest to catch up with the rest of the world, it ought to be Africa. Yet, it is the region of the world that is most laid back. As Africans look for every opportunity to declare public holidays and take time off from work, Asian economies work round-the-clock. Even Chinese businesses that operate in Africa work round-the-clock. While African businesses usually rush to close down on Sundays and public holidays, including public holidays that honor Western saints, Chinese businesses stay open seven days a week, 365 days a year. Until Africans declare war against under-development and move to fight it with a heightened sense of urgency, it will be difficult to achieve

13   http://www.sudval.org/

development. Any nation at war that puts in just eight hours of fighting a day will never win that war. Tackling underdevelopment with the same sense of urgency with which nations fight wars means that Africans must organize their economies into three shift workdays. An 8-hour workday is simply too short for any country or region of the world that truly wants to develop.

Reducing Africa's Dependence on Foreign Aid

In some countries in Africa, as much as 70% of public revenues come from foreign aid. Knowing that aid is there for the asking, there is little reason for these governments to govern with fiscal discipline or explore alternative means of generating public revenues. Instead of noticeable growth, aid to Africa has produced but increased poverty, with more than 50% of the population living on less than $1 a day.[14] Despite the more than $1 trillion of development-related aid that was transferred to the continent in the past half century, real per-capita income in Africa is lower today than it was in the 1970s. Aid that ought to be directed to helping the most destitute in Africa ends up supporting corrupt bureaucrats and bureaucracies. In 2002, the African Union estimated that corruption was costing the continent $150 billion a year. Just weeks ahead of the 2005 G8 conference that had Africa at the top of its agenda, the IMF itself presented a report cautioning that "Aid Will Not Lift Growth in Africa,"[15] therefore, the various stakeholders should be modest in their claims that increased aid will solve Africa's problems. Despite this caution, no serious efforts have been made to wean and redirect Africa away from this vicious cycle. Even after the very intensive debt-relief campaigns of the mid-2000s, African countries still pay as much as $20 billion in interest on debt every year. The repayments are often made at the expense of investments in education, healthcare, and other services that are needed to bring sustainable development.

In some cases, foreign aid forces Africa to develop at a pace it cannot manage, thus, creating a perpetual culture of dependency. The donation of a dozen hospital beds or transportation vehicles to an African country may be well intended and meaningful, but it stifles the creative abilities of that country's citizens in developing long term solutions to the problems that are addressed by such temporary donations. If one looks at foreign aid as a form of welfare, one is prompted to see that while Western nations are working to reduce welfare dependency at home, they are at the same time

14 Goal 1 – Eradicate Hunger & Poverty, http://techalive.mtu.edu/meec/module20/Goal1. htm (accessed 3/8/2011).

15 International Monetary Fund: Report on Africa aid should not be seen as IMF view, Letter to the Editor By Damian Ondo Mañe, Executive Director, and Peter Gakunu, Alternate Executive Director, http://www.imf.org/external/np/vc/2005/070805.htm (accessed 8/9/2010)

working to promote and perpetuate it in Africa.

Independence as a reality implies self-reliance. However, since achieving independence, most African countries have not become self-reliant, they have become increasingly reliant on foreign aid. It is similar to an 18-year old who claims he is an adult and moves out to live on his own, only to keep turning back to his parents to borrow money to pay his bills. This is exactly what foreign aid does to Africa's relationship with its former colonial rulers. It gives a false sense of independence. No nation or individual who depends on donor assistance can truly say that he is independent. Just as it is rare to see a panhandler become financially self-sufficient, it is difficult to see an aid-dependent country develop and become financially self-sufficient. The lesson here is that economies that rely on open-ended commitments of aid almost universally fail, while those that do not depend on aid succeed. Credit for the much talked about economic achievements in China and India goes not to donors of foreign aid but to well thought-out macro-economic policies. The same is true even for some of the stable economies on the continent of Africa. The stable and growing economies of Botswana and South Africa have more to do with internal macroeconomic policies than with externally provided aid.

Just as domestic welfare programs in advanced industrial countries have not been successful in eliminating poverty, foreign aid to Africa and much of the underdeveloped world has not been successful in eliminating underdevelopment. If anything, foreign aid hinders poor nations from becoming self-supporting. It denies Africa the underlying inspiration in the classic maxim that sees "necessity is the mother of invention." If necessity is the mother of invention, then foreign aid saps directly into the spirit of that "necessity." Foreign aid appears to have done for Africa what nicotine does for a cigarette smoker. It creates a habit of dependence and militates against self-reliance. Thus, maybe the lesson here is that, aid is the wrong formula. No amount of externally driven assistance will produce development unless those directly impacted feel the impulse or necessity to invent, create and develop.

Among the vindicating and self-redeeming justification of Europe's exploitation of Africa is a slogan that was euphemistically referred to as "civilizing mission." When it was all said and done, Africa and the world realized that Europe had lied about its real intentions. If Europe is known to have lied about its true intentions in Africa, why should Africa today believe that Europe's foreign aid policies are well intended? In 50 years of foreign aid, Africa has nothing to show but a burden of debt. Not too many financial institutions in the West will continue to grant new loans to a business that has had a 50-year record of failure? But this is exactly what the West has been doing to Africa. It has been granting loans, knowing fully well that these loans were creating no positive impact on Africa, and knowing also that many of the recipient countries were not in a position to repay. No Western bank will approve a loan to a borrower who does not have the ability to repay. That the West has been repeatedly approving such loans for Africa raised concerns that the whistle-blower, John Perkins, in his book *Confessions of an Economic Hitman*,[16] saw as a racketeering ring masterminded by Western governments and Western multinational corporations.

In yet another rather publication, this a Wall Street Journal article titled *Why Foreign Aid Is Hurting Africa,* Dambisa Moyo blames the cycle of corruption, slower economic growth and poverty in Africa on foreign aid. Cutting off the flow, she argues trade would be far more beneficial as "evidence overwhelmingly demonstrates that aid to Africa has made the poor poorer, and the growth slower. The insidious aid culture has left African countries more debt-laden, more inflation-prone, more vulnerable to the vagaries of the currency markets and more unattractive to higher-quality investment. It has increased the risk of civil conflict and unrest (the fact that over 60% of sub-Saharan Africa's population is under the age of 24 with few economic prospects is a cause for worry). Aid is an unmitigated political, economic and humanitarian disaster."[17]

In 2008, Americans had a taste of two of the policies that the IMF and the World Bank had been aggressively pushing on Africa for more than a half century – the high debt that led to the collapse of the housing industry. The aggressive lending practices that granted sub-prime mortgage loans to unqualified home-buyers in the United States were exactly the same practices that were used to impose debt burdens on Africa. In the *Confessions of an Economic Hitman*, John Perkins exposes some of the strategies that the West uses to entrap less developed countries into a vicious circle of debt. The circle begins with a solicited invitation to resource-rich Third World countries to obtain loans from Western lenders. Once obtained, Western corporations are invited to bid for contracts to execute the loans. When the loan is exhausted, the U.S. government and international financial institutions start to demand repayment. Countries that are unable to repay with hard currency are compelled to open up their natural resources for exploitation by Western companies.[18] For countries with the hard currency to repay, just keeping up with interest payment often means sacrificing vital basic human needs such as education and healthcare. From the mid-1990s to the mid-200s, as much as 40% of Cote d'Ivoire's gross national income went

16 Perkins, John, *Confessions of an Economic Hitman*, New York: Ebury Publishing, 2011.
17 Dambisa Moyo, "Why Foreign Aid Is Hurting Africa," The Wall Street Journal, Sunday, March 22, 2009, http://online.wsj.com/article/SB123758895999200083.html
18 John Perkins, *Confessions of an Economic Hit Man*, New York: Penguin Books, 2006.

into making payments on the country's foreign debt.[19] It is hard to imagine how a country can really develop, if close to half of its gross national income is spent on debt servicing.

As pointed out above, countries that are unable to keep up with their loan repayments are quickly granted new loans so they can continue to make payment on the accumulating interest. It was a debt cycle so vicious that, in the late 1990s, the international civil society, led by U2 Singer Bono, was forced to mount an ardent campaign for debt cancellation.[20] By the mid-2000s, Western financial institutions had moved to provide debt relief.

Just as credit card companies make money by loaning money, initially there was a lot of money to be made by loaning money to African countries. From the 1970s through to the 1990s, it was common to find credit card companies on college and university campuses, soliciting credit card applications from 18-year-old students. Newly away from home, and about to enjoy the freedom of living alone for the first time, credit card companies saw the youngsters as easy targets for the lifelong debt trap of "spend now and pay later." Usually with usurious interest rates, the earlier a person gets drawn into this lifestyle, the more money credit card companies stood to make over that person's lifetime. With mom and dad not around to advise or warn their children about the pitfalls of credit cards, college was seen as the most vulnerable environment to get these students hooked on this addiction.

Still too immature to understand the long-term implications of credit card debt, the kids were maxing out credit card after credit card. Before long, some of them were spending more hours working to pay credit card debt. Thanks to the Credit Card Accountability Responsibility and Disclosure Act of 2009, on-campus marketing techniques have largely dried up. A Government Accountability Office report published in 2014 found that credit card marketing to college students had gone down, and in some cases, disappeared altogether.[21]

Just as American college students were spending time working to pay for credit card debt, some African countries too were spending more time extracting their resources to sell and raise the revenues that were needed to make payments on foreign loans. Investments in education, healthcare and other development priorities were suspended so that payments should

19   Economic watch: Ivory Coast (Cote d'Ivoire) Economic Statistics and Indicators, (accessed 10/7/2016); http://www.economywatch.com/economic-statistics/country/Ivory-Coast/

20   *The Scotsman*, Bono Still Hasn't Found What he is Looking for – Debt Relief (accessed, 2/16/2015); http://www.atu2.com/news/bono-still-hasnt-found-what-he-is-looking-for-debt-relief.html

21   Marketing to College Students Appears to Have Declined, https://www.gao.gov/assets/670/661121.pdf

be made on the loans. For the IMF, the World Bank and other Western financial institutions, Africa was as ideal environment for the entrapment of newly independent countries as the American university environment was for the entrapment of newly enrolled college students. These institutions obviously saw that African rulers had the immaturity and vulnerability of American college students. For Western financial institutions, there were hundreds of billions of dollars to be made from granting the loans, and the sooner they got Africans trapped into the debt trap, the more money there was to be made. Even if some of countries defaulted, just as some individuals default on their credit card payments, on the aggregate Western financial institutions still came out ahead.

These loan tactics have led revisionist scholars to come to the rather cynical conclusion that the World Bank and the IMF are institutions of neocolonialism. As the campaign for decolonization forced colonial powers to pull out of Africa, they quickly found subtle ways to continue to exploit the continent indirectly. He who controls a country's finances controls that country. International financial institutions provided the indirect, backdoor way to the continuous exploitation of Africa. It is hard not to refute that what the IMF and the World Bank are seemingly doing to Africa today what European colonial powers did to Africa in colonial times. The strategy may not be the same, but the end result is the same – perpetuating underdevelopment and extracting profits, this time in the form of interest payments on loans. If Western financial institutions were genuinely committed to helping promote sustainable development in Africa, they should have by now realized that money is not what will make it happen. It is apparent therefore that international financial institutions are not seriously interested in cutting off the umbilical cord that keeps the South permanently dependent on the North. If they were, they would have long worked to come up with alternatives to foreign aid. But what is even more disturbing is that, even after discovering that the West hid behind the subterfuge of a "civilizing mission" to colonize and exploit the continent, Africans continue to believe that foreign aid is genuinely in their best interest. What could have occurred in the interim to make Africans think that the West had gone from being a predator to being a philanthropist? Had the United States, at independence, depended on foreign aid from Britain to develop, America would to this day remain underdeveloped.

Generally, when a sizeable percentage of the money that is used in governing a country comes from foreign donors, the rulers of that country will naturally give greater allegiance to the foreign donors than to their domestic constituencies. In other words, if your source of power is external rather than internal, there will be no reason for any African ruler to honor the will of his people. It is only by eliminating foreign aid that African governments would be forced to show respect and greater allegiance to domestic economic actors – as these actors can through the taxes they pay, become the principal sources of government revenues. Instead of promoting domestic predatory policies, African governments will begin to promote policies that are friendly to the domestic economy.

In an article on *Foreign Aid and Underdevelopment in Africa*, the Gambian journalist/writer, Mathew K. Jallow laments that despite the massive injection the rough equivalence of four Marshall Plans ($500 billion) in Africa between 1960 and 1997, rather than achieve economic growth, Africa became more dependent, with a net decline in living standards. Citing a study by *The Oxford International Group*, Jallow points out that the external stock of capital held by Africans in foreign banks was between $700 billion and $800 billion in 2005. Between 1981 and 1991 alone, as much as $20 billion was provided by The World Bank for structural adjustment programs in Africa. As much as 40% of Africa's aggregate wealth was stacked in overseas bank accounts.[22]

From 1975 to 2000, the continent's per capita GDP declined by an average of 0.59% each year. This caused a variety of think-tanks, including the Heritage Foundation to come to the conclusion that foreign aid is not the answer to Africa's economic problems. In 1985, the Heritage Foundation pointed out that aid was actually contributing to the underdevelopment of Africa.[23] It has retarded and continues to retard the process of economic growth and the accumulation of wealth. The findings were confirmed by the United Nations Conference on Trade and Development, which admitted that despite many years of aid and policy reform, no Sub-Saharan African country has completed its adjustment program or achieved any sustained economic growth. The Foundation argued aid dependency pulls entrepreneurship and intellectual capital into non-productive activities, thereby blunting the entrepreneurial spirits of many Africans.

In her book, *Dead Aid*, Dambisa Moyo, a Zambian economist, similarly argues that reducing aid radically will force governments to ease curbs on business, develop better relations with emerging powers, such as India and China, and raise more money from international markets. Mike Kendrick, founder of the *Mineseeker Foundation* and aide to Nelson Mandela, warned that foreign aid has not only increased the hardship faced by the poor in Africa, it has made Africa the 'spoilt child of the planet.' "In the past few decades the West has provided several trillion dollars in aid, yet the average

---

22 Mathew K. Jallow, "Foreign Aid and Underdevelopment in Africa," Sat, 17 Apr 2010, Modern Ghana (http://www.modernghana.com/news/271860/1/foreign-aid-and-underdevelopment-in-africa.html) (accessed August 20, 2011).

23 ibid.

African is now twice as poor as he was before all that started."[24] He uses former Prime Minister Gordon Brown's project to supply £100million of mosquito nets to Africa to illustrate how such well-meaning initiatives can have damaging unintended consequences. The manufacturing and repair of mosquito nets is an industry that provides employment opportunities to many Africans. A foreign aid program that sends millions of dollars of mosquito nets to a country in Africa does not only cause layoffs, it creates unemployment, poverty and dependence.[25] Despite the various findings that point to the negative impact of foreign aid, British Prime Minister David Cameron drastically reduced domestic spending in 2011, while increasing spending on international aid by as much as 34%.

In lieu of foreign aid, a more realistic alternative would be for the West to direct resources to solving the African brain-drain crisis, by facilitating the return of African professionals to Africa. This should, in the long run, do more in promoting sustainable development than the current aid formula. But instead of providing incentives that encourage Western-educated African professionals to return to the continent, what we see are programs that lure them away from Africa. Among them are the American DV Lottery, the Canadian "Citizenship and Immigration Canada (CIC) programs. While such programs may at the micro level be beneficial to individual Africans, at the macro level it is systematically depleting Africa of the indigenous human talent that is needed to produce sustainable development.

Fair Trade in Lieu of Foreign Aid

At an August 2000 speech to a UN Delegation of heads of states, Nobel Peace Prize Laureate and former president of Costa Rica, Oskar Arias pointedly quipped that "We, the developing countries don't want your handouts; we want the right to (freely) sell our products in world markets!" The right that Arias was referring to here is a right that is enjoyed by every developed country. Echoing Arias' plea, T. Baldwin argued in a *London Times* report that what Africa badly needs from the West today are fair terms of trade, generous development aid and the speedy provision of debt relief.[26] Not only is Africa's ability to compete globally restricted by its mono-crop economies, its impoverished farmers are stuck in the production of commodities whose prices are dictated by the buyers – all of whom are in distant parts of the world. In any market where the price is determined by the buyer rather than by the seller, prices are bound to decline or at best remain stagnant. In the

---

24 Jason Groves, 28th May 2011, Mandela aide: Lavish handouts are making Africa the 'spoilt child of the planet',http://www.dailymail.co.uk/news/article-1391714/Mandela-aide-Handouts-making-Africa-spoilt-child.html#ixzz1Nn6ukaVf
25 Ibid.
26 T. Baldwin, *The Times* (London), February 6, 2002.

specific case of Africa, the prices of its commodities have since independence been steadily declining. Weighted for inflation, African producers earn less for their coffee, cocoa, cotton and rubber today than they did in colonial times. In 1966, the price of cocoa was at 37% of its price in 1952.[27] Of course much of Africa was owned by European colonial powers in 1952, and Africa's cocoa then was produced and sold by Europeans. Cocoa buyers made sure they paid fair market prices then. But when Africa became independent and cocoa was now produced by African farmers, the price of the commodity began a downward spiral. By 1966, a mere six years after independence, it had fallen by as much as 63%. Today, in just one online transaction, a commodities' trader in Chicago who does not own a cocoa farm and has probably never seen a cocoa bean can earn in one minute what an African cocoa farmer would earn in a lifetime. Overall, the amount of money that is lost to unfair commodity pricing is much higher than the amount of money Africa receives in foreign aid. The bottom line is that if Africans were paid fair market prices for their raw materials, they will not need foreign aid.

The same is true with market access. Western protectionist trade policies in agriculture and textiles have a deleterious effect over all forms of foreign assistance to Africa, including foreign aid. Agriculture is the one area where Africa can be competitive in the world market. Given direct, unimpeded access to the major markets of the world, Africa can become a competitive player in the global economy. So far, in terms of trade with the U.S., not a single African nation is included among America's top 15 trading partners. In a goodwill attempt to turn this around, the United States established the African Growth and Opportunity Act (AGOA) in May 2000 to help increase African imports to the American market.

Adopting an Open Immigration Policy

Modern nation-states are inherently restrictive to freedoms. There was actually greater freedom of movement in pre-colonial Africa than in colonial and post-colonial Africa. The institution of the modern state has reduced rather than expanded the freedom of movement that Africans enjoyed before the coming of Europeans. Prior to the intrusion of European rule, much of Africa had no state or national boundaries. Africans did not need visas to travel to other parts of the continent. Today, colonially imposed boundaries make Africans aliens in parts of their continent.

Contrary to popular belief, immigration is not a liability for host nations. It is an enterprise that brings in talent, entrepreneurial potential, and people who come in with a readiness and determination to work. Canada and the

---

27   J. B. Knight, Rural-Urban Income Comparisons and Migration in Ghana, Bulletin of the Oxford University Institute of Economics and Statistics, 1972, 34:199-228.

United States are good illustrations of the positive contributions that immigrants can bring to a country.

Labor is one of the four essential means of production. The other three are land, capital and entrepreneurial skills. Among all four, only land is fixed. The rest are mobile. This means that there is the potential that immigrants can bring with them labor, capital, entrepreneurial skills. If the "land resources" (defined to include domestic political stability) of a given country are fertile enough to attract the "mobile resources" of labor, capital and entrepreneurial skills from other parts of the world, it should accelerate economic growth – growth that would benefit the host country.

Restricting immigration means keeping out the potential contributions that immigrant labor, capital and entrepreneurial skills could make to the national economy. More frequently than not, immigrants see in their host country opportunities that natives either do not see, or see but take for granted. The earliest European immigrants to the United States, for example, saw productive potentials that Native Americans did not see, or saw but took for granted. An open immigration policy in Africa, a continent with astronomically high unemployment rates, will potentially open up economic opportunities that so far remain unknown, or known but taken for granted. Because of their motivation and high determination to succeed in their new country, immigrants are more predisposed to working harder and for less money than local citizens. Frequently, the low pay can sometimes push some immigrants to find niches for self-employment. Self-employment in free enterprise economies means bringing together the factors of production – land, labor, capital and entrepreneurial skills - to produce goods and services. It turns the self-employed immigrant into an employer. As his business grows and expands, he/she is now able to employ citizens of his host country. Had s/he been denied immigration into that country, s/he would not have had the opportunity to create jobs or pay business taxes to his host country.

Among all advanced industrial economies, the United States is known to have the most liberal immigration policy. For most immigrants, the primary pull is employment. If the claim that immigrants take jobs away from Americans were true, one would expect that America's liberal immigration policy will cause high unemployment in the United States. Yet, from the last half of the 20th century to the first half of the 21st century, the unemployment rate in the United States has been lower than employment rates in other advanced countries. In the 1990s, while the U.S. unemployment rate averaged 4%, the unemployment rate in Western Europe hovered between 10 to 12%. With some of the strictest anti-immigration laws, one would have expected that the unemployment rate in Europe would be lower. In France the unemployment rate in the early 20002 was so high that the French government voted to reduce the workweek from 40 to 35 hours, in the hope that it will open up more job opportunities for unemployed French citizens.

A 2000 study of US Census data by State University of New York sociologist, John R. Logan, found that black immigrants from Africa ranked highest in educational achievement - outperforming all other immigrant groups, including European and Asian immigrants. As much as 43.8% of African immigrants had university degrees – compared to 42.5% Asian-Americans, 28.0% for immigrants from Europe, Russia and Canada and 23.1% for the U.S. population in general.[28] If African immigrants can compete successfully in a country where opportunities for minorities have historically been limited, they would excel if allowed to freely immigrate and live in any part of Africa where opportunity calls. As they prosper, so too will the economies of their host countries prosper.

The reality in the past half century however is that it is often difficult for Africans to be admitted as immigrants in other African countries. In some cases, it is more difficult for African immigrants to be welcomed in other countries in Africa, than for them to be welcomed in Europe or the United States. While a Nigerian can immigrate to the United States and become an American citizen, the same Nigerian will be denied immigration and citizenship status in neighboring Equatorial Guinea. Even in cases where an African is born of immigrant parents in an African country, the baby is not allowed to acquire the citizenship of its country of birth. Among the triggers of political instability in Cote d'Ivoire in the 2000s were attempts to challenge the citizenship status of native-born Ivorians of Burkinabe ancestry. From what is known of Africa today, it would be extremely difficult for a potential Einstein or Nobel Prize winner from Cameroon to be granted citizenship status in Equatorial Guinea or Gabon.

Non-Aid Approaches to Development

At the launching of the Millennium Development Goals, rich countries committed to spending 0.7% of GDP on overseas development assistance (ODA). By 2010, they were lagging behind by 0.34%. In 2010, the UN estimated the gap between funds promised and funds delivered at $20 billion for the one year alone. Sixteen billion dollars of this shortfall was for development aid that was pledged for Africa. This led experts to cast doubts on conventional approaches to poverty reduction. At a 2010 summit to assess progress in the Millennium Development Goals, world leaders were quick

---

28 *Real Clear Politics*, March 19, 2007, Clarence Page, Black Immigrants, An Invisible 'Model Minority' (accessed 2/18/2009) http://www.realclearpolitics.com/articles/2007/03/black_immigrants_an_invisible.html

to warn that the current approach to foreign aid needed total rethinking.[29]

There is virtually no correlation between the volume of foreign aid that has been given to Africa over the years and the development impact it has produced on the ground. As a result, revisionist scholars in the development community argue that the international system must work in making aid a thing of the past. Their call for an end to foreign aid is based on the old wisdom that if we keep doing the same thing and keep getting the same results, then it is about time we rethink and start doing things differently. If aid has so far proven ineffective in developing Africa, and yet we continue to rely on it as our main policy for development on the continent, then we are in reality promoting failure and not success.

Global economic crises, from the OPEC-triggered oil shocks of the early 1970s to the late 1980s collapse of world commodity prices, to the global financial collapse of the late 2000s were demonstration of Africa's vulnerability to the volatility of the global economy. If Africa has learned any lesson from these crises, it is that Africa cannot continue to depend on outside sources of funding to finance its development. For development to be sustainable, solutions have to be internal, not external. Africa's development is ultimately the responsibility of Africans, and after fifty years of external efforts, Africa ought to know by now that the international community, including passionate supporters of Africa, has grown tired of the argument that Africa is too poor to finance its own development. As the most helpless victim of repeated global economic shocks, Africa ought to know better than anyone that foreign sources and resources for development are typically volatile and distinctively unreliable. To reduce reliance on foreign resources for development therefore, Africa would need to find ways to mobilize its domestic resources and put them to service in the interest of Africa.[30]

Ultimately, domestic resources that need mobilizing include education, healthcare, and the physical infrastructure. Currently, in Africa, there is a serious mismatch between skills that are taught in schools, and skills that are in demand in the economy. As pointed out above, there is need for a permanent and ongoing collaboration between industry and educational institutions to address this mismatch. Other strategies will need to include investments that can transform the structure of African economies from capital intensive natural resource extraction to high-employment labor-intensive manufacturing. For example, it is known that oil pipelines are vulnerable to bunkering and sabotage, particularly in organized crime and

29 Daniel Howden, World leaders warned that approach to African aid needs a total rethink, http://www.independent.co.uk/news/world/politics/world-leaders-warned-that-approach-to-african-aid-needs-a-total-rethink-2083864.html
30 Economic Report on Africa 2010 http://uneca.org/eca_resources/Publications/books/era2010

conflict-ridden zones. So instead of using pipelines to funnel oil to shipping ports, resources could be directed at building railways and superhighways that will put the local labor force to work in transporting these resources. Other strategies that can wean Africa off of foreign aid and help promote sustainable development include:

Refining Africa's Oil in Africa

One of the largest and most important exports from Africa is oil. The oil is largely exported in crude form, denying Africa the value-added income that can be generated from refining the oil in Africa. Paradoxically, many of the countries to which Africa's oil is exported are the very countries that have come to the realization that foreign aid does not work. In our effort to find alternatives to foreign aid, we see the construction of oil refineries in Africa as one of such alternatives. Indeed, building oil refineries in Africa could actually be much cheaper than sending foreign aid to Africa. Some of the aid that the West sends to Africa comes from the taxes that are paid from the profits that are generated by oil refineries. In place of foreign aid, private companies that build refineries in Africa will be given special incentives in the form of tax breaks or direct financial assistance. Transforming the 0.7% GDP that rich countries pledged in the Millennium Development Goals to spend on overseas development assistance (ODA) into tax breaks for foreign corporations that invest in Africa should be a win-win for all. It allows them to achieve their stated foreign policy goals without taking money out of their national treasuries, while at the same time allowing private corporations to earn profits abroad. Finally, not only would the construction of oil refineries in Africa produce value added income for Africa's crude, it will create jobs and bring about the stability and higher incomes that will enhance Africa's ability to import and consume Western made consumer goods.

Transforming Ghana and Cote d'Ivoire into the World's Largest Exporters of Chocolate

Ghana and Cote d'Ivoire are unquestionably the world's largest producers of cocoa. Cocoa is the main raw material that is used in the production of chocolate. As the world's two top producers of this raw material, one would expect these two countries to be among the world's top exporters of chocolate. It is not. It is a paradox that has gone unquestioned for a long time. Foreign aid donors, including international financial institutions such as the IMF and the World Bank, whose assigned mission is to promote economic growth and development in Africa have never cared to question the paradox. Neither have Africans themselves questioned the paradox. Meanwhile, if we take a quick look elsewhere in the world, we would see that Asia's economic rise was largely attributed to value-added production. For Africa hopes to catch up with the rest of the world, it must start by working to transform its economy from extractive industries to manufacturing industries.

Denying African Rulers Personal Banking Rights in Foreign Banks

We have seen here above that the amount of money that leaves Africa annually in the form of ill-gotten wealth far exceeds the amount that comes in as foreign aid. A report by Global Financial Integrity estimates total illicit outflows of money from Africa to approximately $1.8 trillion between 1970 and 2008. Sub-Saharan African countries suffered the bulk of illicit financial outflows. Among countries with egregiously high outflows were Nigeria ($89.5 billion), Egypt ($70.5 billion), Algeria ($25.7 billion), Morocco ($25 billion), and South Africa ($24.9 billion).[31] Egyptian President, Hosni Mubarak's family fortune alone was estimated at $70 billion, with much of it hidden in British and Swiss banks or tied up in real estate in London, New York, Los Angeles and in luxury properties along the Red Sea coast.[32] Overall, illicit financial outflows from the entire region outpaced official development assistance at a ratio of at least 2 to 1. In a rather belated move, the Swiss government had the Deputy State Secretary of the Swiss Federal Ministry of Foreign Affairs, Pierre Helg, declare in Abuja in June 2010 that Switzerland was going to henceforth make it difficult for people who loot state treasuries to save their loot in Swiss banks.[33]

The looting of state funds has substantially contributed to underdevelopment in Africa. It smacks of double standards for Western countries to label African leaders as corrupt, while at the same time providing a safe hideout for Africa's looted funds. While Africans are hiding away the money that is badly needed development at home, they at the same time go to international financial institutions to request loans for development. One of the major democratic reforms that the West has called on Africa to carry out has been transparency in the conduct of public affairs. Besides its tradition of neutrality in world politics, Switzerland is also one of the most democratic countries in the world. That its banking secrecy laws stand squarely in the face of the very transparency that the West has been preaching to Africa smacks of hypocrisy. Shouldn't the democratic transparency that Switzerland and the rest of the West demands of Africa be extended to banking

---

31   Global Financial Integrity: Illicit Financial Flows; (accessed 8/2/2014) http://www.gfip. org/index.php?option=com_content&task=view&id=300&Itemid=75

32   *The Guardian*, Feb 4, 2011, Philip Inman, Mubarak family fortune could reach $70bn, says expert (accessed 2/5/2016) http://www.guardian.co.uk/world/2011/feb/04/ hosni-mubarak-family-fortune

33   AllAfrica.com: Nigeria: Swiss Banks And Looted Funds, (accessed 9/5/2016) http:// allafrica.com/stories/201006080152.html

transparency in Switzerland? Such hypocrisy defeats the professed push to transform African states from kleptocracies to democracies.

The most important foreign aid that the international community can give Africa should be to deny banking privileges to African dictators. Preventing African rulers from banking or hiding away Africa's stolen wealth in the West will reduce the stealing and transfer of Africa's hard-earned currency. Just as the West has put in place sophisticated banking laws to prevent money transfers and money laundering, it equally has the ability to set up laws that will prevent Western banks from becoming safe havens for Africa's stolen wealth. If the West can actively pursue and track down laundered drug monies, and successfully arresting and prosecuting drug traffickers, then it can equally track down African rulers who loot and stash away Africa's wealth in European and American banks.

Tracking down Africa's stolen wealth should actually be easier than tracking down drug money. Banking laws in the United States require that all deposits over $10,000 to be reported to the U.S. government. Money stolen from Africa usually comes in the millions. African rulers are basically public servants. For an American or European bank to accept millions of dollars in deposits from an African public servant, it makes the bank an accessory to the theft.

Expanding the Peace Corps to Include an "Entrepreneurial Corps"

Africa's lack of the can-do spirit is evidenced in everyday activities. In cases where such infrastructures as airports, bridges and highways already exist, one would think Africans would be able to follow existing blueprints and build similar infrastructures. After a half century of independence, Africans still contract out to foreign contractors the construction of most of its infrastructures – from roads to bridges to highways, airports, and even football stadiums. Even in the service industry, most African countries depend on foreign providers in the transportation and hospitality industries. Few African countries own transcontinental airline companies, and even few own five-star hotels. Nigeria, which is the wealthiest and most populous country in Africa – a country with tremendous intellectual potential – has not succeeded in owning an airlines company that can provide steady and reliable services to major destinations outside Africa.

Western societies are driven by the ideology that economies are most efficient if they are organized and run by the private sector. The propelling force in private enterprise economies are entrepreneurs. These are individuals who bring all of the means of production together to produce the goods and services that generate wealth and wellbeing. Where they see resources, they instinctively see opportunities for business. Given the abundance of people with entrepreneurial skills in the West, if foreign aid programs such as the Peace Corps can be extended to include entrepreneurs such as retired CEOs, this could do more to help accelerate the development of Africa than loans from the World Bank. At retirement, most American CEOs are still relatively young and independently wealthy, and thus in a position to share their professional experiences with Africans, if given the opportunity. Having spent their careers managing the production and distribution of resources, they are now in a good position to share their accumulated entrepreneurial experiences. Now in the sunset of life, the CEO who spent a lifetime pursuing wealth and profit may now be eager to extend his legacy by helping make life better for people in other parts of the world. He therefore may see an invitation to volunteer in Africa as an opportunity to leave behind a legacy that crosses international boundaries. The desire to give inauspiciously develops as individuals with wealth grow old. Giving retired CEOs an opportunity to serve in the Peace Corps in Africa could open up an unexpected outlet for philanthropy. Most African businesses seldom outlast their founders. This is an area where retired entrepreneur or business executives in the West can help. Among other things, they can share their management experiences on franchising, branding, and business succession with African entrepreneurs. Expanding the American Peace Corps to include an entrepreneurial corps can help address these needs.

The monopolistic practices that were implemented by African governments at independence have proven detrimental to the African private sector, as they sapped the entrepreneurial spirit in the private citizen. Redirecting foreign aid to the development of entrepreneurship can help reverse this. Besides inviting Western CEOs as volunteers in Africa, entrepreneurial skills can be developed by linking successful foreign entrepreneurs with local African entrepreneurs. The process may require that local chambers of commerce identify potential local business entrepreneurs that are interested in developing working ties with established foreign entrepreneurs. Through such partnering, Africa would be able to gradually develop a modern work ethic, management know-how, capital, entrepreneurial skills, and a network of external clientele.

Hyundaing Honda and Samsuing Sony

Development in various parts of the world has come about not from the reinvention of the wheel, but from copyrighting, refining and readapting the wheel to conditions that are uniquely local. Up until the 19th century, Japan was behind the West in industrial development. Determined to catch up, Japan gradually began emulating the West in a process that I here refer to as "hyundaing Honda and Samsuing Sony." From automobiles to electronics and household appliances, Japan started an industrialization process that was largely based on copying and perfecting American and European technologies. In the 1970s, Japanese products exported to the United States were initially shunned and ridiculed as cheap plastics. The first Japanese cars that were sold in the United States were actually referred to pejoratively as cardboard boxes. Through persistence and perfection, the quality of Japanese manufacture improved and eventually went on to set benchmarks in electronics and automobile production. Honda, Toyota, Sony, and Panasonic became the new standard bearers that producers globally strove to meet. Among the countries that modeled their production after Japan was Korea. For one of its product lines, a Korean automobile company actually took a name that phonetically sounded like the Japanese standard bearer, Honda. The same is true for Korea's flagship electronics company. Its name, Samsung, phonetically sounded very much like Japan's Sony – the electronics standard bearer from the 1960s to the 1990s. By the 2000s, Korea had overtaken Japan in the production and marketing of cellphones and other electronics. How Korea achieved this milestone, we cannot rule out reverse engineering. Reverse engineering is an absolutely legal manufacturing strategy that any manufacturer, including African manufacturers are welcome to resort to.

While Korea is yet to catch up with Japan economically, the one country that has already caught up and even overtaken Japan is China. Leveraging on its large domestic market and a highly disciplined workforce, China succeeded in moving from a Third World communist-driven economy to a global economic behemoth in less than half a century. In the same half century, Africa has had nothing to show. But had Africa at independence invested in development strategies that included reverse engineering efforts that redesign and reproduce existing foreign goods to serve domestic needs, it could today be in the same league with Korea and other net-exporters of consumer technologies.

While it may be true that modern inventions and creative works are generally protected by strict patent and copyright laws, it is also true that some of the most successful inventions and creative works have become benchmarks or industry standard. There are no patent or copyright laws against striving to attain such industrial benchmarks. Among the most disturbing of Africa's failures is Africa's failure to try. The wheel has already been invented. All Africa needs to do is follow existing blueprints and redesign the wheel to serve the unique conditions that are on the ground in Africa.

Maintaining Good Credit

All of the efforts that are directed at carving out a niche and attracting foreign investments to Africa would be naught unless Africans are taught the importance of maintaining good credit. In the early years of independence, all that a prospective African businessperson needed to start an import/ export business was a letter of credit from a local bank. Not before long, the privilege was abused by fraud and deception. This made life hard for everyone else. Whether it is in government or in the private sector, Africans do need to understand that in the modern economy, having credibility or good credit is sometimes preferable to having money in the pocket. All modern business transactions require credibility. Credibility in one area, such as good financial credit, readily transfers to credibility in other areas of business dealings. Not too many people would want to sign a business contract with a person who has had a record of defaulting or of failing to honor contractual agreements. However, a supplier would be willing to sign a contractual agreement to supply goods and services to any individual with good credit, even if that individual is just starting out and does not have money at hand. Thus, while credit tells us something about a person's character, cash in the pocket does not – no matter the amount. The discipline with which an individual manages his personal credit naturally transfers to the discipline with which he will manage his business affairs with others.

It is important to point out here that credibility and good credit are not values that are totally alien in African culture. Africans have sometimes raised business capital through individual contributions that come with no collateral or guarantee for repayment. It generally works as follows: An association of say 12 members will come together once a month and contribute about a thousand dollars each. The total of $12,000 is collected and given to one member. The collection for the following month is given to the next member until all 12 members receive a collection. There is no collateral or in most cases, no written agreement. The transaction is based entirely on faith and blind trust. As informal as this may seem, default seldom occurs. Not even in the case where a member who has received the contribution dies unexpectedly. His estate will generally honor the unwritten obligation and pay off the remaining recipients.

It is obvious therefore that the foundations of credit and credibility are already in place in Africa. All that is needed now is to figure out how to transfer and integrate this communal sense of trust to the modern way of transacting business. This may require going back and studying those core traditional values that guaranteed trust and stability in precolonial Africa.

Curbing Corruption

In a hearing before the U.S. Senate Committee on Foreign Relations in May 2004, Northwestern University's Jeffrey Winters revealed that the World Bank had participated in the corruption of approximately $100 billion of the money it loaned out for the development of Africa.[34] Prior to that, a 2002 report by the African Union, an organization of African nations, estimated that corruption was costing the continent $150 billion a year, as international donors were apparently turning a blind eye to the simple fact that aid money was inadvertently fueling graft.[35]

Corruption is among the many ills that impede economic development in Africa. It is so pervasive on the continent, it causes undue delays and substantial surcharge in the cost of doing business. Money that should go into investment and productive activity is wasted away in under-the-table payments to corrupt officials. Combined with a convoluted bureaucracy, corruption produces red tape, and red tape stymies economic growth. While it takes an average of six days to obtain a business license in the United States, in much of Africa it takes months, and sometimes years. Prior to the advent of cell phones, it often took approximately a year to get business or residential phone service.

Among other things, low income is often given as one of the reasons why corruption is endemic in Africa. The irony however is that most of those who are corrupt are not low-income earners. They are often the most well-to-do and the most highly placed in society. They generally would include the head of state, government ministers, judges, bankers, military and police officials. Meanwhile, the poor and unemployed are among those who are most preyed upon by corrupt officials. The unemployed university graduate who does not yet have a source of income is expected to pay a bribe before he can get hired. Even when the bribe is paid, there is still no guarantee that he or she will get hired. To bid for a government contract, or to simply get a document signed in a government office, one is expected to pay a bribe.

In some African countries, corruption has become so endemic that even if salaries were raised to first world standards, the problem will not go away. The one measure that could cause it to go away would be to pass laws that would make the cost of corruption higher than the benefit. Employment termination and prison sentences have proven ineffective in some countries. The death sentence appears however to work in some countries. It worked in Ghana in the 1980s, when the country's president, Jerry Rawlings, sentenced all of the country's corrupt government officials, including cabinet ministers, to death and had them all executed by public firing squad.

The Ghanaian experience leads us to see corruption as a rationale act, It is an act that involves a cost-benefit analysis. If the benefits are higher

---

34   Isegoria, Wednesday, March 25th, 2009, Why Foreign Aid Is Hurting Africa; http://www. isegoria.net/2009/03/why-foreign-aid-is-hurting-africa/ (accessed August 31, 2011).

35   Dambisa Moyo, *The Wall Street Journal*, Why Foreign Aid Is Hurting Africa, http:// online.wsj.com/article/SB123758895999200083.html (accessed August 31, 2011)

than the costs, many people will participate in it. However, if the costs are higher than the benefits, no one will want to participate in corruption. An individual who is faced with the decision of whether to accept a $5 million bribe or not, may want to start by looking at the punishment he will get if caught. If it is a prison term of say five years, then rationally he might say that losing five years for a $5 million income is well worth the risk. However, if the punishment is a death penalty, then a rational person would see that the cost is higher than the benefits and would reason that it is not worth accepting the bribe. This is certainly the case in China where capital punishment is the standard penalty for most egregious acts of corruption. In Africa, politically connected government officials who are accused of corruption seldom get prosecuted. Those caught are simply reassigned to other government functions or at the most relieved of their functions. If relieved of their functions, they take their millions of stolen dollars away with them. No doubt therefore that corruption is endemic in Africa. Until the punishment for corruption is draconian, the lesson will always be that corruption pays.

Other less draconian measures that could be adopted to help stem corruption in Africa can include the distribution of customer satisfaction survey forms at all government service centers, for customers to fill out and anonymously mail out to a non-governmental watchdog organization; annual civil servant rewards to officials voted the least corrupt by both the public and their peer; and whistle-blower programs that allow employees to report acts of corruption at their places of employment.

Avoiding the Environmental Mistakes of Advanced Industrial Societies

In the relentless push for industrialization and modernization, the West failed to consider the long-term environmental consequences of some of its pollution spewing factories. By the second half of the 20th century, it became evident that the West was headed towards an apocalypse of environmental self-destruction, if nothing was done to reduce pollution. It was not until at the start of the 21st century that advanced industrialized nations began to take these warnings seriously.

The alarm was raised in time for Africa to take heed. The prophesied, though distant, environmental doomsday forecast offers Africa an unprecedented future economic opportunity. As environmental conditions in the West continue to decay, Westerners obsessed about living in a toxic-free environment may want to retire to parts of the world that are pristine and pollution-free. Africa is naturally one of such regions. Should it become a destination of choice for those escaping pollution in the West, it could lead to rapid economic growth on the continent.

For people who believe in the scientific and religious teachings that human life began in Africa, humans may eventually wind up returning to Africa, as industrialization and economic development make living in the heavily industrialized parts of the world unlivable.

Making the Consumption of "Made in Africa" a Status Symbol

In almost every other part of the world, there is a natural preference for the consumption of locally produced goods. Even when priced higher, locals still buy and consume with pride. In Africa, the reverse is true. Here, the general preference is for foreign-made goods. Foreign-made goods are generally seen as a status symbol. While it may be excusable to import such goods as automobiles, electronics, and various high-tech goods that Africa does not yet have the ability to produce, there is no excuse for importing such basic consumer goods as beverages, food, clothing, and household products. It makes it hard for people in other parts of the world to buy and consume African goods, if Africans themselves are unwilling to buy and consume their own goods. Ultimately, when there is low or no demand for African-made goods, it causes unemployment and declining standards of living. This is exactly what is happening in Africa today.

Until "made in Africa" is made a status symbol, it will be hard to overcome these challenges. In the mid-1980s, as America was losing market share to imports from Asia, a similar "Made in America" campaign slogan was launched. It succeeded in stimulating demand for domestic products, enabling U.S. manufacturers to regain market share. A similar campaign will definitely work in helping stimulate the African economy.

Promoting Regional Trade

African rulers have done nothing to change the colonially imposed boundaries and export-oriented economies that were imposed by colonial rulers. If anything, they have been faithful guardians of the status quo, and as faithful guardians, they have made the boundaries sacrosanct. As in the colonial era, African economies continue to depend largely on single commodity exports, making the continent's producers vulnerable to the vagaries of the global economy. Economies whose key infrastructures, from rail systems to highways, are directed to the extraction and export of raw materials out of Africa will by default neglect the domestic and regional economies. If the EU or NAFTA member-countries were not able to trade among themselves because their colonizers had transformed them into producers of similar commodities, the two regions will to this day remain underdeveloped. This has been the plight of Africa.

As currently structured, internal African markets are too small to permit the development of sustainable economies. This means that African systems must look beyond their restrictive borders to develop regional markets. Logi-cally, Africa does need to learn to compete regionally before it can compete globally. To qualify to play in the Olympics, athletes first must compete and qualify in regional competitions. It was not until 1989, almost thirty years after independence, that the World Bank and the United Nations Economic Commission for Africa began talking about the need for increased intra-African trade. [36]

The economic version of the Olympics is globalization. Several years prior to the globalization of the international economy, many countries, including such influential economic powers as the US, Britain, France and Germany knew that effective participation in the new global economic system required an economic clout that is greater than that of the single nation-state. As Europe worked to bring together various European states to form the European Union, North America negotiated an agreement that brought Canada, Mexico and the United States under regional trading blocs. In Asia and Latin America, similar regional economic rearrangements were equally concluded to consolidate and prepare for the upcoming global economic Olympic.

As in everything else, Africa remains structurally unprepared to compete in the global economy. Compared to other regions around the world, the volume of trade among African countries is very low. Yet, they are expected to compete in the global economic Olympic that is called globalization. Indi-vidually, the economies of African states are so infinitesimally small, they can barely stand on their own. The average African country has less than 15 million people. Some, like Gambia, Equatorial Guinea and Sao Tome have populations that are below one million. Some countries are landlocked and have no direct access to the open seas. For them to trade with the outside world, they have to depend on the goodwill of neighboring countries that have access to the ocean. The extra costs incurred for overland shipment through neighboring countries hurts the ability of landlocked countries to participate as full partners in the new global economy.

There is no faster way to economic development than regional trade. If European countries did not trade with one another, and if the United States, Canada and Mexico did not freely trade together, these countries would never have evolved to become major players in the global economy. In failing to include in its structural adjustment plans recommendations for increased intra-African trade, it gives reason to doubt how well-intentioned the policies of the IMF and the World Bank really are.

The UN Economic Commission on Africa reported in its 2002 "Annual

---

36 Douglas Rimmer, in Pierre Hugo, ed., Redistribution and Affirmative Action, Pretoria: Southern Book Publishers, 1992, p. 20.

Report on Integration in Africa" that trade among African countries only accounted for about 10% of their external trade. Even though Gambia is entirely surrounded by Senegal, there is minimal economic activity between the two countries. Senegal's largest trading partner remains France, and Gambia's remains Britain. To grow this trade, these countries do need to diversify trading partners, regionally as well as globally. This of course is going to require the diversification of their economies. They will have to go beyond raw material and monocrop production to the production of finished and semi-finished goods.

It is also going to require specialization in the production of the goods and services for each country has a comparative advantage, and the discontinuation of the current economic system where neighboring countries such as Cote d'Ivoire and Ghana are both producers of cocoa. Trade is impractical between two neighboring countries that produce the same commodity. Besides being producers of the same commodity, Cote d'Ivoire and Ghana also have two different currencies. Unless the two countries can agree to jointly reform their economies and create a common currency, trade between them will continue to remain limited. In European bilateral trade, the largest trading partners in the EU are France and Germany. If these countries produced exactly the same goods and did not share a common currency, trade between them will be seriously limited.

Many of the major roads and railways that are in Africa today are developments that were put in place by European colonial powers. Developed to advance the interest of the colonizer, the roads and railways all lead away from the continent. Today, after more than half a century of independence, these roads and railways continue to lead away from the continent. With poor or no intra-African transportation networks, no doubt therefore that intra-African trade remains at a paltry 10%. Where there are no roads, there certainly will be no trade. Luckily, today, there is a slow but steady realization among African states that to increase intra-African trade, they will have to start by developing an intra-African transportation infrastructure. Just as the trans-American railroad system produced unprecedented economic growth in the United States, a trans-African highway or railway system that goes from Cairo to Cape Town and from Dakar to Nairobi will produce unprecedented economic growth across Africa.

From every perspective, the most effective way to promote growth in extractive and mono-crop economies is to promote manufacturing. Manufacturing produces economic diversity, and diversity increases intra-regional trade. The IMF's 50-plus years of structural adjustment programs in Africa refused to include a push for manufacturing or intra-continental trade. If anything, the IMF frowned at Africa's import-substitution programs, disqualifying them as inefficient and anti-free trade. IMF and World Bank policies that advised Africa to specialize in the production of raw materials were influenced largely by the neoliberal belief in the global division of labor. The rationale was that such specialization was going to produce efficiency and, through trade, specialization was going to lead to increased global output. While there has been an increase in global output, the increase came not so much from Africa's trade with the West, but from Asia's trade with the West.

Led by China, Asia's growth was not influenced by the neoliberal policies of division of labor or specialization and trade, but by a determined defiance of neoliberal policies that advise against the development of import-substitution industries. China and its Asian neighbors aggressively pushed for the adoption of a manufacturing industry that produced virtually the same consumer goods that were produced and consumed in the West. This allowed them to "import-substitute," and once their domestic consumer needs were met, they began to export their surpluses to the outside world. Initially, goods made-in-China were shunned and dismissed in the West as cheap and inferior. With time, China and other Asian manufacturers improved on the quality, and before long China overtook the West in manufacturing and export. Had they abided by the IMF's neoliberal policy and specialized mainly in the production of raw materials and semi-finished goods, China would today be as poor, if not poorer than Africa.

Cultivating the Can-do-it Spirit

It's amazing how the psyche of an entire nation can be emasculated by colonization and oppression. It was not until Africans fought alongside whites in World War II that they developed the confidence and self-esteem that enabled them to begin a campaign for independence. In Myron Echenberg's book, *Colonial Conscripts: The Tirailleurs Senegalais in French Wes Africa*, a soldier is quoted as saying, "we are stronger than the whites. That bullet that hit my tooth would have killed a white. When the shooting came, the whites ran. They knew the area and we did not, so we stayed."[37] They were emboldened even more by watching a non-white army, the Japanese, mount a frontal military attack against the Allies. Prior to this, Africans were taught to believe that the European was invincible. More destructive than the physical exploitation of Africa was the psychological toll colonialism had on the people. It was so intense and so emasculating that it caused Africans to lose faith and confidence in their own abilities. It took Europe's struggle for survival in World War II, and Africa's intervention to help them survive, for Africans to become aware of their ability and potential to free themselves

---

37   Myron Echenberg's book, *Colonial Conscripts: The Tirailleurs Senegalais in French Wes Africa*, 1857-1960 , Portsmouth: Heinemann Publishers, 1991, p. 92.

from the yoke of colonial domination. If this regained self-esteem can be cultivated and extended to other areas, it will enable Africans to develop the can-do-it spirit that will allow them to rely primarily on themselves for the development of their continent.

A National Service that Glamorizes Farming

No country has ever aspired to achieving industrial development without first achieving self-sufficiency in food production. For Africa to achieve food self-sufficiency, it first will have to come up with policies that make farming alluring to the youth. If it can succeed in doing so, it possibly will lead to two important achievements – 1.) domestic sufficiency in food supply and 2.) a curb in youth unemployment. The youth population is one of Africa's most valuable assets. In most countries, it represents as much as 70% of the population. As youthful and as energetic as they are, they suffer the highest unemployment rate on the continent. Africa's septuagenarian and octogenarian rulers are occupying economic and political positions that should be providing employment opportunities to Africa's youths. With their rights to dignified employment usurped, African youths are forced to fetch for opportunities in the informal economy. Many here are forced to indulge into fraud, thievery, Internet scams, prostitution, banditry and armed robbery. Many end up finding early death. As the prostitute finds early death from the epidemic of AIDS, the armed robber finds his in the epidemic of vigilantism and mob justice that has become the answer of the masses who are frustrated with Africa's dysfunctional judicial system.

As a profession, farming is a lot more dignifying than many of these informal activities that bring early death to Africa's youths. Not only would instituting a national youth service that requires African youths to be involved in farming help end the risky activities that cause hardship and early death, it will make farming both glamorous and alluring to the youth. This can be best accomplished by including farming as a discipline in the educational curriculum, and getting youths involved in it at a very early age. On completion of their educational career, one of the preconditions for employment would be for graduates to serve as farmers for two years as part of a government run national service program. Those that complete the service and decide to stay on as career farmers will be given start-up capital that will include land, tractors, and ongoing outreach mentoring and technical support. The stable life that will be produced by such an opportunity should enable young Africans to settle, get married, raise families, and possibly pass on better economic opportunities to their off-spring. In the long run, this newfound love in farming could very well be the epiphany that will place Africa on the path to global competitiveness.

Harnessing the African Diaspora Community

The African diaspora is Africa's least tapped resources. It is a resource that is composed of Africans who have taken up residence in other parts of the world. Many have acquired foreign citizenships and are doing well socially and economically in their adopted countries. As comfortable as they may be, there is always a nostalgic yearning to stay connected with their country of origin. The challenge for Africa is to harness this nostalgia and create conditions that will facilitate the development of good working ties between Africa and its diaspora populations.

Establishing such conditions would require African governments to fully embrace Africans in the diaspora. Such embrace can come through the granting of dual citizenship, voting rights and the right to equal participation in national policy-making. African countries which have extended such privileges to their citizens have enjoyed steady political and economic development. Cape Verde, for example, dual citizenship and grants visa-free entry to anyone in the diaspora whose ancestry is traceable to Cape Verde. It also grants parliamentary seats to regions of the world that have sizeable concentrations of the Cape Verdean diaspora. North America for example has two parliamentary seats; Africa two; Europe two; and Latin America two. Democratically, this has made Cape Verde the most progressive and forward-looking democratic nation in Africa.

With full participatory rights in shaping the political destiny of their countries of origin, Africans in diaspora will be motivated to work in helping develop an Africa that has the best that their various adopted countries have to offer. Eventually, Africans in the diaspora could be the magic wand that will bring sustainable development to the continent. Just as the Chinese diaspora was the driving force behind foreign investments in China, the African diaspora could, given the right political environment, become the most important driver of foreign investment in the African environment. Their potential contributions go beyond the contribution of tangible financial resources, to include the contribution of such intangibles as intellect, passion, hands-on experience, and business connections. With the experience of living in the developed world, they see and understand firsthand the culture and mental processes that produce sustainable development. Should they decide to return to invest or live in Africa, they certainly would want to replicate the working and living conditions that they are accustomed to in the developed world. If they are accustomed to driving on pothole-free highways, they will work to make sure that the roads they drive on in Africa remain pothole-free. In living in a culture where upward mobility is determined not by nepotism but by merit, and where the rule of law prevails over despotic rule, they will push to establish similar values in Africa, and could be the force what will end corruption in Africa. On healthcare, they will demand nothing less than the quality of healthcare that they are accustomed to in the developed world.

Conclusion

None of the things that Africa needs to do to pull itself out of underdevelopment today needs to be invented or reinvented. Everything is already in place, and all that is needed is the ability to copy, adopt, replicate, emulate, duplicate, innovate, perfect, and produce. Whether it is in the private or public sector, the formula for success has already been conceived, tested and proven. There are no copyright laws against copying or imitating the economic or political system of another country. There also no copyright laws against reverse-engineering and re-manufacturing at home, many of the consumer products that Africa needs to produce to raise its standard of living.

Not only will adopting these proven models enable Africa to leapfrog the West, they will help Africa avoid the costly efforts of trying to reinvent the wheel.

Appendixes

Our assessment of Africa's political performance in the first half century of independence and self-rule will be incomplete without eavesdropping on what Africa's external stakeholders are saying about Africa. From her former colonial powers, to international financial institutions, to present-day global economic powers, Africa has a host of external stakeholders. Since it is not materially possible to find out what everyone of them thinks about Africa, we can preview the thoughts of at least one of them. Who better to listen to, than the United States – leader of the free world, and a nation whose development model Africa and much of the rest of the world seek to emulate. In the decade when a majority of countries in Africa was celebrating the 50th anniversary of their independence, its President, Barack Obama paid two official visits to the continent. During both visits, he had the opportunity to address Africans publicly. Speaking as the voice of the free world, President Obama was blunt. He said things that the entrenched oligarchies in Africa did not want to hear, but things that they needed to hear.

In return, Africa too had the opportunity to address the outside world. Speaking for Africa was Ghanaian President Nana Akufo–Addo, president of sub-Sahara Africa's first independent country. In his address, President Akufo-Addo, speaking for Africa said things that had so far never been said to Africa's external stakeholders, but things that needed to be said. It certainly took long to come, but these two new worlds that were forcibly incorporated into the orbit of the Western world in the late 1490s are now directly talking to each other.

Africa may not have achieved much in its first half century of independence, but by standing tall and speaking truth to power, there is no denying that Africa has now come of age. The dialog has begun, and no one knows where it is going to lead. We hope however that these two longtime partners are listening to each other in good faith. If they are, then there is hope that future generations will come along and build on the aspirations that Obama and Akufo-Addo have averred.

Nothing holds more sway in history than a first-person narrative. To give these speeches the weight they deserve, we here present them in full text.

Appendix 1. U.S. President Barack Obama's First Official Address to Africa

Good morning!

It is an honor for me to be in Accra, and to speak to the representatives of the people of Ghana. I am deeply grateful for the welcome that I've received, as are Michelle, Malia, and Sasha Obama. Ghana's history is rich, the ties between our two countries are strong, and I am proud that this is my first visit to sub-Saharan Africa as President of the United States.

I am speaking to you at the end of a long trip. I began in Russia, for a Summit between two great powers. I traveled to Italy, for a meeting of the world's leading economies. And I have come here, to Ghana, for a simple reason: the 21st century will be shaped by what happens not just in Rome or Moscow or Washington, but by what happens in Accra as well.

This is the simple truth of a time when the boundaries between people are overwhelmed by our connections. Your prosperity can expand America's. Your health and security can contribute to the world's. And the strength of your democracy can help advance human rights for people everywhere.

So I do not see the countries and peoples of Africa as a world apart; I see Africa as a fundamental part of our interconnected world - as partners with America on behalf of the future that we want for all our children. That partnership must be grounded in mutual responsibility, and that is what I want to speak with you about today.

We must start from the simple premise that Africa's future is up to Africans.

I say this knowing full well the tragic past that has sometimes haunted this part of the world. I have the blood of Africa within me, and my family's own story encompasses both the tragedies and triumphs of the larger African story.

My grandfather was a cook for the British in Kenya, and though he was a respected elder in his village, his employers called him "boy" for much of his life. He was on the periphery of Kenya's liberation struggles, but he was still imprisoned briefly during repressive times. In his life, colonialism wasn't simply the creation of unnatural borders or unfair terms of trade - it was something experienced personally, day after day, year after year.

My father grew up herding goats in a tiny village, an impossible distance away from the American universities where he would come to get an education. He came of age at an extraordinary moment of promise for Africa. The struggles of his own father's generation were giving birth to new nations, beginning right here in Ghana. Africans were educating and asserting themselves in new ways. History was on the move.

But despite the progress that has been made - and there has been considerable progress in parts of Africa - we also know that much of that promise has yet to be fulfilled. Countries like Kenya, which had a per capita economy larger than South Korea's when I was born, have been badly outpaced. Disease and conflict have ravaged parts of the African continent. In many places, the hope of my father's generation gave way to cynicism, even despair.

It is easy to point fingers, and to pin the blame for these problems on others. Yes, a colonial map that made little sense bred conflict, and the West has often approached Africa as a patron, rather than a partner. But the West is not responsible for the destruction of the Zimbabwean economy over the last decade, or wars in which children are enlisted as combatants. In my father's life, it was partly tribalism and patronage in an independent Kenya that for a long stretch derailed his career, and we know that this kind of corruption is a daily fact of life for far too many.

Of course, we also know that is not the whole story. Here in Ghana, you show us a face of Africa that is too often overlooked by a world that sees only tragedy or the need for charity. The people of Ghana have worked hard to put democracy on a firmer footing, with peaceful transfers of power even in the wake of closely contested elections. And with improved governance and an emerging civil society, Ghana's economy has shown impressive rates of growth.

This progress may lack the drama of the 20th century's liberation struggles, but make no mistake: it will ultimately be more significant. For just as it is important to emerge from the control of another nation, it is even more important to build one's own.

So I believe that this moment is just as promising for Ghana - and for Africa - as the moment when my father came of age and new nations were being born. This is a new moment of promise. Only this time, we have learned that it will not be giants like Nkrumah and Kenyatta who will determine Africa's future. Instead, it will be you - the men and women in Ghana's Parliament, and the people you represent. Above all, it will be the young people - brimming with talent and energy and hope - who can claim the future that so many in my father's generation never found.

To realize that promise, we must first recognize a fundamental truth that you have given life to in Ghana: development depends upon good governance. That is the ingredient which has been missing in far too many places, for far too long. That is the change that can unlock Africa's potential. And that is a responsibility that can only be met by Africans.

As for America and the West, our commitment must be measured by more than just the dollars we spend. I have pledged substantial increases in our foreign assistance, which is in Africa's interest and America's. But the true sign of success is not whether we are a source of aid that helps people scrape by - it is whether we are partners in building the capacity for transformational change.

This mutual responsibility must be the foundation of our partnership. And today, I will focus on four areas that are critical to the future of Africa and the entire developing world: democracy; opportunity; health; and the peaceful resolution of conflict.

First, we must support strong and sustainable democratic governments.

As I said in Cairo, each nation gives life to democracy in its own way, and in line with its own traditions. But history offers a clear verdict: governments that respect the will of their own people are more prosperous, more stable, and more successful than governments that do not.

This is about more than holding elections - it's also about what happens between them. Repression takes many forms, and too many nations are plagued by problems that condemn their people to poverty. No country is going to create wealth if its leaders exploit the economy to enrich themselves, or police can be bought off by drug traffickers. No business wants to invest in a place where the government skims 20 percent off the top, or the head of the Port Authority is corrupt. No person wants to live in a society where the rule of law gives way to the rule of brutality and bribery. That is not democracy, that is tyranny, and now is the time for it to end.

In the 21st century, capable, reliable and transparent institutions are the key to success - strong parliaments and honest police forces; independent judges and journalists; a vibrant private sector and civil society. Those are the things that give life to democracy, because that is what matters in peoples' lives.

Time and again, Ghanaians have chosen Constitutional rule over autocracy, and shown a democratic spirit that allows the energy of your people to break through. We see that in leaders who accept defeat graciously, and victors who resist calls to wield power against the opposition. We see that spirit in courageous journalists like Anas Aremeyaw Anas, who risked his life to report the truth. We see it in police like Patience Quaye, who helped prosecute the first human trafficker in Ghana. We see it in the young people who are speaking up against patronage, and participating in the political process.

Across Africa, we have seen countless examples of people taking control of their destiny, and making change from the bottom up. We saw it in Kenya, where civil society and business came together to help stop post-election violence. We saw it in South Africa, where over three quarters of the country voted in the recent election - the fourth since the end of Apartheid. We saw it in Zimbabwe, where the Election Support Network braved brutal repression to stand up for the principle that a person's vote is their sacred right.

Make no mistake: history is on the side of these brave Africans, and not with those who use coups or change Constitutions to stay in power. Africa doesn't need strongmen, it needs strong institutions.

America will not seek to impose any system of government on any other nation - the essential truth of democracy is that each nation determines its own destiny. What we will do is increase assistance for responsible individuals and institutions, with a focus on supporting good governance - on parliaments, which check abuses of power and ensure that opposition voices are heard; on the rule of law, which ensures the equal administration of justice; on civic participation, so that young people get involved; and on concrete solutions to corruption like forensic accounting, automating services, strengthening hotlines, and protecting whistle-blowers to advance transparency and accountability.

As we provide this support, I have directed my Administration to give greater attention to corruption in our Human Rights report. People everywhere should have the right to start a business or get an education without paying a bribe. We have a responsibility to support those who act responsibly and to isolate those who don't, and that is exactly what America will do.

This leads directly to our second area of partnership - supporting development that provides opportunity for more people.

With better governance, I have no doubt that Africa holds the promise of a broader base for prosperity. The continent is rich in natural resources. And from cell phone entrepreneurs to small farmers, Africans have shown the capacity and commitment to create their own opportunities. But old habits must also be broken. Dependence on commodities - or on a single export - concentrates wealth in the hands of the few, and leaves people too vulnerable to downturns.

In Ghana, for instance, oil brings great opportunities, and you have been responsible in preparing for new revenue. But as so many Ghanaians know, oil cannot simply become the new cocoa. From South Korea to Singapore, history shows that countries thrive when they invest in their people and infrastructure; when they promote multiple export industries, develop a skilled workforce, and create space for small and medium-sized businesses that create jobs.

As Africans reach for this promise, America will be more responsible in extending our hand. By cutting costs that go to Western consultants and administration, we will put more resources in the hands of those who need it, while training people to do more for themselves. That is why our $3.5 billion food security initiative is focused on new methods and technologies for farmers - not simply sending American producers or goods to Africa. Aid is not an end in itself. The purpose of foreign assistance must be creating the conditions where it is no longer needed.

America can also do more to promote trade and investment. Wealthy nations must open our doors to goods and services from Africa in a meaningful way. And where there is good governance, we can broaden prosperity through public-private partnerships that invest in better roads and electricity; capacity-building that trains people to grow a business; and financial services that reach poor and rural areas. This is also in our own interest - for if people are lifted out of poverty and wealth is created in Africa, new markets will open for our own goods.

One area that holds out both undeniable peril and extraordinary promise is energy. Africa gives off less greenhouse gas than any other part of the world, but it is the most threatened by climate change. A warming planet will spread disease, shrink water resources, and deplete crops, creating conditions that produce more famine and conflict. All of us - particularly the developed world - have a responsibility to slow these trends - through mitigation, and by changing the way that we use energy. But we can also work with Africans to turn this crisis into opportunity.

Together, we can partner on behalf of our planet and prosperity, and help countries increase access to power while skipping the dirtier phase of development. Across Africa, there is bountiful wind and solar power; geothermal energy and bio-fuels. From the Rift Valley to the North African deserts; from the Western coast to South Africa's crops -Africa's boundless natural gifts can generate its own power, while exporting profitable, clean energy abroad.

These steps are about more than growth numbers on a balance sheet. They're about whether a young person with an education can get a job that supports a family; a farmer can transfer their goods to the market; or an entrepreneur with a good idea can start a business. It's about the dignity of work. It's about the opportunity that must exist for Africans in the 21st century.

Just as governance is vital to opportunity, it is also critical to the third area that I will talk about - strengthening public health.

In recent years, enormous progress has been made in parts of Africa. Far more people are living productively with HIV/AIDS, and getting the drugs they need. But too many still die from diseases that shouldn't kill them. When children are being killed because of a mosquito bite, and mothers are dying in childbirth, then we know that more progress must be made.

Yet because of incentives - often provided by donor nations - many African doctors and nurses understandably go overseas, or work for programs that focus on a single disease. This creates gaps in primary care and basic prevention. Meanwhile, individual Africans also have to make responsible choices that prevent the spread of disease, while promoting public health in their communities and countries.

Across Africa, we see examples of people tackling these problems. In Nigeria, an Interfaith effort of Christians and Muslims has set an example of cooperation to confront malaria. Here in Ghana and across Africa, we see innovative ideas for filling gaps in care - for instance, through E-Health initiatives that allow doctors in big cities to support those in small towns.

America will support these efforts through a comprehensive, global health strategy. Because in the 21st century, we are called to act by our conscience and our common interest. When a child dies of a preventable illness in Accra, that diminishes us everywhere. And when disease goes unchecked in any corner of the world, we know that it can spread across oceans and continents.

That is why my Administration has committed $63 billion to meet these challenges. Building on the strong efforts of President Bush, we will carry forward the fight against HIV/AIDS. We will pursue the goal of ending deaths from malaria and tuberculosis, and eradicating polio. We will fight neglected tropical disease. And we won't confront illnesses in isolation - we will invest in public health systems that promote wellness, and focus on the health of mothers and children.

As we partner on behalf of a healthier future, we must also stop the destruction that comes not from illness, but from human beings - and so the final area that I will address is conflict.

Now let me be clear: Africa is not the crude caricature of a continent at war. But for far too many Africans, conflict is a part of life, as constant as the sun. There are wars over land and wars over resources. And it is still far too easy for those without conscience to manipulate whole communities into fighting among faiths and tribes.

These conflicts are a millstone around Africa's neck. We all have many identities - of tribe and ethnicity; of religion and nationality. But defining oneself in opposition to someone who belongs to a different tribe, or who worships a different prophet, has no place in the 21st century. Africa's diversity should be a source of strength, not a cause for division. We are all God's children. We all share common aspirations - to live in peace and security; to access education and opportunity; to love our families, our communities, and our faith. That is our common humanity.

That is why we must stand up to inhumanity in our midst. It is never justifiable to target innocents in the name of ideology. It is the death sentence of a society to force children to kill in wars. It is the ultimate mark of criminality and cowardice to condemn women to relentless and systematic rape. We must bear witness to the value of every child in Darfur and the dignity of every woman in Congo. No faith or culture should condone the outrages against them. All of us must strive for the peace and security necessary for progress.

Africans are standing up for this future. Here, too, Ghana is helping to point the way forward. Ghanaians should take pride in your contributions to peacekeeping from Congo to Liberia to Lebanon, and in your efforts to resist the scourge of the drug trade. We welcome the steps that are being taken by organizations like the African Union and ECOWAS to better resolve conflicts, keep the peace, and support those in need. And we encourage the vision of a strong, regional security architecture that can bring effective, transnational force to bear when needed.

America has a responsibility to advance this vision, not just with words, but with support that strengthens African capacity. When there is genocide in Darfur or terrorism in Somalia, these are not simply African problems - they are global security challenges, and they demand a global response. That is why we stand ready to partner through diplomacy, technical assistance, and logistical support, and will stand behind efforts to hold war criminals accountable. And let me be clear: our Africa Command is focused not on establishing a foothold in the continent, but on confronting these common challenges to advance the security of America, Africa and the world.

In Moscow, I spoke of the need for an international system where the universal rights of human beings are respected, and violations of those rights are opposed. That must include a commitment to support those who resolve conflicts peacefully, to sanction and stop those who don't, and to help those who have suffered. But ultimately, it will be vibrant democracies like Botswana and Ghana which roll back the causes of conflict, and advance the frontiers of peace and prosperity.

As I said earlier, Africa's future is up to Africans.

The people of Africa are ready to claim that future. In my country, African-Americans - including so many recent immigrants - have thrived in every sector of society. We have done so despite a difficult past, and we have drawn strength from our African heritage. With strong institutions and a strong will, I know that Africans can live their dreams in Nairobi and Lagos; in Kigali and Kinshasa; in Harare and right here in Accra.

Fifty-two years ago, the eyes of the world were on Ghana. And a young preacher named Martin Luther King traveled here, to Accra, to watch the Union Jack come down and the Ghanaian flag go up. This was before the march on Washington or the success of the civil rights movement in my country. Dr. King was asked how he felt while watching the birth of a nation. And he said: "It renews my conviction in the ultimate triumph of justice."

Now, that triumph must be won once more, and it must be won by you. And I am particularly speaking to the young people. In places like Ghana, you make up over half of the population. Here is what you must know: the world will be what you make of it.

You have the power to hold your leaders accountable, and to build institutions that serve the people. You can serve in your communities, and harness your energy and education to create new wealth and build new connections to the world. You can conquer disease, end conflicts, and make change from the bottom up. You can do that. Yes you can. Because in this moment, history is on the move.

But these things can only be done if you take responsibility for your future. It won't be easy. It will take time and effort. There will be suffering and setbacks. But I can promise you this: America will be with you. As a partner. As a friend. Opportunity won't come from any other place, though - it must come from the decisions that you make, the things that you do, and the hope that you hold in your hearts.

Freedom is your inheritance. Now, it is your responsibility to build upon freedom's foundation. And if you do, we will look back years from now to places like Accra and say that this was the time when the promise was realized - this was the moment when prosperity was forged; pain was overcome; and a new era of progress began. This can be the time when we witness the triumph of justice once more. Thank you.

Appendix 2. U.S. President Barack Obama's Second Official Address to Africa

The President: Thank you. Thank you so much. Madam Chairwoman, thank you so much for your kind words and your leadership. To Prime Minister Haile-mariam, and the people of Ethiopia - once again, thank you for your wonderful hospitality and for hosting this pan-African institution. To members of the African Union, distinguished guests, ladies and gentlemen - thank you for welcoming me here today. It is a great honor to be the first President of the United States to address the African Union.

I'm grateful for this opportunity to speak to the representatives of more than one billion people of the great African continent. We're joined today by citizens, by leaders of civil society, by faith communities, and I'm especially pleased to see so many young people who embody the energy and optimism of today's Africa. Hello! Thank you for being here.

I stand before you as a proud American. I also stand before you as the son of an African. Africa and its people helped to shape America and allowed it to become the great nation that it is. And Africa and its people have helped shape who I am and how I see the world. In the villages in Kenya where my father was born, I learned of my ancestors, and the life of my grandfather, the dreams of my father, the bonds of family that connect us all as Africans and Americans.

As parents, Michelle and I want to make sure that our two daughters know their heritage - European and African, in all of its strengths and all of its struggle. So we've taken our daughters and stood with them on the shores of West Africa, in those doors of no return, mindful that their ancestors were both slaves and slave owners. We've stood with them in that small cell on Robben Island where Madiba showed the world that, no matter the nature of his physical confine-ment, he alone was the master of his fate. For us, for our children, Africa and its people teach us a powerful lesson - that we must uphold the inherent dignity of every human being.

Dignity - that basic idea that by virtue of our common humanity, no matter where we come from, or what we look like, we are all born equal, touched by the grace of God. Every person has worth. Every person matters. Every person deserves to be treated with decency and respect. Throughout much of history, mankind did not see this. Dignity was seen as a virtue reserved to those of rank and privilege, kings and elders. It took a revolution of the spirit, over many centuries, to open our eyes to the dignity of every person. And around the world, generations have struggled to put this idea into practice in laws and in institutions.

So, too, here in Africa. This is the cradle of humanity, and ancient African kingdoms were home to great libraries and universities. But the evil of slavery took root not only abroad, but here on the continent. Colonialism skewed Africa's economy and robbed people of their capacity to shape their own destiny. Eventually, liberation movements grew. And 50 years ago, in a great burst of self-determination, Africans rejoiced as foreign flags came down and your national flags went up. As South Africa's Albert Luthuli said at the time, "the basis for peace and brotherhood in Africa is being restored by the resurrection of national sovereignty and independence, of equality and the dignity of man."

A half-century into this independence era, it is long past time to put aside old stereotypes of an Africa forever mired in poverty and conflict. The world must recognize Africa's extraordinary progress. Today, Africa is one of the fastest-growing regions in the world. Africa's middle class is projected to grow to more than one billion consumers. With hundreds of millions of mobile phones, surging access to the Internet, Africans are beginning to leapfrog old technologies into new prosperity. Africa is on the move, a new Africa is emerging.

Propelled by this progress, and in partnership with the world, Africa has achieved historic gains in health. The rate of new HIV/AIDS infections has plummeted. African mothers are more likely to survive childbirth and have healthy babies. Deaths from malaria have been slashed, saving the lives of millions of African children. Millions have been lifted from extreme poverty. Africa has led the world in sending more children to school. In other words, more and more African men, women and children are living with dignity and with hope.

And Africa's progress can also be seen in the institutions that bring us together today. When I first came to Sub-Saharan Africa as a President, I said that Africa doesn't need strongmen, it needs strong institutions. And one of those institutions can be the African Union. Here, you can come together, with a shared commitment to human dignity and development. Here, your 54 nations pursue a common vision of an "integrated, prosperous and peaceful Africa."

As Africa changes, I've called on the world to change its approach to Africa. So many Africans have told me, we don't want just aid, we want trade that fuels progress. We don't want patrons, we want partners who help us build our own capacity to grow. We don't want the indignity of dependence, we want to make our own choices and determine our own future.

As President, I've worked to transform America's relationship with Africa - so that we're truly listening to our African friends and working together, as equal partners. And I'm proud of the progress that we've made. We've boosted American exports to this region, part of trade that supports jobs for Africans and Americans. To sustain our momentum - and with the bipartisan support of some of the outstanding members of Congress who are here today - 20 of them who are here today - I recently signed the 10-year renewal of the African Growth and Opportunity Act. And I want to thank them all. Why don't they stand very briefly so you can see them, because they've done outstanding work.

We've launched major initiatives to promote food security, and public health and access to electricity, and to prepare the next generation of African leaders and entrepreneurs -investments that will help fuel Africa's rise for decades to come. Last year, as the Chairwoman noted, I welcomed nearly 50 African presidents and prime ministers to Washington so we could begin a new chapter of cooperation. And by coming to the African Union today, I'm looking to build on that commitment.

I believe Africa's rise is not just important for Africa, it's important to the entire world. We will not be able to meet the challenges of our time - from ensuring a strong global economy to facing down violent extremism, to combating climate change, to ending hunger and extreme poverty - without the voices and contributions of one billion Africans.

Now, even with Africa's impressive progress, we must acknowledge that many of these gains rest on a fragile foundation. Alongside new wealth, hundreds of millions of Africans still endure extreme poverty. Alongside high-tech hubs of innovation, many Africans are crowded into shantytowns without power or running water - a level of poverty that's an assault on human dignity.

Moreover, as the youngest and fastest-growing continent, Africa's population in the coming decades will double to some two billion people, and many of them will be young, under 18. Now, on the one hand, this could bring tremendous opportunities as these young Africans harness new technologies and ignite new growth and reforms. Economists will tell you that countries, regions, continents grow faster with younger populations. It's a demographic edge and advantage - but only if those young people are being trained. We need only to look at the Middle East and North Africa to see that large numbers of young people with no jobs and stifled voices can fuel instability and disorder.

I suggest to you that the most urgent task facing Africa today and for decades ahead is to create opportunity for this next generation. And this will be an enormous undertaking. Africa will need to generate millions more jobs than it's doing right now. And time is of the essence. The choices made today will shape the trajectory of Africa, and therefore, the world for decades to come. And as your partner and your friend, allow me to suggest several ways that we can meet this challenge together.

Africa's progress will depend on unleashing economic growth - not just for the few at the top, but for the many, because an essential element of dignity is being able to live a decent life. That begins with a job. And that requires trade and investment.

Many of your nations have made important reforms to attract investment - it's been a spark for growth. But in many places across Africa, it's still too hard to start a venture, still too hard to build a business. Governments that take additional reforms to make doing business easier will have an eager partner in the United States.

And that includes reforms to help Africa trade more with itself - as the Chairwoman and I discussed before we came out here today - because the biggest markets for your goods are often right next door. You don't have to just look overseas for growth, you can look internally. And our work to help Africa modernize customs and border crossings started with the East African Community - now we're expanding our efforts across the continent, because it shouldn't be harder for African countries to trade with each other than it is for you to trade with Europe and America.

Now, most U.S. trade with the region is with just three countries - South Africa, Nigeria and Angola - and much of that is in the form of energy. I want Africans and Americans doing more business together in more sectors, in more countries. So we're increasing trade missions to places like Tanzania, Ethiopia Mozambique. We're working to help more Africans get their goods to market. Next year, we'll host another U.S.-Africa Business Forum to mobilize billions of dollars in new trade and investment - so we're buying more of each other's products and all growing together.

Now, the United States isn't the only country that sees your growth as an opportunity. And that is a good thing. When more countries invest responsibly in Africa, it creates more jobs and prosperity for us all. So I want to encourage everybody to do business with Africa, and African countries should want to do business with every country. But economic relationships can't simply be about building countries' infrastructure with foreign labor or extracting Africa's natural resources. Real economic partnerships have to be a good deal for Africa - they have to create jobs and capacity for Africans.

And that includes the point that Chairwoman Zuma made about illicit flows with multinationals - which is one of the reasons that we've been a leading advocate, working with the G7, to assist in making sure that there's honest accounting when businesses are investing here in Africa, and making sure that capital flows are properly accounted for. That's the kind of partnership America offers.

Nothing will unlock Africa's economic potential more than ending the cancer of corruption. And you are right that it is not just a problem of Africa, it is a problem of those who do business with Africa. It is not unique to Africa - corruption exists all over the world, including in the United States. But here in Africa, corruption drains billions of dollars from economies that can't afford to lose billions of dollars - that's money that could be used to create jobs and build hospitals and schools. And when someone has to pay a bribe just to start a business or go to school, or get an official to do the job they're supposed to be doing anyway - that's not "the African way." It undermines the dignity of the people you represent.

Only Africans can end corruption in their countries. As African governments commit to taking action, the United States will work with you to combat illicit financing, and promote good governance and transparency and rule of law. And we already have strong laws in place that say to U.S. companies, you can't engage in bribery to try to get business - which not all countries have. And we actually enforce it and police it.

And let me add that criminal networks are both fueling corruption and threatening Africa's precious wildlife - and with it, the tourism that many African economies count on. So America also stands with you in the fight against wildlife trafficking. That's something that has to be addressed.

But, ultimately, the most powerful antidote to the old ways of doing things is this new generation of African youth. History shows that the nations that do best are the ones that invest in the education of their people. You see, in this information age, jobs can flow anywhere, and they typically will flow to where workers are literate and highly skilled and online. And Africa's young people are ready to compete. I've met them - they are hungry, they are eager. They're willing to work hard. So we've got to invest in them. As Africa invests in education, our entrepreneurship programs are helping innovators start new businesses and create jobs right here in Africa. And the men and women in our Young African Leaders Initiative today will be the leaders who can transform business and civil society and governments tomorrow.

Africa's progress will depend on development that truly lifts countries from poverty to prosperity - because people everywhere deserve the dignity of a life free from want. A child born in Africa today is just as equal and just as worthy as a child born in Asia or Europe or America. At the recent development conference here in Addis, African leadership helped forge a new global compact for financing that fuels development. And under the AU's leadership, the voice of a united Africa will help shape the world's next set of development goals, and you're pursuing a vision of the future that you want for Africa.

And America's approach to development - the central focus of our engagement with Africa - is focused on helping you build your own capacity to realize that vision. Instead of just shipping food aid to Africa, we've helped more than two million farmers use new techniques to boost their yields, feed more people, reduce hunger. With our new alliance of government and the private sector investing billions of dollars in African agriculture, I believe we can achieve our goal and lift 50 million Africans from poverty.

Instead of just sending aid to build power plants, our Power Africa initiative is mobilizing billions of dollars in investments from governments and businesses to reduce the number of Africans living without electricity. Now, an undertaking of this magnitude will not be quick. It will take many years. But working together, I believe we can bring electricity to more than 60 million African homes and businesses and connect more Africans to the global economy.

Instead of just telling Africa, you're on your own, in dealing with climate change, we're delivering new tools and financing to more than 40 African nations to help them prepare and adapt. By harnessing the wind and sun, your vast geothermal energy and rivers for hydropower, you can turn this climate threat into an economic opportunity. And I urge Africa to join us in rejecting old divides between North and South so we can forge a strong global climate agreement this year in Paris. Because sparing some of the world's poorest people from rising seas, more intense droughts, shortages of water and food is a matter of survival and a matter of human dignity.

Instead of just sending medicine, we're investing in better treatments and helping Africa prevent and treat diseases. As the United States continues to provide billions of dollars in the fight against HIV/AIDS, and as your countries take greater ownership of health programs, we're moving toward a historic accomplishment - the first AIDS-free generation. And if the world learned anything from Ebola, it's that the best way to prevent epidemics is to build strong public health systems that stop diseases from spreading in the first place. So America is proud to partner with the AU and African countries in this mission. Today, I can announce that of the $1 billion that the United States is devoting to this work globally, half will support efforts here in Africa.

I believe Africa's progress will also depend on democracy, because Africans, like people everywhere, deserve the dignity of being in control of their own lives. We all know what the ingredients of real democracy are. They include free and fair elections, but also freedom of speech and the press, freedom of assembly. These rights are universal. They're written into African constitutions. The African Charter on Human and Peoples Rights declares that "every individual shall have the right to the respect of the dignity inherent in a human being." From Sierra Leone, Ghana, Benin, to Botswana, Namibia, South Africa, democracy has taken root. In Nigeria, more than 28 million voters bravely cast their ballots and power transferred as it should - peacefully.

Yet at this very moment, these same freedoms are denied to many Africans. And I have to proclaim, democracy is not just formal elections. When journalists are put behind bars for doing their jobs, or activists are threatened as governments crack down on civil society - then you may have democracy in name, but not in substance. And I'm convinced that nations cannot realize the full promise of independence until they fully protect the rights of their people.

And this is true even for countries that have made important democratic progress. As I indicated during my visit to Kenya, the remarkable gains that country has made with a new constitution, with its election, cannot be jeopardized by restrictions on civil society. Likewise, our host, Ethiopians have much to be proud of - I've been amazed at all the wonderful work that's being done here - and it's true that the elections that took place here occurred without violence. But as I discussed with Prime Minister Hailemariam, that's just the start of democracy.

I believe Ethiopia will not fully unleash the potential of its people if journalists are restricted or legitimate opposition groups can't participate in the campaign process. And, to his credit, the Prime Minister acknowledged that more work will need to be done for Ethiopia to be a full-fledged, sustainable democracy.

So these are conversations we have to have as friends. Our American democracy is not perfect. We've worked for many years, but one thing we do is we continually reexamine to figure out how can we make our democracy better. And that's a force of strength for us, being willing to look and see honestly what we need to be doing to fulfill the promise of our founding documents.

And every country has to go through that process. No country is perfect, but we have to be honest, and strive to expand freedoms, to broaden democracy. The bottom line is that when citizens cannot exercise their rights, the world has a responsibility to speak out. And America will, even if it's sometimes uncomfortable - even when it's sometimes directed toward our friends.

And I know that there's some countries that don't say anything - (laughter) - and maybe that's easier for leaders to deal with. (Laughter.) But you're kind of stuck with us - this is how we are. We believe in these things and we're going to keep on talking about them.

And I want to repeat, we do this not because we think our democracy is perfect, or we think that every country has to follow precisely our path. For more than two centuries since our independence, we're still working on perfecting our union. We're not immune from criticism. When we fall short of our ideals, we strive to do better. But when we speak out for our principles, at home and abroad, we stay true to our values and we help lift up the lives of people beyond our borders. And we think that's important. And it's especially important, I believe, for those of us of African descent, because we've known what it feels like to be on the receiving end of injustice. We know what it means to be discriminated against. We know what it means to be jailed. So how can we stand by when it's happening to somebody else?

I'll be frank with you, it can't just be America that's talking about these things. Fellow African countries have to talk about these things. Just as other countries championed your break from colonialism, our nations must all raise our voices when universal rights are being denied. For if we truly believe that Africans are equal in dignity, then Africans have an equal right to freedoms that are universal - that's a principle we all have to defend. And it's not just a Western idea; it's a human idea.

I have to also say that Africa's democratic progress is also at risk when leaders refuse to step aside when their terms end. Now, let me be honest with you - I do not understand this. (Laughter.) I am in my second term. It has been an extraordinary privilege for me to serve as President of the United States. I cannot imagine a greater honor or a more interesting job. I love my work. But under our Constitution, I cannot run again. (Laughter and applause.) I can't run again. I actually think I'm a pretty good President - I think if I ran I could win. (Laughter and applause.) But I can't.

So there's a lot that I'd like to do to keep America moving, but the law is the law. And no one person is above the law. Not even the President. And I'll be honest with you - I'm looking forward to life after being President. (Laughter.) I won't have such a big security detail all the time. (Laughter.) It means I can go take a walk. I can spend time with my family. I can find other ways to serve. I can visit Africa more often. The point is, I don't understand why people want to stay so long. (Laughter.) Especially when they've got a lot of money. (Laughter and applause.)

When a leader tries to change the rules in the middle of the game just to stay in office, it risks instability and strife - as we've seen in Burundi. And this is often just a first step down a perilous path. And sometimes you'll hear leaders say, well, I'm the only person who can hold this nation together. (Laughter.) If that's true, then that leader has failed to truly build their nation.

You look at Nelson Mandela - Madiba, like George Washington, forged a lasting legacy not only because of what they did in office, but because they were willing to leave office and transfer power peacefully. And just as the African Union has condemned coups and illegitimate transfers of power, the AU's authority and strong voice can also help the people of Africa ensure that their leaders abide by term limits and their constitutions. Nobody should be president for life.

And your country is better off if you have new blood and new ideas. I'm still a pretty young man, but I know that somebody with new energy and new insights will be good for my country. It will be good for yours, too, in some cases.

Africa's progress will also depend on security and peace - because an essential part of human dignity is being safe and free from fear. In Angola, Mozambique, Liberia, Sierra Leone, we've seen conflicts end and countries work to rebuild. But from Somalia and Nigeria to Mali and Tunisia, terrorists continue to target innocent civilians. Many of these groups claim the banner of religion, but hundreds of millions of African Muslims know that Islam means peace. And we must call groups like al Qaeda, ISIL, al-Shabaab, Boko Haram - we must call them what they are - murderers.

In the face of threats, Africa - and the African Union -has shown leadership. Because of the AU force in Somalia, al-Shabaab controls less territory and the Somali government is growing stronger. In central Africa, the AU-led mission continues to degrade the Lord's Resistance Army. In the Lake Chad Basin, forces from several nations - with the backing of the AU - are fighting to end Boko Haram's senseless brutality. And today, we salute all those who serve to protect the innocent, including so many brave African peacekeepers.

Now, as Africa stands against terror and conflict, I want you to know that the United States stands with you. With training and support, we're helping African forces grow stronger. The United States is supporting the AU's efforts to strengthen peacekeeping, and we're working with countries in the region to deal with emerging crises with the African Peacekeeping Rapid Response Partnership.

The world must do more to help as well. This fall at the United Nations, I will host a summit to secure new commitments to strengthen international support for peacekeeping, including here in Africa. And building on commitments that originated here in the AU, we'll work to develop a new partnership between the UN and the AU that can provide reliable support for AU peace operations. If African governments and international partners step up with strong support, we can transform how we work together to promote security and peace in Africa.

Our efforts to ensure our shared security must be matched by a commitment to improve governance. Those things are connected. Good governance is one of the best weapons against terrorism and instability. Our fight against terrorist groups, for example, will never be won if we fail to address legitimate grievances that terrorists may try to exploit, if we don't build trust with all communities, if we don't uphold the rule of law. There's a saying, and I believe it is true - if we sacrifice liberty in the name of security, we risk losing both.

This same seriousness of purpose is needed to end conflicts. In the Central African Republic, the spirit of dialogue recently shown by ordinary citizens must be matched by leaders committed to inclusive elections and a peaceful transition. In Mali, the comprehensive peace agreement must be fulfilled. And leaders in Sudan must know their nation will never truly thrive so long as they wage war against their own people - the world will not forget about Darfur.

In South Sudan, the joy of independence has descended into the despair of violence. I was there at the United Nations when we held up South Sudan as the promise of a new beginning. And neither Mr. Kiir, nor Mr. Machar have shown, so far, any interest in sparing their people from this suffering, or reaching a political solution.

Yesterday, I met with leaders from this region. We agree that, given the current situation, Mr. Kiir and Mr. Machar must reach an agreement by August 17th - because if they do not, I believe the international community must raise the costs of intransigence. And the world awaits the report of the AU Commission of Inquiry, because accountability for atrocities must be part of any lasting peace in Africa's youngest nation.

And finally, Africa's progress will depend on upholding the human rights of all people - for if each of us is to be treated with dignity, each of us must be sure to also extend that same dignity to others. As President, I make it a point to meet with many of our Young African Leaders. And one was a young man from Senegal. He said something wonderful about being together with so many of his African brothers and sisters. He said, "Here, I have met Africa, the [Africa] I've always believed in. She's beautiful. She's young. She's full of talent and motivation and ambition." I agree.

Africa is the beautiful, talented daughters who are just as capable as Africa's sons. And as a father, I believe that my two daughters have to have the same chance to pursue their dreams as anybody's son - and that same thing holds true for girls here in Africa. Our girls have to be treated the same.

We can't let old traditions stand in the way. The march of history shows that we have the capacity to broaden our moral imaginations. We come to see that some traditions are good for us, they keep us grounded, but that, in our modern world, other traditions set us back. When African girls are subjected to the mutilation of their bodies, or forced into marriage at the ages of 9 or 10 or 11 - that sets us back. That's not a good tradition. It needs to end.

When more than 80 percent of new HIV cases in the hardest-hit countries are teenage girls, that's a tragedy; that sets us back. So America is beginning a partnership with 10 African countries - Kenya, Lesotho, Malawi, Mozambique, South Africa, Swaziland, Tanzania, Uganda, Zambia and Zimbabwe - to keep teenage girls safe and AIDS-free. And when girls cannot go to school and grow up not knowing how to read or write - that denies the world future women engineers, future women doctors, future women business owners, future women presidents - that sets us all back. That's a bad tradition - not providing our girls the same education as our sons.

I was saying in Kenya, nobody would put out a football team and then just play half the team. You'd lose. The same is true when it comes to getting everybody and education. You can't leave half the team off - our young women. So as part of America's support for the education and the health of our daughters, my wife, Michelle, is helping to lead a global campaign, including a new effort in Tanzania and Malawi, with a simple message - Let Girls Learn - let girls learn so they grow up healthy and they grow up strong. And that will be good for families. And they will raise smart, healthy children, and that will be good for every one of your nations.

Africa is the beautiful, strong women that these girls grow up to become. The single best indicator of whether a nation will succeed is how it treats its women. When women have health care and women have education, families are stronger, communities are more prosperous, children do better in school, nations are more prosperous. Look at the amazing African women here in this hall. If you want your country to grow and succeed, you have to empower your women. And if you want to empower more women, America will be your partner.

Let's work together to stop sexual assault and domestic violence. Let's make clear that we will not tolerate rape as a weapon of war - it's a crime. And those who commit it must be punished. Let's lift up the next generation of women leaders who can help fight injustice and forge peace and start new businesses and create jobs - and some might hire some men, too. (Laughter.) We'll all be better off when women have equal futures.

And Africa is the beautiful tapestry of your cultures and ethnicities and races and religions. Last night, we saw this amazing dance troupe made up of street children who had formed a dance troupe and they performed for the Prime Minister and myself. And there were 80 different languages and I don't know how many ethnic groups. And there were like 30 different dances that were being done. And the Prime Minister was trying to keep up with - okay, I think that one is - (laughter) - and they were moving fast. And that diversity here in Ethiopia is representative of diversity all throughout Africa. And that's a strength.

Now, yesterday, I had the privilege to view Lucy - you may know Lucy - she's our ancestor, more than 3 million years old. In this tree of humanity, with all of our branches and diversity, we all go back to the same root. We're all one family - we're all one tribe. And yet so much of the suffering in our world stems from our failure to remember that - to not recognize ourselves in each other.

We think because somebody's skin is slightly different, or their hair is slightly different, or their religious faith is differently expressed, or they speak a different language that it justifies somehow us treating them with less dignity. And that becomes the source of so many of our problems. And we think somehow that we make ourselves better by putting other people down. And that becomes the source of so many of our problems. When we begin to see other as somehow less than ourselves - when we succumb to these artificial divisions of faith or sect or tribe or ethnicity - then even the most awful abuses are justified in the minds of those who are thinking in those ways. And in the end, abusers lose their own humanity, as well.

Nelson Mandela taught us, "to be free is not merely to cast off one's chains, but to live in a way that respects and enhances the freedom of others."

Every one of us is equal. Every one of us has worth. Every one of us matters. And when we respect the freedom of others - no matter the color of their skin, or how they pray or who they are or who they love - we are all more free. Your dignity depends on my dignity, and my dignity depends on yours. Imagine if everyone had that spirit in their hearts. Imagine if governments operated that way. Just imagine what the world could look like - the future that we could bequeath these young people.

Yes, in our world, old thinking can be a stubborn thing. That's one of the reasons why we need term limits - old people think old ways. And you can see my grey hair, I'm getting old. (Laughter.) The old ways can be stubborn. But I believe the human heart is stronger. I believe hearts can change. I believe minds can open. That's how change happens. That's how societies move forward. It's not always a straight line - step by halting step - sometimes you go forward, you move back a little bit. But I believe we are marching, we are pointing towards ideals of justice and equality.

That's how your nations won independence - not just with rifles, but with principles and ideals. That's how African Americans won our civil rights. That's how South Africans - black and white - tore down apartheid. That's why I can stand before you today as the first African American President of the United

States.

New thinking. Unleashing growth that creates opportunity. Promoting development that lifts all people out of poverty. Supporting democracy that gives citizens their say. Advancing the security and justice that delivers peace. Respecting the human rights of all people. These are the keys to progress - not just in Africa, but around the world. And this is the work that we can do together.

And I am hopeful. As I prepare to return home, my thoughts are with that same young man from Senegal, who said: Here, I have met Africa, the [Africa] I've always believed in. She's beautiful and young, full of talent and motivation and ambition. To which I would simply add, as you build the Africa you believe in, you will have no better partner, no better friend than the United States of America.

God bless Africa. God bless the United States of America. Thank you very much, everybody. Thank you.

Appendix 3. Ghanaian President, Nana Akufo–Addo's Address to the West

(Given at the National Governors' Conference in Washington, DC. on February 25, 2018).

I must, at the outset, express my sincere gratitude to the Chair of the National Governors Association, Governor Brian Sandoval of Nevada, and the Vice Chair, Governor Steve Bullock of Montana, and, indeed, the entire membership of this Association, for the honor of this invitation to deliver this address at the National Governors Association 2018 Winter Meeting.

The Ghanaian people, the first in sub-Saharan Africa to free themselves from colonial rule some 61 years ago, and pacesetters, today, in the development of the principles of democratic accountability, respect for human rights and the rule of law on the African continent, are truly appreciative and deeply humbled by your choice of their leader and principal servant to be given the opportunity to address this important annual meeting, which groups together all 50 Governors, Republican and Democrat, of the states of this great federation, the United States of America.

I recognize the significance of the moment, as being the first leader from the continent to speak at this meeting. I hope that my country, Ghana, and, indeed, the African continent, will not be judged by any deficiencies of mine. Those are purely personal to me, and not at all representative.

Let me also express the gratitude of all freedom-loving peoples of the world to the men and women of this great country, the United States of America – the land of the free and the home of the brave. In the 20th century, the United States was largely responsible for seeing to it that the threats to freedom, posed by totalitarian ideas, such as Nazism, fascism, and communism, were defeated.

With the rapid spread of democratic values around the world, consequent upon that, America's responsibility in this 21st century is to remain "the shining city upon a hill", the force of whose ideas inspire greater chapters in man's development in freedom. The space for democratic engagement, importantly in Africa, has certainly widened. In my country, we have decided to make a full fist of it.

In the era of the 4th Republic, we have experienced the longest, uninterrupted period of stable, constitutional governance in our history, banishing the specter of instability that disfigured the early years of our nation's existence.

Indeed, on 7th January last, we celebrated its Silver Jubilee.

Democracy, equality of opportunity and respect for human rights, ideals which have stood the test of time, have now found firm anchor in our body politic. We have had 5 successive Presidents in the 4th Republic, with peaceful transfers of power from a governing to an opposition party on three separate occasions, the latest being in 2016, which brought me to office.

Ghana Beyond Aid - capable of mobilizing its own material and human resources - generating prosperity for her people,

Ladies and Gentlemen, my party, the New Patriotic Party, and I won the 2016 elections because the Ghanaian people were dissatisfied with their living conditions and the direction in which Ghana's economy, and, indeed, the country was headed. They believed we were different, and could put in place the requisite measures to improve their living conditions.

My government's program of economic transformation is hinged on restructuring the institutions of our governance, modernizing our agriculture to enhance its productivity, a clear industrial policy, and rationalizing the financial sector so that it supports growth in agriculture, and growth in manufacturing and industry. In my view, that is the way we can build a resilient economy, and lead Ghana to a situation beyond aid. That is, indeed, our goal – a Ghana Beyond Aid; a Ghana capable of mobilizing its own material and human resources to build a strong economy capable of generating prosperity for the mass of her people, a Ghana no longer dependent on hand-outs and charity.

To this end, and over the past 13 months, the period of stay of my government in office, we have begun to work on the fundamentals of the economy, because we believe that an improved macro-economy is a basic requirement for stimulating the investments we need for the rapid expansion and growth of the Ghanaian economy, and the generation of wealth and jobs. This has led to the growing strength of the economy, from a growth rate of 3.6% in 2016 to 7.9% in 2017; the stabilization of our currency, the cedi; reduction in inflation from 15.6% at the end of 2016 to its current level of 10.3%; a revival of Ghanaian industry, from a growth rate of -0.5% in 2016 to 17.7% in 2017; reduction in interest rates, and the fiscal deficit from 9.3% to 5.6% of GDP; and the abolition of nuisance taxes, with the aim of shifting the focus of the Ghanaian economy from an emphasis on taxation to an emphasis on production. We are also putting in place strong measures to increase revenue mobilization, by plugging leaks and reforming the existing tax exemption regime.

This process of economic and industrial transformation is going along with ensuring that the most basic elements of social justice are met. We have begun to make quality basic education, i.e. education from kindergarten through to secondary school, accessible to all of Ghana's children.

Through my government's policy of free secondary education in our public schools launched in September 2017, at the beginning of this academic year,

90,000 more children gained access to senior high school in 2017, than they did the year before. Equally, accessible healthcare to all our citizens, through an efficient and financially self-sustaining National Health Insurance Scheme, is a crucial goal of my government. We do all this to promote a culture of incentives and opportunity, to unleash the considerable ingenuity, creativity and entrepreneurial talents of our people, especially of our youth.

This is the surest path to national prosperity, bolstered by an enhancement of public accountability. Last Friday, before my departure for this visit, I appointed the first Special Prosecutor in our history, a known, respected anti-corruption crusader, whose task will be to deal, exclusively, with issues of corruption, and hold public officials, past and present, accountable for their stewardship of our nation's public finances.

A key challenge of our economy, like many other economies in Africa, is our infrastructural deficit. We are embarking on an aggressive public-private-partnership program to attract investment in the development of both our road and railway infrastructure. We are hopeful that, with solid private sector participation, we can develop a modern railway network with strong production center linkages, and with the potential to connect us to our neighbors to the north, i.e. Burkina Faso, the west, i.e. Cote d'Ivoire, and to the east, Togo. Apart from prosecuting the agenda of building, with the private sector, at least one factory in each district of Ghana, the time has come for Ghana to develop strategic industries out of its abundant natural resources of bauxite and iron ore.

We shall, shortly, establish an Integrated Bauxite/Aluminum Development Authority to assemble the relevant financial resources for the systematic exploitation and development of our bauxite deposits. By the same token, we have decided to exploit our substantial iron ore and manganese deposits, situated in the Western and Northern regions of our country, to build an integrated steel industry to serve the needs of our country and region.

Opportunity for American capital, technology & enterprise in Ghana and Africa

We are making systematic efforts to develop our new oil and gas industry, into which ExxonMobil has just appeared, signing on 18th January, this year, a major offshore oil and gas exploration and production agreement with Ghana. We are determined also to establish the relevant petrochemical industries to take advantage of the growth of our oil and gas industry.

There is a lot of opportunity for American capital, technology and enterprise in Ghana, and, indeed, in Africa, and we welcome companies from all your states to participate in the exceptional opportunities that exist in our country and on the continent.

We appreciate the continuing support offered to our country, and to the financing of our budgets by the American people and their government. Thus, towards the holding of the 2016 elections in Ghana, the election which brought me to office, the United Stated contributed some $7 million towards the holding of that election.

We received $547 million from Millennium Challenge Compact I, negotiated by the Kufuor Government with the Bush Government, when I was Ghana's Foreign Minister. It was satisfactorily completed. Under MCC Compact II, negotiated by the successor Mills/Obama governments, nearly $500 million is being invested in Ghana to improve power generation. Nonetheless, I believe, the time has come for a new form of relationship between Ghana and the United States of America. We are not disclaiming aid, but we do want to discard a mind-set of dependency; it is unhealthy both for the giver and for the receiver. We want our relations with the United States to be characterized by a substantial increase in trade and investment co-operation. This is the way to develop healthy relations between our two countries, and, thereby, strengthen our economies, and raise the living standards of our two peoples.

Ladies and gentlemen, I urge you not to ignore our continent. Many people say that this is the Asian century, but I believe strongly that this can be Africa's century. Our growth in 2015 was second only to that of Asia. According to the World Bank, six of the world's ten fastest growing economies, this year, are in Africa. We are rich in natural resources, and in possession of nearly 30 percent of the earth's remaining mineral resources.

We have a vibrant young population, and, though we still have important security challenges, we are more at peace than before, despite the distressing events in DR Congo, leading to the displacement of hundreds of thousands of innocent people. The African Union has to rise to the occasion, and mobilize the global community to find a peaceful, democratic outcome to the crisis. We now see the beginnings of meaningful intra-regional trade, which is about to be given an institutional framework by the historic decision of the African Union to bring into being, on 21st March, 2018, the Continental Free Trade Area. In my own region of ECOWAS, for the first time since its establishment, all 15 member countries have democratically elected governments, which gives us a great opportunity to prosecute vigorously the agenda of regional integration, not just with words, but with concrete regional projects that will benefit our populations. This is the time to look at Africa.

Africa cannot continue travelling the worn path of being exporters of raw materials.

Yes, it is disheartening to find that African youths do not see a future in their respective countries, and are willing to cross the Sahara desert on foot and drown in the Mediterranean Sea, in a desperate bid to reach the mirage of a better life in Europe. With the majority of African economies dependent on the production and export of raw materials, who can blame them for wanting to leave? These economies cannot produce wealth and prosperity for the masses on the continent. It, therefore, drives the determination to seek a much better standard of living out of Africa, thereby, fueling the refugee crises and the numerous counts of illegal migrations. The large wave of migrations into the United States from Ireland and Italy, in the 19th century, has completely subsided because the economies of the two countries are working properly.

We, in Africa, cannot continue travelling the worn path of limited success of being exporters of raw materials. Our problems require that we think outside of the box. Our thinking and approach to solving problems must be different from the thinking and approach that brought about the problems in the first place. The only way to ensuring prosperity in Africa and jobs for our young populations is through value addition activities, in a transformed and diversified, modern economy, in which we take full advantage of the digital revolution. In other words, the industrial development of our continent, and we are determined to ensure the realization of this, so that our young people can stay and devote their great energies to the building of a great Africa.

It is worth recounting, at this juncture, the inspiring words of the American politician, William Jennings Bryan that: "Destiny is not a matter of choice. It is not a thing to be waited for, it is a thing to be achieved."

There are many amongst us who cannot accept that it is only Asians who can engineer, in a generation, their transition from poverty to prosperity. We are determined to do that in our generation in Ghana, on the continent, and ensure that succeeding generations will be neither victims nor pawns of the global order. This will serve as the impetus for re-shaping the continent and charting a new path of growth and development in freedom, which will lift the long suffering African masses out of poverty into the realms of prosperity and dignified existence.

In conclusion, let me reaffirm the commitment of my government and Ghana in standing shoulder to shoulder with the United States in the promotion of human rights on the African continent, and across the globe. We stand shoulder to shoulder with the United States in the rejection of terrorism as a legitimate means of resolving political issues.

We appreciate the courageous commitment and the lead role being played in the fight against terrorism by the United States in several parts of the world, including the Sahel region of West Africa. We stand shoulder to shoulder with the United States in attempting to develop our economies to provide opportunities for its citizens to fulfil their aspirations, especially the youth. We stand ready to renew and deepen our relations with the United States of America for the prosperity and progress of our two peoples.

May God bless us all, and the peoples of the United States of America and Ghana. I thank you for your attention and wish you fruitful deliberations.

Index

Abacha, Sani 97, 108, 138, 155
Abiola, Moshood 2, 113, 127
Achebe, Chinua 131
Afghanistan 40, 42, 44, 45
Africa and Afghanistan 44
Africa and China 28, 29, 154
Africa Command. *See* Africom
African Americans 33, 34, 135, 152, 265
African-born scientists 166
African bureaucracies 65
African Charter on Human and Peoples
   Rights 260. *See also* Human rights
African diaspora 167, 243
African Growth and Opportunity Act 226,
   257
African heads of states 46, 104, 105, 107,
   111, 113, 120, 128, 129, 138
African intellectuals 39, 66, 95, 118, 150,
   167
African markets 238
African military command 40
African private sector 71, 166, 178, 194,
   199, 200, 233
African public sector 66, 163, 166, 178,
   180, 192, 194, 218
African renaissance 3
African rulers 2, 3, 18, 20, 22, 23, 30, 53,
   55, 56, 60, 66, 73, 91, 92, 95, 97, 98,
   99, 101, 103, 105, 106, 109, 110,
   111, 114, 115, 117, 118, 119, 120,
   126, 138, 150, 155, 158, 167, 179,
   203, 216, 223, 232, 238
African trade 56, 63, 113, 168, 239, 240
African Union 56, 117, 219, 236, 252, 255,
   256, 257, 262, 270
Africa Partnership Station 41
Africa's First World War 38
Africom 39, 40, 41, 42, 43, 44, 45, 46, 47,
   49
Afrobarometer xii
Afrocentricism 100. *See also* Afrocentric

scholars
Afrocentric scholars xv
Ahidjo, Ahmadou 19, 104, 120, 157, 185.
   See also Cameroon
Akufo-Addo, President Nana xvi, 245. *See
   also* Ghana
Algeria 14, 44, 101, 112, 145, 146, 231
Al Qaeda 40, 42, 43. *See also* international
   terrorism
Al Shabab 43. *See also* terrorism
American Civil War 32
American colonies 13, 14, 32
American constitution 18
American DV Lottery 225
American Revolution, The 32, 34, 124, 169
Amin, Idi 155
Amin, Samir 94
Amish 85, 87, 88, 89
Anglo-Saxon 18
Angola 6, 14, 44, 97, 112, 118, 138, 152,
   154, 160, 258, 262
Annan, Koffi 180
anti-Americanism 42, 45, 46
apartheid 76, 113, 114, 115, 161, 265
Arab colonizers 30
Arab Spring 102
archeological treasures 99
Argentina 213, 215
Articles of Confederation 16
Asia 5, 11, 13, 30, 35, 41, 44, 48, 64, 113,
   142, 151, 162, 184, 193, 230, 238,
   239, 241, 259, 270
Asian Tigers 162
autocratic bureaucracies 56
autocratic rule 20, 61, 184
autocratic systems 20, 157
Ayittey, George 217

Bakongo xv, 153. *See also* Angola, Queen
   Nzinga

Banda, Hastings Kamuzu 180, 184. *See also* Malawi
Bangladesh 142, 173
bankruptcy 14, 95, 97, 109, 125, 178
Bedouin 61
Belgium 13, 36, 72, 118, 133, 137, 144, 155
Benevolent Dictators 183, 184, 185, 186, 188, 191
Benin 112, 260
Berlin Conference, 1884 34, 40, 41, 123, 139
Bill Gates 109, 118, 150
Bill of Rights, American 7, 179
Bin Laden, Osama 40, 45, 46
Biya, Paul 2, 19, 60, 96, 102, 104, 105, 108, 120, 127, 155, 157, 169, 182, 184
Black Americans 30, 35, 36
Black Man Time 124
Black soldiers 32, 33
Blair, Tony 11, 190
Boer settlers 152. *See also* Apartheid
Boigny, Houphouet 96, 105
Bokassa, Jean-Bédel 2, 52, 72, 104, 139, 155, 157, 184, 185
Boko Haram 43, 262. *See also* terrorism
Bongo, Ali 101
Bongo, Omar 101, 102, 157
Bosnia 183
Boston Tea Party 15
Botswana 57, 112, 114, 217, 220, 253, 260
Bouteflika, Abdelaziz 101
brain-drain 118, 150, 151, 166, 167, 225
Brazil 143, 203, 212, 213
Brazzaville 61, 112, 133
Britain 6, 13, 14, 16, 20, 22, 23, 31, 32, 35, 36, 40, 55, 56, 69, 72, 85, 86, 134, 136, 146, 153, 155, 156, 162, 166, 173, 174, 177, 201, 212, 223, 239, 240
British colonial policy 135
British colonies 21, 35, 217
British monarchy 124, 168
British neocolonial exploitation 15
Buffalo Soldiers 33
Buhari, Muhammadu 182. *See also* Nigeria
Burkina Faso 2, 104, 112, 157, 185, 269
Burma Campaign 36
Burundi 55, 60, 112, 175, 176, 183, 187, 262
Bush, George 39, 58

Cabral, Amilcar 5, 104
Cambodia 183
Cameron, David 225
Cameroon 2, 19, 60, 64, 72, 80, 96, 97, 102, 103, 104, 105, 107, 108, 109, 112, 120, 127, 132, 155, 157, 165, 168, 174, 182, 184, 185, 212, 213, 214, 228
  CamAir 97
  Douala 64, 96
Canada 118, 173, 209, 215, 225, 226, 228, 239
  Citizenship and Immigration Canada 225
Cape of Good Hope 11, 13
Cape Verde 25, 55, 81, 85, 104, 112, 117, 121, 160, 213, 217, 243
capitalism 2, 5, 14, 15, 47, 69, 70, 75, 140, 164
Capitalism without Capital 69
cartography 11
Castro, Fidel 160
Catholic Church, The 96, 137, 143
Center for Global Development 35, 118
Central African Republic 2, 107, 184
Central America 12
Chad 55, 64, 107, 112, 127, 262
Chieftaincy 22
China 5, 14, 28, 29, 39, 40, 42, 43, 45, 46, 47, 48, 49, 53, 67, 99, 106, 117, 122, 129, 133, 134, 135, 153, 154, 160, 162, 163, 201, 203, 206, 208, 211, 215, 220, 224, 234, 237, 241, 243
  Chinese workers 13
Chinese Emperor 154
Chirac, Jacques 38, 52, 103
Chissano, Joaquim 128. *See also* Mozambique
Christianity 141, 145
Christian missionaries 30, 161. *See also* Catholic Church, The
civilization 3, 51, 89, 125, 140, 141, 151
civilizing mission 3, 41, 54, 60, 77, 87, 139, 146, 155, 220, 223
civil society 9, 58, 157, 161, 167, 191, 192, 222, 248, 249, 255, 259, 260
Civil War 16, 32, 38, 147
climate change 251, 257, 260
Clinton, Bill 63, 190

Clinton, Hillary 58, 102
Cold War 1, 2, 4, 5, 16, 38, 39, 40, 42, 47,
	48, 100, 106, 110, 157, 183
colonial conquest 87, 141, 146
colonialism 3, 9, 23, 37, 40, 41, 62, 72, 73,
	74, 75, 76, 79, 91, 119, 123, 131,
	132, 133, 134, 140, 145, 149, 152,
	154, 155, 174, 193, 241, 247, 256,
	261
colonial rule xii, 2, 3, 13, 14, 16, 21, 23, 24,
	54, 55, 56, 61, 63, 66, 73, 74, 76, 77,
	80, 87, 92, 94, 95, 111, 113, 121,
	128, 129, 135, 137, 139, 142, 144,
	145, 150, 152, 155, 157, 158, 159,
	160, 161, 163, 173, 174, 175, 177,
	184, 185, 207, 267. See also coloni-
	alism
Colorado 24, 55, 63, 94
Columbus, Christopher 11
Combatant Commands 39, 45
Communism 14, 75. See also Marx, Karl
communist bloc states 160
Communist Manifesto 14, 15. See
	also Marx, Karl
community colleges 196, 197
Compaore, Blaise 2, 104, 157
concentration of power 18
Confessions of an Economic Hit Man 221.
	See also Perkins, John
Confucius 141, 193
	Confucian culture 141
Congo xv, 2, 3, 4, 5, 19, 21, 36, 38, 39, 60,
	61, 80, 94, 100, 104, 109, 112, 118,
	127, 133, 144, 148, 152, 153, 155,
	159, 160, 172, 187, 189, 252, 270
Congolese civil war 172. See also Demo-
	cratic Republic of Congo
Constantinople 30
Copernicus 86
corruption xii, 3, 42, 56, 73, 78, 93, 95, 100,
	108, 128, 147, 164, 169, 183, 184,
	185, 186, 192, 193, 200, 219, 221,
	235, 236, 237, 243, 248, 250, 258,
	259, 269
Costa Rica 225
Cote d'Ivoire 21, 67, 80, 96, 97, 102, 104,
	105, 127, 132, 182, 221, 222, 228,
	230, 240, 269
	Yamoussoukro 96
Cuba 107, 159, 160, 161. See also Castro,
	Fidel

cycle of debt 92, 93

Daewoo 122
da Gama, Vasco 12
Darfur 3, 61, 76, 183, 252, 263. See also Su-
	dan
Davidson, Basil 6, 7, 16, 17, 57, 98, 131,
	140, 141, 145, 152, 153, 165
Deby, Idriss 127. See also Chad
Declaration of Independence 31, 134, 135
decolonization 2, 20, 55, 72, 223
de Gaulle, Charles 4, 139. See also France
delayed gratification 161, 207
democracy xiv, 6, 7, 8, 15, 19, 20, 21, 22,
	23, 45, 48, 56, 57, 58, 75, 76, 104,
	127, 132, 133, 138, 139, 140, 141,
	155, 156, 157, 159, 160, 161, 168,
	172, 176, 183, 184, 185, 186, 188,
	189, 190, 191, 192, 214, 247, 248,
	249, 250, 260, 261, 266
	constitutional democracy 15, 23
	democratic governance 7, 55, 161, 184,
	185
Democratic Republic of Congo xv, 3, 4, 21,
	38, 80, 94, 109, 118, 133, 144, 147,
	148, 159, 187
Deng, Xiaoping 53. See also China
dependency school xv, 94, 95
Dias, Bartholomew 11
diasporazation 81, 95. See also migration
Dibango, Manu 213. See also Cameroon
Digital Opportunity Task Force 209
Diseases
	AIDS xii, 93, 97, 109, 242, 251, 252, 256,
	260, 264
	Ebola 260
	HIV/AIDS 93, 251, 252, 256, 260
	tuberculosis 252
Djenne 57. See also Mali
Djibouti 42, 112, 133
Doe, Samuel 97
Douglas, Frederick 33, 92, 93, 124, 151,
	239
driving habits, Africa 126
dual citizenship 243
Dubois, W.E.B. 135, 151

East Africa 30, 40, 45, 57, 85, 89, 145, 182,

187, 213
East Asian nations 76
Eastern bloc states 75, 157, 159, 160, 161
Economic Commission for Africa 10, 56,
   239
economic development xiv, 5, 8, 17, 29, 62,
   64, 68, 71, 85, 89, 92, 93, 103, 107,
   128, 131, 157, 194, 195, 214, 236,
   238, 239, 243
  development is a mental 17, 125
economic Olympic 239. *See also* economic
   development
Economic Partnership Agreements 123.
   See also Berlin Conference
economies of scale 24, 134
ECOWAS 252, 270
Edinburgh University 155, 156
education ix, 9, 45, 71, 93, 98, 99, 103,
   128, 139, 156, 163, 167, 169, 190,
   194, 195, 196, 201, 203, 217, 219,
   221, 222, 229, 247, 250, 251, 252,
   253, 259, 264, 268. *See also* higher
   education
Egypt 35, 81, 101, 109, 112, 139, 157, 164,
   213, 231
Electoral Fraud 111
electricity 66, 71, 81, 87, 89, 94, 106, 110,
   250, 257, 259
  blackouts 79, 126
England 6, 27, 57, 87, 88, 93. *See also* Britain
entrepreneurial skills 64, 181, 194, 195,
   227, 233
entrepreneurial spirit 65, 233
environmental self-destruction 237
Equatorial Guinea 19, 25, 101, 102, 112,
   118, 184, 213, 228, 239
Eritrea 3, 112, 174
  Eritrea's secession 174
Ethiopia 46, 63, 81, 112, 121, 133, 168, 174,
   175, 177, 255, 258, 261, 265
Ethiopian Constitution 175
ethnicity 22, 62, 252, 265
European Enlightenment 137
European Union, The 24, 215, 239
Europe's colonial legacy 169
Eyadéma, Gnassingbé 101. *See also* Togo

famine 95, 121, 146, 251
Fanon, Frantz 94, 140

Fascism 37
Fela Ransom-Kuti 213. *See also* Nigeria
feudal lords 72
Fighter Group, 332nd 36
financial capital 199, 210
Florida 58, 151, 210
foreign aid xii, xvi, 83, 95, 100, 187, 201,
   216, 219, 220, 221, 223, 224, 225,
   226, 229, 230, 231, 232, 233
Forgotten Army, The 37
Fort Knox 151
France 4, 13, 15, 34, 35, 38, 56, 57, 72, 80,
   83, 104, 105, 118, 121, 153, 162,
   212, 227, 239, 240
  French franc 15
Frank, Andre Gunder 94
Franklin, Benjamin 124, 135, 150
Frazer, Jendayi 127
Freedom House xii, 112, 113
free market 92, 101, 157
free press 58, 191
French champagne 165

Gabon 44, 101, 105, 112, 118, 157, 228
Gaddafi, Muammar 46, 101, 102, 121, 158.
   See also Libya
Gambia 97, 112, 116, 184, 185, 239, 240
Garvey, Marcus 34, 102, 135. *See also* pan-
   Africanism
Gates, Bill 109, 118, 150
Gates, Robert 39, 60
Gbagbo, Laurent 97, 102, 104, 127, 158,
   182
gentrification 167
George III, King 134
Germany 13, 34, 44, 96, 134, 154, 184, 188,
   206, 239, 240
Ghana 5, 6, 7, 37, 39, 52, 54, 76, 94, 112,
   118, 132, 185, 186, 191, 224, 226,
   230, 236, 240, 247, 248, 249, 250,
   251, 252, 253, 260, 267, 268, 269,
   270, 271
  Ashanti 6, 7, 153
  Ashanti State 7
  Ghanaian Parliament 158
Giscard d'Estaing, Valery 103
globalization 1, 2, 3, 4, 9, 23, 24, 25, 83,
   171, 205, 206, 239
Gnassingbé, Faure 101. *See also* Togo,
   Eyadéma

Gold Coast 37, 132. *See also* Ghana
Good Credit 234
good governance xvi, 119, 128, 132, 155, 166, 182, 183, 248, 250, 259
goodwill 41, 59, 77, 129, 226, 239
Gore, Al 58, 63
Government budgets 82
Great Britain 31, 85
Great Depression 16, 54
gross national income 221, 222. *See also* See GNI
Guinea Bissau 61, 76, 94, 112, 160
Guinea-Bissau 5, 118
Guinea Conakry 61
Gulf of Guinea 41, 43, 116

Haiti 27
half century x, xi, xii, xiv, xv, 3, 52, 73, 78, 81, 94, 101, 110, 117, 118, 119, 178, 183, 192, 209, 219, 221, 228, 232, 234, 245
harmony with nature 84
Hatshepsut, Queen 139
Hausa 173. *See also* Nigeria
health 45, 66, 80, 93, 98, 114, 118, 128, 166, 167, 207, 210, 219, 247, 249, 251, 252, 256, 257, 260, 264
    healthcare 9, 68, 71, 92, 93, 95, 96, 98, 100, 108, 114, 150, 163, 169, 190, 197, 201, 203, 204, 207, 208, 210, 221, 222, 229, 243, 244, 269
    public health systems 252, 260
higher education ix, 99, 156, 195, 217
Hill & Knowlton 102
HIV 93, 251, 252, 256, 260, 264
Hobbes, Thomas 16, 168, 179
Honda 197, 233, 234
Hong Kong 203, 217
honorary degree 155, 156
Horn of Africa 42, 43, 174
hospitality industries 232
House of Commons 140
House of Lords 140. *See also* traditional institutions
housing industry 221
How Europe Underdeveloped Africa 91. *See also* Rodney, Walter
Hughes, Langston xiv
humanitarian crisis 3
human rights 41, 102, 113, 128, 156, 173,
182, 183, 186, 247, 263, 266, 267, 268, 271
Hutus 136, 137, 173, 175, 176

Ibo 173. *See also* Nigeria
Ibrahim Index of African Governance 128
Ibrahim, Mo 128, 180
Illinois 55, 89
IMF xi, 9, 66, 67, 69, 70, 71, 72, 92, 100, 102, 163, 164, 165, 166, 167, 168, 169, 178, 186, 200, 216, 219, 221, 223, 230, 239, 240, 241
immigrants 18, 115, 116, 117, 227, 228, 253
immigration 74, 93, 115, 187, 226, 227, 228
imperialism 23, 35, 41, 42, 45, 138, 140
independence and self-rule xi, xii, xiii, 73, 77, 78, 79, 94, 128, 150, 192, 245
independent electoral commissions 181, 182
Index of Economic Freedom 217
India 12, 13, 43, 54, 99, 142, 173, 208, 220, 224
Indian military 99
individualism 85, 88, 207
individual liberties 61, 216
Industrial Revolution 27, 67, 86, 192, 201, 214
intellectual capital 208, 224
inter-ethnic conflicts 21
international financial institutions xiii, 9, 66, 92, 163, 164, 167, 178, 199, 216, 221, 223, 230, 231, 245
International Maritime Bureau 43
International Maritime Organization 43
International Monetary Fund 166, 199, 219. *See also* IMF
International Relief Committee 38
international terrorism 42. *See also* terrorism
Iran 43
Iraq 21, 147
iron curtain 76
Israel 107

Jammeh, Yahya 97, 184, 185
Japan 23, 36, 107, 203, 206, 209, 215, 233, 234

Japanese 33, 35, 107, 234, 241
Jefferson, Thomas 31, 134, 150
Johnathan, Goodluck 182. *See also* Nigeria

Kabila, Joseph 182
Kagame, Paul 60, 185, 186, 187, 188, 189,
    190, 191. *See also* Rwanda
Kennedy, President John F. 78
Kenya 20, 21, 30, 43, 57, 60, 63, 64, 70, 76,
    80, 81, 112, 118, 120, 127, 131, 133,
    135, 136, 145, 181, 211, 247, 248,
    249, 255, 260, 264
  Kenyan elections 20
  Mombasa 64
Kenyatta, Jomo 20, 120
Kia automobile 197
Kibaki, Mwai 60, 127, 181. *See also* Kenya
Kikuyu 20, 136. *See also* Kenya
"Kip" Ward, General 45
Kissinger, Henry 131
kleptocracy 56
Korea 76, 94, 107, 121, 122, 129, 162, 184,
    191, 203, 206, 208, 234, 248, 250
Korean Police Action 33
Korea's per capita GDP 94
Kraybill, Donald 87, 88
  legacy of dissent 87

Latin America 41, 113, 162, 214, 239, 243
Leopold, King 2, 133, 144, 145, 153, 155
Leviathan 58, 158
Liberal institutions 172
Liberia 21, 97, 107, 109, 112, 118, 138, 180,
    252, 262
libraries 202, 256
Libya 46, 80, 101, 102, 104, 109, 112, 116,
    161, 183
Life expectancy xv
lifespan, Africa xv, 9, 197
Lincoln, Abraham 32, 150, 212
Livingstone, David 30, 141
Locke, John 16, 158, 168
London 6, 8, 24, 91, 104, 134, 139, 141,
    152, 212, 225, 231
Lord Dunmore's Ethiopian Regiment 32.
    See also Ethiopia
Lord's Resistance Army 42, 262. *See
    also* terrorism

Los Angeles 231
Louis XIV 169
Lumumba, Patrice 2, 4, 5, 39, 104, 113,
    120, 159
Luo 20, 136. *See also* Kikuyu, Kenya

Madagascar 112, 122
made in Africa 68, 238
Maghreb 43
Magna Carta 124
Makeda, Queen 139
malaria 114, 207, 251, 252, 256
Malawi 70, 92, 112, 122, 180, 184, 264
Malaysia 76
Malcolm X 135
Mali xv, 55, 57, 112, 174, 262, 263
Mandela, Nelson 2, 3, 113, 161, 224, 225,
    262, 265
Mansa Musa, King xv
Mao, Tse Tung 53. *See also* communism,
    China
Marshall Plan 216. *See also* World War II
Marx, Karl 14, 15, 53, 75
Maslow, Abraham 47
Mauritius 112, 217
Mayo Institute 207
McCain, Senator John 59, 60
medieval times 86, 127
Mediterranean Sea 116, 270
mercantilism 2, 11, 20. *See also* capitalism
Mercedes, cars 98, 165, 197
Mexican Expedition 33
Mexico 43, 239
Michael Jordan, Teeshirts 151, 213
Michigan 55
micro-states 14, 17, 24, 25
middle class xiv, 48, 63, 68, 106, 162, 214,
    215, 256. *See also* economic devel-
    opment
Middle East 30, 41, 44, 46, 257
  Arabs 30
migrant workers 13
Military Command 39, 46
military coups 22, 179
  factional warfare 22
  military rule 20
Milla, Roger 213, 214
Millennium Development Goals 228, 230.
    See also MDGs, economic develop-
    ment

Minerals 67
mission civilizatrice 139, 162
Mitterrand, Francois 103, 169
Mobutu, Sese Seko 2, 19, 39, 72, 97, 100,
    101, 103, 104, 108, 119, 120, 133,
    138, 155, 157, 159, 160, 185. *See
    also* Zaire, DRC
Modernity vii, 3, 17, 22, 79, 81, 83, 84, 85,
    86, 87, 88, 89, 125, 141, 144
    modernization 66, 70, 84, 85, 86, 87, 125,
    129, 134, 138, 141, 163, 194, 202,
    217, 237
modern state system 62, 146, 147, 148, 149
Moi, Daniel Arab 120
Monroe Doctrine 214. *See also* Latin
    America
Montana 33, 55, 267
morbidity rate 207. *See also* healthcare
Morocco 112, 231
Morrill Land Grant Act 195
Mortality rates 28
Moyo, Dambisa 221, 224, 236
Mubarak, Hosni 101, 120, 157, 164, 231
Mugabe, Robert 19, 60, 80, 97, 133, 138,
    155, 156, 181, 184. *See also* Zim-
    babwe
multiparty democracies 19, 93, 183
Museveni, Yoweri 190. *See also* Uganda
Muslim 30, 44, 45, 46, 176. *See also* reli-
    gion
Muzenda, Simon 94

NAFTA 24, 215, 238. *See also* North
    American Free Trade Area
Namibia 57, 112, 217, 260
Nandi, Queen 139
Napoleonic Wars 34
National Democratic Congress 186. *See
    also* Jerry Rawlings
National Health Service 166
nationalist leaders 80, 104
nationalization 70, 71
nation-builders 16
Nation Building 16, 18
Native Americans 28, 227
NATO 43, 160
natural resources 8, 48, 49, 51, 55, 64, 67,
    73, 79, 81, 84, 107, 114, 115, 132,
    133, 144, 152, 154, 195, 196, 210,
    211, 215, 217, 221, 250, 258, 269,

270
Naval Center for Contemporary Conflict
    42
Nazism 37, 267
Ndi, John Fru 127, 182
Nehanda, Queen 139
neocolonial exploitation 15, 40
neocolonialism 9, 15, 23, 42, 119, 223. *See
    also* colonialism
Newton, Isaac 86
New World Order 1, 194
New York 1, 4, 7, 8, 17, 32, 33, 35, 36, 38,
    43, 57, 60, 93, 94, 97, 102, 122, 131,
    132, 135, 140, 141, 160, 161, 184,
    217, 221, 228, 231
New Zealand 209
Nguema, Macias 101
Nguesso, Denis Sassou 60. *See also* Repub-
    lic of Congo
Niger 35, 55, 112, 118
Nigeria xiii, xv, 2, 43, 45, 57, 60, 61, 64, 70,
    76, 80, 97, 105, 107, 108, 112, 123,
    127, 132, 138, 142, 146, 147, 155,
    168, 172, 173, 174, 176, 177, 212,
    231, 232, 251, 258, 260, 262
    Abuja 105, 231
    Fulani 61
    Igbo 61, 142
    Lagos 105, 253
    Nigerian stock markets 114
Nigerian-Biafran War 61
Nkrumah, Kwame 5, 39, 52, 53, 54, 171,
    248. *See also* Ghana, pan-African-
    ism
Nkurunziza, Pierre 60. *See also* Burundi
Nobel Peace Prize 128, 225
North America 2, 11, 14, 16, 88, 98, 114,
    117, 151, 197, 212, 213, 239, 243
North American Free Trade Agreement
    214
Nyerere, Julius 1. *See also* Tanzania
Nzinga, Queen xv, 154. *See also* Angola,
    Bakongo

Obama, President Barack vii, xvi, 1, 58,
    59, 60, 102, 109, 111, 150, 158, 186,
    190, 245, 247, 255, 270
Obasanjo, Olusegun 60, 127. *See also* Ni-
    geria
Obiang Nguema Mbazogo, Teodoro

101. *See also* Equatorial Guinea, Nguema, Macias

Odinga, Raila 60, 91, 127, 181. *See also* Kenya

official development assistance 231

Olajuwon, Akeem 151

one-party dictatorships 93, 155, 157

OPEC 229

Organization of African Unity 55, 114. *See also* OAU

Ottoman Empire, The 11, 29, 30

Ouattara, Alassane 127. *See also* Cote d'Ivoire

overseas development assistance 228, 230

Pakistan 21, 142, 173

partnership 5, 41, 43, 44, 47, 190, 212, 247, 249, 250, 256, 258, 263, 264, 269

Peace Corps 232, 233

peacekeepers 262

Pearl Harbor 35

Perestroika 76

Perkins, John 221

Pham, J Peter 147, 172, 173

pharmaceutical industry 204

Philippines 162

piracy attacks 43

piratization 72

political kingdom 52, 53, 54

political mismanagement 128

political power 7, 171, 176

pollution 204, 209, 237

Portugal 11, 12, 13, 30, 35, 72, 118, 138, 154, 160, 161, 162

post 9/11 era 44

post-Cold War era 39, 183

post-colonial, Africa xii, xiv, 2, 3, 17, 61, 66, 73, 76, 80, 95, 103, 104, 113, 132, 136, 139, 148, 156, 158, 173, 178, 226

poverty 8, 51, 56, 74, 80, 92, 95, 128, 136, 147, 169, 172, 188, 217, 219, 220, 221, 225, 228, 249, 250, 256, 257, 259, 266, 271

precolonial 95, 146, 147, 148, 153, 235

Privatization 70, 71, 72, 92, 163, 164, 166, 187, 199, 200

public utilities 70, 71

public works departments 200

Rawlings, Jerry 185, 186, 191, 236. *See also* Ghana

Reagan, President Ronald 35, 36

referendum 171, 174, 177

Religion
  Buddhism 193
  Islam 30, 262

Renaissance 3, 86, 188

republicanism 15, 16, 168

research and development 79, 202, 203, 204, 205

revisionist scholars 223, 229

Rhodes, Cecil 30, 72, 123, 133, 155

Rodney, Walter 91. *See also* dependency school

Rousseau, Jean-Jacques 16, 57, 139, 168

rule of law 58, 73, 127, 128, 136, 158, 167, 172, 183, 187, 243, 249, 250, 259, 263, 267

Russia 15, 43, 135, 188, 228, 247

Rwanda 3, 21, 52, 60, 61, 76, 112, 118, 127, 135, 136, 137, 172, 175, 176, 183, 185, 186, 187, 188, 189, 190, 191
  Rwandan genocide 103, 135, 172, 175, 176, 189

Sahara Desert 92, 116, 117

Sall, Macky 182. *See also* Senegal

Sankara, Captain Thomas 104, 185

Sao Tome 25, 112, 213, 239

Sarkozy, Nicolas 103

Saudi Arabia 40, 46, 121, 122

Savimbi, Jonas 97. *See also* Angola

Schraeder, Peter 7, 57

science 86, 98

scramble for Africa, The 5, 29, 34, 121, 123, 131

secession 174, 175, 176, 177

Second World War 76

self-aggrandizement 95, 96, 97, 100, 101, 103, 104, 110, 113

Senegal 35, 104, 112, 132, 182, 240, 263, 266
  Senegalese veterans 38

Sierra Leone 21, 57, 109, 112, 118, 166, 260, 262

Sierra Leonean medical doctors 166

Simpson, O. J. 137

Singapore 107, 162, 184, 187, 188, 191, 217, 250

slave raiders 154. *See also* slavery

slavery 9, 23, 28, 31, 41, 80, 92, 93, 116, 123, 134, 137, 145, 150, 152, 153, 154, 155, 256

slave trade 13, 27, 30, 40, 115

sleeping giant, Africa xiv

Smith, Adam 14, 15, 206

soccer museum 213

social contract 16, 18, 139

socialist philosophy 94. *See also* Marxism

software development 208

Somali 42, 147, 148, 149, 262

Somalia xv, 3, 21, 42, 43, 57, 76, 107, 112, 133, 135, 147, 148, 168, 252, 262

Somaliland 133

South Africa 2, 13, 45, 55, 61, 76, 81, 112, 113, 114, 115, 118, 131, 139, 145, 152, 160, 161, 168, 189, 211, 213, 215, 217, 220, 231, 249, 251, 256, 258, 260, 264

Southern Africa 57, 72, 85, 97, 155, 161, 182. *See also* Zimbabwe, South Africa, Mozambique

Southern Rhodesia 131, 132. *See also* Zimbabwe

South Korea 76, 94, 121, 122, 162, 184, 191, 203, 208, 248, 250. *See also* Samsung, Kia, Hyundai

South Sudan 3, 55, 121, 122, 123, 263

sovereignty 135, 173, 174, 182, 183, 256

Soviet Union 14, 39, 48, 157, 159

Spain 11, 13, 35, 72, 116, 118, 162

stock markets 114

street addresses 82

structural adjustment plan 164, 199

Sudan xv, 2, 3, 35, 40, 55, 57, 58, 61, 102, 109, 112, 118, 121, 122, 123, 138, 180, 184, 263

superpower rivalry 1, 42, 132

superpowers 1, 4, 5, 15, 39, 40, 156

sustainable development 120, 125, 168, 179, 196, 202, 203, 216, 219, 223, 225, 230, 243. *See also* MDGs

Suzuki 197

Swahili 30, 57

Swiss banks 231

Switzerland 67, 201, 206, 207, 231, 232

Syria 183

Taiwan 107, 162, 203

Tanzania 1, 57, 112, 121, 187, 189, 258, 264

telecommunications 29, 46, 110, 180, 203

term limits 19, 21, 60, 101, 102, 126, 127, 128, 167, 183, 262, 265

terrorism xiv, 5, 29, 39, 42, 43, 44, 52, 102, 123, 252, 263, 271

Texas 33, 35, 105, 121, 122, 151, 210

Thailand 23, 76

think-tanks 202, 215, 216, 217, 224

Third World exports 65

Timbuktu 57. *See also* Mali

Tirailleurs 38, 241

Toll highways 210

totalitarian political systems 93

Toure, Sekou 80, 185. *See also* Guinea Conakry

Touré, Sekou 4, 80. *See also* Guinea Conakry

tourism 85, 187, 205, 211, 212, 213, 259

traditional African political systems 57

traditional institutions 22, 138, 140

traffic lights 82, 126

trans-Atlantic slave trade 40. *See also* slavery

Transparency International xii

transportation 31, 71, 76, 98, 134, 201, 203, 213, 219, 232, 240

Tshisekedi, E. 182

Tsvangirai, Morgan 60, 182. *See also* Zimbabwe

Tuareg 61

Tunisia 101, 109, 112, 217, 262

Tunka Manin, Emperor 7

Turner, Ted 109

Tuskegee Airmen 36

Tutsis 136, 137, 173, 175, 176. *See also* Hutus

Uganda 2, 21, 42, 64, 72, 76, 80, 102, 112, 118, 155, 157, 184, 190, 264

umuganda 190. *See also* Paul Kagame, Rwanda

underdevelopment xv, 8, 9, 16, 76, 79, 94, 95, 107, 125, 149, 169, 181, 195, 197, 202, 204, 206, 209, 219, 220, 223, 224, 231, 244

Union of Soviet Republics 216

United Nations 10, 56, 180, 224, 239, 263
United States iv, x, xi, xii, xiv, xvi, 4, 5, 13,
        14, 15, 16, 17, 18, 24, 25, 28, 29, 32,
        33, 34, 39, 42, 43, 44, 45, 46, 47, 49,
        51, 55, 57, 58, 60, 69, 78, 81, 82, 86,
        88, 102, 108, 109, 115, 124, 133,
        143, 150, 151, 158, 159, 160, 161,
        166, 173, 174, 186, 187, 192, 196,
        207, 209, 210, 214, 215, 216, 218,
        221, 223, 226, 227, 228, 232, 234,
        236, 239, 240, 245, 247, 255, 258,
        259, 260, 261, 262, 265, 266, 267,
        270, 271
University of Illinois 89
University of Pennsylvania 89
UN Secretary General 52
UN Security Council 182
Urban II, Pope 29
USAID 41
U.S. Constitution 18
U.S. foreign policy 43, 47, 49
U.S. Military 39, 46
U.S. Military Command 39, 46
U.S. Presidential debate 39
U.S. presidential elections 62, 111
U.S. Senate Committee on Foreign Rela-
        tions 164, 235

Van de Walle, Nicolas 24
Vatican 173
Venezuela 43
visionary leadership 17, 113, 204

Wade, Abdoulaye 182
Wallerstein, Immanuel 94. See also de-
        pendency school
waltmartization 25
Washington, George 150, 262
Wealth of Nations, The 14
Western democracies 20, 58, 60, 160
Western multinationals 24
Western myopia 48
Western nations 3, 46, 215, 219
Western world 70, 95, 159, 201, 245
white man's burden, the 139. See also Basil
        Davidson
white supremacy 137
wildlife 84, 211, 212, 259. See also tourism

winds of democracy 19, 20, 21, 75, 76, 161,
        186
Wisconsin 34, 55
World Bank, The xi, 9, 35, 51, 66, 67, 69,
        70, 71, 72, 92, 100, 102, 122, 163,
        164, 166, 167, 169, 178, 186, 188,
        209, 211, 216, 221, 223, 224, 230,
        233, 235, 239, 240, 270
World Cup soccer 151
World Development Index xii
World Health Organization 207. See
        also health
World Trade Organization 69
    WTO 69
World War II 4, 14, 15, 36, 37, 38, 39, 54,
        55, 77, 107, 129, 136, 241
World War III 1, 110

Yaoundé 165. See also Cameroon
yibana mayele 100. See also Mobutu Sese
        Seko
Yorubas 146, 173, 177. See also Nigeria

Zaire 18, 72, 97, 100, 101, 103, 108, 119,
        138, 155, 157, 159, 160, 184. See
        also Democratic Republic of Congo
Zambia 92, 112, 129, 132, 264
Zaria, Queen xv
Zimbabwe 19, 21, 80, 97, 107, 112, 127,
        132, 133, 138, 139, 145, 155, 156,
        182, 183, 184, 249, 264
    Zimbabwean elections 60
Zulu 57, 153. See also South Africa